# Mass Media
## and
## Political Thought

# Mass Media
# and
# Political Thought

an information-processing approach

### Edited by
## Sidney Kraus
## Richard M. Perloff

**SAGE** PUBLICATIONS
Beverly Hills   London   New Delhi

*This book is dedicated to our parents—to Robert and Evelyn Perloff, and to the memory of Joseph and Lillian Kraus and Neddie Masters.*

*For information address:*

SAGE Publications, Inc.
275 South Beverly Drive
Beverly Hills, California 90212

SAGE Publications India Pvt. Ltd.
M-32 Market
Greater Kailash I
New Delhi 110 048 India

SAGE Publications Ltd
28 Banner Street
London EC1Y 8QE
England

Printed in the United States of America

**Library of Congress Cataloging in Publication Data**

Main entry under title;

Mass media and political thought.

Includes index.
1. Communication in politics—Addresses, essays, lectures. 2. Mass media—Psychological aspects—Addresses, essays, lectures. I. Kraus, Sidney. II. Perloff, Richard M.
JA74.M37    1985        306'.2        85-14190
ISBN 0-8039-2516-6

FIRST PRINTING

# CONTENTS

# PREFACE

WE BEGAN THIS PROJECT in 1983 when we observed that a rapidly increasing number of studies of political information processing were being conducted by scholars in several different disciplines. Our goal was to bring together a representative cross section of these cross-disciplinary ventures so as to bridge and integrate different concepts, methods, and ideas.

We first identified the major steps of the political communication process, from input of the message to cognitive processing of its content to output in terms of effects on the individual and the larger political system. We then used this as one basis for selecting our contributors, trying to make certain that each step in the process was covered in the volume. Undoubtedly, as research continues, new steps and new processes will be discovered and additional studies will be conducted and published. This volume is, as they say, just the beginning.

For our part, we have found the process of developing ideas, editing papers, and integrating concepts to be challenging, rewarding, and at times frustrating, but mostly rewarding and stimulating. Both coeditors participated equally in the development and preparation of the book; the order of authorship is alphabetical. And we'd both do it again (and may!).

—R.M.P.
S.K.

# INTRODUCTION
## Political Communication
## Processes and Effects

### Richard M. Perloff
### Sidney Kraus

"THE WORLD THAT we have to deal with politically," wrote an early student of political cognition, "is out of reach, out of sight, out of mind." In *Public Opinion,* Lippmann added what has since become a classic statement on the nature of political beliefs: "We shall assume that what each man does is based not on direct and certain knowledge, but on pictures made by himself or given to him" (Lippmann, 1922/1947). In *Public Opinion* and the books that followed, Lippmann proceeded to outline a theory of political thinking in the new age of mass communication.

Today, some sixty years after the publication of Lippmann's seminal works, there is renewed interest in his ideas, for they suggest to scholars useful directions for research in the burgeoning field of political information processing. There is, it seems, a new intellectual ferment: conferences are being held, rump groups have been formed, and research on political information processing is being published at an ever-increasing rate in the journals of several different disciplines including communication, political science, psychology, and sociology.

These research efforts have been stimulated by recent developments in cognitive psychology and in the study of human information processing. In recent years, rapid advances have been made in our understanding of how people go about decoding, interpreting, storing, retrieving, and utilizing the information they encounter. These new theories, findings, and methods have suggested exciting new directions for research in political communication. And they come at a time when there is increasing dissatisfaction with older approaches to voter psychology, such as those based on party identification, group norms, and so forth. Today, rather than focusing solely on the cognitive effects political messages exert, as did researchers in the 1970s (see Becker et al., 1975), scholars are increasingly investigating the processes by which these effects are achieved. By specifying the nature of these mediating processes, and the factors that lead to the use of one or another cognitive mechanisms, researchers hope to gain a greater understanding of the nature of political media effects.

Lest we be accused of reinventing the wheel (or the processes by which wheels were reinvented), we hasten to remind the reader that the study of the symbiotic relationship between mass communication processes and effects can be traced back from Lazarsfeld et al. (1944) through Schramm (1955) and to Klapper (1960). Klapper noted that the processes of selective exposure, perception, and retention served to minimize media effects. However, there are several important differences between the research of today and that of Lazarsfeld's, Schramm's, and Klapper's era. First of all, contemporary scholars believe that voters play a more active role in the reality construction process than did their predecessors. Second, reseachers today have developed a more extensive and precise terminology to study processes, differentiating between cognitive, affective, and psychophysiological phenomena. Finally, and perhaps most important, researchers today believe that cognitive processes help explain why communications *do* exert certain types of effects, as well as why they serve to minimize media influences.

The present volume reflects this new enthusiasm about studying the cognitive psychology of political communication. The chapters in this book mirror the diversity of approaches to political information processing, ranging from macrosociological to microcognitive to the unabashedly affective, as well as the different methods (experimental, survey, field experimental, and case study). The chapters also reflect the shortcomings in our ability to study and measure cognitive processes: We have begun to conceptualize research problems in information processing terms, but we still lack the methods and the terminology to adequately measure and differentiate the various mediating factors.

The book is divided into three sections. The first set of chapters is concerned with the basic structure of political cognition and the methods by which political information is processed. Building on these foundations, the second portion of the book focuses more directly on the cognitive (and affective) influences of political communications and the processes by which these effects are achieved. The final section takes a more macro focus, examining the interface between systems-level variables and micropolitical cognitions, as well as exploring the implications of our knowledge of political cognition for real-world electoral issues.

In the first chapter, John Herstein, Jr., articulates the cognitive processing assumptions that underlie contemporary models of voting behavior. Herstein argues that these models make assumptions that are in large part inconsistent with what we know about how people make decisions, and he outlines and tests a new cognitive processing model of political decision making. In the chapter that follows, Richard Lau and Ralph Erber extend the literature on information processing differences between experts and novices by studying how political experts and political novices differ in their political decision making. Lau and Erber then discuss the implications of their research for mass media effects. Martin Fishbein, Susan Middlestadt, and Jean-Kyung Chung apply Fishbein and Ajzen's theory of reasoned action to a new behavioral domain—the explanation and prediction of voting participation (e.g., the intention *not* to vote for candidates) among first-time participants in the 1980 U.S. presidential election.

The first two chapters in Part II focus on the new interest in affective responses to political communications and the relationship between affect and cognition. John Lanzetta, Denis Sullivan, Roger Masters, and Gregory McHugo review the results of a series of experiments on the impact of politicians' nonverbal displays. Shanto Iyengar and Donald Kinder next discuss the findings from several experiments designed to uncover the psychological underpinnings of agenda-setting.

Tom Tyler and Paul Lavrakas focus on a different type of media effect—the impact of media reports of crime. Their discussion centers around the distinction between two cognitive antecedents of behavioral responses to crime: beliefs about personal risk and beliefs about the social problem. The next three chapters focus primarily on the processes and effects of political media under different motivational conditions. Klaus Schoenbach and David Weaver, in a panel study of a West German election, explore the effects of interest and uncertainty on the structuring of political information. Based in part on cognitive response research, Richard Perloff examines the relationships between personal relevance and both the nature of respondents' political cognitions and their information seeking; he then suggests some interrelationships between cognitive response studies and the literature on self-interested political behavior. In the next chapter, Gina Garramone focuses on the processes that underlie the uses and gratifications of political media. She reports the results of several studies in which motives are experimentally manipulated to determine their effects on the processing of mass communications.

Russell Neuman and Ann Fryling begin Part III by discussing the "constructive tension" that exists between macro research on public opinion and more molecular studies of political information processing. Arthur Miller and Kent Asp examine what individuals at different levels of education and political partisanship learn from television and newspapers in the United States and Sweden. Miller and Asp apply research and constructs from cognitive psychology to help illuminate and explain their findings. Philip Tetlock describes his studies of political thinking among policy elites; guided by integrative complexity theory, he discusses several extensions of his research program and suggests some possible linkages with the mass media. Finally, in Part IV Sidney Kraus critically reviews the studies, discussing their findings in light of behavior in previous elections and the real world of politics. His chapter is guided by both the "critical events" and participant/observer approaches, and is organized under a schematic approach developed by the editors.

As a whole, the book reflects the present state of theory and research in the area of political information processing. When we started this project in 1982, there were a handful of interdisciplinary studies on political information processing. By 1985 that number has multiplied. We hope that this book will stimulate further borrowing, bridging, and integration of concepts from different fields so that by the time another set of researchers decides to put together an edited volume, we will have an even more comprehensive body of knowledge on the cognitive processing and effects of political media.

## REFERENCES

BECKER, L. B., M. E. McCOMBS, and J. M. McLEOD (1975) "The development of political cognitions," pp. 21-64 in S. H. Chaffee (ed.) Political Communication: Issues and Strategies for Research. Beverly Hills, CA: Sage.

KLAPPER, J. T. (1960) The Effects of Mass Communication. New York: Free Press.

LAZARSFELD, P. F., B. BERELSON, and H. GAUDET (1944) The People's Choice. New York: Columbia University Press.

LIPPMANN, W. (1922/1947) Public Opinion. New York: Macmillan. (originally published 1922)

SCHRAMM, W. (1955) "How communication works," pp. 3-26 in W. Schramm (ed.) The Process and Effects of Mass Communication. Urbana: University of Illinois Press.

# PART I

## COGNITIVE FOUNDATIONS

Chapter 1

# VOTER THOUGHT PROCESSES
# AND VOTING THEORY

## John A. Herstein, Jr.

THE VOTER IS mysterious, sometimes seeming aloof, wise, and calculating, other times appearing simple, amusing, and vulnerable. Are these
two creatures the same? Sometimes the voter blandly sweeps an unsatis-
factory president from office, other times the voter meekly gives sanction
to foregone circumstance. How might this mystery be solved? Perhaps
there is no solution, but if there is a solution it must begin with knowledge of the voter's mind. In pursuit of this answer this chapter delineates
the cognitive processing assumptions that are inherent in five traditional
models of voting. Next, the chapter reviews psychological perspectives
on decision making and discusses the implications for voter thought
processes. Finally, it concludes with a discussion of a cognitive processing model of voting and presents data from three tests of the model.

## COGNITIVE PROCESSING ASSUMPTIONS
## UNDERLYING TRADITIONAL MODELS OF VOTING

At the risk of ignoring important contributions to the theory of
voting, this treatment of traditional models is confined to those accom-

AUTHOR'S NOTE: I would like to thank Susan T. Fiske for her scholarly
guidance through the literature on political psychology and her many suggestions.
I would also like to thank Margaret S. Clark and John R. Hayes for the many hours

panied by data. These models are classified as basically nonrational, rational, or somewhere in between. In this chapter, rational refers to logical and goal-oriented symbol manipulation.

## NONRATIONAL VOTING

The first major empirical investigation of voting emphasized factors other than reason. In their book, *The People's Choice,* Lazarsfeld et al. (1944) argue that social characteristics determine political preference. Lazarsfeld et al. never explicitly present an integrated model, but they do examine the effects of various factors on the vote and even describe a process called activation. Figure 1.1 shows a representation of the cognitive processes implicit in Lazarsfeld et al.'s analysis. The model reduces to two rather simple processes: (1) political predispositions are activated and then (2) candidates are matched to political predispositions. The candidate who matches is the candidate who receives the vote.

The model of the vote decision presented by Campbell et al. (1960) in *The American Voter* is more explicit than that of *The People's Choice,* but still appeals to social characteristics as the ultimate determinant of the vote. Predispositions do not enter directly into their hypothesized voting process but supposedly determine party identification. Party identification then determines attitudes toward political objects, which in turn determine the vote. Consequently, the cognitive processes posited by Campbell et al. leading up to the point of choice are almost as simple as those underlying Lazarsfeld et al.'s analysis (see Figure 1.2). These processes can also be described in a two-stage model: (1) attitude formation and (2) comparisons of attitudes.

Both models, rooted in social determinism, assume that a fairly simple set of mental operations are involved in the vote decision. This is largely because much of the process is predetermined. Political predispositions are already formed and attitudes derive from stable party identification. Rational models tend to assume much more complicated cognitive processes.

they spent editing earlier versions of this chapter. In addition, thanks go to Kristi J. Anderson, Herbert B. Asher, William Gabrenya, and Stuart J. Thorson for useful discussions and comments. Special thanks are due John S. Carroll with whom many of the important ideas presented in this chapter were first developed.

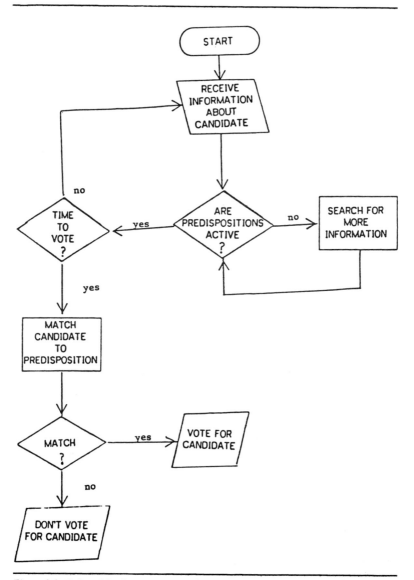

**Figure 1.1 A Cognitive Process Interpretation of Lazarsfeld, Berelson, and Gaudet**

**RATIONAL VOTING**

Modern theoretical conceptions of the rational voter have existed since Downs's (1957) *An Economic Theory of Democracy.* Downs borrows from the economists' model of human behavior and proposes a voter who maximizes benefits and minimizes costs in the act of voting. Shapiro (1969) operationalized and tested a model based on a synthesis of Downsian ideas and social psychological theory. The cognitive processing assumptions of Shapiro's model are representative of those processing assumptions made by most cost-benefit or spatial models: An evaluation of each candidate is based on the proximity of the candidate to the voter's self or ideal candidate along various dimensions. As can be seen in Figure 1.3, quite a bit of calculation is required for a rational voter of this type to arrive at a decision. The more informed such a voter, the more calculations that voter must perform in order to arrive at a vote.

More recent versions of spatial models are even more complex in form (Enelow and Hinich, 1982), but the underlying processing assumptions are, I believe (after rubbing the mathematical smoke from my eyes), the same.

Fishbein and Coombs (1974) have proposed a model of attitudes toward candidates that has a structure vaguely similar to those in the Downsian tradition. Instead of a distance between the candidate and voter in a multidimensional space, they speak of an overall attitude. Instead of various unidimensional distances, they speak of evaluations or attitudes toward various specific objects (like political parties, personal characteristics, or issue stances). Their model is reminiscent in this respect of *The American Voter* model. Instead of dimension weights, they speak of the strength of beliefs or subjective probabilities that link the politician and various attitude objects. Thus one may strongly positively value an improved economy while believing that there is only one chance in ten that such improvement is a genuine concern of a given politician. Finally, instead of computing Euclidean distances, the probabilitized evaluations are simply summed. In this respect Fishbein and Coombs's model is simpler than the spatial models, but still posits unlikely cognitive processes.

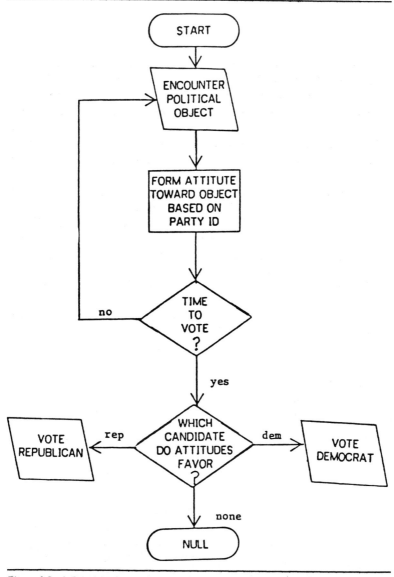

**Figure 1.2   A Cognitive Interpretation of Campbell, Converse, Miller, and Stokes**

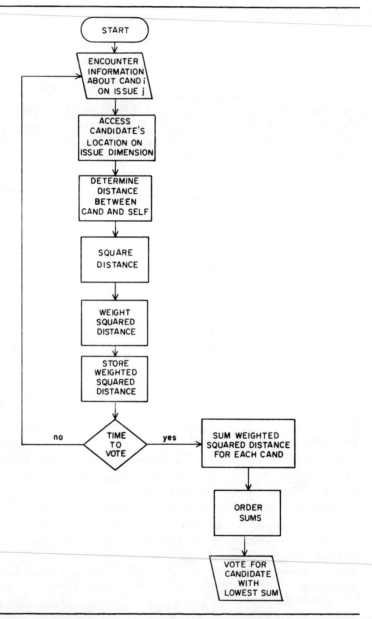

**Figure 1.3  Spatial Model**

## HEURISTIC VOTING

More recent formulations of the voting process focus on reasonable rules by which voters may decide, rather than on the information on which they base their decisions or the rationality of the process. Brody and Page (1973) suggest a heuristic illustrated in Figure 1.4. Voters simply choose the candidate they evaluate most highly. If a voter likes all candidates equally, he or she votes at random. This model posits simple cognitive processes without appealing to social determinism.

Kelley and Mirer (1974) proposed to improve upon previous explanations of voter's choices. They prefaced their analysis by describing three basic characteristics of a better explanation of voting: (1) it should have a higher statistical association with voter choice than competing explanations, (2) it should be a more believable account of the way a voter may arrive at a vote than competing explanations, and (3) it should permit more accurate predictions of voting than competing explanations. They cite the model presented in *The American Voter* as the current theory coming closest to meeting these criteria. But, as Kelley and Mirer put it, although Campbell et al. provided the basic ingredients, they left out the recipe for mixing them. Kelley and Mirer looked for this recipe by examining a large number of heuristics for predicting the vote. The best was another relatively simple rule: The number of reasons for voting for a candidate minus the number of reasons for voting against a candidate gives a score to each candidate. The candidate with the highest net positive reasons is the choice. Party identification breaks ties. Figure 1.5 is a flow diagram of the Kelley and Mirer rule.

Miller and Miller (1977) give a comprehensive analysis of rational choice in the 1976 presidential election. Although they present no rule for integrating political information, they do show that no one type of information, such as party identification or issues, can alone account for the vote. Both issue voting and partisan loyalty played weaker roles in the 1976 election, whereas assessment of candidate performance played a stronger role. Miller and Miller point out that the election outcome must be analyzed in terms of all these factors and their possible interactions.

Each of these analyses of the voting process supports aspects of both sides of the rational voter controversy. Brody and Page (1973) find support in their data for both the rational model assumption that voters maximize utility and the "funnel of causality" metaphor used by Campbell et al. to describe the effects of prior perceptions on political objects.

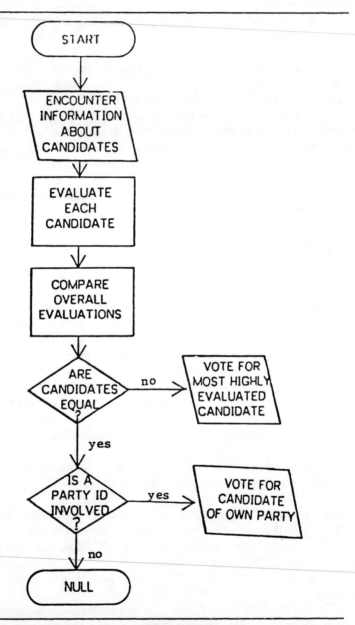

**Figure 1.4   A Flowchart of the Brody and Page Heuristic**

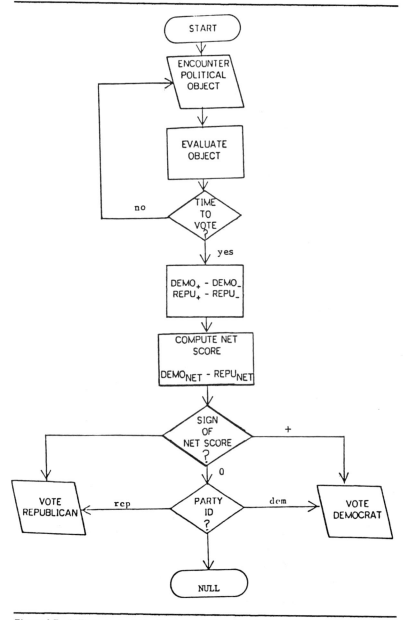

**Figure 1.5  A Flowchart of the Kelley and Mirer Heuristic**

Kelley and Mirer (1974) complement *The American Voter* but see their own rule as rational. Miller and Miller (1977) emphasize the need to identify the conditions under which issue voting will be important and when it will not. It seems that researchers have come to the reasonable conclusion that the voter is neither completely rational nor completely nonrational, but somewhere in between.

Much of the rational voter controversy may be the result of a paradigm clash (Kuhn, 1962), a paradigm being defined here as a meta-theoretical set of assumptions shared by a scientific community. Two theories coming out of different paradigms may explain the same data equally well, and there is probably no crucial test to support one while falsifying the other. What is now needed is a new way to view the voter: a paradigm that can account for both the rational and nonrational aspects of the voting process.

## SOCIAL COGNITIVE RESEARCH ON
## RATIONALITY AND THE VOTING PROCESS

Rational models of decision making tend to view people as choosing among alternative actions by using available information to identify the optimal choice. However, substantial evidence exists indicating that this rational model is simply incorrect. People are unreasonably influenced by concrete, personalized information (Nisbett et al., 1976); they judge probability by envisioning concrete instances (Tversky and Kahneman, 1973); multiattribute judgments and decisions are based on only part of the available information (Slovic, 1975; Payne, 1976). Even expert decision makers use the same simplifying strategies producing the same errors as do laypeople (Dawes, 1976; Slovic et al., 1976).

In order to choose optimally, humans would be expected to take into account all available relevant information. In fact, people are severely limited in the amount of information they can process (Miller, 1956; Newell and Simon, 1972). Large amounts of information are not only difficult to process but can actually reduce the effectiveness of a decision while increasing the decision maker's confidence (Payne, 1976).

Any model of voting that assumes exhaustive search or full utilization of all information in the voter's memory must be modified. Shapiro's (1969) model and Kelley and Mirer's (1974) heuristic are particularly vulnerable to this criticism. Shapiro assumed voters acquired and integrated information about a large number of issues, and Kelly and Mirer used all the attitudes voters output in order to make their vote predictions. In fact, Kelly and Mirer report that the accuracy of their predictions decrease as the number of attitudes voters mention increase. This decrement in accuracy of prediction as a function of the number of attitudes voters hold would be expected if voters used only a small number of attitudes in making their decisions. As the number of attitudes in memory increase, the scientist's ability to predict which attitudes will actually be drawn into the choice process decreases.

Limited processing capacity presents special problems for spatial models of voting. As was shown earlier, the numerical calculations required to arrive at a vote using the processes suggested by these models are formidable. The processing capacity required to square, store, and sum even a few values for each of two candidates is beyond that of most people. Highly practiced individuals using sophisticated strategies may be able to cope with these calculations (Hunter, 1968), but the average voter does not have such capabilities.

Decision making research suggests that any model of voting that posits first an evaluation and then a comparison of candidates is flawed. Two of the models discussed earlier suffer from this flaw—Brody and Page's (1973) heuristic and the spatial model of Shapiro (1969). Brody and Page offer no hypothesis as to how an evaluation is made, but their proposed process is a comparison of candidate evaluations, not a series of comparisons of particular attributes of the candidates. Shapiro's model clearly assumes a candidate-by-candidate computation of distance from some ideal in a multidimensional space.

The reader may have noted that rational models of voting have fared especially badly in our process analysis. This is not surprising, given that Simon's (1957) formulation of bounded rationality was in part a reaction to the economists' models of human decision making. These models' susceptibility to attack may be attributed to the same qualities that have enhanced their attractiveness—they are well-specified, rigorous formulations. But there is ample evidence that these elegant machines are bad representations of cognitive processes.

One might argue that the original Downsian conception sought only a predictive device or a linkage between candidate and voter behavior rather than a model of the psychological processes involved in voting, but this seems unlikely in view of the following psychological assumptions Downs (1957) makes concerning decision makers. For example:

(1) The voter can always make a decision when confronted with a range of alternatives.

(2) The voter ranks all alternatives in order of preference.

(3) The voter's preference ranking is transitive.

(4) The voter always chooses from among the possible alternatives that alternative ranking highest in his or her preference ordering.

(5) Faced with the same alternatives the voter always makes the same decision.

Assumption 1 seems reasonable, given that the option of not voting is considered an alternative. Assumption 2 is unlikely given the poor memory subjects have for comparisons of alternatives (Johnson, 1978). Assumption 3 is probably mistaken, inasmuch as intransitivity of preference has been observed (Tversky, 1969). Slovic (1966) presents data that cast doubt on assumption 4, that is, that choice makers have been observed choosing an alternative that would rationally be ranked below another alternative. Assumption 5 runs afoul of the possibility that voters may shift their choices as they focus on different attributes of the candidates. In short, the psychological assumptions on which the economic-spatial model is based are currently in question. Similarly, the other models also make assumptions about human decision making that are inconsistent with what we know about how people make choices.

## A NEW APPROACH TO
## DATA ABOUT VOTER BEHAVIOR

Traditional models of voting pay little or no attention to thought processing assumptions. Why is it important to consider assumptions at the processing level? Isn't a highly predictive theory good enough? No. Not if we wish to know how the media and other stimuli affect voter thought processes. Not if we are intent on improving political information processing capabilities.

### GENERAL FEATURES OF A PROCESS MODEL

Given the limited information processing capability of voters, it is reasonable to assume that fairly simple decision processes are used in choosing a candidate. The kinds of processes a voter undertakes can be generally described at this point, without postulating a specific process model of the vote decision.

Any decision process must normally begin with the acquisition of information. Information is either sought or incidentally acquired, and then is represented in long-term memory. For the voter this information may include each candidate's position on important issues, past performance, party, physical appearance, and so forth. When called upon to make a choice, the voter must access part or all of this information from memory and process it. On the basis of previous decision-making research, we could guess that the actual process involves partial information and simple comparisons.

A general class of methodologies known as process tracing has shown itself to be particularly helpful in the study of decision making (Payne et al., 1978; Ericsson and Simon, 1980; Russo and Rosen, 1975; and Wilkens, 1967).

The first steps in tracing the processes involved in a vote decision have already been taken (Herstein, 1981). Using process tracing data and previous work in decision making, a model of the cognitive processes involved in voting was constructed.

## A MODEL OF VOTE DECISIONS

Let's pretend that we have looked into the mind of the voter. Granted, we can only observe shadows of reflections, but let's pretend. Such observations suggest the following criteria for any model of voter thought processes: (a) the model should posit that the voter compares candidates along attribute dimensions first rather than evaluating each candidate on all attribute dimensions and then making comparisons; (b) the model should include a central role for negative overall evaluations of candidates (i.e., negative "gut" feelings); and (c) processing limitations must be incorporated into the model.

Based on the preceding criteria, the heart of this model of voter cognition can be represented as follows:

(1) If candidate has negative overall evaluation, vote against the candidate.

(2) Otherwise, compare candidates on a few particular items and select the better candidate.

Figure 1.6 shows a detailed representation of this process.

It should be stressed here that although the general features of a process model were developed prior to the process tracing study, the complete model was developed post hoc in light of the data; the model was not a hypothesis that was tested using the process tracing data. However, tests of the model's validity were made and will be described

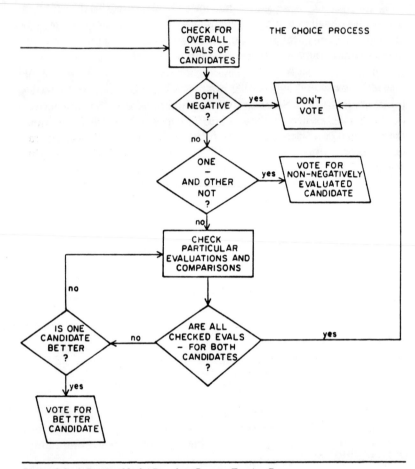

THE CHOICE PROCESS

**Figure 1.6   A Process Model Based on Process-Tracing Data**

later in this chapter. Directly below the reader will find a brief summary of the process tracing study.

Twenty Carnegie-Mellon University undergraduates were placed in front of an information display and asked to vote for one of two candidates in three simulated elections. The information display offered 45 items of information about each candidate. Subjects were told to access as much or as little information as they wished before making a decision.

Data from process tracing studies are extremely rich, but below are summarized only findings that correspond to the criteria for a model of voter thought processes stated above. (1) The model should posit that voters give prominence to particular attribute comparisons rather than evaluating each candidate on an attribute dimensions and then comparing the candidates. This hypothesis was confirmed by the prevalence of intraitem searching of the information display. (2) The central role for overall negative evaluations was not hypothesized, but observed in the process tracing data. Negative overall evaluations were the only perfect predictors of choice in these data. However, they are fairly rare, appearing in only 25 percent of the verbal protocols. (3) The incorporation of processing limitations is basic to any model of human thought. These limitations are reflected in the process tracing data by the fact that only 17.1 of the 45 information items were accessed, on average, and a mean of only five items was remembered as being important in retrospective reports. (For a complete report of these data see Herstein, 1981.)

## TESTS OF THE MODEL

Three tests of the process model have been conducted since the process tracing study. The data for these tests were gathered prior to actual elections in the Fall of 1978, the Spring of 1980, and the Fall of 1980. I will describe the test in the Spring of 1980 first, mainly because this study includes a comparison with some of the traditional models.

### OHIO, SPRING 1980

The presidential primary in Ohio provided an opportunity to compare five voting models: Kelley and Mirer's rule, Brody and Page's heuristic, my cognitive process model, an issue space model, and a standard model derived from Lazarsfeld et al.'s work in *The People's Choice.*

A questionnaire that focused on four candidates for president of the United States—two Democrats and two Republicans (Carter, Kennedy, Reagan, and Bush)—was filled out by 64 voting-age undergraduates at Ohio State University. Each of the models requires a particular type of input.

The input for the Kelley and Mirer rule was obtained by inviting subjects to express their likes and dislikes for each of the four candidates in an open-ended format. In other words, subjects simply listed their positive and negative feelings about the candidates. In order to compute the model's vote prediction we substracted the number of negative feelings from the number of positive feelings and selected the candidate with the largest difference, using party identification (ID) to break ties when appropriate (see Figure 1.5).

The input for the Brody and Page heuristic consisted of four thermometer measures, one for each of the candidates. A thermometer measure is a measure of affective warmth. It ranges from 0° to 100°. The warmest candidate was considered the model's selection (see Figure 1.4).

The input for my cognitive process model was taken in two parts: (1) subjects were afforded an opportunity to express overall evaluations about each of the candidates, and (2) subjects were asked which candidate they preferred on a number of particular topics. Subjects were also asked to rate each of the topics for importance on a 1 to 10 scale. The vote prediction was computed by first ruling out any candidate for whom a negative overall evaluation was expressed, and, as in most cases, if no such expression was made the candidates were compared on a small number of particular topics. Subjects were asked to circle the name of the candidate they preferred on each of 11 topics. The actual number of topic comparisons used as input for the model depended on the number that were rated highly important (usually 4 or 5). Party ID was used to break ties when appropriate. This feature of the model was added after the 1978 study (Herstein, 1981). The candidate with no negative overall evaluation and the most favorable comparisons on the few important topics was the model's vote prediction (see Figure 1.6).

Input for the issue space voting model was obtained by having subjects rate themselves, an ideal candidate, and each of the four presidential candidates on a series of seven-point scales that indicated issue stances. With these data a point representing the self and a point representing each of the candidates was located in a multidimensional issue space. The candidate the least distance from the self in the issue space was predicted to be the voter's choice (see Figure 1.3).

The input for Lazarsfeld et al.'s model was obtained by asking each subject to indicate his or her family income, religion, and place of residence. With these data we calculated an Index of Political Predisposition (IPP). The index ranges from 1 to 7; 1 indicates high income, rural residence, and Protestant religion—a total Republican predisposition; 7 indicates low income, urban residence, and Catholic religion—a total Democrat predisposition. The index was calculated for each subject by adding one point for urban residence, one point for being Catholic, and between one and four points for income level—the lower the income, the more points added. Finally, we necessarily had to adapt the index predictions to a four candidate choice, with two candidates from each party. We treated 1 and 2 IPPs as predictions for Reagan, 2.5 to 3.5 IPPs as predictions for Bush, 4 to 5.5 IPPs as predictions for Carter, and 6 and 7 IPPs as predictions for Kennedy (see Figure 1.1).

There were four orders in which the inputs were gathered. The open-ended question about the likes and dislikes for the Kelley and Mirer model came last in every case, whereas the order in which the other four question sets appeared was counterbalanced. An equal number of subjects received each of the orders.

Brody and Page's heuristic did best of all the models, correctly predicting 76.5 percent of the subjects' expressed voting intentions. My model was the next most accurate, predicting 68.8 percent of the voting intentions (which is actually not significantly different from 76.5 percent by the Newman-Keuls test). Several different versions of the issue space model were tested; the most accurate involved choosing the candidate closest to the self (rather than the ideal candidate) in unweighted issue space. This model predicted 50 percent of the intentions correctly (which is significantly different from 68.8 percent by Newman-Keuls). Kelley and Mirer's model predicted only 40.6 percent of the voting intentions, and Lazarsfeld et al. did even worse, predicting 26.5 percent correctly.

None of these models did very well by conventional standards. Voting models typically predict over 85 percent of the vote correctly; our best predictor, the Brody and Page heuristic, correctly predicted just 76 percent of our subjects' preferences. These poor showings are probably due to the relatively large number of candidates the subjects had to choose from and lack of party ID as a tie-breaker in many cases. Kelley and Mirer's model was especially affected by the fact that many ties could not be broken by party identification; for example, an equal number of net positive attitudes toward Carter and Kennedy would remain a tie because they are both Democrats.

Nevertheless, the findings that emerge from this first comparison of five voting models indicate that the process model is a reasonable predictor of voting choice. Its performance is not significantly worse than the best and is significantly better than the other three models. Furthermore, as my earlier discussion indicated, the process model better reflects our knowledge of human decision making than do the other four models. The results from this lab study were encouraging, but somewhat suspect due to the small sample size. In the final study reported in this chapter, a larger sample was selected and interviewed;

this study, along with the one described below, tests only my cognitive process model.

## PENNSYLVANIA, 1978

Chronologically, the 1978 Pennsylvania gubernatorial election provided the first opportunity to test the model using registered voters. Respondents (107) were telephoned and asked questions about their feelings and thoughts concerning the two major candidates. Respondents' answers to these questions revealed any negative overall evaluations and identified what the most salient campaign topics were for each voter. Respondents also provided particular preferences on each campaign topic; in other words, they indicated which candidate they preferred on each campaign topic. In addition, respondents were asked to express a vote preference.

In order to assess the predictive power of the model, information about negative overall evaluations, topic salience, and particular comparisons were plugged into the model at appropriate places in order to simulate the hypothesized decision processes of each of the respondents (see Figure 1.6). Predictions were compared to the vote preferences that respondents indicated. Of the 107 respondents, 70 percent expressed a vote preference. The model makes a prediction for 86 percent of these voters. The model matches the indicated vote preference of 94 percent of these cases.

## OHIO, FALL 1980

This third test of the model involved the general election of 1980. Stuart Thorson and Kristi Anderson graciously allowed me to suggest items for a survey conducted by the Polimetrics Lab at Ohio State University. This test differs in two important respects from the other tests. First, the operationalization of the model was greatly streamlined. Second, the sample size was much larger.

In previous tests of the model, negative overall evaluations were tapped by open-ended questions about candidates. In this test a standard feeling thermometer question was used, and feelings of less than 50° (on a 0°-100° scale) were assumed to be reflections of overall negative evaluations.

In previous tests of the model the measurement of topic salience and the comparisons of the candidates on each topic was measured using a lengthy closed-ended procedure. Respondents were asked to rate how important each of several topics were on a numerical scale and which candidate they preferred on each topic. In this study the respondents were asked simply to name the issues that seemed most important to them and then asked to compare the candidates on the issues they named.

A common complaint about the work of the psychologist in the realm of political science is that of sample size. This complaint can be dealt with by pointing out that the processing variables have much lower distribution dispersion than attitudes or demographics. But in this case no arguments are necessary: The Polimetrics Lab interviewed 976 respondents.

Of this nice-sized sample, 88 percent expressed a clear preference and some prediction was made for them by the model. Another 8 percent of the sample expressed no preference and the remaining 4 percent of the sample expressed a preference but no prediction was made for them by the model. It should be noted that these are predictions of a modified version of the model in which party identification is assumed to be a salient topic in case of ties. Of the 857 cases who expressed a preference and for whom a prediction was made, 87 percent were correctly predicted.

## DISCUSSION

This chapter began with a critique of the traditional models of voting behavior. It was argued that these models make certain assumptions about human thought processes. Some of these assumptions, especially those of the rational models, are simply inconsistent with what we know about how people go about making choices. In order to help remedy this situation, a cognitive process model was proposed that differed from these other approaches in two ways: (1) it allocates a central role to negative overall evaluations of the candidates (i.e., negative gut feelings); and (2) it posits that voters compare candidates along attribute dimensions first rather than evaluating each candidate on all attribute dimensions and then making comparisons. This model emerged post hoc from a laboratory process tracing study. In this experiment, negative overall evaluations played an important role in voters' choices, emerging as the only perfect predictor of choice. In addition, key processing limitations were also observed, as evidenced by the fact that subjects recalled only 5 of 45 items as being important factors in retrospective reports.

Subsequent tests indicate that the model compares favorably to others, statistically as good as the best, and in the context of a large survey performs quite well. Although future studies are needed that pit Brody and Page and other models against my own in larger sample surveys, the present results are encouraging.

The relative predictive power of the cognitive process model in comparison with the other models not only encourages the use of process tracing techniques, but also supports one of the assumptions on which the model is based—that voters are quite limited in their information processing capacities. Given the validity of this assumption, an interesting question can be posed: How deficient is the voter of bounded rationality compared to the optimal (but nonexistent) rational voter? Given the uncertain world in which we live, optimizing equations cannot predict outcomes much better than human judges. Both equation and human judge are terrible at making such relatively simple predictions as success in graduate school (Dawes, 1976). In the more complex domains of world and domestic affairs both types of judges are likely to do even worse. The question now becomes one of preference. Are the voters at least voting for the candidate they really want? The answer to this question is "most of the time." The three, four, or five items a voter takes into account will usually be the ones he or she considers most important. The only danger is that the media or some cognitive fluke will make relatively unimportant items salient at the time of decision. (For a discussion of media effects on salience ratings, see Iyengar and Kinder's chapter in this volume.)

Recall for a moment the basics of the cognitive process model: (a) vote against candidates evoking a negative "gut" reaction, and (b) compare all other candidates on a few topics. The media may affect these processes in three ways. First, as mentioned above, the media may determine what topics are salient at the time of the election. Second, the media may provide the needed commensurate information so that the voter may make a comparison. Thus, a voter may approve of candidate A's energy policy, but this approval may not enter into the decision process unless the media provide similar information about candidate B's energy policy. Third, the media may provide such negative news about a candidate that regardless of one's initial evaluation the voter will tag the candidate with a negative overall evaluation.

# REFERENCES

BRODY, R. A. and B. I. PAGE (1973) Indifference, alienation and rational decision. Public Choice 15: 1-17.

CAMPBELL, A., P. E. CONVERSE, W. E. MILLER, and D. E. STOKES (1960) The American Voter. New York: John Wiley.

DAWES, R. M. (1976) "Shallow psychology," in J. S. Carroll and J. W. Payne (eds.) Cognition and Social Behavior. Hillsdale, NJ: Lawrence Erlbaum.

DOWNS, A. (1957) An Economic Theory of Democracy. New York: Harper & Row.

ENELOW, J. M. and M. J. HINICH (1982) "Twenty-five years after Downs: the future of the spatial theory of elections." Paper presented at the 1982 Annual Meeting of the American Political Science Association, Denver, Colorado, September 2-5.

ERICSSON, K. A. and H. A. SIMON (1980) "Verbal reports as data." Psychological Review, 87: 215-251.

FISHBEIN, M. and F. S. COOMBS (1974) "Basis for decision: An attitudinal analysis of voting behavior." Journal of Applied Social Psychology 4: 95-124.

HERSTEIN, J. A. (1981) "Keeping the voter's limits in mind: a cognitive process analysis of decision making in voting." Journal of Personality and Social Psychology 40; 843-861.

HUNTER, I.M.L. (1968) "Mental calculation," in P. C. Wason and P. N. Johnson-Laird (eds.) Thinking and Reasoning. Baltimore: Penguin.

JOHNSON, E. J. (1978) "Decision making: what we know about process." Unpublished manuscript, Carnegie-Mellon University.

KELLEY, S., Jr. and T. W. MIRER (1974) "The simple act of voting." American Political Science Review 61: 572-591.

KUHN, T. S. (1962) The Structure of Scientific Revolutions. Chicago: University of Chicago Press.

LAZARSFELD, P., B. BERELSON, and M. GAUDET (1944) The People's Choice. New York: Columbia University Press.

MILLER, A. H. and W. E. MILLER (1977) "Partisanship and performance: 'rational' choice in the 1976 Presidential election." Manuscript prepared for delivery at the 1977 Annual Meeting of the American Political Science Association, Washington, DC, September 1-4.

MILLER, G. A. (1956) "The magical number seven plus or minus two: some limits on our capacity for processing information." Psychological Review 63: 61-97.

NEWELL, A. and H. A. SIMON (1972) Human Problem Solving. Englewood Cliffs, NJ: Prentice-Hall.

NISBETT, R. E., E. BORGIDA, R. CRANDALL, and H. REED (1976) "Popular induction: information is not necessarily informative," in J. S. Carroll and J. W. Payne (eds.) Cognition and Social Behavior. Hillsdale, NJ: Lawrence Erlbaum.

PAYNE, J. W. (1976) "Task complexity and contingent processing in decision making: an information search and protocol analysis." Organizational Behavior and Human Performance 16: 366-387.

———M. L. BRAUNSTEIN, and J. S. CARROLL (1978) "Exploring predecisional behavior: an alternative approach to decision research." Organizational Behavior and Human Performance 22: 17-44.

RUSSO, J. E. and L. D. ROSEN (1975) "An eye fixation analysis of multi-alternative choice." Memory and Cognition 3: 267-276.

SHAPIRO, M. J. (1969) "Rational political-man: a synthesis of economic and social-psychological perspectives." American Political-Science Review 63: 1106-1119.

SIMON, H. A. (1957) Models of Man. New York: John Wiley.

SLOVIC, P. (1975) "Choice between equally valued alternatives." Journal of Experimental Psychology: Human Perception and Performance 1: 280-287.

———(1966) Cue-consistency and cue-utilization in judgment. American Journal of Psychology 79: 427-434.

SLOVIC, P. and S. LICHTENSTEIN (1971) "Comparison of Bayesian and regression approaches to the study of information processing in judgment." Organizational Behavior and Human Performance 6: 649-744.

SLOVIC, P., B. FISCHOFF, and S. LICHTENSTEIN (1976) "Cognitive processes and societal risk taking," in J. S. Carroll and J. W. Payne (eds.) Cognition and Social Behavior. Hillsdale, NJ: Lawrence Erlbaum.

THORNGATE, W. and J. MAKI (1976) "Decision heuristics and the choice of political candidates." Unpublished manuscript, University of Alberta.

TVERSKY, A. (1972) Elimination by aspects: A theory of choice. Psychological Review, 79: 281-299.

———(1969) "Intransitivity of preferences." Psychological Review, 76: 31-48.

———and D. KAHNEMAN (1973) "Availability: a heuristic for judging frequency and probability." Cognitive Psychology 5: 207-232.

WILKINS, L. (1967) Social Deviance. Englewood Cliffs, NJ: Prentice-Hall.

Chapter 2


# POLITICAL SOPHISTICATION
## An Information-Processing Perspective


Richard R. Lau
Ralph Erber


TO FULLY APPRECIATE and understand any area of knowledge, one must study how experts think about that topic. By definition, experts *know* more than nonexperts about any area. They have had more experience thinking about it, and they presumably have learned the most efficacious ways of grouping, categorizing, or organizing information in that domain. In many areas of knowledge, the only relevant actors are experts (plus perhaps novices becoming experts). Theoretical physics is a domain reserved chiefly for experts; novices play little part, and in fact most of us nonexperts are totally unaware that the game is even being played. Such is not the case with politics, however. Unlike theoretical physics, unless one lives in a cave high up on a mountain, one is very unlikely to be completely oblivious to politics.

Over the past decade cognitive psychology has begun to study basic information processing differences between experts and novices. Starting with a brief review of that literature, this chapter will examine how the field of political behavior has studied political expertise, or "political sophistication," to use the more popular term. As we shall see, political science implicitly has taken a much more narrow or domain-specific

AUTHORS' NOTE: We would like to thank Susan Fiske, Karen Hartman, and Jim Sidanius for commenting on an earlier version of this chapter. Please address all correspondence to Richard R. Lau, Department of Social Sciences, Carnegie-Mellon University, Pittsburgh, PA 15213.

view of expertise than has cognitive psychology. After offering a more general measure of political expertise, we will present evidence of significant information processing differences between experts and novices during the 1980 U.S. presidential campaign. We will conclude with a brief discussion of the implications of our findings for the political process.

## INFORMATION PROCESSING DIFFERENCES BETWEEN EXPERTS AND NOVICES

In any domain, experts and novices differ from each other in at least two aspects. The first difference lies in the amount of knowledge they have. Grandmasters in chess know more about the game than ordinary players. Physics professors know more about their field than sophomores. This expert-novice difference is hardly arguable. Of more ιterest, however, experts and novices differ not ony in the amount of knowledge they have but also in the ways they *structure and organize* it in memory. This difference can account for what is sometimes called "the paradox of the expert" (Smith et al. 1978; Reder and Anderson, 1980). Although experts have *more* knowledge, they also have an easier time applying it to their domain because of the manner in which it is structured and organized.

Before we can discuss differences in how experts and novices structure and organize knowledge, we must briefly introduce some fundamental assumptions about how people process information in general. The minds of both experts and novices do not consist simply of carbon copies of sensory information. Instead, people impose structure on what reaches their senses. This structuring has two advantages. First, previously stored knowledge can be more easily brought to mind. A good analogy is the ease of retrieving something from a filing system in which the information is stored according to topics rather than randomly. The structure greatly facilitates retrieval. Second, new information can be related to and interpreted in terms of prior knowledge. These preexisting knowledge structures have been called "schemas" (Hastie 1981; Rumelhart and Ortony, 1977; Taylor and Crocker, 1981; see Fiske and Taylor, 1984, for a good review). In keeping with Rumelhart and Ortony, we think of schemas as knowledge structures representing generic concepts in some stimulus domain that specify the interrelations assumed to exist between the attributes of each concept. In addition, schemas are related to specific instances of the concept.

The concepts represented by a schema can vary in their degree of abstraction. One can have a schema for generic politicians that includes all the attributes that politicians are believed to have in common (e.g., dishonest, power hungry, have opinions on issues, are usually lawyers). On a lower level of abstraction, one can have concepts representing specific types of politicians (presidential candidates, congresspersons, foreign and local politicians). Yet a lower level of abstraction can include concrete exemplars, or specific instances of the concept (Ronald Reagan, Jesse Jackson, Tip O'Neill). Finally, the schema includes knowledge about the attributes of a concept and specifies the relationship that is assumed to exist among those attributes. We know, for example, that a liberal is likely to oppose defense spending and cuts in social programs, and that Republicans are likely to center their economic policies on control of inflation even at the expense of increased unemployment.

An instructive way to think about the overall structure of a schema is in terms of a hierarchically organized network of concepts and attributes (nodes) that are interconnected through associations (links). What distinguishes a schema from other parts of memory is that there are more and stronger interconnections among the elements of the schema than there are between those elements and elements of other parts of the larger associative network. The hierarchical organization of the schema allows us to process information in a top-down fashion. When we think about a politician, the top node receives activation, which then spreads through the network (Collins and Loftus, 1975), and schema knowledge "comes to mind" as a unit. Figure 2.1 illustrates a possible schema representation of knowledge about Ronald Reagan.

Note how the concepts represented in the schema decrease in their levels of abstraction. For example, the generic concept politician is linked to the concept president, and that concept is linked to an attribute of his personality (competence). Competence, in turn, is linked to a set of more specific attributes that together make up competence. Similarly, the concept conservative is linked to a number of specific issue positions. These links allow for a great deal of inference. That is, if we know that a particular politician is conservative, we can be pretty sure that she or he favors increased defense spending and cuts in social programs even in the absence of specific information about that person's issues positions. This inference comes about because the concepts and attributes of schema have "default values" (Rumelhart and Ortony, 1977). When the schema is incompletely instantiated, missing information is inferred

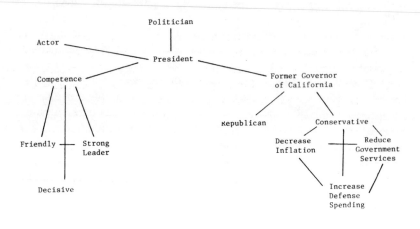

Figure 2.1   **Possible Schema Representation of Knowledge About Ronald Reagan**

from those default values. Thus, in any area in which a person has well-developed schemas, inference is often top-down or "theory-driven" rather than bottom-up or "data-driven."

In this chapter, we propose that experts and nonexperts in politics (as in any other knowledge domain) differ in the extent to which they have well-developed schemas about politics in general, and politicians in particular. More specifically, we propose that the schemas of experts differ from those of nonexperts on at least three dimensions. First, the schemas of experts have more and stronger links among the concepts and their attributes. Second, the concept represented by experts' schemas consist of larger units, or "chunks," of knowledge (Fiske, et al., 1983). Third, experts' chunks are organized in a more meaningful— functional or task-relevant—way. There is evidence for all three propositions from research on expert-novice differences in cognitive psychology.

Most of the evidence for experts having more cohesive schemas than novices comes from computer simulations of expert and novice problem solving (e.g., Larkin et al., 1980). Perhaps the most direct evidence for experts having more and stronger links among concepts and their attributes, however, comes from a study that looked at expertise within a single subject. Chi and Koeske (1983) compared a child's representation of familiar and unfamiliar dinosaurs. The child was an expert with regard to one class of dinosaurs, namely, those with which he had previous experience. The same child was a novice with regard to a different class of dinosaurs, those with which he had little or no experience. First, the subject was asked to list as many dinosaurs as possible. It was assumed that those dinosaurs that were mentioned in succession without a pause were interconnected via concept-concept links. Second, the number of multiple links of attributes (such as "eats plants") to concepts (dinosaurs) was assessed by asking the subject to describe each dinosaur named and by looking at the number of times the same attribute was ascribed to various concepts (such as "eats plants" to Brachiosaur, Stegosaur, Triceratops). The results of the two tasks supported the idea that within an area of expertise there are more interconnections between similar concepts and their attributes.

A memory task administered one year after the initial study sheds some light on the importance of the strength of the interconnections. The subject was presented with models of dinosaurs from the familiar and unfamiliar sets and asked to name them. He correctly named (remembered) 55 percent of the dinosaurs he had been familiar with a year ago, but he remembered only 10 percent of the unfamiliar dinosaurs. One explanation for the superior retention and recognition of the familiar dinosaurs is that the links among concepts were stronger in this set, which prevented forgetting.

The study has two important implications for differences between experts and novices. First, the knowledge of experts seems more cohesive, more tightly organized. Second, and as a result of the greater cohesiveness, experts' knowledge can be more easily brought to mind and is less likely to be forgotten.

The most persuasive evidence that experts' schemas consist of larger chunks of knowledge comes from Chase and Simon's (1973) work on expert-novice differences in chess. Chase and Simon argued that the differences in the performance of grandmasters and ordinary players may be explained in terms of how they represent board configurations in memory. Experts presumably organize configurations into larger chunks than do novices. This difference in chunking, in turn, facilitates the recognition of a given configuration and decreases the amount of information that has to be retained in short-term memory while deciding on the proper move. To test their assertion about chunking differences, a grandmaster, a class A master, and a beginner were asked to reconstruct board configurations representing middle games (with 24-26 pieces on the board) and end games (with 12-15 pieces on the board). Some of the configurations were meaningful, that is, they were actual positions selected from chess magazines; other configurations were constructed randomly.

The results showed remarkable differences in the ability of the three players to accurately reconstruct the meaningful board configurations. The grandmaster was about twice as accurate in his reconstruction of the configurations (measured as the number of pieces correctly placed) compared to the master, and both were more accurate than the beginning player. The difference was pronounced for the middle games, which consisted of twice as many pieces. All three players were equally poor reconstructing the random configurations, however, regardless of whether they were middle or end games. People have the same short-term memory constraints irrespective of expertise, and therefore after five seconds of exposure all subjects were equally poor in their reconstruction of random patterns. However, the expert was able to divide the meaningful patterns into large chunks and compare them with chunks stored in long-term memory. Indeed, the expert placed more pieces on the board before taking a pause than the less skilled players, suggesting that he recalled larger chunks of the configuration in a sequence. Chunk size is thus another dimension on which experts and novices may vary. Having fewer and larger chunks facilitates both the ability to retrieve information from long-term memory and the efficiency with which new information is related to existing knowledge, because chunking helps to overcome the limitations of short-term memory.

Furthermore, it seems that expert and novice chunks differ not only quantitatively but also qualitatively. Expert chunks are organized in a more functional, perhaps hierarchical fashion. A recent study of computer programmers (McKeithen, et al., 1981) at three levels of skill (beginners, intermediates, and experts) showed that beginners tend to make use of mnemonic devices in representing the programming language. Expert chunks, on the other hand, were organized according to the meaning of the commands in the programming language, such as their descriptive functions and in terms of "if-then" relationships. In addition, knowledge that is organized in a functional way should promote the ways in which it is applied to a problem domain. Mnemonics may facilitate retrieval to a certain extent, but because they are irrelevant to the task, they may interfere with the application of the knowledge (see Anderson, 1982).

The differences in the schemas of experts and nonexperts discussed above should have similar effects in the domain of politics. If we define political expertise in purely cognitive terms, we would expect experts to differ from nonexperts in terms of the amount and strength of interrelations within their schemas, as well as the size and organization of knowledge chunks. The schema illustrated in Figure 2.1 depicts a moderate expert in politics. It is easy to imagine a schema for a novice by deleting some of the concepts, attributes, and interconnections between them. As for chunk size, a nonexpert may think of a politician's personality in terms of single, isolated personality traits, whereas an expert may think of a candidate's personality in terms of concepts such as competence and integrity that are made up of several interconnected traits. Finally, a nonexpert may organize chunks around domain-irrelevant criteria, whereas an expert uses a criterion that is relevant to politics. For example, one may organize a chunk of knowledge about Ronald Reagan around his career as an actor or, alternatively, around the fact that he was formerly the governor of California.

## PREVIOUS TREATMENTS OF POLITICAL SOPHISTICATION

### IDEOLOGY AS POLITICAL SOPHISTICATION

Since at least Lippmann's time, political commentators have noted how widely people vary in their apparent political sophistication (Lippmann, 1922). However, the most influential treatment of political sophistication was not presented until *The American Voter* (Campbell et al., 1960). Based on answers to open-ended survey questions, Campbell et al. categorized respondents into four "levels of conceptualization."

It is difficult to exaggerate the importance of the levels of conceptualization and the subsequent research it inspired for understanding political ideology (see Bennett et al., 1979; Bishop and Frankovic, 1981; Conover and Feldman, 1981; Hagner and Pierce, 1982; Lane, 1973; Leviton and Miller, 1979; Smith, 1980; Wychoff, 1980). It is not our purpose to review that work here (see Converse, 1975; Kinder and Sears, 1985).[1] There is, however, one serious drawback to accepting the levels of conceptualization as a measure of political sophistication: Those levels are ordered in terms of the ability to think about policy issues. This may well be the best way to think about political *ideology*, which was the intent of the levels of conceptualization. But it is a very limited way to think about political *sophistication*. As our review of the cognitive literature has suggested, sophistication or expertise has more generally been defined in terms of knowledge and experience in a certain domain. Certainly political expertise would include knowledge of political issues, but it would also include knowledge about other aspects of the political world, such as candidates, leaders and governments of foreign countries, past experience participating in politics, and paying attention to politics more generally. (Empirically, these factors all covary strongly; Milbraith and Goel, 1977.) Therefore, the levels of conceptualization are tapping only one aspect of political sophistication.

## KNOWLEDGE-BASED MEASURES OF SOPHISTICATION

Fiske and Kinder (1981; Fiske et al., 1983) define political sophistication not in terms of ideology but rather in terms of knowledge. Political knowledge was operationalized only indirectly, however: paying attention to politics and performing political behaviors. Fiske and Kinder reason that the limits of short-term memory are the same for everyone, but if experts' knowledge is more tightly organized, they can consider more consistent information in making a judgment in their area of expertise. Therefore, given a specified amount of information, experts are much more likely than novices to consider *both* consistent *and* (because there is more cognitive "room" in short-term memory) inconsistent information when making judgments. To test this hypothesis, Fiske et al. (1983) described an unknown third-world country (Mauritius) which was labeled as either "democratic" or "Communist." The description, which was the same for all subjects except for the initial label, included information that was both consistent and inconsistent with the label. As predicted, novices had a bias to recall information that was consistent with the initial democratic/Communist label, although experts showed no such bias. Moreover, the inferences that were drawn by the novices seemed to be based on the information in the description that was consistent with the initial label, whereas experts made inferences based on information that was inconsistent with the initial label. Fiske et al. conclude that the organization of knowledge in memory (as distinct from the *amount* of knowledge in memory) has important effects on how new information is utilized.

Using a somewhat different knowledge-based measure of expertise, Lau et al., (1983) examined the beliefs of political experts and novices regarding Massachusetts' Proposition 2½, a property-tax reduction measure. Lau et al. defined political sophistication in terms of political knowledge and involvement (rudimentary knowledge of Reagan's proposed federal budget, holding an opinion on a variety of political issues, having a party identification, placing oneself on a liberalism-conservatism scale, being registered to vote, and always or usually voting) and cognitive ability (or its surrogate, education). Notice that this operationalization of political sophistication has a cognitive basis, although it does include elements of ideology (liberalism-conservatism self-placement, awareness of political issues).

The primary hypothesis reasoned that because the political schemas of experts are more hierarchically organized that those of novice, attitudes toward Proposition 2½ would be more highly correlated with general political values like party identification and liberalism-conservatism in experts than in novices. This hypothesis was strongly supported: The average correlation for experts was .32, for novices only .06. A related hypothesis was that the opinions of experts toward Proposition 2½ would be more closely tied to their background characteristics and past political socialization than those of novices, who would base their opinions solely on proximal beliefs. By "proximal beliefs," we meant attitudes that are tied closely to support or opposition to the proposition, such as beliefs that state and local governments are wasteful, that government employees are inefficient and overpaid, and opinions about more government spending. Again, the hypothesis was based on the greater organization and structure of the political schemas of experts, compared to the "morselizing" of narrowly defined political topics by novices. This hypothesis too was strongly supported. Overall, less than 17 percent of the variance in novices' attitudes toward Proposition 2½ could be explained, whereas 45 percent of the variance in experts' attitudes was explained.

The analyses presented here will continue the line of research defining political sophistication in cognitive, knowledge-based terms. We will refine the measure of political sophistication so that it includes knowledge, performance, and interest. Then we will use this measure to examine information processing differences of experts and novices during the 1980 U.S. presidential campaign. A presidential campaign provides a good opportunity to study information processing differences between political experts and novices for a number of reasons. First, although nonexperts may be more or less oblivious to the everyday business of politics, they do participate in elections, and we can expect them to have at least a rudimentary knowledge of the candidates and the issues. Second, there is a huge amount of information that has to be processed by both experts and nonexperts. On the basis of our previous discussion of expert-novice differences in terms of schema development, we can make three predictions about information processing differences.

(1) Experts should display more stability in their political attitudes and their evaluations of particular candidates. When experts encounter informa-

tion that is somewhat inconsistent with their existing schema, they should be better able than novices to relate it to the schema. Experts and novices may differ in the extent to which they *assimilate* new information into their existing schema or *accommodate* their schema to new information (Piaget, 1952; Piaget and Inhelder, 1973). An expert who has a highly developed and cohesive schema should be more likely to assimilate new information without making major revisions in the overall knowledge structure. On the other hand, a novice with a more rudimentary schema should be more likely to accommodate the new information by revising the schema.

(2) The greater number of interconnections among the attributes of experts' schemas should be reflected in stronger associations between the concepts of the schema and the overall affective evaluation of the candidates. That is, more information should be brought to bear in experts' candidate evaluations, and that information should be more strongly associated with those evaluations compared to evaluations made by novices.[2]

(3) Finally, following Fiske et al. (1983), experts should be better able to perceive specific information about candidates that is inconsistent with their party identification. We must, of course, expect that any candidate perceptions will be strongly influenced by partisanship. Republicans are likely to think of their candidate as more competent and honest than his or her Democratic opponent, and vice versa. Because experts organize their knowledge more hierarchically and efficiently, however, they should be able to make use of information that is inconsistent with their party identification in ascribing traits to candidates. Therefore, if a major issue during a campaign focuses on the competence or integrity of a particular candidate, this focus should be reflected in the candidate evaluations of expert Democrats and Republicans alike, regardless of whether the information is consistent or inconsistent with partisan predispositions.[3]

## EXPERTS AND NOVICES DURING A PRESIDENTIAL CAMPAIGN

### MEASURING POLITICAL SOPHISTICATION

The setting for our study is the 1980 National Election Study conducted by the University of Michigan Center for Political Studies (CPS).[4] We used the data from four waves of a panel conducted in

February (before the first primary), June (after the primaries but before the conventions), September (after the conventions), and November (after the election). We wanted to construct a measure of expertise that primarily reflects information processing differences between experts and novices. In other words, we did not want our operational definition of expertise to be tied exclusively to ideology. Therefore, the first set of variables included in our measure of political sophistication are variables indicating campaign-relevant knowledge of all types. Consequently, familiarity with the candidates and the issues as well as awareness of the polls (every "knowledge" variable available) all enter into our measure of political expertise. In the February wave, respondents were asked how familiar they were with a number of prominent political figures, primarily candidates running on the Democratic and Republican tickets. The political figures included Howard Baker, Jerry Brown, George Bush, Jimmy Carter, John Connally, Phillip Crane, Robert Dole, Gerald Ford, Edward Kennedy, George McGovern, Walter Mondale, Ronald Reagan, and George Wallace. We counted the proportion of candidates that respondents had at least heard of at that time. Respondents were also asked for their position on seven specific issues (four in the first wave, one more in the second wave, and two more in the third wave): (1) trade-offs between reducing unemployment or reducing inflation (even if the other would go up); (2) decreasing or increasing defense spending; (3) whether government should provide fewer public services or continue providing the services it currently does; (4) how strongly we should try to get along with Russia; (5) whether government should focus more on the rights of minorities; (6) whether government should be concerned that everybody has a job; and (7) whether abortion should be legalized. As was done in the assessment of candidate familiarity, we again calculated the proportion of issues on which respondents held an opinion. Knowledge of the polls was our third knowledge variable. In June, respondents were asked which of the three candidates—Reagan, Carter, and Anderson—was leading in the polls and by what margin (narrow or wide). We again calculated the extent to which respondents correctly judged the standings in the polls.

Our operational definition of political sophistication is not limited to pure knowledge-related variables, however, There is another important aspect of expertise that is often underestimated. Experts should be more motivated than novices to *engage in* activities within their domain of expertise. A grandmaster in chess, for example, is more likely to spend considerable time playing the game as well as keeping up with the field by reading the relevant literature. Similarly, political experts should be more likely to become involved in a candidate's campaign by wearing a campaign button, providing financial support, and so on (Milbraith and Goel, 1977). Consistent with Fiske et al. (1983), we also expect political experts to pay more attention than novices to news about the campaign in the media. To assess involvement, we calculated the proportion of political activities respondents performed during the campaign (wearing a campaign button, persuading other people how to vote, giving financial support to a candidate, going to political rallies, displaying a bumper sticker, voting in the 1980 election). Subjects were also asked how much attention they paid to campaign news on television, radio, newspapers, and magazines. We calculate the average amount of attention respondents paid to the media. In addition to involvement and attention, two direct items asking respondents how generally interested they were in politics and how much they cared about the outcome of the election were also included.

Our measure of political sophistication then, is a summary index composed of the following components: familiarity with issues and candidates, knowledge of the polls, campaign-related behavior supporting a candidate, exposure to campaign news in the media, general interest in politics, and caring about the outcome of the election. Each item was standardized and then summed into an index of political sophistication.[5]

The seven components of our sophistication index were submitted to a factor analysis to make sure that they indeed represent parts of the same concept. All seven variables loaded highly (at least .56) on the first unrotated factor. Table 2.1 depicts the intercorrelations among the seven variables. As can be seen, they are all moderately high, and with the exception of two, are all significantly different from zero. The reliability of the political sophistication index computed from the internal consistency of these seven items proved to be quite adequate (alpha = .75).

The summary political sophistication index was then correlated with several other criteria. Our operationalization of political sophistication explicitly excluded ideology (although it does involve knowledge of issues). Therefore, we expected the measure of sophistication to be uncorrelated with the extent to which respondents described themselves as liberal or conservative. The standard CPS measure of ideology (in which respondents place themselves on a seven-point scale from "extremely liberal" to "extremely conservative") was folded at its midpoint to represent extremity of ideological self-identification. The Pearson product-moment correlation between political sophistication and extremity of ideology showed that they are indeed uncorrelated ($r = .05$). We also folded the standard seven-point CPS measure of party

TABLE 2.1
Correlations Between Indicators of Political Sophistication

|  |  | 1 | 2 | 3 | 4 | 5 | 6 | 7 |
|---|---|---|---|---|---|---|---|---|
| (1) | Familiarity with candidates | — | | | | | | |
| (2) | Familiarity with issues | .46 | — | | | | | |
| (3) | Knowledge of polls | .37 | .46 | — | | | | |
| (4) | Political behavior index | .43 | .42 | .36 | — | | | |
| (5) | Following politics in media | .33 | .27 | .23 | .33 | — | | |
| (6) | General interest in politics | .40 | .30 | .26 | .43 | .52 | — | |
| (7) | Caring about outcome of election | .10 | .02* | .04* | .16 | .28 | .23 | — |

NOTE: Table entries are Pearson product-moment correlations. All are significant, p < .001, except those marked with an asterisk (*).

identification (from "strong Democrat" to "strong Republican") in the middle, reflecting respondents' strength of party identification. Political sophistication is slightly correlated with strength of party identification (ID) (r = .08; this correlation is barely statistically significant due to the large n). Not unexpectedly, however, our index of political sophistication is highly correlated with education (r = .42, p < .001) and income (r = .26, p < .001).

## TEMPORAL STABILITY OF POLITICAL BELIEFS

We hypothesized that political experts would be more consistent over time in two types of ratings. First, we expected them to be more consistent in their party identification and their issue stands. Second, experts were hypothesized to have more stable overall evaluations of the candidates and more stable ratings of their competence and integrity.

To test this hypothesis, we computed separate Pearson product-moment correlations of experts' and novices' party identification, issue positions, and affective evaluations and trait ratings of the candidates between February and September. Our analysis is restricted to the three candidates for whom data were available in both February and September (Jimmy Carter, Ronald Reagan, and Edward Kennedy). Overall affective evaluations of the candidates were measured by 100-point "feeling thermometers." Prior to the analysis we created a competence index for each candidate by averaging respondents' ratings of how knowledgeable, weak, and inspiring each candidate was, and the extent to which each was seen as providing strong leadership (measured on 4-point scales). Similarly, subjects' ratings of how honest, moral, and

TABLE 2.2
**Political Sophistication and Consistency of Political Attitudes**

| | Experts | Novices | Differences |
|---|---|---|---|
| Party identification | .89 | .80 | .09** |
| Self-placement on issues | | | |
| Inflation/unemployment | .37 | .24 | .13 |
| Defense spending | .42 | .52 | −.10 |
| Size of government | .56 | .36 | .20* |
| Relations with Russia | .54 | .56 | −.02 |
| Liberalism-conservatism | .64 | .48 | .16** |
| Affective evaluations of candidates | | | |
| Jimmy Carter | .68 | .43 | .25** |
| Ronald Reagan | .62 | .48 | .14* |
| Edward Kennedy | .76 | .54 | .22** |
| Competence ratings of candidates | | | |
| Jimmy Carter | .73 | .62 | .11* |
| Ronald Reagan | .54 | .42 | .12* |
| Edward Kennedy | .63 | .59 | .04 |
| Integrity ratings of candidates | | | |
| Jimmy Carter | .52 | .48 | .04 |
| Ronald Reagan | .55 | .55 | .00 |
| Edward Kennedy | .67 | .59 | .08 |

NOTE: Table entries are Pearson correlations between data collected in the February survey and data collected in September.
*$p < .05$; **$p < .001$.

power hungry they considered the candidates to be were combined into a single index of integrity (see Abelson et al., 1982).

Our analysis of respondents' self-placement on the issues is restricted to those issues that were asked in February and September: (1) trade-offs between reducing unemployment or reducing inflation (even if the other would go up substantially), and between (2) decreasing or increasing defense spending; (3) whether government should provide many fewer services or continue providing the services it currently does; (4) how strongly we should try to get along with Russia; and (5) general liberalism-conservatism. Each of these items were 7-point scales.[6]

For all analyses we used the bottom and top third of the distribution on the political sophistication index as novices and experts, respectively, in order to get a sharper distinction between experts and novices. Table 2.2 depicts the simple stability correlations for experts and novices in the two categories of judgment. As predicted, these correlations are higher for experts than for novices. More specifically, experts are significantly more consistent over time in their party identification, how they place themselves on the issue of government size, and whether they consider themselves to be liberals or conservatives. In addition, experts are also more consistent in how they evaluate the three candidates affectively and in how they rate the competence of the two front runners, Carter and Reagan. There is also a tendency for experts to be more consistent about Kennedy's competence. On the other hand, there is a curious and unpredicted absence of that tendency for integrity ratings.

Overall, our analysis provides fairly strong support for the idea that political experts are more consistent in how they evaluate the candidates during a presidential campaign and in how they place themselves on the issues. Of the 15 comparisons, 12 are in the expected direction, and 8 of those differences are significant. We argued that this was a result of the experts' knowledge being more cohesive. Both experts and novices seem to form an impression of the candidates fairly early in the campaign. During the course of a campaign they may encounter information that is incongruent with their existing knowledge structure. The higher correlations for experts indicate that they are better able to relate this new information to their existing knowledge. Novices, on the other hand, are less able to integrate new information with previous knowledge, and as a result may be more easily swayed in their opinions about political candidates.

## CANDIDATE EVALUATIONS

We have just shown that experts hold more stable political attitudes than novices. Our next and perhaps most important question (for politics, anyway) is whether experts and novices differ in how they evaluate political candidates, and consequently whether they differ in how they reach a vote decision. To answer this question, we examined five sets of predictors of candidate evaluations: party identification, trait ascriptions, "feelings" toward the candidates, respondents' issue positions, and "issue distances" between the respondent's position and perceptions of the candidate's positions on the issues. The party identification variable was the standard CPS index, reduced to five points by collapsing weak partisans and independent leaners together. The trait ascriptions have already been described; both competence and integrity ratings were employed. In addition to the trait ratings, respondents were asked to "think about" each candidate, and report whether that candidate, "because of the kind of person he is, or because of something he has done," had ever made the respondent feel "angry," "hopeful," "afraid of him," "proud," "disgusted," "sympathetic toward him," or "uneasy." For each candidate, the number of positive feelings (hopeful, proud, sympathetic) and the number of negative feelings (angry, afraid, disgusted, uneasy) were counted separately, and these were also used as predictors of candidate evaluations.

In addition to their own positions on the five issues (counting liberalism-conservatism) included in the first wave of interviews, respondents were asked for their perceptions of the positions of several of the important candidates on these same issues. "Issue distances" were then calculated as the absolute value of the difference between the respondent's position and the respondent's perception of the candidates' positions on each issue.

Simple correlations between all of these predictors and the feeling thermometer evaluations of Carter, Reagan, and Kennedy during wave 3 were then computed separately for experts and novices. Each of the predictors came from questions asked during the first wave of interviews, except for the issue distances. These distances were calculated using the respondent's position on the issues from wave 1 and the respondent's perceptions of the candidates' positions from wave 3. Such a procedure was employed to reduce obvious assimilation or contrast in placing liked or disliked candidates on the issues immediately after one had reported one's own position.

The data are presented in Table 2.3 for Carter, Reagan, and Kennedy, respectively. Party identification is significantly correlated with evaluations of all three candidates among both experts and novices. This correlation is significantly higher among experts, however—an average of .21 higher. About 15 percent more of the variance in evaluations of Democratic or Republican candidates is explained by party identification among political experts compared to political novices.

Competence, integrity, and positive and negative feelings are similarly all significantly correlated with candidate evaluations in both experts and novices. These four variables predict evaluations of the three candidates more strongly among experts than among novices, although these differences are not always significant.

The most dramatic differences between experts and novices occur in the number of issues used in evaluating candidates. Generally speaking, experts use three to five issues in forming evaluations of candidates; novices use only one or two. Novices' stands on the proper size of government and government spending was the only issue to correlate significantly with their evaluations of more than one candidate. Reducing government spending (and the concomitant tax cuts) was

**TABLE 2.3**

**Correlates of Affective Evaluations of Presidential Candidates**

| | Jimmy Carter | | | Ronald Reagan | | | Edward Kennedy | | |
|---|---|---|---|---|---|---|---|---|---|
| | Expert | Novice | Difference | Expert | Novice | Difference | Expert | Novice | Difference |
| Party identification[a] | -.46* | -.27* | .19 | .49* | .23* | .26* | -.44* | -.25* | .19 |
| Candidate personality | | | | | | | | | |
| Competence | .67* | .53* | .14 | .49* | .36* | .13 | .60* | .55* | .05 |
| Integrity | .44* | .26* | .18* | .50* | .33* | .17 | .64* | .55* | .09 |
| Feelings toward candidate | | | | | | | | | |
| Positive | .56* | .38* | .18* | .57* | .32* | .25* | .66* | .52* | .14 |
| Negative | -.55* | -.38* | .17* | -.49* | -.20* | .29* | -.53* | -.49* | .04 |
| Issue positions[b] | | | | | | | | | |
| Inflation/unemployment | -.19* | -.27* | -.08 | .10 | .07 | .03 | -.22* | -.15* | .07 |
| Defense spending | .11 | .05 | .06 | .20* | .18* | .02 | -.12* | -.09 | .03 |
| Size of government | -.27* | -.09 | .18* | .21* | .23* | -.02 | -.28* | -.23* | .05 |
| Relations with Russia | -.08 | .04 | .12 | .14* | .07 | .07 | -.11* | -.00 | .11 |
| Liberalism/conservatism | -.15* | .02 | .17* | .35* | .04 | .31* | -.26* | -.15 | .11 |
| Average | -.16 | -.07 | .09 | .20 | .12 | .08 | -.20 | -.12 | .08 |
| Issue distances | | | | | | | | | |
| Inflation/unemployment | -.14* | -.04 | .10 | -.13* | .01 | .14 | -.17* | .03 | .20 |
| Defense spending | -.24* | -.20* | .04 | -.30* | -.10 | .20* | .01 | .01 | .00 |
| Size of government | -.21* | .00 | .21* | -.23* | -.06 | .17 | -.36* | -.04 | .32* |
| Relations with Russia | -.14* | -.03 | .11 | -.26* | -.01 | .25* | .30* | .07 | .37* |
| Liberalism-conservatism | -.13* | -.02 | .12 | .46* | -.13* | .33* | -.31* | -.24* | .07 |
| Average | -.17 | -.06 | .12 | -.28 | -.06 | .22 | -.23 | -.03 | .19 |

NOTE: The dependent variable is the feeling thermometer evaluation of the candidate from wave 3. All predictors are measured during wave 1, except the issue distances, in which perceptions of the candidate's position are from wave 3.

a. Republican high.

b. Conservative high.

*p < .05.

Reagan's major campaign issue. Novices evidently responded to this major theme of the campaign. Experts also evaluated the candidates at least partially in terms of their stand on this issue, but in addition experts were concerned with the economy, defense spending, and relations with Russia. The most notable difference between experts and novices, however, is in experts' use of their liberal-conservative position in evaluating the candidates. Of the five issues, liberalism-conservatism has on average the highest correlation with candidate evaluations. Experts' stands on the issues are in general more highly correlated with candidate evaluation than are the stands of novices, but this difference is statistically significant only three times across the different candidates; two of these three instances involve liberalism-conservatism. These last data are of course very consistent with the ideological view of political sophistication.

The picture of greater issue voting on the part of experts only gets stronger when issue distances (the difference between the respondent's stand and the respondent's perception of the candidates' stands on each issue) are examined. Almost all (14 of 15) of these issue distances are significantly correlated with candidate evaluation among experts, but only a handful (3 of 15) are significant for novices.

Of course bivariate correlations like those shown in Table 2.3 do not indicate *unique* variance explained by each predictor. If there is a good deal of shared variance among the predictors, then the bivariate correlations shown in Table 2.3 could be overstating the differences between experts ad novices. Indeed, we expect these predictors to be more highly intercorrelated among experts, because the schemas of experts have more interconnections among the elements that make up those schemas. To test this expectation directly, we examined intercorrelations among perceptions of a candidate's positions on the five issues (including liberalism-conservatism), and intercorrelations among all ratings of the candidate (competence, integrity, positive and negative feelings) separately for experts and novices. The average intercorrelations for each candidate are shown in Table 2.4. As expected, constraint is higher—more than 12 points higher—for experts compared to novices. This greater constraint in experts' beliefs is found not only in perceptions of issue positions, as Converse has shown, but also in perceptions of the candidates' personalities. Consequently, the simple bivariate analyses reported in Table 2.3 must be repeated, controlling for the shared variance of the set of predictors.

To examine the unique contribution of each predictor, the feeling thermometers for each candidate were regressed on the set of variables employed in Table 2.3. (Perceived issue distances rather than the

TABLE 2.4
Constraint in Experts' and Novices' Candidate Perceptions

|  | Experts | Novices | Differences |
|---|---|---|---|
| Perceptions of Carter's issue positions | .098 | .000 | .098 |
| Ratings of Carter's personality and feelings | .493 | .387 | .106 |
| Perceptions of Reagan's issue positions | .268 | .154 | .114 |
| Ratings of Reagan's personality and feelings | .585 | .378 | .207 |
| Perceptions of Kennedy's issue positions | .298 | .168 | .110 |
| Ratings of Kennedy's personality and feelings | .516 | .407 | .103 |
| Average | .375 | .249 | .123 |

respondent's own position on each issue were used because this seems to be more common practice in political behavior research.) These results are shown in Table 2.5. As expected, there is apparently a good deal of shared variance among these predictors, particularly for experts, because the regression coefficients representing the unique contribution of each predictor are not always larger for experts compared to novices. Nevertheless, most (20 of 30) of the regression coefficients are still larger for experts, a pattern that does differ significantly from chance ($p < .03$). About 18 percent more of the variance in candidate evaluations can be explained by the set of predictors among experts compared to novices. Considering the individual coefficients, there are two predictors that produce consistently large differences between experts and novices across the three candidates: Competence ratings explain more unique variance in the candidate evaluations of novices, whereas positive feelings explain more unique variance in the evaluations of experts. This result was not predicted, and it defies easy explanation.

## DISCUSSION AND IMPLICATIONS

In this chapter we have tried to present a case for measuring political sophistication in cognitive, knowledge-based terms rather than with the more traditional (for political scientists) "levels of conceptualization." There is no need to think of the levels of conceptualization as measuring political sophistication as opposed to ideological sophistication, yet they are often mistakenly used in that way. Operationalizing sophistication in terms of knowledge, performance, and interest, as we have done here, brings the measure more in line with both common understanding and with measures in other social sciences (e.g., cognitive psychology).

## TABLE 2.5
### Predicting Candidate Evaluations

|  | Jimmy Carter | | | Ronald Reagan | | | Edward Kennedy | | |
|---|---|---|---|---|---|---|---|---|---|
|  | Expert | Novice | Difference | Expert | Novice | Difference | Expert | Novice | Difference |
| Party ID | -2.16*** | -2.34** | -.18 | 2.81** | 2.81** | .53 | -1.59** | -1.56* | .03 |
| Competence | 13.12*** | 15.15*** | -2.03 | 3.97@ | 9.09* | -5.12* | 3.10 | 7.12* | -4.02@ |
| Integrity | 2.14 | -.20 | 2.34 | 6.47** | 4.25 | 2.22 | 9.06*** | 6.61** | 2.45 |
| Positive feelings | 6.12*** | 4.22** | 1.90@ | 5.73*** | 3.70* | 2.03 | 7.43*** | 4.77*** | 2.66@ |
| Negative feelings | -4.94*** | -3.83** | 1.11 | -3.68*** | -2.33@ | 1.35 | -3.34*** | -3.39** | -.05 |
| Issue distances |  |  |  |  |  |  |  |  |  |
| Inflation/unemployment | -.46 | .24 | .70 | -.20 | -.03 | .17 | -.56 | .67 | 1.13 |
| Defense spending | -1.49* | -1.68* | -.19 | -1.57@ | -1.70* | -.13 | -.33 | .47 | .80 |
| Size of government | .14 | .96 | .82 | 1.01 | -.62 | -1.63 | -1.17@ | .72 | 1.89@ |
| Relations with Russia | -.33 | -.51 | -.18 | -1.35@ | -.15 | 1.20 | -1.91** | .66 | 2.57* |
| Liberalism-conservatism | -1.23@ | .08 | 1.31 | -2.40** | -.37 | 2.03@ | -1.04 | -3.04*** | -2.00@ |
| $R^2$ | .58 | .40 | .18@ | .50 | .24 | .26* | .58 | .46 | .12@ |
| N | 295 | 248 |  | 291 | 188 |  | 295 | 224 |  |

NOTE: Entries are unstandardized regression weights.
@p < .10; *p < .05; **p < .01; ***p < .001.

56

It also eliminates the necessity of making what can only be a value judgment that a belief system structured in terms of liberalism-conservatism is somehow more sophisticated than belief systems organized in some other way. The measure of political sophistication offered here was purposely a very general one, utilizing familiar and widely available questions. Although the specific items constituting the various knowledge indices are unique to the 1980 survey, comparable measures are available in every CPS election survey since 1972. Moreover, our measure of political sophistication is certainly far easier to construct than the levels of conceptualization.

We illustrated three important differences in how political experts and novices process political information. First, experts hold more stable political attitudes over time. This stability, we should add, is not simply a function of greater cognitive ability per se. Partialling education out of the correlations shown in Table 2.2 changes the reported coefficients only one or two points. Thus, this effect of political sophistication must be understood as a function of something other than greater overall cognitive ability (or intelligence). These findings are quite in line with Converse's attitudes and nonattitudes (1970). We have argued that these differences can be explained in terms of the level of development of experts' and novices' political schemas. The hierarchical organization and stronger links between concepts in experts' schemas makes any bit of knowledge, including a political attitude, easier to retrieve. Moreover, the cohesive structure of an expert's schemas makes it highly likely that any new information will be assimilated into an existing schema without radical changes in the schema (Anderson et al., 1980). Thus, even in a changing political environment, experts will usually hold more stable political beliefs.

The findings for candidate evaluations underline another important difference between our view of political sophistication and the more traditional levels of conceptualization. According to the traditional view, only experts—or ideologues and near ideologues—are capable of voting on the issues. People in the second group benefits category might also be capable of voting on the issues via an "ideology by proxy," but certainly people in the lowest category—the no-issue content category—should not be able to use issues to evaluate candidates. Our cognitive view of sophistication focuses not so much on what type of information but rather on *how much* information is brought to bear on the relevant evaluation or decision. Because of superior organization or "chunking" of information, experts are able to utilize more information in their evaluations or decisions. Consistent with our view, we found that (1) experts apparently use more issues in evaluating candidates, but (2) novices nonetheless can still employ one or two issues—probably the one or two most salient issues during a campaign—in candidate evaluations.

On the other hand, our data do not support a view of political experts dispassionately considering the candidates' stands on a host of issues—carefully computing some rational calculus of how much they agree with each one—while the great mass of nonexperts blindly pull the lever of party identification and vote their self-interest or "gut" feelings. On the contrary, although experts did consider more issues in evaluating the candidates, both party identification and feelings were more important in their evaluations than in those of novices. Again, these data are somewhat at odds with a purely ideological view of political sophistication.

The results of one final analysis provide some interesting insights into expert-novice differences in the perception of political candidates. At the time the data were collected, Jimmy Carter had been in office for almost four years. His handling of the economy in general, and the Iranian hostage crisis in particular, left severe doubts about his competence. On the other hand, nobody doubted that he was an honest man of high moral standards. Supplemental analysis confirmed our expectations. Experts perceived Carter as less competent than did novices, but there was no effect of expertise on ratings of Carter's integrity.

The pattern of results was just the opposite for Kennedy. Expertise predicted ratings of Kennedy's integrity but not of his competence. The fact that Kennedy's integrity ratings dropped as a function of expertise can of course be accounted for by Chappaquiddick and related incidents in the past that cast long shadows on his integrity. These supplemental results therefore suggest that experts are more sensitive to any relatively unique characteristic of a candidate. In general, incumbents in highly visible offices like the presidency are more likely to stand out because of competence information; they have, after all, been in office for almost four years at the time of the next election. Because there is in general little relevant competence information available about challengers, however, they will by default stand out in terms of some other characteristic like integrity, if at all.

## IMPLICATIONS FOR MEDIA RESEARCH

Our data raise some obvious questions for future media research. First, it should be obvious that our measure of political expertise overlaps substantially with any measure of overall media consumption. One of the seven scales constituting our expertise measure is a direct item counting how many different media respondents use in following politics. And three of the scales measure familiarity with different aspects of politics—the candidates, the issues, and the polls—that could only have been achieved through using some media. So already one does not have to make too great a leap of faith if one wanted to translate many of the expert-novice differences reported above into high versus low media usage differences.

One can make some finer distinctions about what type of media political experts and political novices use, however, and the remainder of our comments will focus on these distinctions. In particular, it has been found that highly educated people and those with higher incomes rely on newspapers for most of their political information, whereas the less educated and those with lower income rely much more heavily on television (e.g., Patterson and McClure, 1976). Given the moderately high correlations between education and income, on the one hand, and our measure of political sophistication, on the other (.42 and .26, respectively), it is not too much of an overgeneralization to assume that the majority of political experts rely chiefly on newspapers for their political information, whereas most political novices rely chiefly on television. If this assumption is granted, then the differential media usage could help explain some of the expert-novice differences in information processing that we have observed.

More specifically, one could argue that it generally is easier to *selectively attend to* or *ignore* different stories in a newspaper than on a TV news program because it is easier to turn the page of a newspaper than to get up and switch the station. Thus, it is easier for someone to shape their reading environment than for someone to shape their viewing environment. If this is the case, then one reason for the greater stability of expert's political views could be their more biased (selectively chosen) information environments, which presumably include mostly consistent information. However, it seems unlikely that experts would maintain their political beliefs through selectively attending to inconsistent information. As Fiske and Kinder (1981) have suggested, one of the differences between political experts and novices lies in their abilities to deal effectively with information that is inconsistent with their beliefs.

More specifically, due to their rich and well-organized previous knowledge, experts may be better able to assimilate inconsistencies into their existing knowledge structures as long as these inconsistencies are moderate. It may be that reading the newspaper rather than watching television promotes exactly this process in the case of political experts.

There is evidence that the processing of belief-inconsistent information takes more time, relative to the processing of consistent information (Brewer et al., 1981), especially when the information matters (Erber and Fiske, 1984). Certainly, one can devote more time to a piece of political information when it is printed in the newspaper than when it is shown on television. Political experts who, by our definition, care more about such news, may spend this additional time assimilating inconsistent information into their existing knowledge structure. One way this could be accomplished is by generating situational attributions for the inconsistent information (see Crocker et al., 1983; Kulik, 1983). For example, a political expert who believes that a candidate is competent may discount news about flashes of incompetence and thus maintain his or her belief. Political novices, on the other hand, who mainly rely on relatively fast-paced television news, may lack the knowledge and the time necessary to do this. As a result, they should be more easily swayed by inconsistent information, and their political beliefs should be less stable than those of experts.

One of the most striking expert-novice difference in our data is the relatively greater influence of negative feelings vis-à-vis positive feelings in the candidate evaluations of novices compared to those of experts (see Table 2.5). Across all three candidates, positive feelings are far more important in the evaluations by experts than are negative feelings, but these differences are much smaller in the evaluations by novices. If we again assume that novices chiefly are watching television, do we have some evidence that they are suffering from Robinson's (1976) "video-malaise," a "greater sense of cynicism and distrust" (p. 418), whereas political experts—because they depend less on television—are relatively sheltered from it?

A related issue involves the media's role in "agenda-setting." Although a "minimal effects" model most accurately describes the media's ability to change opinions, recent research has shown that the media can play a much larger role in telling us what to think about, if not what to think (Cook et al., 1983; Iyengar et al., 1982). We are unaware of any research suggesting that agenda-setting is accomplished more by television than newspapers, although we would guess that that would be the case. If so, then political novices should more strongly show the effects of television's agenda-setting proclivities compared to experts. Even if the visual and print media are more or less equal in their ability to set the agenda,[7] if readers can more easily selectively choose what they see compared to television news watchers, then, again, agenda-setting might be a phenomenon limited chiefly to political novices.

## CONCLUSION

If democratic theory requires good citizens to be attentive primarily to the day's political issues and the policy stands of parties and candidates, then it is not unreasonable to define political sophistication in terms of the ability to understand political issues in a meaningful way. This is fundamentally what the levels of conceptualization, with their ideological focus, measure. As Converse (1975) and others have noted, however, the trials and tribulations of day-to-day living have far more immediate consequences for all of our lives, and therefore demand far more attention, than anything that goes on in Washington. A good citizen, we would argue, is one who pays enough attention to politics to be at least moderately aware of the major candidates and issues of the day. He or she participates in the political process during elections, and on rare occasions between elections by contacting elected officials. When the political situation demands more attention, the good citizen is able to give it. He or she has the cognitive structures available to process and assimilate new and perhaps different political information. *Understanding the new information in ideological terms is not required, however.* Indeed, a strong ideology might even hinder the assimilation of new information or new issues if those issues are not easily categorized as liberal or conservative. If people understand politics in terms of ideology, that is fine; but it is equally fine to process political information by its relevance to one's personal self-interest or to one's group's interests. It is equally reasonable to evaluate candidates by personality factors, for who would deny that a candidate's personality could influence his or her performance in office? The measure of political sophistication offered here taps this broader definition of good citizenship. It is a more optimistic view of the public, for although no cutoffs or criteria for distinguishing experts from novices are offered, they would certainly be more lenient or inclusive than the ideology category of the levels of conceptualization. And this broader view makes more realistic demands on what we would normatively ask of good citizens.

## NOTES

1. Elsewhere we have presented an alternative schematic model of how people think about politics (Lau, 1985), a model that differs in several important ways from the levels of conceptualization, but a model that is by no means incompatible with those levels.

2. See Fiske and Pavelchak (1984) for a thorough discussion of the role of affect in schemas.

3. Indeed, there is some evidence that when people with well-developed schemas focus attention on schema-relevant information, their judgments tend to become polarized in the direction implied by the schema (Strack et al., 1982; Tesser, 1978).

4. The data were provided by the Interuniversity Consortium for Political and Social Research. The n for the initial survey was 1008. It dropped to 843, 769, 764 on subsequent waves of the panel. We, of course, bear all responsibility for the analyses and interpretations presented in this chapter.

5. Three missing values were allowed.

6. The analyses were by necessity restricted to respondents who reported an opinion on the issue at both time points. One of the criteria distinguishing experts from novices was the proportion of such issues on which respondents held an opinion. Consequently, novices were disproportionately excluded from the analyses due to missing data. This exclusion introduces a conservative bias into the analyses, for it minimizes one of the important expert-novice differences.

7. We would suspect (again, with no evidence) that news magazines like *Time* and *Newsweek* are closer to television news than to daily newspapers in the extent to which they help set the political agenda for the day.

# REFERENCES

ABELSON, R. P., D. R. KINDER, M. D. PETERS, and S. T. FISKE (1982) "Affective and semantic components in political person perception." Journal of Personality and Social Psychology 42: 619-630.

ANDERSON, J. R. (1982) "Acquisition of cognitive skill." Psychological Review 89: 369-406.

———M. R. LEPPER, and L. ROSS (1980) "Perseverance of social theories: the role of explanation in the persistence of discredited information." Journal of Personality and Social Psychology 39: 1037-1049.

BENNETT, S. E., R. OLDENDICK, A. J. TUCHFORBES and G. F. BISHOP (1979) "Education and mass belief systems: an extension and some new questions." Political Behavior 7: 53-72.

BISHOP, G. F. and K. A. FRANKOVIC (1981) "Ideological consensus and constraint among party leaders and followers in the 1978 election." Micropolitics 1: 87-112.

BREWER, M. B., V. DULL, and L. LUI (1981) "Perceptions of the elderly: stereotypes as prototypes." Journal of Personality and Social Psychology 41: 656-670.

CAMPBELL, A., P. E. CONVERSE, W. E. MILLER, and D. E. STOKES (1960) The American Voter. New York: John Wiley.

CHASE, W. G. and H. A. SIMON (1973) "Perception in chess." Cognitive Psychology 4: 55-81.

CHI, M.T.H. and R. KOESKE (1983) "Network representation of a child's dinosaur knowledge." Developmental Psychology 19: 29-39.

COLLINS, A. M. and E. S. LOFTUS (1975) "A spreading activation theory of semantic processing." Psychological Review 82: 407-428.

CONOVER, P. J. and S. FELDMAN (1981) "The origins and meaning of liberal/conservative self-identifications." American Journal of Political Science 25: 617-645.

CONVERSE, P. E. (1975) "Public opinion and voting," in F. Greenstein and N. Polsby (eds.) Handbook of Political Science (Vol. 4). Reading, MA. Addison-Wesley.

———(1970) "Attitudes and non-attitudes: continuation of a dialogue," in E. R. Tufte (ed.) The Quantitative Analysis of Social Problems. Reading, MA. Addison-Wesley.

COOK, F. L., T. R. TYLER, E. G. GOETZ, M. T. GORDON, D. PROTESS, D. R. LEFF, and H. L. MOLOTCH (1983) "Media and agenda setting: effects on the public, interest group leaders, policy makers, and policy." Public Opinion Quarterly 47: 16-35.

CROCKER, J., D. B. HANNAH, and R. WEBER (1983) "Person memory and causal attributions." Journal of Personality and Social Psychology 44: 56-66.

ERBER R. and S. T. FISKE (1984) "Outcome dependency and attention to inconsistent information." Journal of Personality and Social Psychology 47: 709-726.

FISKE, S. T. and D. R. KINDER (1981) "Involvement, expertise, and schema use: evidence from political cognition," in N. Cantor and J. Kihlstrom (eds.) Personality, Cognition, and Social Interaction. Hillsdale, NJ: Lawrence Erlbaum.

FISKE, S. T. and M. A. PAVELCHAK (1984) "Category-based versus piecemeal-based affective responses: developments in schema-triggered affect," in R. U. Sorrentine and E. T. Higgins (eds.) The Handbook of Motivation and Cognition. New York: Guilford.

FISKE, S. T. and S. E. TAYLOR (1984) Social Cognition. Reading, MA: Addison-Wesley.

FISKE, S. T., D. R. KINDER, and W. M. LARTER (1983) "The novice and the expert: knowledge based strategies in political cognition." Journal of Experimental Social Cognition Psychology 19: 381-400.

HAGNER, P. R. and J. C. PIERCE (1982) "Correlation characteristics of levels of conceptualization in the American public, 1956-1976." Journal of Politics 44: 779-807.

HASTIE, R. (1981) "Schematic principles in human memory," in E. T. Higgins, P. Herman, and M. Zanna (eds.) Social Cognition. Hillsdale, N.J.: Lawrence Erlbaum.

IYENGAR, S., M. D. PETERS, and D. R. KINDER (1982) Experimental demonstrations of the "not-so-minimal" consequences of television news programs. American Political Science Review 76: 848-858.

KINDER, D. R., and D. O. SEARS (1985) "Political behavior," in E. Aronson and G. Lindzey (eds.) The Handbook of Social Psychology (3rd ed.). Reading, MA: Addison-Wesley.

KULICK, J. A. (1983) "Confirmatory attribution and the perpetuation of social beliefs." Journal of Personality and Social Psychology 44: 1171-1181.

LANE, R. E. (1973) "Patterns of political belief," in J. Knutson (Ed.) Handbook of political psychology. San Francisco: Jossey-Bass.

LAU, R. R. (1985) "Political schemas, candidate evaluations, and voting behavior," in R. R. Lau and D. O. Sears (eds.) Political Cognition. Hillsdale, NJ: Lawrence Erlbaum.

———R. F. COULAM, and D. O. SEARS (1983) "Proposition 2½ in Massachusetts: self-interest, antigovernment attitudes, and political schemas." Presented at the annual meeting of the Midwest Political Science Association, Chicago.

LEVITON, T. E., and W. E. MILLER (1979) "Ideological interpretations of presidential elections." American Political Science Review 73: 751-771.

LIPPMANN, W. (1922/1947) Public Opinion. New York: Macmillan. (originally published 1922)

McKEITHEN, K. B., J. S. REITMAN, H. H. RUETER, and S. C. HIRTLE (1981) "Knowledge organization and skill differences in computer programmers." Cognitive Psychology 13: 307-325.

MILBRAITH, L. W., and M. L. GOEL (1977) Political Participation. Chicago: Rand McNally.

PATTERSON, T. E. and R. D. McCLURE (1976) The Unseeing Eye. New York: G. P. Putnam's.

PIAGET, J. (1952) The Origins of Intelligence in Children. New York: International Universities Press.

———and B. INHELDER (1973) Memory and Intelligence. New York: Basic Books.

REDER, L. M. and J. R. ANDERSON (1980) "A partial resolution of the paradox of interference: The role of integrating knowledge." Cognitive Psychology 86: 447-472.

ROBINSON, M. J. (1976) "Public affairs television and the growth of political malaise: the case of 'The Selling of the Pentagon.' " American Political Science Review 70: 409-432.

RUMELHART, D. E., and A. ORTONY (1977) "The representation of knowledge in memory," in R. C. Anderson, F. J. Spiro, and W. E. Montague (eds.) Schooling and the Aquisition of Knowledge. Hillsdale, NJ: Lawrence Erlbaum.

SMITH, E. E., N. ADAMS, and D. SCHOOR (1978) "Fact retrieval and the paradox of interference." Cognitive Psychology 10: 438-464.

SMITH, E.R.A.N. (1980) "The levels of conceptualization: false measures of ideological sophistication." American Political Science Review 74: 685-696.

STRACK, F., R. ERBER, and R. A. WICKLUND (1982) "The effects of salience and time pressure on ratings of social causality." Journal of Experimental Social Psychology 18: 581-594.

TAYLOR, S. E. and J. CROCKER (1981) "Schematic bases of social information processing," in E. T. Higgins, P. Herman, and M. Zanna (eds.) Social Cognition. Hillsdale, NJ: Lawrence Erlbaum.

TESSER, A. (1978) "Self-Generated Attitude Change," in L. Berkowitz (ed.) Advances in Experimental Social Psychology (vol. 11). New York: Academic.

WYCHOFF, M. L. (1980) "Belief system constraint and policy voting: a test of the unidimensional consistency model." Political Behavior 2: 115-146.

Chapter 3

# PREDICTING PARTICIPATION
# AND CHOICE
### First-Time Voters in
### U.S. Partisan Elections

Martin Fishbein
Susan E. Middlestadt
Jean-Kyung Chung

MOST ANALYSES of voting behavior in partisan elections make a clear distinction between the citizen's *participation* in the electoral process and the voter's *choice* of for whom to vote. Although researchers have been remarkably successful in predicting which choice a voter will make among candidates, they have been quite unsuccessful at predicting whether or not an individual will cast a ballot. Often regarded as the indispensable attribute of citizenship in a democratic society, the act of voting provides the average citizen with the opportunity to become involved directly in the political process. Yet, this act, more than any other, has remained an enigma to political scientists. As Crittenden succinctly stated, "No one has satisfactorily explained why some people vote and others do not" (1982: 178). Using data gathered from potential first-time voters in the 1980 U.S. presidential election, the primary purpose of this chapter is to suggest a way to predict and explain voting participation as well as voting choice.

The most widely accepted view of *voting choice* is that put forth by Campbell et al. in *The American Voter* (1960). According to this perspective, voting choice is determined primarily by short-term partisan attitudes toward candidates, parties, and issues that are in turn affected by the long-term influence of a person's party identification.

Although researchers have been largely successful in predicting voting choice from these variables, even the strongest devotee of this approach will readily admit that partisan attitudes and party identification do not provide adequate explanations of *voting participation*. In order to explain this latter behavior, a number of additional concepts—such as political efficacy, interest, and involvement—have been considered. Although these variables do account for some of the variation in participation, they cannot be viewed as determinants of that behavior.

As explained elsewhere (Fishbein, 1967, 1980; Fishbein and Ajzen, 1975; Ajzen and Fishbein, 1980), the theory of reasoned action assumes that behaviors under an individual's volitional control are predictable from a knowledge of a person's intentions. These intentions are in turn viewed as a function of attitudes and subjective norms. In a recent series of articles (Fishbein and Coombs, 1974; Bowman and Fishbein, 1978; Fishbein, Ajzen, and Hinkle, 1980; Fishbein, Bowman et al., 1980; Fishbein and Ajzen, 1981) the theory of reasoned action has been applied to an understanding of *voting choice*. Consistent with the theory, these studies have shown the following:

(1) Voting choice is accurately predicted from voting intentions; that is, people vote for the candidate toward whom they have the strongest voting intention.

(2) The intention to vote for a given candidate is in turn predictable from knowledge of the person's attitude toward voting for that candidate and his or her subjective norm concerning voting for that candidate.

(3) Attitudes toward voting for a given candidate and the subjective norm with respect to voting for that candidate are themselves predictable from a knowledge of the person's behavioral and normative beliefs. More specifically, attitudes toward voting for a candidate are accurately predicted from a knowledge of the voter's beliefs that voting for the candidate will lead to various outcomes and his or her evaluations of those outcomes. Similarly, the subjective norm—the person's belief that "most people who are important to me think I should (or should not) vote for candidate X"—is accurately predicted from beliefs about the normative prescriptions of relevant individuals or groups and the voter's motivation to comply with those relevant referents.

The implications of these findings for a theory of voting behavior have been spelled out elsewhere (see Fishbein, Ajzen, and Hinkle, 1980; Fishbein and Ajzen, 1981). There are, however, two key points that are particularly relevant to this chapter. First, according to the theory, variables other than those described above are viewed as external variables that can influence behavior only indirectly. Thus, in contrast to most theories of voting behavior, partisan attitudes and party identification do not serve as primary determinants of voting choice. Consistent with the theory of reasoned action, these external variables have been shown to influence voting choice only indirectly by affecting the attitude toward voting for the candidate and the subjective norm concerning voting for the candidate (Fishbein, Ajzen, and Hinkle, 1980; Fishbein and Ajzen, 1981).

Second, unlike other theories of voting behavior, our approach is not limited to the prediction of voting choice in partisan elections. Its applicability to choice in nonpartisan elections has already been demonstrated (Bowman and Fishbein, 1978). In this chapter we investigate the utility of the theory of reasoned action to the prediction of voting participation. Instead of assuming that different processes and thus different variables are needed to explain participation and choice, the theory views the behavior of not voting—like the behavior of voting for a particular candidate—as an alternative confronting the potential voter. For example, with respect to state or local referenda, a voter may cast his or her ballot for the proposition, against the proposition, or may choose to not vote. Similarly, in partisan elections for political office, the potential voter might vote for one of the candidates on the ballot, write in some other candidate, or abstain from voting. Given a set of behavioral alternatives, the theory assumes that people will form intentions with respect to each of the alternatives and will perform the behavior toward which they have the strongest intention.

In the context of the 1980 U.S. presidential election, potential voters could be viewed as having five behavioral alternatives available to them: not voting, voting for John Anderson, voting for Jimmy Carter, voting for Ronald Reagan, and voting for some other candidate. According to the theory, potential voters will form intentions with respect to each of these five behavioral alternatives. And, although direct measures of these intentions should be the best single predictors of whether or not the respondent performed the behavioral alternative in question, the most accurate predictor of the person's behavior in this choice situation should be a relative measure that is based on a consideration of intentions with respect to each alternative. One simple decision rule to use in combining multiple intentions is to predict that the person will engage in the behavioral alternative toward which he or she holds the strongest intention. Because voting requires more effort than not voting, we developed a more complex decision rule. More specifically, we assumed that a potential voter will participate in the electoral process only if he or she had a positive intention to vote for at least one candidate *and* a negative intention to not vote. Potential voters meeting this criterion should choose to vote for the candidate toward whom they have the strongest intention. This decision rule reflects our belief that participation will occur only if the potential voter is positively motivated to vote for at least one of the available candidates.

Assuming that participation and choice can, in fact, be predicted from a consideration of intentions to perform each of the available alternatives, the next step in an analysis of voting behavior and hence the next purpose of this chapter is to understand the factors influencing each of the intentions. As indicated above, according to the theory of reasoned action, each intention is a function of two primary determinants, one personal or attitudinal in nature and the other social or normative. More specifically, an individual's intention to perform any given behavior is determined by (1) his or her attitude toward performing the behavior in question *and/or* (2) his or her subjective norm concerning the performance of that behavior. For example, the intention *to not vote* should be a function of the potential voter's attitude toward "my voting for Ronald Reagan" and his or her subjective norm that "most people who are important to me think I should (or should not) vote for Ronald Reagan." Similarly the intention to *not vote* should be a function of the potential voter's attitude toward "My not voting" and his or her subjective norm that "Most people who are important to me think I should not (or should) vote in the presidential election."

Note, however, that attitudes and subjective norms concerning *not voting* are unlikely to show much variance. That is, because of the special importance placed on voting in a democratic society, most people accurately will perceive that their important others think they should vote in the election and will also recognize the social undesirability of holding a negative attitude toward voting. Thus, most respondents will report negative attitudes and subjective norms with respect to nonparticipation, and measures of these variables are unlikely to account for a substantial proportion of the variance in the intention to not vote.

Recall, however, that according to our approach, voting participation does not occur in isolation but occurs in the context of the full range of behavioral alternatives that, in the case of partisan elections, includes the choices among candidates. Given that the five alternatives outlined to the potential voter are mutually exclusive and exhaustive, it seems reasonable to assume that the intention to not vote will reflect, at least in part, the candidate-oriented intentions. For example, someone who has not formed a positive intention toward any of the available candidates should hold a *positive* intention to not vote; whereas someone with a positive intention to vote for one candidate and negative intentions to vote for the remaining candidates should hold a strong *negative* intention to not vote. The remaining respondents are expressing some degree of uncertainty in their intentions to vote for the various candidates. For example, they may have formed equally or almost equally strong intentions to vote for two of the candidates. Although their positive intentions to vote for one or more candidates should lead to a negative intention toward not voting, the conflict or uncertainty may lead at least some of these people to intend to not vote. Hence, we would expect this uncertain group to fall somewhere between the above two groups with respect to not voting. A third purpose of this chapter is to explore the relationship between the intention to not vote and the pattern of intentions to vote for each of the candidates.

A final purpose of this chapter is to replicate earlier findings concerning the distinction between the attitude toward a candidate and the attitude toward voting for that candidate. As mentioned previously, one of the more important implications of the theory of reasoned action is that it points out that it is the attitude toward *voting for the candidate*, not the attitude toward *the candidate per se* that serves as a primary determinant of voting intentions and voting choice. Indeed, it is our contention that the attitude toward a candidate is only related to voting intention and behavior indirectly, through its relationship with attitudes toward voting and subjective norms. It follows from this that considerations of attitudes toward candidates in addition to attitudes toward voting for those candidates will not improve prediction of either intention or behavior.

To summarize, the purpose of this chapter is fourfold: (1) to determine whether participation, as well as choice, can be predicted from intentions; (2) to investigate the extent to which intentions to not vote, as well as intentions to vote for a given candidate, can be predicted from attitudes and subjective norms; (3) to explore the relationship between the intention to not vote and intentions to vote for the various candidates; and (4) to provide further support for the distinction between attitudes toward a candidate and attitudes toward voting for that candidate.

## METHOD AND PROCEDURES

In order to ensure a sample of potential first-time voters, all of the respondents consisted of undergraduate students at the University of Illinois who participated in partial fulfillment of a course research requirement. A lengthy closed-ended self-completion questionnaire was administered to this group two weeks prior to the election and a short (10-minute) follow-up interview was conducted by telephone in the week immediately after the election.

The pre-election questionnaire assessed the components of the theory of reasoned action with respect to the five behavioral alternatives of not voting, voting for John Anderson, voting for Jimmy Carter, voting for Ronald Reagan, and voting for some other candidate. *Intentions* were measured with single seven-point likely-unlikely scales. The *attitudinal* component of the model was assessed with two seven-point evaluative semantic differential scales that were summed. The *normative* component was measured with single seven-point should-should not scales.

In addition to the above measures of the model variables of intention, attitude toward the behavior and subjective norm, several standard measures of partisan attitudes, and party identification were included in the pre-election questionnaire. *Party identification* was assessed following the procedure from Campbell et al. (1960). That is, respondents were first asked to classify themselves as Republican, Democrat, or Independent. Those reporting a party affiliation were then asked if they saw themselves as a strong or weak Republican or Democrat; and Independents were asked if they leaned more toward the Democratic or Republican parties. This procedure assigns respondents to one of seven categories: Strong Republican, Republican, Republican Leaner, Independent, Democratic Leaner, Democrat, and Strong Democrat. *Liberalism-conservatism* was assessed with a multiple-choice item that simply asked respondents to indicate whether they saw themselves as liberal, moderate, or conservative. *Attitude toward the candidate* was measured with the same two seven-point evaluative semantic differential scales used to measure the attitude toward voting for the candidate.

Finally, measures of the demographic variables of age, sex, and perceived social class were obtained. *Social class* was assessed with a multiple-choice self-report item. That is, respondents were asked to indicate whether they considered themselves to be members of the upper, middle, working, or lower class.

*Voting behavior* was measured with three questions in the follow-up telephone interview. All respondents were asked, "Did you vote in last Tuesday's election?" Those who responded affirmatively were asked, "Did you vote for a presidential candidate?" Those who said they voted for a presidential candidate were asked, "For whom did you vote?"

# RESULTS AND DISCUSSION

*The sample.* The pre-election questionnaire was completed by 125 undergraduate students. These respondents were all potential first-time voters; that is, they were U.S. citizens between 18 and 21 years of age and none had been eligible to vote in the 1976 election. Despite repeated callbacks, 14 respondents could not be reached for the follow-up telephone interview. In addition, 3 of those who were recontacted did not have complete data. Thus the sample for the present study consisted of 108 potential first-time voters, 49 men and 59 women. The majority of these respondents were 18 years of age. More specifically, 81 (75 percent) reported they were 18, 19 (18 percent) said they were 19, and the remaining six were 20 or 21. In terms of social class, 12 (11 percent) considered themselves upper class, 84 (78 percent) middle class, 11 (10 percent) working class, and 1 (1 percent) lower class. Although the respondents were all undergraduate students from primarily middle-class backgrounds, they did span the political spectrum from Liberal to Conservative and Democratic to Republican to Independent.

## VOTING BEHAVIOR

Of the 108 respondents with complete data, 42 reported they did not vote, 27 voted for Anderson, 17 for Carter, and 22 for Reagan. Thus, consistent with previous findings, a substantial proportion (almost 40 percent) of those eligible to vote for the first time chose not to do so.

*Predicting voting behavior.* The first purpose of this chapter is to demonstrate that participation as well as choice can be predicted from a knowledge of intentions. Recall that all respondents were asked to indicate on a seven-point likely-unlikely scale their intentions with respect to each of the five behavioral alternatives available in the 1980 U.S. presidential election. A relative intention measure was created based on these five direct measures of intention. Specifically, following the decision rule outlined earlier, respondents with a positive intention to vote for at least one candidate *and* a negative intention to not vote were classified as intending to vote for the candidate toward whom they

**TABLE 3.1**
The Relationship Between Relative Voting Intention
and Voting Behavior (N = 108)

| | Reported Behavior | | | |
|---|---|---|---|---|
| Relative Intention | Not Vote | Vote Anderson | Vote Carter | Vote Reagan |
| Not vote | 33** | 1 | 2 | 1 |
| Vote Anderson | 1 | 18 | 2 | 0 |
| Vote Carter | 3 | 2 | 12 | 0 |
| Vote Reagan | 2 | 2 | 0 | 20 |
| Vote other | 0 | 2 | 0 | 0 |
| VAR* | 1 | 1 | 0 | 0 |
| VCR | 2 | 0 | 0 | 1 |
| VCO | 0 | 0 | 1 | 0 |
| VACR | 0 | 1 | 0 | 0 |

*Tie between intention to vote for Anderson and Reagan; **Number of respondents who intended to not vote who did not vote.

had the strongest intention. Respondents with equally strong positive intentions to vote for two or more candidates were placed in tie categories. All other respondents were classified as intending to not vote.

Table 3.1 shows the relationship between this relative intention measure and the respondents' self-reports of their voting behavior. It can be seen that intentions are accurate predictors of voting behavior. Ignoring for a moment the 7 respondents with equally strong intentions to vote for two or more candidates, Table 3.1 shows that consideration of a person's intention with respect to all of the behavioral alternatives available accurately predicted the voting behavior of 83 of the 101 (82 percent) respondents. Note that for voters with unambiguous intentions, choice among candidates was predicted accurately in 50 of 58 cases (86 percent); and for the total sample participation was predicted with equal accuracy, that is, in 95 of 108 cases (88 percent).

It is also possible to investigate the relationship between voting intentions and voting behavior by analyzing separately the performance or nonperformance of each behavioral alternative. To accomplish this, four dichotomous behavior measures were created, one for each behavioral alternative. (Because no respondent indicated voting for "some other candidate," this alternative was not included in these analyses.) For example, to create a behavior measure to assess the alternative of voting for Anderson, respondents were given a score of one if they reported voting for Anderson and a score of zero if they did not (that is, if they voted for Reagan or Carter or if they did not vote). With respect to the alternative of not voting, respondents were assigned a score of one if they did not vote and a score of zero if they did. Similarly, the overall relative intention measure described above and presented in Table 3.1 was used to create a relative intention measure for each behavioral alternative. For example, with respect to the relative intention to vote for Reagan, respondents were given a score of 1 if their relative intention was to vote for Reagan and only Reagan, a score of .50 if their relative intention was a tie between Reagan and one other candidate, and a score of .33 if their relative intention was a tie between Reagan and two other candidates. The remaining respondents held relative intentions to vote for one or more of the other candidates or not to vote and were assigned a score of zero.

Table 3.2 shows the relationship between voting intentions and voting behavior separately for each behavioral alternative. For each alternative, the table gives the correlation between the dichotomous behavior measure and the relative intention measure. For comparative purposes, it also presents the correlation between the behavior measure and the direct measure of intention using a seven-point likely-unlikely scale. Consistent with expectations, it can be seen that both relative and direct measures of intentions are strongly and significantly related to voting behavior. Moreover, the relative measures (which take into consideration a person's intentions with respect to all the available alternatives) consistently provide more accurate predictions of voting behavior. These results give strong support for the contention that participation as well as choice can be predicted accurately from a knowledge of intentions. Indeed, even the direct measure of the intention to not vote allows one to quite accurately predict electoral participation ($r = .709$, $p < .001$).

*The effect of external variables.* One question that may be raised at this time is whether consideration of other variables would improve the prediction of voting behavior. According to the theory of reasoned action, intentions are the sole determinants of behavior. Although consideration of other variables might help to explain why people behave the way they do, these variables should not contribute to behavioral prediction. In order to test this notion with respect to voting for each of the three major candidates, the dichotomous behavior measures were regressed on the respective relative intention measure and the following three external variables: attitude toward the candidate, party identification, and liberalism-conservatism. The simple

TABLE 3.2

**Relative Versus Direct Intentions as Predictors of the Performance of Each Behavioral Alternative (N = 108)**

| | Correlation with | |
|---|---|---|
| *Behavioral Alternative* | *Relative Intention* | *Direct Intention* |
| Not vote | .745* | .709 |
| Vote Anderson | .714 | .624 |
| Vote Carter | .653 | .573 |
| Vote Reagan | .831 | .667 |

*All correlations significant, p < .01.

correlations, standardized beta weights, and multiple correlations for these analyses are presented in Table 3.3. It can be seen that although these three external variables are related significantly to the behavior measure for one or more of the behavioral alternatives, none of them significantly improves behavioral prediction. In addition, although not shown in the table, the consideration of party identification, liberalism-conservatism, and perceived social class—in addition to the relative intention to not vote—did not improve the prediction of voting participation.

## VOTING INTENTIONS

*Predicting voting intentions from attitudes and subjective norms.* Given that voting intentions predict voting behavior, we can now consider the determinants of these intentions. According to the theory of reasoned action, the intention to perform any given behavior is determined by a person's attitude toward performing that behavior and his or her subjective norm with respect to performing that behavior. Table 3.4 presents strong support for this hypothesis with respect to intentions to vote for a given candidate. The multiple correlations ranged from .750 with respect to predicting the intentions to vote for Jimmy Carter to .805 with respect to predicting the intention to vote for Ronald Reagan. In marked contrast, although significant (R = .441, p < .01), the prediction of the intention to not vote was only moderately successful. We shall return to this point shortly.

First, however, note that consistent with previous findings from U.S. presidential elections (Fishbein and Ajzen, 1981; Fishbein, Ajzen, and

**TABLE 3.3**
**Relative Intentions and External Variables as Predictors of
the Performance of Behavioral Alternatives (N = 108)[a]**

| Behavioral Alternative | Simple Correlations | | | | Standardized Beta Weights | | | | Multiple R |
|---|---|---|---|---|---|---|---|---|---|
| | $RI$ | $A_o$ | $PI$ | $L$-$C$ | $RI$ | $A_o$ | $PI$ | $L$-$C$ | |
| Vote Anderson | .714** | .329** | .212* | −.216* | .660** | .075 | −.053 | −.101 | .727** |
| Vote Carter | .653** | .308** | .312** | −.043 | .605** | .050 | .115 | .047 | .666** |
| Vote Reagan | .831** | .467** | −.447** | .310** | .794** | −.024 | −.074 | .048 | .834** |

a. RI = relative intention; $A_o$ = attitude toward the candidate; PI = party identification; L-C = liberalism-conservatism.
*p < .05; **p < .01.

TABLE 3.4
**TABLE 3.4**
**Prediction of Voting Intentions from Attitudes**
**Toward Voting and Subjective Norms (N = 108)[a]**

| Direct Intention | Simple Correlations[b] | | Standardized Beta Weights | | Multiple Correlations[b] |
|---|---|---|---|---|---|
| | $A_b$ | SN | $A_b$ | SN | |
| Not vote | .428 | .400 | .366** | .126 | .441 |
| Vote Anderson | .738 | .592 | .600** | .226** | .759 |
| Vote Carter | .743 | .548 | .660** | .132 | .750 |
| Vote Reagan | .794 | .487 | .725** | .148* | .805 |

a.  $A_b$ = attitude toward behavior; SN = subjective norm.
b.  All simple and multiple correlations significant, $p < .01$.
*$p < .05$;  **$p < .01$.

Hinkle, 1980) attitudinal considerations are more important determinants of intentions to vote for a given candidate than are normative considerations. Although not anticipated, it is also interesting to note that, relatively speaking, normative considerations were more important determinants of the intention to vote for John Anderson than of the intentions to vote for either Ronald Reagan or Jimmy Carter. This suggests that, at least in the context of U.S. presidential elections, one may pay more attention to others in forming one's intention to vote for a third party candidate than in arriving at intentions regarding the candidates of the Democratic and Republican parties.

*Attitude toward behavior versus attitude toward object.* One of the major predictions of the theory of reasoned action is that it is the attitude toward the behavior and *not* the attitude toward the object of the behavior that is the major determinant of the intention to engage in the behavior. In the context of predicting voting intentions, this means that it is the attitude toward *voting for the candidate* rather than the attitude toward *the candidate per se* that serves as the major determinant of the intention to vote for the candidate.

Table 3.5 shows the simple correlations between attitudes toward each candidate, attitudes toward voting for each candidate, and intentions to vote for each candidate. Consistent with expectations, attitudes toward voting for a candidate are better predictors of voting intentions than are attitudes toward the candidates. Furthermore, it can be seen that the correlation between the attitude toward the candidate and voting intention is related strongly to the correlation between the attitude toward the candidate and the attitude toward voting for the candidate. The stronger this latter correlation, the better the prediction

## TABLE 3.5
### Prediction of Voting Intentions from Attitudes Toward Voting, Attitudes Toward Candidates, and Subjective Norms (N = 108)[a]

| Direct Intention | Simple Correlations[b] | | | Standardized Beta Weights | | | Multiple $R$[b] | Simple Correlations[b] |
|---|---|---|---|---|---|---|---|---|
| | $A_b$ | $A_o$ | SN | $A_b$ | $A_o$ | SN | | $A_b$ with $A_o$ |
| Vote Anderson | .738 | .566 | .592 | .543** | .094 | .215** | .762 | .677 |
| Vote Carter | .743 | .606 | .548 | .555** | .158 | .122 | .759 | .700 |
| Vote Reagan | .794 | .736 | .487 | .582** | .168 | .140* | .809 | .870 |

a. $A_b$ = attititude toward behavior; $A_o$ = attitude toward object; SN = subjective norm.
b. All simple and multiple correlations significant, p < .01.
*p < .05; **p < .01.

of intentions from the attitude toward the candidate. More specifically, it can be seen that the correlation between the attitude toward the candidate and the attitude toward voting for the candidate varies across the three candidates. Although attitude toward Reagan is highly correlated with the attitude toward voting for Reagan (r = .870), the correlation between these two attitudes with respect to Anderson is only .677. Because it is the attitude toward voting for a candidate that serves as a primary determinant of the intention to vote for the candidate, the attitude toward Reagan is a better predictor of voting intentions (r = .736) than is the attitude toward Anderson (r = .566).

To demonstrate further the indirect role of these traditional attitude measures, the attitudes toward the candidate were included as a third variable (along with the two model components of attitude toward voting for the candidate and subjective norm) in the prediction of intentions. The results of these analyses are also shown in Table 3.5. Consistent with expectations, consideration of attitudes toward the candidates did not significantly improve prediction of intentions to vote for that candidate.

*The prediction of intention to not vote.* As we saw above in Table 3.4 the intention to not vote was predicted with only moderate accuracy (R = .441) from a consideration of attitudes and subjective norms. It should be recalled that this relatively low multiple correlation was not unexpected. It was assumed that there would be relatively little variance in both the attitude toward not voting and the subjective norm concerning not voting. Indeed, only 5 of 108 respondents indicated positive attitudes toward not voting and only 1 of the 108 perceived that their important others thought they should not vote. Given these restrictions in range, it is surprising that these two variables predicted the intention to not vote as well as they did.

Be that as it may, the fact remains that our measures of attitudes and subjective norms with respect to not voting do not provide satisfactory explanations of the intention to not vote. As discussed earlier however, it seems reasonable to assume that one's intention to not vote will be, at least in part, related to the pattern of one's intentions with respect to the various candidates. In order to examine this relationship, respondents were assigned to one of three categories on the basis of their four candidate-oriented intentions. Respondents with positive intentions with respect to one candidate and negative intentions with respect to the remaining candidates were given a score of one. These respondents were viewed as having a clear and unambiguous intention to vote for one and only one candidate and were expected to form a *negative* intention to not vote. At the other extreme, respondents with negative or neutral intentions with respect to all four candidates were assigned a score of three and were expected to hold *positive* intentions to not vote. The remaining respondents received a score of two. This group consisted of individuals who held positive intentions to vote for two or more candidates or who had a positive intention to vote for one candidate and were uncertain with respect to another. These respondents were expected to fall between the two extreme groups in their intentions to not vote. That is, although the positive intentions to vote for at least one candidate should imply a negative intention to not vote, potential voters' conflict or ambiguity with respect to the candidates may lead some of them to hold positive intentions to not vote.

Table 3.6 shows the relationship between the three-category pattern variable based on the candidate-oriented intentions and intention to not vote. It can be seen from the frequencies presented in Table 3.6 that respondents with a clear and unambiguous intention to vote for one and only one candidate were least likely to intend to not vote (that is, were most likely to form negative intentions); whereas those with negative or neutral intentions to vote for all candidates were most likely to intend to not vote (that is, were most likely to form positive intentions toward not voting). Those expressing some conflict or ambiguity with respect to their intentions to vote for the various candidates were intermediate in their intentions to not vote ($\chi^2 = 37.0$, df = 2, p < .01). Viewed in another way, the correlation between the pattern of intentions to vote for the various candidates and the intention to not vote was .566 (df = 106, p <

TABLE 3.6
Relationship Between Intention to Not Vote and
Pattern of Intentions to Vote for the Candidate (N = 108)

| Pattern of Candidate Intentions | Intention To Not Vote | |
|---|---|---|
| | Positive or Neutral | Negative |
| Negative or neutral toward all candidates | 18 | 3 |
| Uncertain | 9 | 26 |
| Positive toward one and only one candidate | 7 | 45 |

.01). Thus, one can better predict the intention to not vote from a consideration of one's intentions *to vote* for the various candidates than from measures of one's attitudes and subjective norms with respect to not voting (R = .44). Considering all three of these variables simultaneously, the intention to not vote is predicted with reasonable accuracy (R = .599, p < .01), with the pattern of intentions vis-à-vis the candidates ($\beta$ = .461, p < .01) and the attitude toward not voting ($\beta$ = .177, p = .07) contributing most to the prediction. The relatively small increment in predictability (from .566 to .599) reflects the fact that the pattern of intentions to vote for the various candidates is significantly correlated with both the attitude toward (r = .468, p. < .01) and the subjective norm concerning (r = .315, p < .01) not voting.

## SUMMARY AND CONCLUSIONS

One of the main unresolved problems in studies of voting behavior has been the prediction and explanation of political participation. Perhaps our main contribution in this chapter is the finding that participation as well as choice can be accurately predicted from a knowledge of the potential voter's intentions to engage in each of the alternatives available in the election in question. A direct measure of the intention to perform each alternative did lead to quite accurate predictions of whether or not one performed that alternative. But, more important, a measure of relative intention, based on a consideration of all of the person's intentions, provided significantly improved prediction. Stated another way, although one is most likely to vote for the candidate toward whom one has the strongest intention, participation is likely to occur only if one has a positive intention to vote for at least one of the candidates and a negative intention not to vote.

Given that voting behavior can be predicted accurately from voting intentions, we next turned to the determinants of these intentions. As expected according to the theory of reasoned action, the intention to vote for a given candidate can be predicted accurately from a knowledge of the person's attitudes toward voting for that candidate and his or her subjective norm concerning voting for that candidate. However, although significant, the model components of attitudes and subjective norms with respect to the alternative of not voting provided only moderate prediction of the intention to not vote. This moderate relationship, in part due to the restricted range of the two predictor variables, leaves us in the position of being unable to fully explain the intention to not participate. We have found, however, that the intention to not vote is also related to the pattern of a person's intentions to vote for the various candidates. More specifically, when one has a strong unambiguous intention to vote for one and only one of the candidates, one is unlikely to intent to not vote. In contrast, when one has negative intentions with respect to all candidates, one is likely to intend to not vote.

At this point it becomes important to ask how the pattern of a person's candidate-oriented intentions exerts its influence on intentions to not vote. In this and other work we have found that external variables, like demographic variables and political attitudes, do not influence intentions or behavior directly, but indirectly by way of their effect on the attitudinal and normative model components. To a certain extent, because people with clear and unambiguous intentions to vote for one and only one candidate have a negative attitude and subjective norm concerning not voting, the pattern of candidate intentions operates by way of its influence on the attitudinal and normative components. However, in contrast to the theory of reasoned action, this pattern variable appears to have an effect on the intention to not vote that is over and above its effect on the model components. Whether this finding qualifies as a case of an external variable directly influencing intention or is merely an artifact of the restricted range of our measures can only be answered by further research.

In conclusion, from our perspective most citizens in a democratic society are aware of the importance that society places upon participation in the electoral process. Almost all believe that their important others think they should vote and feel an almost moral obligation to vote (i.e., they have negative attitudes toward not voting; they evaluate not voting as "bad" and "foolish"). Within the context of any given election, there is probably a small proportion of eligible voters who, for reasons of protest or otherwise, place a positive value on not voting and thus form intentions to not vote. For the remainder of the population, however, their attitudes and subjective norms concerning not voting should lead to negative intentions to not vote. According to our data, this does not happen unless one has someone to vote *for*. That is, in addition to forming attitudes and subjective norms toward not voting, the potential voter forms attitudes and subjective norms toward *voting for* each candidate. Based on these attitudes and subjective norms, the potential voter arrives at an intention to vote for each candidate. If none of these candidate-oriented intentions is positive, the person is likely to form an intention to not vote. In contrast, when the intention to vote for one candidate is positive and the intentions to vote for the remaining candidates are negative, (i.e., when one has a clear and unambiguous intention to vote for a particular candidate) one is unlikely to intend to not vote.

These findings suggest a very different view of the processes influencing behavior in a partisan election than typically is assumed. As discussed previously, most scholars of voting behavior have made a clear distinction between participation and choice. Moreover, they have implicitly or explicitly viewed voting behavior as a two-step process in which one first decides whether to participate, and then if this decision is positive, the decision of one's voting choice is made. In marked contrast, the data presented above suggest that potential voters consider simultaneously all the alternatives available to them; and their ultimate decision to vote for a given candidate or to abstain from voting reflects their intentions with respect to each of these alternatives. In fact, these data can be taken to indicate that if there is anything like a two-step process, it occurs in an order opposite to that described above. That is, nonparticipation may, in part, reflect the fact that one has not formed a positive intention to vote for any of the potential candidates.

## REFERENCES

AJZEN, I. and M. FISHBEIN (1980) Understanding Attitudes and Predicting Social Behavior. Englewood Cliffs, NJ: Prentice-Hall.

BOWMAN, C. H. and M. FISHBEIN (1978) "Understanding public reactions to energy proposals: an application of the Fishbein model." Journal of Applied Social Psychology 8: 319-340.

CAMPBELL, A., P. E. CONVERSE, W. E. MILLER, and D. E. STOKES (1960) The American Voter. New York: John Wiley.

CRITTENDEN, J. A. (1982) Parties and Elections in the U. S. Englewood Cliffs, NJ: Prentice-Hall.

FISHBEIN, M. (1980) "A theory of reasoned action: some applications and implications," in H. Howe and M. Page (eds.) Nebraska Symposium on Motivation, 1978. Lincoln: University of Nebraska Press.

———(1967) "Attitude and the prediction of behavior," pp. 477-492 in M. Fishbein (ed.) Readings in Attitude Theory and Measurement. New York: John Wiley.

———and I. AJZEN (1981) "Attitudes and voting behavior: an application of the theory of reasoned action," pp. 253-313 in G. M. Stephenson and J. M. Davis (eds.) Progress in Applied Social Psychology (vol. 1) New York: John Wiley.

———(1975) Belief, Attitude, Intention, and Behavior: An Introduction to Theory and Research. Reading, MA: Addison-Wesley.

FISHBEIN, M. and F. S. COOMBS (1974) "Basis for decision: attitudinal analysis of voting behavior." Journal of Applied Social Psychology 4: 95-124.

FISHBEIN, M., I. AJZEN, and R. HINKLE (1980) "Predicting and understanding voting in American elections: effects of external variables," pp. 173-195 in I. Ajzen and M. Fishbein (eds.) Understanding Attitudes and Predicting Social Behavior. Englewood Cliffs, NJ: Prentice-Hall.

FISHBEIN, M., C. H. BOWMAN, K. THOMAS, J. J. JACCARD, and I. AJZEN (1980) "Predicting and understanding voting in British elections and American referenda: illustrations of the theory's generality," pp. 196-216 in I. Ajzen and M. Fishbein (eds.) Understanding Attitudes and Predicting Social Behavior. Englewood Cliffs, NJ: Prentice-Hall.

# PART II

## POLITICAL MEDIA
## PROCESSES AND EFFECTS

Chapter 4

# EMOTIONAL AND COGNITIVE
# RESPONSES TO TELEVISED IMAGES
# OF POLITICAL LEADERS

John T. Lanzetta
Denis G. Sullivan
Roger D. Masters
Gregory J. McHugo

IT IS GENERALLY AGREED that television has transformed some aspects of politics in industrialized societies of the West. For example, it is a commonplace of American journalism and political science that party identification today plays less of a role in voting—and the personalities of candidates have become more important—than a generation ago. These changes may be related to the role of the media in politics. Because television brings images of political leaders into the homes of citizens on a daily basis, it may tend to elicit emotional responses to individuals and thus favor viewer involvement in the candidates as "personalities" rather than in the parties they represent or the issues they espouse. Because television may be a particularly viewer-involving medium (Andreoli and Worchel, 1978), its increased importance as the source of political information might help explain these changes. TV provides detailed information on leaders' facial images along with verbal messages—and these nonverbal cues are known to communicate emotion and to provide information for trait evaluations.

AUTHORS' NOTE: Research conducted under grants from the National Science Foundation, Harry Frank Guggenheim Foundation, and Dartmouth College. We thank Alice Feola and Basil Englis for their help in various stages of the experimental research reported here.

Psychologists have long recognized the face as the primary channel for affective communication (e.g., Argyle, 1969, 1975; Ekman et al. 1972; Izard, 1971). Facial expressions influence viewers' expectations regarding the future behavior of another (e.g., Camras, 1980) or regarding environmental events (e.g., Lanzetta and Orr, 1980, 1981). Moreover, the communicative effects of facial expressions involve the vicarious instigation of an emotion in the viewer (e.g., Englis et al., 1982; Krebs, 1975; Vaughan and Lanzetta, 1980).

Ethologists have also studied the ways in which expressive displays influence social behavior, but they have tended to focus on leader-follower relationships and the role of displays in establishing and maintaining status (Lorenz and Leyhausen, 1973; van Hooff, 1973). Chance (1976a, 1976b) has shown, for example, that the dominant individual in groups of primates utilizes varied mixtures of agonic (threat) and hedonic (playful exhibition) displays. Similar phenomena are evident not only in human children (Montagner, 1978; Barner-Barry, 1981), but in adult politics as well (Masters, 1976, 1981).

It would, of course, be naive to assume that humans respond reflexively when they see expressive displays of political leaders. From earlier research on stereotypes and prejudice to more recent conceptualizations of "schemas" (e.g., Leventhal, 1984), "scripts" (e.g., Abelson, 1976, 1981), and "networks" (e.g., Bower, 1981), it has been well recognized by psychologists that cognition can play a powerful role in emotional responses.

As is well known, most Americans have developed a broad basis of political information and opinion by the time they reach young adulthood (Greenstein, 1960; Easton and Dennis, 1969). It can therefore be assumed that cognitive structures (attitudes, ideology, party identification) will be linked directly to affective responses toward politicians. As a result, variables of the sort routinely analyzed by political scientists provide an excellent basis for studying the way prior cognition influences present emotional responses, and the reciprocal influence of evoked emotional responses on information processing and attitude change.

## EMPIRICAL STUDIES OF VIEWERS' EMOTIONAL AND COGNITIVE RESPONSES TO LEADERS' FACIAL DISPLAYS

We have based our work primarily on three kinds of expressive displays that social psychologists and ethologists have found generally

## TABLE 4.1
### Criteria for Classifying Facial Displays

|  | *Anger/Threat* | *Fear/Evasion* | *Happiness/Reassurance* |
|---|---|---|---|
| Eyelids | Opened wide | Upper raised/ lower tightened | Wide or normal or slightly closed |
| Eyebrows | Lowered | Lowered and furrowed | Raised |
| Eye orientation | Staring | Averted | Focused then cut off |
| Mouth corners | Forward or lowered | Retracted, normal | Retracted and/or raised |
| Teeth showing | Lower or none | Variable | Upper or both |
| Head motion: | | | |
| Lateral | None | Side-to-side | Side-to-side |
| Vertical | None | Up-down | Up-down |
| Head orientation: | | | |
| To body | Forward from trunk | Turned from vertical | Normal to trunk |
| Angle to vertical | Down | Down | Up |

to be involved in social interaction. The definitions of these displays —which we call "happy/reassurance," "anger/threat," and "fear/evasion"—were based on a combination of Ekman's criteria for facial expressions of anger, fear, and happiness and ethological descriptions of threat, evasion, and reassurance displays. The reasons for this procedure have been explained in detail elsewhere (Masters et al., 1984; Sullivan et al., 1984b); our criteria are summarized in Table 4.1. Although some important features of these three types of displays are dynamic, they are recognized easily even in still photographs (Figure 4.1) and are reliably distinguished cross-culturally (Ekman, 1972; Keating et al., 1981).

## FACIAL DISPLAYS AND VERBAL RESPONSES (EXPERIMENTS 1 AND 2)

Preliminary studies employed a common procedure to see whether videotape excerpts of different facial displays by the same (known) leader would produce distinct emotional and cognitive reactions. We began with images of President Reagan because he was a powerful figure known to all subjects.

Figure 4.1   Still Frames from Videotape Excerpts Used in Experiments 1-5 (A and B) and in Experiment C.

NOTE: President Reagan is shown expressing happiness/reassurance (A) and anger/threat (B). Senator Hart is shown in a happiness/reassurance (C) and a neutral (D) excerpt.

**Figure 4.1 Continued**

## Experimental Design

Videotape excerpts were chosen from actual TV news coverage to produce segments with an understandable verbal message and a full-screen image of a facial display of happiness/reassurance, anger/threat, or fear/evasion that met the criteria described in Table 4.1. The resulting excerpts, ranging from 25 to 150 seconds in length, were comparable to those routinely shown on television. In our first experiments, small groups of adults and college students viewed a random sequence of three examples of President Reagan exhibiting each of the three types of expressive behavior being studied. Following each of the nine excerpts, subjects first described the intensity of the President's emotional state on nine scales (e.g., joyful-happy-amused; angry-irritated-mad). Then subjects used similar scales to rate the intensity of their own emotional responses to the same excerpt. To determine the relative contribution of facial display and spoken message to the viewer's impressions and emotional responses, different groups of subjects were exposed to one of three media conditions: sound-only, image-only, and sound-plus-image (experiment 1). To discriminate the independent effects of paravocal cues and verbal message, two further media conditions—filtered-sound-plus-image and transcript-only—were added to these three (experiment 2).

## Findings

In order to assess the underlying dimensions of the viewers' descriptions, the correlation matrix of subjects' descriptive scale ratings of the nine videotaped displays was factor analyzed. The results revealed a striking structural consistency in viewers' descriptions (Table 4.2). For both experiments 1 and 2, descriptive scale ratings were reducible to three easily identified factors: happiness/reassurance (factor 1), anger/threat (factor 2), and fear/evasion (factor 3). In each sample, the factors were robust, accounting for over 70 percent of the total variance; each factor was correlated with only the descriptive ratings predicted by these three dimensions of displays behavior.

Viewers' descriptions of the displays were not significantly correlated with their prior attitude toward President Reagan. In other words, even those individuals whose emotional responses to a political leader may be strongly influenced by their opinions and partisanship provided accu-

## TABLE 4.2
### Factor Structure of the Descriptions of President Reagan's Happiness/Reassurance, Anger/Threat, and Fear/Evasion Displays for All Media Conditions Combined

| | Factor 1 Happiness/Reassurance Experiment | | Factor 2 Anger/Threat Experiment | | Factor 3 Fear/Evasion Experiment | | Communality Experiment | |
|---|---|---|---|---|---|---|---|---|
| | #1 | #2 | #1 | #2 | #1 | #2 | #1 | #2 |
| Strong | .59 | .46 | .37 | .32 | −.55 | −.69 | 79 | 78 |
| Joyful | .80 | .61 | −.04 | −.42 | .05 | −.28 | 64 | 62 |
| Comforting | .74 | .70 | −.12 | −.28 | −.35 | −.31 | 68 | 66 |
| Interested | .74 | .90 | −.07 | .04 | −.18 | −.12 | 59 | 82 |
| Angry | −.10 | −.05 | .90 | .92 | −.01 | −.13 | 83 | 86 |
| Disgusted | −.03 | −.17 | .83 | .88 | .25 | .08 | 75 | 80 |
| Fearful | −.32 | −.21 | .12 | .25 | .75 | .75 | 67 | 66 |
| Confused | −.21 | −.19 | −.03 | −.08 | .88 | .87 | 82 | 80 |
| Evasive | .05 | −.09 | .29 | .01 | .77 | .70 | 69 | 50 |
| Percentage variance accounted for | 25 | 22 | 20 | 23 | 27 | 28 | | |

NOTE: Principal components analysis with Varimax rotation. (N = 65 in experiment 1, and N = 145 in experiment 2.) Underlined loadings were used to interpret the factors.

**TABLE 4.3**
**Factor Structure of Emotional Responses to President Reagan's**
**Happiness/Reassurance, Anger/Threat, and Fear/Evasion Displays**
**for All Media Conditions Combined**

| | Experiment 1 (N = 65) | | Experiment 2 (N = 145) | |
|---|---|---|---|---|
| | Positive | Negative | Positive | Negative |
| Joyful | .70 | −.06 | .69 | −.34 |
| Comforted | .83 | −.26 | .83 | −.29 |
| Supportive | .83 | −.30 | .84 | −.25 |
| Interested | .71 | −.02 | .81 | .09 |
| Angry | −.05 | .87 | −.05 | .84 |
| Disgusted | −.21 | .81 | −.25 | .79 |
| Fearful | −.11 | .86 | −.17 | .81 |
| Confused | −.20 | .68 | −.15 | .58 |
| Percentage variance accounted for | 31 | 35 | 33 | 33 |

NOTE: Principal components analysis with Varimax rotation. Underlined loadings were used to interpret the factors.

rate descriptions of that leader's nonverbal expressions. To examine the effects of nonverbal and verbal channels separately, we analyzed responses to each media condition using three distinct procedures: (1) a factor analysis to examine the structure of responses on all nine descriptive scales; (2) differences in mean profiles of standardized factor scores; and (3) a "centroid" cluster analysis to assess viewers' descriptive accuracy, on the assumption that our characterization of the expressive displays was correct. These analyses generally confirmed the distinctiveness of these three types of expressive displays, and indicated an extraordinary degree of similarity in facial, verbal, and paravocal cues of emotion.

Turning to verbal self-reports of the emotions felt while watching the displays (Table 4.3), subjects used emotional terms in much the same way voters did in a presidential preference survey (Abelson et al., 1982). Furthermore, when separate factor analyses were done for each channel of communication in experiments 1 and 2, the two-factor solution was remarkably stable across subsamples. We therefore conclude that viewers respond emotionally to televised displays of a political leader along the same positive (hedonic) and negative (agonic) dimensions identified by social psychologists and ethologists.

Unlike descriptions, however, the self-reported emotional responses were highly influenced by viewers' pre-experimental attitudes toward

President Reagan. As subjects' descriptions of the displays were consistent with our definition of the expressive behavior, these variations in the verbal self-reports of emotion cannot be accounted for in terms of differential perception of the stimuli. In Figure 4.2, factor scores for positive and negative emotional responses to the three kinds of expressive displays are plotted as a function of prior attitude toward President Reagan, with the results from all groups in experiment 2 combined.

Whereas happiness/reassurance excerpts generated very strong positive responses in the president's supporters and neutral reactions from his opponents, fear/evasion excerpts generated little positive affect from any viewers; anger/threat excerpts were intermediate, generating moderately positive responses from supporters but not from critics. Negative affect was roughly inverted: Agonistic excerpts generated more negative responses in critics than in supporters, whereas happy/reassurance excerpts reduced negative emotional responses in critics and even more so in supporters (see Masters et al., 1984; Sullivan et al., 1984b).

## FACIAL DISPLAYS AND PSYCHOPHYSIOLOGICAL RESPONSES (EXPERIMENT 3)

The initial studies were based entirely on verbal self-reports. Our third experiment was designed to clarify the meaning of these responses and their relationship to both media condition and prior attitude. How does a subject's initial attitude toward a communicator combine with exposure to an expressive display in eliciting an emotional response? To answer this question, we felt the need for continuous and less "reactive" measures of emotion. Consequently, subjects in experiment 3 were exposed to the same kinds of displays as before, but we measured emotional responses at both the physiological and self-reported levels. Autonomic and facial electromyographic (EMG) responses were obtained continuously before, during, and after stimulus exposure. Such psychophysiological measures have been used widely to assess emotional response (Schwartz et al., 1976; Ekman et al., 1983; Cacioppo and Petty, 1979; Englis et al., 1982) and in developing political attitude scales (Tursky et al., 1979).

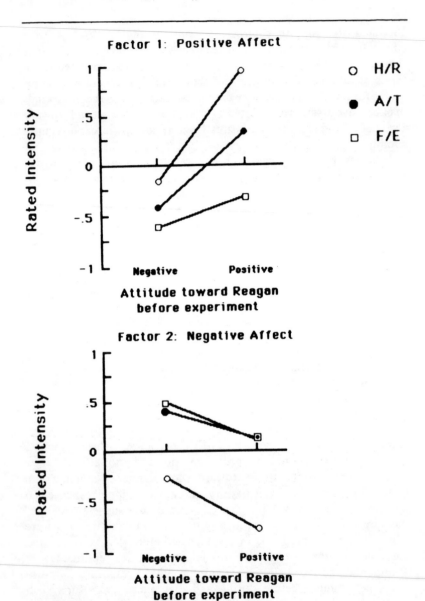

**Factor 1: Positive Affect**

○ H/R
● A/T
□ F/E

Rated Intensity

Negative    Positive

Attitude toward Reagan
before experiment

**Factor 2: Negative Affect**

Rated Intensity

Negative    Positive

Attitude toward Reagan
before experiment

NOTE: H/R = happiness/reassurance; A/T = anger/threat; and F/E = fear/evasion.
On a 100-point thermometer scale 1-49 is negative and 51-100 is positive.

Figure 4.2   Positive and Negative Emotional Response (as Factor Scores) to President
Reagan's Happiness/Reassurance, Anger/Threat, and Fear/Evasion Displays as a Function of Attitude Toward Reagan Before Experiment 2

Theoretical Rationale

Competing theories predict different relationships between prior affective dispositions, stimulus-produced physiological responses, and self-report measures of emotion. Consistency theories suggest, for example, that the congruence of attitude evoked by the political leader and self-report of emotion evoked by his or her expressive behavior is the result of pressures toward cognitive consistency (Rosenberg, 1968). Regardless of the nature of the expressive display, or whether subjects judge it to express a positive or negative emotion, they would report emotional responses consistent with prior attitude toward the expressor. Thus, the differences between pro- and anti-Reaganites in reported emotion may have been a consequence of cognitive adjustments in which Reagan supporters exaggerated, and Reagan opponents minimized, the extent to which Reagan's happy face, for example, gave them pleasure. This model suggests that the cognitive process of adjusting self-reported emotion to prior attitude may require distortion of or inattention to responses on the psychophysiological level.

In contrast to the simple consistency interpretation, others (e.g., Mandler, 1975, 1980; Schachter, 1964; Schachter and Singer, 1962) postulate that physiological arousal is accurately assessed, but that it is not the primary determinant of the *nature* of emotional experience. In this view, physiological arousal indicates an emotional experience, but subjects use information from the situation and past experience—not differences in autonomic and skeletal responses—to report which emotion has been experienced. These two-factor theories imply that a leader's facial display may generally be arousing on the physiological level, but that prior attitude toward the leader may determine the nature of the emotion (whether positive or negative) the viewer reports. Thus Reagan supporters and opponents would be similarly aroused by his expressive displays, but supporters would report a positive and opponents a negative emotional response.

In discrete emotion theories, self-reports and physiological measures should covary because emotional responses are biologically rooted and culturally shaped patterns of behavior (Izard, 1971, 1977; Tompkins, 1962, 1963; Ekman and Friesen, 1975). Facial expressive displays usually evoke autonomic and facial muscle changes (Dimberg, 1982; Vaughan and Lanzetta, 1980), and different subjective reports of emotion covary with different expression conditions (Englis and Lanzetta, 1984). Thus, type of expressive display and viewer attitude toward the communicator should influence both the pattern and the intensity of autonomic and facial muscle responses, because both factors are associated with different subjective reports of emotion. From this perspective, one would predict that both positive and negative attitude groups should have similar psychophysiological profiles for each expressive display, but the amplitudes should differ in ways that reflect the blending of the affective component of prior attitude with the emotions evoked by the display itself.

## Experimental Design

In an experiment designed to explore these hypotheses, the primary factors were media condition (image-only compared to sound-plus-image), facial display, and prior attitude toward President Reagan. Each of forty Dartmouth undergraduates saw eight excerpts: four displays (neutral, happy/reassurance, anger/threat, and fear/evasion) in two media conditions. Emotional responses during the viewing session were assessed by measures of autonomic activity (changes in heart rate and skin resistance) and of facial expressive behavior (corrugator supercilii [brow] and zygomaticus major [cheek/mouth] EMG); after the presentation of each facial display, verbal self-reports of emotion were obtained. (For a full description of the experimental methods and the findings, see McHugo et al., 1984.)

## Findings

The results confirmed that facial displays elicited distinct patterns of psychophysiological response. EMG measurements showed that zygomatic muscles were activated by happy/reassurance displays and relaxed by displays of either anger/threat or fear/evasion; corrugator EMG, although activated during the viewing of all displays, was most responsive to anger/threat and least responsive to happy/reassurance displays (Figure 4.3a). Although these differences were evident in the sound-plus-image media condition, they were amplified when subjects viewed the stimuli in the image-only condition (Figures 4.4a and 4.4b). Electrodermal activity indicated that, although the stimuli were not highly arousing, the most activation occurred during anger/threat displays and the least during happy/reassurance displays (Figure 4.3a). Heart rate changes reflected an interaction between media and display

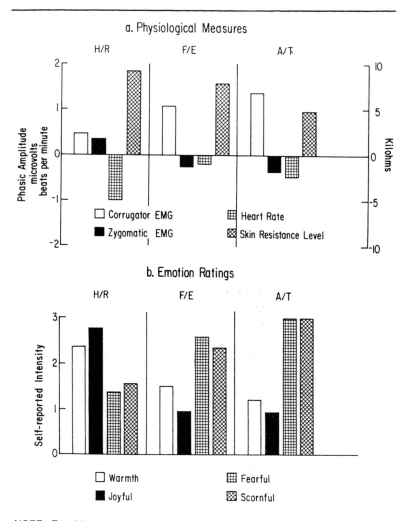

a. Physiological Measures

Figure 4.3 Mean Phasic Psychophysiological Responses During, and Self-Report Profiles Following H/R, F/E, and A/T Expressive Displays by President Reagan

NOTE: For abbreviations, see note in Figure 4.2.

condition; the usual decelerative response was reversed during sound-plus-image presentations of both fear/evasion and anger/threat excerpts (Figure 4.4c). Generally speaking, there was no systematic relationship between display condition and prior attitude toward Reagan on the four psychophysiological measures.

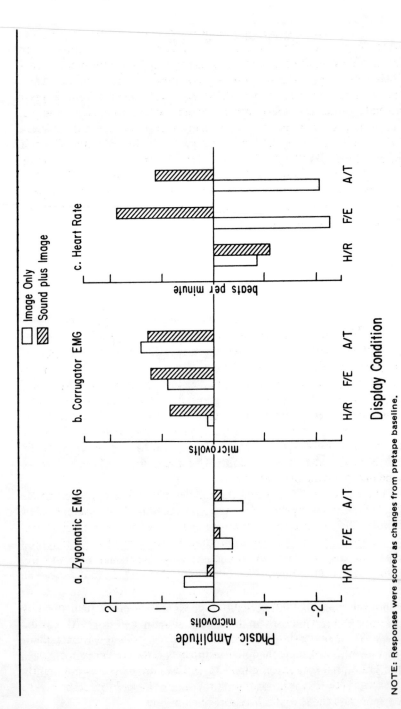

NOTE: Responses were scored as changes from pretape baseline.

Figure 4.4 Display by Media Interaction for Corrugator and Zygomatic EMG and for Heart Rate

Subjects' self-reported emotional responses to expressive displays were consistent with our prior experiments in both direction and interaction with prior attitude. In general, happy/reassurance displays elicited more positive and less negative emotions than either anger/threat or fear/evasion (Figure 4.3b). As in experiments 1 and 2, prior attitude influenced these verbal reports of emotion (for example, supporters felt more positive after seeing anger/threat than did critics). Whereas cognitive reports of emotion after the fact showed effects of prior attitude [$F(12,88) = 2.44$; $p = .009$], the only effect of attitude on physiological response resulted from a post hoc blocking limited to extreme attitude groups, and reflected an interaction between prior attitude and media condition only for corrugator EMG and heart rate responses (McHugo et al., 1984).

## Discussion

The strong effects of prior attitude on verbal self-reports, combined with the absence of comparable effects of prior attitude on the physiological level, suggest that subjects modified their initial emotional responses to the expressive displays over the viewing period. The attenuated amplitude of facial EMG responses in the sound-plus-image condition is consistent with this possibility, insofar as a stimulus that combines a verbal message with a facial display should activate cognitive processes and dampen immediate emotional reactions, whereas an image-only stimulus may be processed first as an emotionally evocative cue and only subsequently compared to relevant cognitive schemas involving prior attitudes.

These findings suggest that the competing theories discussed above need not be mutually exclusive. Although the Mandler-Schacter models capture the distinction between immediate psychophysiological response and self-report of emotion, they do not predict the differential effect of displays on autonomic systems and facial masculature. Conversely, even though discrete emotion theories fail to describe the full complexity of cognitive processing of emotional responses to political leaders' display behavior, they seem to be partly confirmed by the different physiological patterning due to agonic and hedonic displays. Finally, although predictions derived from consistency theories may underestimate the relationship between differences in displays and emotional responses, cognitive consistency pressures apparently intervene between the immediate autonomic or facial EMG responses to a display and the verbal self-report of emotion.

## COGNITIVE EFFECTS OF REPEATED EXPOSURE
## TO A LEADER'S DISPLAYS (EXPERIMENTS 4 AND 5)

The three experiments described above placed viewers in an artificial situation in part because the stimuli were discrete excerpts. Although the data showed the effectiveness of facial displays in eliciting emotional responses and cognitive assessments of a leader, they also revealed complex interactions between the kind of display seen, the channel of communication, and the characteristics of the viewer. But does it matter that cognitive and emotional processes interact in the responses to leaders' expressive displays? Can facial displays in a more typical setting actually influence political attitudes?

### Theoretical Rationale

From the inception of our research program, we assumed that expressive displays would have minimal effects on strongly anchored attitudes toward, and trait attributions to, political leaders. Such effects could be anticipated only after repeated exposure to a particular display over a moderately long period of time. And even then, the effects may be complex and obtained only for those with neutral or unstable attitudes. These deliberations led to an experimental design in which subjects with different prior attitudes were exposed repeatedly to expressive displays known to be emotionally evocative.

It has been difficult to specify a single theoretical model that would generate unambiguous predictions for our data. We have therefore drawn upon three different theoretical perspectives that might predict the way facial displays could produce enduring changes in attitudes toward, and traits attributed to, a powerful leader like President Reagan.

The first perspective—an emotional mediating process—predicts that expressive displays evoke emotional responses in viewers that, in turn, modify more enduring attitudes and trait attributions. Within this perspective, there are two different subtheories—attraction and expectancy theory. To apply attraction theory (Byrne, 1971; Lott and Lott, 1972), one must assume that specific displays evoke either positive or negative emotions in the viewer. Lott and Lott (1972) have summarized the evidence that liking for another is a direct function of the positive reinforcements experienced when one is in that person's presence. As reinforcers, expressive displays may thus contribute to the positive or negative valence of the leader. Although Lott and Lott cite not evidence on the reinforcing power of expressive displays and do not deal explicitly with leaders, the work of Vaughan and Lanzetta (1980) indicates that facial displays of emotion do function as conditioned reinforcers. The extension of the Lott and Lott model to political leadership is thus plausible, and predicts that expressive displays evoking positive affect (e.g., happy/reassuring displays) should increase liking for, and dispositions to support, a leader, whereas expressive displays that elicit negative affect (e.g., fear/evasion) should decrease liking and support.

The other emotional mediating process approach—an instrumental or expectancy model—interprets facial displays as providing the viewer with information about future behaviors of the leader, behaviors that have either positive or negative consequences for the viewer (Englis et al., 1982). If the expectancy dimension of prior attitude is salient, viewers might interpret a leader's facial displays as indicating negative or positive policy consequences for themselves or groups with which they identify. For viewers with extremely strong attitudes, the cue value of a facial display may be decodable even in the absence of a message suggesting a target. For example, viewers who intensely dislike the leader may decode the leader's smile or threat as indicating a negative consequence for self and friends; conversely, a leader's fear/evasion display may evoke pleasure (or at least relief) in the viewer because it signals a reduced probability of harm. Indirect support for these assumptions is provided in studies demonstrating that emotional reactions to the expressive displays of an ingroup member or a cooperative partner tend to be empathic, whereas the same displays evoked indifference or counterempathy when emitted by an outgroup member or a competitor (Lanzetta and Englis, 1982; Englis and Lanzetta, 1984).

A second major theoretical perspective—which might be called a rational appraisal model—treats a leader's expressive displays as potentially useful cues in interpreting what the leader says and is likely to do. According to this model, viewers use whatever information seems most appropriate for inferring traits associated with leadership or policy outcomes. Although the facial display might be a reliable indicator of a leader's competence or strength, verbal messages could be a more salient source of information (at least for informed viewers). In this perspective, predictions as to facial display effects cannot be made in the absence of information about the prior attitudes of the viewer and the messages. The emotional response might indeed change attitudes, but there would be no one-to-one relationship between the nature of the display and the resulting attitude. In some ways, a rational appraisal model of this sort is an extension of Popkin's work on the rationality of voting decisions based on attributions of traits like competence (Popkin et al., 1976).

The third major perspective—ethology—assumes that facial displays trigger or release specific responses in the viewer, responses that have a long evolutionary history (Lorenz and Leyhausen, 1973; Plutchik, 1980; Hinde, 1982). In terms of our experimental paradigm, this approach suggests that viewers should decode and respond to displays quite independently of the accompanying message. This is consistent with the findings in experiment 3, which showed that at the psychophysiological level, immediate responses are largely independent of prior attitude. Thus exposure to combinations of reassuring (hedonic) and determined or threatening displays should strengthen dominance attributions, whereas exposure to fear/evasion displays should weaken them. In particular, threat displays should be especially salient as means of bonding supporters and leaders (Lorenz, 1966).

It is clear that these theoretical approaches differ not only in their assumptions about the mediating mechanisms, but also in the class of dependent variables upon which they focus. The Lott and Lott hypothesis predicts that the hedonic valence of the expressive displays of a leader should influence the positive or negative affect elicited by him or her and that this in turn should influence the strength of support dispositions. The expectancy model treats expressive displays as signals that influence expectations of positive or negative outcomes; it is the hedonic valence of these predicted consequences that determines the strength of support for a leader. The ethological perspective postulates direct emotional reactions to a display, but it assumes that these responses are functionally linked to perceptions of dominance or to the status and prior experiences of the observer. Thus, leaders whose displays support attributions of dominance are viewed more favorably than leaders whose displays are perceived as indicating submissiveness; threat displays should elicit different responses depending on the relation between the leader and the viewer. Finally, the rational appraisal model predicts that prior attitude, facial display, and message content may on occasion be differentially weighted in forming impressions of a leader. Because of the mediating role of trait attributions of competence, strength, and warmth, this model does not predict simple effects of the displays on support dispositions without reference to prior attitude or message content.

## Experimental Stimuli

The theoretical concerns cited above prompted the choice of a repeated exposures paradigm similar to that adopted by Iyengar et al. (1982). To ensure ecological validity and at the same time achieve precise experimental control, we embedded different expressive displays by President Reagan within short TV news excerpts. In each excerpt, while newscasters deliver a verbal message containing presidential news, an expressive display is substituted for part of the visual background of the story. There are two advantages to this editing technique. First, the stimulus figure's gestures—in this case those of President Reagan—accompany the naturally occurring flow of text presented by the newscaster. Second, as Reagan is seen but not heard (thus avoiding confounds of tone of voice and other paravocal cues), this procedure is a powerful test of the hypothesis that a leader's expressive displays can influence attitudes and trait attributions. Excerpts were standardized so that the introduction of an expressive display made sense to the viewer, and the commentary was edited to match the 16-22 second expressive displays that were inserted. Using this approach, we carried out experiment 4 to test our stimuli and experiment 5 to explore more fully the repeated exposures design.

## Experiment 4

This experiment pretested the emotional and cognitive effects of the experimental stimuli described above. Full analyses of eight stories showed within-subject main effects for President Reagan's expressive displays on emotional responses to the excerpts. Other factors, of course, were important regardless of the nature of the display: The stories evoked different emotional reactions, and viewers who were warm toward Reagan on the thermometer scale reported more joy and more reassurance than those who were cold. More interesting, the effect of the different facial displays interacted with the viewers' prior attitudes; that is, as in earlier experiments, differences in President Reagan's expressive displays modified the emotional responses of supporters much more than of critics.

## Experiment 5

Having shown that a leader's expressive displays embedded in news excerpts can influence a viewer's emotional responses apart from the topic being presented—even when the leader is not speaking—we felt justified in using such stimuli in a repeated exposure experiment over three days. Three sets of twenty news stories were created, so that different groups of subjects could be presented with identical stories varying solely in the overall proportions of different facial displays of the President shown in the background. In each set, half of the news stories had a mixed expressive display, and the other half had either a happy/reassurance display, an anger/threat display, or a neutral display. A different group of subjects saw each set of news stories over a two-day period (five stories with mixed displays, and five with either happy/reassurance, anger/threat, or neutral displays at each session); on the third day, subjects returned for a measurement of posttest attitudes and other variables, such as traits ascribed and emotions evoked. This design made it highly unlikely that any between-group differences would be due to extraneous factors, because the only variable manipulated was the type of expressive displays. (For a fuller account of the experimental procedure and results, see Sullivan et al., 1984a.)

The findings were complex but interesting. Although, as might be expected, the topics covered in the news stories produced different emotional responses in our viewers, the facial displays they saw had an independent effect. There were significant between-group differences in emotional responses, trait attributions, and attitudes toward President Reagan 24 hours after watching the last of the excerpts. That is, merely by varying the mixture of facial displays in the background of newscasts, both emotional and cognitive reactions of viewers could be influenced. These effects were, however, far from simple and straightforward; on the contrary, prior attitude and the gender of the viewer had a major effect not only on responses to each individual news story, but above all on emotions reported, traits attributed, and attitudes changed on the final day of the experiment.

In the posttest questionnaire, 24 hours after the last viewing, subjects were asked to recall the proportion of happy/reassurance, anger/threat, or other displays of Reagan that they had seen. Although for all subjects there were effects of display condition on recall [$F(8,382) = 4.02$; $p <$ .001], males were more accurate than females in recalling the mixture of facial displays to which they had been exposed. Whereas the differences in males' recall by display condition were highly significant [$F(8,200) =$

2.91; p < .001], differences in female recall reached statistical significance only for between-group means adjusted by a covariance analysis
(instead of blocking) to remove the effects of initial attitude toward
Reagan [F(6,190) = 2.29; p < .05].

This difference in recall by gender was paradoxical because immediately after seeing the videotapes and in the posttest, females exhibited
significantly different emotional responses in the three display conditions, whereas male subjects did not show this effect; the feelings of
happiness, sympathy, and disgust toward President Reagan reported by
female viewers varied depending on prior attitude and kind of display
seen. Hence males were *more* accurate than females in describing the
displays to which they had been exposed, but *less* likely to report
different emotional feeling due to these displays. Females seem to have
integrated emotional and cognitive responses in a different way than
males.

This gender difference is underscored by comparing the pretest and
posttest thermometer ratings of President Reagan in the three display
conditions (Figures 4.5a and 4.5b). Whereas seeing different facial
displays in the background did not greatly change the ratings of females
or of male critics and supporters, neutral males exposed to stories into
which happy/reassurance displays had been edited became significantly
more positive, and neutral males who saw the same stories with
anger/threat or neutral images became more negative. Hence males'
cognitive assessments seem to have been more strongly influenced by
nonverbal facial displays than were their emotions, whereas females'
prior attitudes, emotional reactions, and judgments seemed more
closely linked. Moreover, the detailed patterns of trait attribution in
each display condition confirmed the importance of variations in facial
expression as a potential factor in the formation and modification of
attitudes toward leaders.

## Discussion

Once again, our findings suggest that the competing theories of
emotional and cognitive response may all be partially correct because
they refer to different aspects of the phenomena. The ethological
approach, which leads to the prediction that facial displays are
"prepared" stimuli likely to have effects apart from the accompanying
messages, is especially relevant to the response of the male viewers
without strong partisan identification in experiment 5; in addition, the

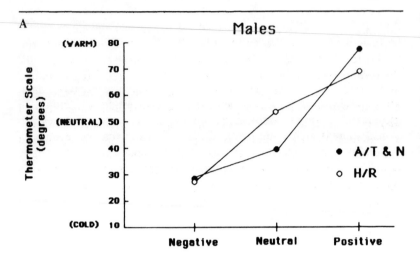

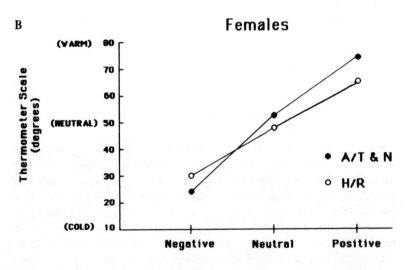

NOTE: Neutral (N) and anger/threat (A/T) combined versus happiness/reassurance (H/R).

Figure 4.5  (A) Male and (B) Female Subjects' Overall Attitude Toward Reagan 24 Hours After Exposure (Mean Thermometer Rating) by Initial Attitude Toward Reagan and by Display Condition different effect of anger/threat displays on supporters and critics is consistent with Lorenz's hypothesis that ritualized threat bonds followers to a leader. Something like rational appraisal seems to describe the responses of those with strong prior attitudes, particularly among male viewers who did not respond to the videotape excerpts with different emotions even though they accurately recalled the kinds of display that they had seen. Finally, the responses of females seem more consistent with emotional mediating processes, because cognition and emotion interact more closely both in descriptive recall and self-reported verbal responses of emotion and trait attribution. Perhaps there is more than one mode of information processing, and this multiplicity itself explains the differential power of affective cues in modifying cognitive responses as well as the difficulties in studying this system in naturalistic settings.

## EXPRESSIVE DISPLAYS IN THE 1984 AMERICAN PRESIDENTIAL CAMPAIGN (EXPERIMENT 6)

### Theoretical Rationale

The exception that properties of the leader might influence politically important viewer responses is based on two hypotheses: First, candidates and leaders *vary* in the kinds of display behavior shown by the media (and, quite probably, in the kinds of displays that they actually exhibit in day-to-day behavior); second, the actual and perceived *status* of a political figure will influence the way that individual's display behavior elicits emotional and cognitive responses from the public (Masters, 1976). The first hypothesis means that television should show significantly different images of each candidate due to variations in behavior or to editorial bias; the second predicts that increases in status should be correlated with increased emotional response to the same display behavior by a single leader. Experiment 6 tested these hypotheses in order to explore whether political parties, individual leaders, or issue positions could modify viewers' emotional and cognitive reactions to expressive displays.

Experimental Design

During the 1984 American presidential campaign, a set of naturally occurring displays of all eight announced Democratic candidates as well as of President Reagan was shown to two samples of subjects, one at the outset of the election year (in January, before the first caucuses or primaries) and the other in October (three weeks before election day). Because the same videotaped excerpts were shown at two different times, between-sample differences can be used as evidence of the effect of changed political status on viewer responses; because each subject saw images of nine different leaders, within-sample responses provide a measure of the variation in expressive display behavior in an actual election campaign.[1]

For each candidate, two displays like those used in our earlier experiments were selected from material actually shown during TV news coverage of the campaign: one excerpt in which the candidate's expressive display behavior was neutral and one containing happy/reassuring facial displays.[2] To control for the contribution of the facial display as distinct from other emotional or verbal factors, each candidate was seen by half of the subjects in the sound-plus-image condition (once emotionally neutral and once exhibiting happiness/reassurance), and by the other half of the subjects in the image-only condition. So that each subject would see a total of 20 videotape excerpts, half with sound and half without, a second pair of displays of Reagan was added; hence each subject saw Reagan in both media formats.

Description of Displays:
Expressive Behavior as a Variable

The descriptive scores given to *neutral* displays were relatively similar for all nine candidates whereas descriptions of *happy/reassurance* displays varied quite sharply from both one candidate to another and each candidate's neutral display. Descriptions of neutral and happy/reassuring displays differed considerably in mean levels, and for ratings of the candidates' happiness, the two display conditions were weakly correlated ($r = .18$).

Exposure to politics over the campaign and changes in political status and attitudes toward the candidates generally did not influence descriptions of their expressive behavior. Nine of the ten statistically significant differences concerned ratings of Reagan and Jackson, who were two candidates whose pretest thermometer ratings by our subjects improved between January and October (see below). The varied descriptive ratings of each candidate's happy/reassurance display were presumably due either to differences in TV news coverage or to differences in the candidates' own expressions of emotion. On the one hand, it is possible that our excerpts reflected bias in the TV networks' selection of only some kinds of expressive behavior on the part of one or more candidate; on the other hand—and perhaps more plausibly— differences in facial configuration, individual display repertoire, or public presentational style could be involved. Although we cannot yet choose among these explanations, our data confirm the first of the two hypotheses stated in this section: The expressive behavior of leaders shown on TV does indeed vary.

## Emotional Responses, Display Intensity, and Leadership Status

Before the Iowa caucuses, self-reported reactions to *neutral* displays showed relatively little emotional response to any of the candidates. Even so, descriptions of happiness in these displays were highly correlated with subjects' emotional feelings of joy ($r = .72$). More important, TV excerpts showing *happiness/reassurance* for each candidate were highly differentiated. The degree of joyful emotion elicited by a happy/reassurance display was almost perfectly correlated with its perceived intensity ($r = .97$).

If we turn to the second wave of our experiment, for most candidates there is no statistically significant difference in the emotional responses to the same videotapes seen at the beginning and at the end of the campaign year. The exceptions are revealing. Only three candidates improved their pretest thermometer ratings if we compare our January and October samples: Hart, Jackson, and Reagan. For all three, this increase in viewer support seems to have been reflected in a greater evocation of joy when seeing that candidate's happy/reassurance displays—and for Reagan and Jackson, even after seeing neutral excerpts. Enhanced status does indeed seem to increase emotional responses to a given expressive display.

## Cognitive Responses: Candidate Recognition, Priming, and Attitude Shifts

In experiment 6, comparison of pretest and posttest thermometer ratings of each candidate provides one measure of the effects of seeing a series of displays by politicians (Table 4.4). These effects are clearest from the net change in percentage giving a candidate *either* a rating between 0 and 40 (significantly negative) *or* a 60-100 score (significantly positive); these changes permit us to record polarization in opposite directions (i.e., movements away from neutral or "no opinion" that are cancelled out in averaging).

At the outset of the campaign, the only candidates whose displays produced a clear shift from negative to positive were Reagan and Jackson, who were both well known before the Iowa caucuses. In contrast, the experience of seeing Mondale in January had a net negative effect (mainly because 15.2 percent of those who had rated Mondale positively before our first experiment no longer did so after seeing the televised displays).

In January, the viewing experience had quite different effects on thermometer ratings of the lesser-known candidates. Viewers' judgments of Hart, Cranston, Askew, and Hollings were polarized by the exposure to the TV displays: substantial portions of our sample (20%-40%) shifted from noncommittal pretest ratings to *either* positive *or* negative judgments on the posttest thermometer scale. Here, we have good evidence of the phenomenon that Iyengar and others have described as "priming": The viewing experience often seems to function primarily as a means of activating prior attitudes and schemas rather than as a means of conversion (Iyengar and Kinder, this volume). Given this general priming function of exposure to lesser-known candidates early in the campaign, the effect of our experiment on attitudes toward Gary Hart was especially interesting: Although he was known by only one-third of our subjects polarization along party lines involved a smaller proportion of our sample for Hart than for Cranston, Askew, or Hollings.

In October 1984, three candidates had pretest thermometer ratings that has increased from our January sample: Reagan, Hart, and Jackson. Of these, two—Reagan and Jackson—elicited even higher thermometer ratings after subjects' experimental viewing of their displays. Once again, therefore, a major finding in our October sample was the enhanced effect of the displays of Reagan and Jackson. Need it be added that between January and October, Hart lost his primary

TABLE 4.4
### Changes in Attitude After Viewing Expressive Displays
(Pretest and Posttest Thermometer Ratings, Experiment 6)

| | January, 1984 | | | | | October |
|---|---|---|---|---|---|---|
| | 0-40 (%) | 45-55 (%) | 60-100 (%) | DK (%) | Average* | Average* |
| **Reagan** | | | | | | |
| Pretest | 23.6 | 1.2 | 61.5 | 0 | 61.6 | 64.0 |
| Posttest | 20.0 | 3.6 | 73.9 | 2.5 | 64.0 | 71.2 |
| Net change | −3.6 | | +12.4 | | | |
| **Mondale** | | | | | | |
| Pretest | 36.3 | 20.0 | 43.8 | 0 | 51.3 | 45.5 |
| Posttest | 37.6 | 30.0 | 28.6 | 2.5 | 47.9 | 46.4 |
| Net change | +1.3 | | −15.2 | | | |
| **Jackson** | | | | | | |
| Pretest | 51.2 | 20.1 | 27.5 | 0 | 41.1 | 46.1 |
| Posttest | 42.4 | 22.5 | 32.4 | 0 | 44.6 | 48.1 |
| Net change | −8.8 | | +4.9 | | | |
| **Hart** | | | | | | |
| Pretest | 18.6 | 37.5 | 28.6 | 15.0 | 52.6 | 59.6** |
| Posttest | 28.7 | 28.8 | 39.8 | 2.5 | 50.9 | 54.5 |
| Net change | +10.1 | | +11.2 | | | |
| **Glenn** | | | | | | |
| Pretest | 15.1 | 33.7 | 49.9 | 1.2 | 54.9 | 50.1** |
| Posttest | 15.0 | 31.1 | 51.1 | 2.5 | 56.9 | 46.1 |
| Net change | −0.1 | | +1.2 | | | |
| **McGovern** | | | | | | |
| Pretest | 50.0 | 23.8 | 23.9 | 2.5 | 42.7 | 40.1 |
| Posttest | 46.7 | 28.7 | 21.2 | 2.5 | 41.1 | 41.2 |
| Net change | −3.3 | | −2.4 | | | |
| **Cranston** | | | | | | |
| Pretest | 23.8 | 46.1 | 16.1 | 13.7 | 45.9 | 40.8 |
| Posttest | 43.6 | 28.7 | 24.9 | 2.5 | 42.8 | 39.9 |
| Net change | +19.8 | | +8.8 | | | |
| **Askew** | | | | | | |
| Pretest | 18.7 | 43.7 | 1.2 | 35.0 | 43.5 | 38.6 |
| Posttest | 41.3 | 34.8 | 21.3 | 2.5 | 43.7 | 40.4 |
| Net change | +22.6 | | +20.1 | | | |
| **Hollings** | | | | | | |
| Pretest | 13.7 | 28.7 | 10.0 | 47.5 | 48.7 | 44.9 |
| Posttest | 36.1 | 42.9 | 21.4 | 2.5 | 44.4 | 40.7 |
| Net change | +22.4 | | +11.4 | | | |

*Don't know (DK) not included in average thermometer ratings; **Difference between January and October is significant (p < .05).

contest with Mondale, whereas Jackson increased his political stature and Reagan's reelection became more assured?

## CONCLUSIONS AND SIGNIFICANCE

Our research to date has already established findings of interest for theories of emotion and information processing, as well as for the study of American politics:

(1) Facial displays of happiness/reassurance, anger/threat, and fear/evasiveness are perceived differently, elicit different psychophysiological responses, and interact with prior attitude and message in generating self-reported emotional or attitudinal reactions.

(2) Prior attitudes—although having little effect on psychophysiological responses to facial displays—interact strongly with self-reported emotional responses and cognitive assessments of the stimulus figure.

(3) Partisanship predicts potency of response to display behavior. Supporters of President Reagan find his nonverbal displays of happiness/reassurance more reassuring than critics, and his displays of anger/threat, which elicit fear and hostility among critical viewers, generate a sense of strength and power among supporters.

(4) Facial displays are capable of arousing and influencing viewers even when embedded in the background of a TV newscast during which the leader's voice is not heard.

(5) Different candidates vary in the way they are perceived and in the emotional responses they elicit.

(6) Although similar emotions are conveyed by the image, the sound, and the combined sound-plus-image presentation, these channels of communication do not seem to contribute equally to the emotional effects on viewers.

Our findings are directly relevant to major theoretical issues in information processing. Rival hypotheses concerning the role of expressive displays in mediating changes in dispositions toward political leaders may each contain an element of validity. On the one hand, expressive displays seem to function as "prepared stimuli," eliciting distinct psychophysiological effects that do not seem to be influenced by prior attitudes; when embedded in the background of newscasts, these cues can modify attitudes (notably of males with neutral pretest opinions). On the other hand, cognitive processing plays an important role in the way these displays elicit emotional and verbal responses; not only do self-reports of emotion interact with prior attitude, but males and females show rather different ways of integrating affective and cognitive cues in establishing attitudes toward political leaders.

In addition to differences among viewers, the character and status of the leader may be a key factor. The different way that individual political leaders exhibit expressive behavior may well be important in determining electoral outcomes. Although expressive displays of unknown candidates seen at the beginning of a political campaign may function to prime partisan attitudes and to associate them with individual names and faces, a well-known politician whose status improves over a campaign seems to become more effective in eliciting emotional responses that further improve viewers' attitudes.

Practical implications of our results confirm three hypotheses that might explain the effect of television in increasing the role of personality in contemporary politics. First, the displays shown on television vary considerably from one candidate to another. Second, the emotional responses to such displays are also variable, and can change due to a leader's political success. Finally, viewers' attitudes toward candidates —at least as measured by a thermometer scale score—can be influenced by the facial displays seen on TV. Expressive displays conveyed by the media might thus play a significant role in the process by which voters' emotional and cognitive responses are integrated to form judgments of leaders.

These findings support—and help explain—the current thrust of much research in political science. Reactions to political leaders and changes in support for candidates are in part a function of the emotions they elicit, and hence are not likely to be determined solely by party identification or issue evaluation. Although affective responses are themselves a function of prior attitudes, the nature of expressive displays is also critically important. Indeed, under certain conditions these nonverbal displays can exert an influence independent of prior attitude on the emotional reactions to and judgments of a political leader. Could these nonverbal cues be the "Teflon" in the "Teflon factor"?

## NOTES

1. Background characteristics of our subjects showed no statistically significant between-sample difference in party identification, ideology, gender, and intention to vote,

although subjects in the second wave were more likely to be paying attention to the campaign and to TV news, watching television, and to be concerned by the outcome of the election than subjects in the first wave; the distribution of partisanship was not radically different from that of the population at large (see Masters et al., 1985).

2. In the period before the campaign began, it was impossible to find usable examples of anger/threat and fear/evasion for most of the Democratic candidates. Although we were able to find at least one instance of a happy/reassurance display for each candidate, we were not able to select stimuli matched for intensity. These differences in the happy/reassurance displays illustrate the variability of display behavior in politics, but they prevented us from measuring directly the difference in emotional response to matched expressive displays by different politicians.

# REFERENCES

ABELSON, R. P. (1981) "Psychological status of the script concept." American Psychologist 36: 715-729.
———(1976) "Script processing in attitude formation and decision making," (pp. 33-45) in J. S. Carroll and J. W. Payne (eds.) Cognition and Social Behavior. Hillsdale, NJ: Lawrence Erlbaum.
———D. R. KINDER, M. D. PETERS, and S. T. FISKE (1982) "Affective and semantic components in political person perception." Journal of Personality and Social Psychology 42: 619-630.
ANDREOLI, V. and S. WORCHEL (1978) "Effects of media, communicator, and message position on attitude change." Public Opinion Quarterly 42: 59-70.
ARGYLE, M. (1975) Bodily Communication. London: Methuen.
———(1969) Social Interaction. Methuen, NJ: Atherton.
BARNER-BARRY, C. (1981) "Longitudinal observation research and the study of basic forms of political socialization," pp. 51-60 in M. Watts (ed.) Biopolitics: Ethological and Physiological Approaches. New Directions for Methodology of Social and Behavioral Sciences 7. San Francisco: Jossey-Bass.
BOWER, G. H. (1981) "Mood and memory." American Psychologist 36: 129-148.
BYRNE, D. (1971) The Attraction Paradigm. New York: Academic.
CACIOPPO, J. T. and R. E. PETTY (1979) "Attitudes and cognitive response: an electrophysiological approach." Journal of Personality and Social Psychology 37: 2181-2199.
CAMRAS, L. A. (1980) "Children's understanding of facial expressions used during conflict encounters." Child Development 51: 879-885.
CHANCE, M.R.A. (1976a) "The organization of attention in groups," in M. von Cranach (ed.) Methods of Inference from Animal to Human Behavior. The Hague: Mouton.
———(1976b) "Social attention: society and mentality," pp. 315-333 in M.R.A. Chance and R. R. Larsen (eds.) The Social Structure of Attention. New York: John Wiley.
DIMBERG, U. (1982) "Facial reactions to facial expressions." Psychophysiology 19: 643-647.
EASTON, D. and J. DENNIS (1969) Children in the Political System. New York: McGraw-Hill.

EKMAN, P. (1972) "Universals and cultural differences in facial expressions of emotion," in J. Cole (ed.) Nebraska Symposium on Motivation, 1971 (vol. 19). Lincoln: University of Nebraska Press.

———and W. V. FRIESEN (1975) Unmasking the Face: A Guide to Recognizing Emotions from Facial Cues. Englewood Cliffs, NJ: Prentice-Hall.

———and P. ELLSWORTH (1972) Emotion in the Human Face. Elmsford, NY: Pergamon.

EKMAN, P., R. W. LEVENSON, and W. V. FRIESEN (1983) "Autonomic nervous system activity distinguishes among emotions." Science 221: 1208-1210.

ENGLIS, B. G. and J. T. LANZETTA (1984, April) "The effects of group categorization on observer's vicarious emotional responses." Presented at the meeting of the Eastern Psychological Association, Baltimore.

ENGLIS, B. G., K. B. VAUGHAN, and J. T. LANZETTA (1982) "Conditioning of counter-empathetic emotional responses." Journal of Experimental Social Psychology 18: 375-391.

GREENSTEIN, F. I. (1960) "The benevolent leader: children's images of political authority." American Political Science Review 54: 934-943.

HINDE, R. A. (1982) Ethology. Glasgow, Scotland: William Collins Sons.

IYENGAR, S., M. D. PETERS, and D. R. KINDER (1982) "Experimental demonstrations of the 'not-so-minimal' consequences of television news programs." American Political Science Review 76: 848-858.

IZARD, C. E. (1977) Human Emotions. New York: Plenum.

———(1971) The Face of Emotion. New York: Appleton-Century-Crofts.

KEATING, C. F., A. MAZUR, M. H. SEGALL, P. G. CYSNEIROS, W. DIVALE, J. E. KILLBRIDE, S. KORMIN, P. LEAHY, B. THURMAN, and R. WIRSING (1981) "Culture and the perception of social dominance from facial expression." Journal of Personality and Social Psychology, 40: 615-626.

KREBS, D. (1975) "Empathy and altruism." Journal of Personality and Social Psychology 32: 1134-1146.

LANZETTA, J. T. and B. G. ENGLIS (1982, April) "The effect of observer expectancies on vicarious emotional responses." Presented at the meeting of the Eastern Psychological Association, Baltimore.

LANZETTA, J. T. and S. P. ORR (1981) "Stimulus properties of facial expressions and their influence on the classical conditioning of fear." Motivation and Emotion 5: 225-234.

———(1980) "Influence of facial expressions on the classical conditioning of fear." Journal of Personality and Social Psychology 39: 1081-1087.

LEVENTHAL, H. (1984) "A perceptual motor theory of emotion," pp. 271-291 in K. R. Scherer and P. Ekman (eds.) Approaches to Emotion. Hillsdale, NJ: Lawrence Erlbaum.

LORENZ, K. (1966) On Aggression. New York: Harcourt, Brace & World.

———and P. LEYHAUSEN (1973) Motivation of Human and Animal Behavior. New York: Von Nostrand Rheinhold.

LOTT, A. and B. E. LOTT (1972) "The power of liking: consequences of interpersonal attitudes derived from a liberalized view of secondary reinforcement," in L. Berkowitz (ed.) Advances in Experimental Social Psychology. New York: Academic.

MANDLER, G. (1980) "The generation of emotion: a psychological theory," pp. 219-243 in R. Plutchik and H. Kellerman (eds.) Emotion: Theory, Research, and Experience. Vol. 1: Theories of Emotion. New York: Academic.

———(1975) Mind and Emotion. New York: John Wiley.

MASTERS, R. D. (1981) "Linking ethology and political science: photographs, political attention, and presidential elections," pp. 61-89 in M. Watts (ed.) Biopolitics: Ethological and Physiological Approaches. New Directions for Methodology of Social and Behavioral Sciences, 7. San Francisco: Jossey-Bass.

————(1976) "Exit, voice, and loyalty in animal and human behavior." Social Science Information 15: 855-878.

————D. G. SULLIVAN, J. T. LANZETTA, and G. J. McHUGO (1985, July) "Leaders' facial displays as a political variable." Presented at the meeting of the International Political Science Association, Paris.

————and B. G. ENGLIS (1984, June) "Facial displays & political leadership." Presented to the Conference on Ethological Contributions to Political Science, Tutzing, West Germany.

McHUGO, G. J., J. T. LANZETTA, D. G. SULLIVAN, R. D. MASTERS, and B. G. ENGLIS (1984) "Emotional reactions to a political leader's expressive displays." Unpublished manuscript.

MONTAGNER, H. (1978) L'enfant et la Communication. Paris: Stock.

PLUTCHIK, R. (1980) Emotion: A Psychoevolutionary Synthesis. New York: Harper & Row.

POPKIN, S., J. W. GORMAN, C. PHILLIPS, and J. T. SMITH (1976) "Comment: what have you done to me lately? Toward an investment theory of voting. American Political Science Review 70: 779-805.

ROSENBERG, M. J. (1968) "Hedonism, inauthenticity, and other goals toward expansion of a consistency theory," pp. 73-111 in R. P. Abelson et al. (eds.) Theories of Cognitive Consistency: A Sourcebook. Chicago: Rand McNally.

SCHACHTER, S. (1964) "The interaction of cognitive and physiological determinants of emotional state," in L. Berkowitz (ed.) Advances in Experimental Social Psychology. New York: Academic.

————and J. SINGER (1962) "Cognitive, social, and physiological determinants of emotional states." Psychological Review 69: 379-399.

SCHWARTZ, G. E., P. L. FAIR, P. SALT, M. R. MANDEL, and G. L. KLERMAN (1976) "Facial muscle patterning to affective imagery in depressed and nondepressed subjects." Science 192: 489-491.

SULLIVAN, D. G., R. D. MASTERS, J. T. LANZETTA, B. G. ENGLIS, and G. J. McHUGO (1984a) "The effect of President Reagan's facial displays on observers' attitudes, impressions, and feelings about him." Presented at the meeting of the American Political Science Association, Washington, DC, September.

SULLIVAN, D. G., R. D. MASTERS, J. T. LANZETTA, G. J. McHUGO, E. F. PLATE, and B. G. ENGLIS (1984b) "Facial displays and political leadership: some experimental findings." Presented at the meeting of the American Political Science Association, Washington, DC, September.

TOMKINS, S. S. (1963) Affect, Imagery, Consciousness. Vol 2: The Negative Affects. New York: Springer.

————(1962) Affect, Imagery, Consciousness. Vol 1: The Positive Affects. New York: Springer.

TURSKY, B., M. LODGE, and R. REEDER (1979) Psychophysiological evaluation of the direction, intensity, and meaning of race-related stimuli." Psychophysiology 16: 452-462.

van HOOFF, J.A.R.A.M. (1973) "A structural analysis of the social behavior of a semi-captive group of chimpanzees," in M. von Cranach and I. Vine (eds.) Social Communication and Movement. New York: Academic.

VAUGHAN, K. B. and J. T. LANZETTA (1980) "Vicarious instigation and conditioning of facial expressive and autonomic responses to a model's expressive display of pain." Journal of Personality and Social Psychology 38: 909-923.

Chapter 5

# PSYCHOLOGICAL ACCOUNTS
# OF AGENDA-SETTING

Shanto Iyengar
Donald R. Kinder

AGENDA-SETTING, as it is typically called by social scientists, has antecedents in the writings of Lippmann (e.g., 1922) and others. Empirical work on agenda-setting, however, is of more recent vintage. Even by 1960, Klapper's comprehensive summary of communication research devoted a mere two pages to agenda-setting. It is true that research on agenda-setting has multiplied prodigiously in the past decade. But to our way of thinking, with some important exceptions this work has been theoretically naive and methodologically unsophisticated (for a review of this literature see Kinder and Sears, 1985).

Over the past several years, we have begun to develop a general understanding of how network news influences the political thinking of ordinary Americans. To test and refine our ideas, we have relied primarily upon experimental methods. The results of more than a dozen experiments, supplemented at key junctures by time-series analysis of national surveys, are unequivocal: By lavishing attention on some problems while ignoring others, television news programs profoundly affect which problems the American public takes seriously. Put more generally, they vindicate Lippmann's suspicion that news media provide compelling accounts of a political world that is otherwise out of reach

AUTHORS' NOTE: We wish to thank the National Science Foundation for its generous support through grants SES 80-12581, 81-21306, and 82-08714.

(Behr and Iyengar, 1985; Iyengar and Kinder 1985a; Iyengar et al., 1982).

This chapter reports on our initial explorations into the psychology of agenda-setting. Although our experimental and time series results testify unambiguously to the power of television news, they do so without specifying precisely *why* television news is so powerful. The answer to this question requires an understanding of the psychology of media influence. We will provide preliminary evidence regarding several alternative psychological explanations. Drawing upon the results of four separate experiments, we test three possibilities in particular: *counterarguing, source credibility*, and *affect*.

Perhaps television news is so powerful because, after carefully and deliberately appraising news stories, viewers find them persuasive. Individuals do not register information passively like well-trained clerks. Instead, the news is evaluated within an established framework of prior knowledge, beliefs, and attitudes. We refer to this as the *counterarguing hypothesis*. Research on persuasion has repeatedly demonstrated that counterarguing conditions the effects of communication. Individuals who actively quarrel with the message are more resistant to persuasion; those who fail to do so are persuaded the most (see Petty et al., 1982; Petty and Cacioppo, 1981). By simple extension, viewers who critically scrutinize news stories about national problems should be less likely to alter their political priorities than viewers who cognitively capitulate to the news.

Counterarguing requires effort and knowledge. To counterargue, viewers must pay at least some attention to the details of individual news stories and they must be able to call up relevant information and analysis of their own. These requirements may outrun what the typical viewer is ordinarily prepared or able to do. It is well known that individuals pay rather casual and intermittent attention to television news (e.g., Neuman, 1976) and that they often are astonishingly ignorant of public affairs (Kinder and Sears, 1985). Consequently, instead of carefully monitoring television's depiction of national and world events, the typical viewer may rely instead on simple shortcuts (for evidence of the pervasiveness of inferential shortcuts in social judgment, see Nisbett and Ross, 1980; Kahneman et al., 1983).

One convenient shortcut would be to follow the apparent credibility of information sources, rather than to scrutinize carefully each and every new piece of information. In fact, according to countless persuasion experiments, the influence exercised by a message does depend significantly on the credibility of its source: Expert and trustworthy sources exert more influence than inexpert, untrustworthy sources (the role of source credibility in the attitude change process is discussed in McGuire, 1981). Thus, television news may be so powerful because viewers generally regard the networks as authoritative. This second alternative explanation for agenda-setting is called the *source credibility hypothesis*. Without having to consider the merits and liabilities of particular stories, viewers who judge the networks to be objective and accurate should be especially persuaded, whereas those who regard the networks as partisan and biased should be persuaded least.

Both counterargument and assessments of source credibility entail deliberation. In the case of the former, viewers in effect ask themselves, "Is this story correct? Is it consistent with what I know?" In the case of the latter, viewers in effect ask themselves, "Does this story have a believable source?" But the impact of television news may also be attributed to emotion. Perhaps television is so powerful because viewers "feel" the news. The vivid pictures and dramatic stories that are the networks' standard fare may evoke strong emotions in viewers, especially because politics is an area of "hot cognition." This *affect hypothesis*, our third possible explanation for agenda-setting, could work in two ways. Affect may itself directly boost the importance viewers assign to national problems. Merely feeling anger, sadness, or fear may cause viewers to alter their political judgments (for evidence consistent with this claim see Zajonc, 1979, 1984). Alternatively, affect may influence political judgment indirectly, by focusing attention on the triggering stimulus—in our research, on news coverage of a particular national problem. Viewers angered, saddened, or otherwise aroused by a news story describing the plight of the unemployed may find their attention drawn to unemployment, and as a consequence may attribute more importance to that problem at the expense of others. (The relationship between affect and attention is discussed in Clarke, 1984; the effects of focused attention on judgment are reviewed in McArthur, 1981; Taylor and Fiske, 1978.)

Counterargument, source credibility, and affect are by no means mutually exclusive mediators of political judgment. Viewers' beliefs about national problems no doubt incorporate some combination of the three. The particular mix will vary with characteristics of the audience and the presentation. Some viewers may rely primarily on their emotional reactions whereas others pursue a more deliberate strategy and consider the strengths and weaknesses of news stories. Similarly, some news stories may prove so arousing as to distract viewers from the details of the coverage thus forcing them to be more reliant on their emotional responses. The analysis to follow will consider both differences in the pattern of mediation associated with viewers' personal circumstances, and with the positioning of news stories within the newscast.

## METHOD

### OVERVIEW

In experiments 1 and 2, participants watched one complete (thirty minute) newscast every day for one week. On the first day of the experiment, participants received instructions about the purposes and procedures of the study. They were instructed that it was necessary for them to watch the news at the university in order to avoid distractions present at home and to ensure that they all watched the same newscast under uniform conditions.

After completing a lengthy questionnaire covering a variety of political topics, participants proceeded to watch an unedited videotape recording of the previous evening's national news drawn from one of the three major networks. Then, over the next four days, participants viewed what appeared to be a recording of the previous evening's national news. In fact, sections of these broadcasts were unobtrusively altered ahead of time in order to manipulate the amount and nature of coverage given particular national problems. In experiment 1, for example, participants randomly assigned to one condition received a mild but steady dose of news regarding arms control; a second group watched newscasts that were identical in all respects except that instead of stories on arms control, we had inserted stories on civil rights; a third group watched newscasts containing stories that stressed unemployment. Because participants in each experimental condition were exposed to sustained coverage of one and only one of the three target problems, each condition served as a control group for the other two. On the sixth and final day of the experiment, participants completed a second questionnaire that repeated key measures of problem importance that had appeared in the first questionnaire, and included measures of counterarguing, source credibility, and affective response that are the core of the analysis presented ahead.

In experiments 3 and 4, participants viewed at a single one-hour sitting a collection of news stories taken from the three networks. Participants were told that the presentations were a cross section of typical news stories broadcast by the three networks during the past year. Immediately after the presentations (and *only* afterwards, in contrast to experiments 1 and 2), participants completed a questionnaire that ranged over many political topics including, for tests of agenda-setting, the priorities participants attached to various national problems. At the very close of the questionnaire, participants were asked to recall their reactions to television news; the thoughts and feelings, if any, that had occurred to them while they watched the newscasts; as well as their appraisal of the accuracy and objectivity of television news in general.

To summarize, participants in experiments 1 and 2 viewed unobtrusively edited newscasts over the course of a week. In experiments 3 and 4, participants watched a single collection of news stories in one session. The former are obviously more realistic than the latter. Moreover, they have the virtue of enabling us to examine *change* in viewers' judgments about national problems. Measures of change are highly useful in studies of mediation. With experiments 1 and 2, we can determine the extent to which change in viewers' judgments about national problems (induced by our experimental variations in television news) are mediated by viewers' appraisals of the news stories themselves (the counterarguing hypothesis), by their assessment of the accuracy and objectivity of network news (the source credibility hypothesis). Although they do not include measures of change in viewers' judgments about national problems, experiments 3 and 4 are still useful to our interest in mediation. Furthermore, their design has one real advantage: It provides the opportunity to construct more complex experimental treatments and therefore to pursue more subtle hypotheses. In experiment 4, for example, we were able to examine whether stories that lead off the broadcast are more persuasive than stories that appear in the middle of the broadcast by moving the *identical story* from one position to the other.

## PROCEDURE

In all four experiments, participants were recruited through advertisements placed in local newspapers and by posters displayed in public buildings. The notices offered payment for participation in "television research." When individuals responded to the advertisements, we obtained information about their demographic characteristics (to exclude students, noncitizens, and those under the age of eighteen) and scheduled them (according to their personal convenience) to one of several daily viewing sessions. As we had hoped, this procedure yielded an experimental population that, in demographic and political terms, is roughly representative of the New Haven community, where the four experiments were conducted. Compared to the national population, our participants were, on average, somewhat better educated, younger, more likely to be minority, Democratic, and liberal, and slightly more involved in political affairs. (For details on the composition of our experimental population, see Iyengar and Kinder, 1985a.)

Depending on the experiment, each condition was represented by at least two and as many as five daily sessions. Sessions were limited to between three and ten participants (average size was five) and were held in buildings on the Yale University campus. After all participants were assigned to a session, each session was then randomly assigned to an experimental condition.

## MANIPULATING THE NETWORKS' AGENDA

A critical aspect of all four experiments is the creation of experimental newscasts that participants find utterly realistic. The procedure is more elaborate in the week-long experiments.

On the evening prior to each daily viewing session, we recorded the broadcasts of two of the major networks. To create slightly different broadcasts for each experimental condition, we then inserted condition-appropriate stories while deleting a story or stories of equivalent length. The stories inserted into the newscasts were actual news stories that had been broadcast six to eight months earlier by the same network. We made certain that these stories contained no clues as to their actual date of broadcast by selecting feature stories that were "timeless" in their content. (In many cases, these stories were themselves edited to remove temporal markers.) To do so we accumulated a large pool of stories, dealing with ten national problems, from the Vanderbilt University Television News Archive and from our own audiovisual facilities at Yale. For each problem, for each network, we collected stories from several reporters introduced by different anchors. Some stories were winter stories and others were summer stories; some implicated the president and others did not; some displayed "talking heads," whereas others featured dramatic action. On any given day, therefore, we had a large and diverse pool of potential treatment stories to insert into the broadcasts.

The treatment story (usually one each day) was inserted during the middle portion of the newscast and usually ran 2-4 minutes. In practice the actual newscasts were left substantially intact except for the insertion of the treatment story and the deletion of a story or two in compensation. Over the course of a week-long experiment, a typical treatment would consist of four stories (between 11 and 17 minutes of news time) spread across the last four days of the experiment. (On the first day we usually did no editing so as to allay any doubts that participants may have entertained about the authenticity of the experimental newscast.)

## AVOIDING EXPERIMENTAL DEMAND

In any experimental procedure it is important to guard against "demand characteristics"—cues in the experimental setting that suggest to participants what is expected of them (Orne, 1962). In order to limit the impact of demand characteristics in our experiments, we undertook several precautions. First, we disguised their purpose. We began all experiments by presenting to participants an entirely plausible but false account of our purpose. Second, to minimize the artificial and perhaps reactive nature of our research setting, we made our experimental manipulations as unobtrusive as possible. Finally, to minimize the prominence of our key measures, we embedded them in a long battery of questions about politics. Participants reported their opinions on current issues, explanations for the nation's problems, perceptions of an ideal president, partisan attachments, political activities, and so forth.

We believe our various precautions were successful. At the conclusion of each experiment (after the questionnaires had been collected and the participants paid), all participants were asked to describe their perceptions of what the experiment was about now that they had completed it, and whether their perceptions were consistent with their initial expectations. In all 14 of our experiments, only two participants expressed skepticism about our real purpose—and they claimed that we were in fact engaged in "market research" for the networks![1]

## MEASURES

*Problem importance.* In experiments 1 and 2 we measured participants' beliefs about the relative importance of various national problems both before and after exposure to the experimental treatment; in experiments 3 and 4, only afterwards.

On all occasions, participants judged the importance of each of a set of national problems (including the experimental target problem), their personal concern for each, the degree to which each was deserving of additional government action, and how strongly they felt about each.[2] Because the four separate ratings were strongly intercorrelated, they were added together to form a composite index of problem importance. The index ranged from four (low importance) to twenty (high importance).[3] To complement the composite index, our experiments also included an open-ended measure of problem importance. Early in the questionnaire, participants were invited to name the "three most important problems facing the nation." In the analysis ahead, we will make use of both the composite ratings and the spontaneous mentions.

*Counterarguing.* We measured the extent of counterarguing by using a "thought listing" procedure. At the close of the experiments, we provided participants with brief and neutral descriptions of one or more of the stories we had included. We then asked them to record the "thoughts, feelings, and reactions" that had occurred to them as they had watched these stories.[4] We coded their comments for the number of counterarguments. We defined counterargument broadly to include simple disaffirmations of the story ("unemployment is not that bad; people who want to work can find it"), expressions of disagreement ("this is not real important"), as well as specific and reasoned refutations of the story ("unemployment is not that bad for the nation because it holds down the inflation rate").

*Source credibility.* We assessed source credibility simply by asking participants to rate the objectivity and accuracy of the national newscasts.[5]

*Affective arousal.* We gauged participants' emotional reactions with an affect battery adapted from research on emotional reactions to presidential candidates (e.g., Abelson et al., 1982). Participants indicated whether they had felt various affects as they had watched specific news stories: hope, happiness, anger, sadness, fear, and disgust. Given the nature of the news stories we used—stories showing rising unemployment, racial inequities, the threat of nuclear war, and so on—negative affects were naturally the rule. Consequently, we concentrated on just the four negative affects, assigning to each participant a score corresponding to the number of emotions he or she reported feeling.[6]

# RESULTS

## EXPERIMENTS 1 AND 2

Experiment 1 was conducted in July 1982 and focused on three problems. Depending on conditions, participants viewed newscasts that emphasized either arms control (n = 21), civil rights (n = 22), or unemployment (n = 22). Experiment 2 followed soon after (in August) and focused on a single problem, unemployment. Participants either viewed a sequence of newscasts that emphasized unemployment (n = 36) or saw no newscasts at all (n = 32).

Our principal objective in these experiments was to test the agenda-setting hypothesis: that those problems paid attention to by television news become the problems the public worries about. The results from experiments 1 and 2 confirmed the hypothesis handsomely. Without exception, problems given steady news coverage became more serious (and significantly so) over the course of the experiment, at least in the minds of our participants. According to these results (as well as others, some experimental, some survey, not reported here: see Iyengar and Kinder, 1985a), network news contributes heavily to the public's beliefs about national priorities.

How should these results be understood in psychological terms? More specifically, to what extent are television news-induced changes in viewers' judgments about national problems mediated by viewers' appraisals of the news stories themselves (the counterarguing hypothesis), by their assessment of the accuracy and objectivity of network news (the source credibility hypothesis), and by the emotions the news stories arouse (the affect hypothesis)? To find out, we analyzed change in viewers' beliefs about the importance of national problems as a function of counterarguing, source credibility, and affect. In this analysis, we combined experiments 1 and 2 and pooled across the four treatments. Thus the dependent variable for participants who watched news about arms control was change in the importance they attributed to arms control; for participants who watched newscasts that provided steady coverage of civil rights, the dependent variable was change in the importance they attributed to civil rights; and so on.[7] The importance of counterarguing, credibility, and affect on change in problem importance was estimated by a two-stage procedure. This takes into account the possibility that counterarguing, credibility, and affect may be consequences as well as causes of change in problem importance (the simultaneity problem), and corrects for biases accompanying autocorrelation. (Space considerations prohibit inclusion of the technical details; these details are available from the authors.) The results are shown in Table 5.1.

These findings are weakest with respect to counterarguing. As Table 5.1 reveals, the amount of critical commentary the stories provoked was unrelated to shifts in composite ratings and was only marginally related to shifts in spontaneous mentions. By these results, agenda-setting appears to have rather little to do with any careful appraisal of the news stories themselves. In contrast, news stories do seem to owe some of their agenda-setting success to the emotions they manage to stir up. According to our analysis, for every three affects elicited by news coverage of a particular problem, change in the composite importance ratings increased by nearly a full point. This is quite a strong effect; however, affect exerted no influence on change in the likelihood of mentioning the problem as one of the country's most important. Finally, the evidence is strongest for the credibility hypothesis. On both measures of problem importance, participants who placed more credibility in television news were influenced more by the stories they saw. Participants who declared the news to be "very accurate and objective" outgained those who declared the news to be "not accurate or objective at all" by more than a full point on the composite index, and by a comparable measure on the likelihood of naming the problem as one of the country's most important. In sum, these results suggest that agenda-setting is mediated rather weakly by counterarguing, moderately by affect, and quite strongly by source credibility.

## EXPERIMENT 3

Experiment 3 was designed to explore the conditions under which agenda-setting is enhanced or weakened. In particular, we examined differences in viewers' personal circumstances that might lead to differences in the priorities they attach to the nation's problems. Many national problems—crime, racial discrimination, unemployment, and others—are also personal problems. It is one thing to learn from the *CBS Evening News* that serious crime is on the increase; it is quite another thing to be mugged. In reaching judgments about national problems, Americans are likely to be influenced by both—evidence

TABLE 5.1
**Determinants of Change in Problem Importance,
Experiments 1 and 2 Pooled**

| *Variable* | *Equation 1*<br>*Composite Ratings* | *Equation 2*<br>*Spontaneous Mentions* |
|---|---|---|
| Counterarguing | − | −.15<br>(.10) |
| Source credibility | .19<br>(.11) | .32<br>(.19) |
| Affect | .31<br>(.14) | − |
| N = 96 | | |

NOTE: Equation 1 was estimated by two-stage least squares; equation 2 by two-stage logit.

from television news, on the one hand, and from their personal experience, on the other.

We used experiment 3 to assess differences in agenda-setting between viewers personally affected and unaffected by the subject of news coverage. The experiment was conducted in September and October of 1981. In a single one-hour session, participants were exposed either to intermediate (two stories) or extensive (four stories) coverage of one of three target problems—civil rights, unemployment, or the threatened financial collapse of social security—and saw no news of the other two. We treated personal experience with the target problem as a simple dichotomy—those vulnerable to racial discrimination, unemployment, or reductions in social security were compared with those not so affected. Thus, half of the participants in the civil rights treatment were employed blacks; half the participants in the unemployment treatment were unemployed white males; half the viewers in the social security treatment were white senior citizens. The remaining participants in each treatment were made up equally of the two groups not affected by the target problem. Within the constraints of an equal division of participants across treatments, these participants were randomly assigned. With the obvious exception of race, age, and gender, participants in the three treatments did not differ from one another in their economic position, social status, or political orientations.

The effects of personal predicaments and news coverage on problem importance are shown in Table 5.2.[8] The most interesting evidence furnished by experiment 3 is that regarding the possible interaction between personal predicaments and news coverage. We had expected to find that the impact of television news would be more pronounced

**TABLE 5.2**
**Impact of News Coverage and Personal Predicaments**
**on Problem Importance:  Experiment 3**

|  | *Percentage Naming Problem as One of Country's Most Important* | | |
|---|---|---|---|
|  | *Viewed No Stories* | *Viewed 2 Stories* | *Viewed 4 Stories* |
| Civil rights | | | |
| Blacks | 47 | 38 | 67 |
| Whites | 7 | 22 | 0 |
| Unemployment | | | |
| Unemployed | 36 | 25 | 100 |
| Employed | 29 | 33 | 46 |
| Social Security | | | |
| Elderly | 19 | 67 | 50 |
| Young | 4 | 13 | 38 |

among those personally affected by the problem given coverage. People who are personally vulnerable to a particular problem should be more sensitive to news about it; they should be more likely to notice and to remember news bearing upon "their" problem (Erbring et al., 1980). Table 5.2 supports this expectation in all three cases. News about civil rights was more influential among blacks than among whites ($F < .10$); news about unemployment was more influential among the unemployed ($F < .10$); news about social security was more influential among the elderly than among the young ($F < .10$).[9]

Those results imply that counterarguing and affect, to the extent they mediate viewers' beliefs about national problems, are dependent upon whether or not viewers are personally affected by the target problem.[10] If the counterarguing hypothesis is correct, those personally affected should quarrel less (or yield more) in response to news stories than those personally unaffected. By the same logic, if the affect hypothesis is correct, those personally affected should report more emotions in response to news stories than those who are not so affected.

As Table 5.3 shows, both these implications are supported for each of the three problems (main effect of personal predicament on the number of yielding responses $< .01$; and on the number of affective responses $< .01$). In the case of news coverage of civil rights, for instance, blacks reported nearly twice as many yielding thoughts, and almost twice as many emotional reactions, as did whites. Similar, if less dramatic, differences emerge in the unemployment and Social Security treatments. In every instance, those personally implicated by the news coverage were

**TABLE 5.3**
**Counterarguing and Affect by Viewers' Personal Circumstances:**
**Experiment 3**

|  | Number of Yielding Responses | | |
|---|---|---|---|
|  | Treatment | | |
|  | *Civil Rights* | *Unemployment* | *Social Security* |
| Ss affected by target problem | 1.59 | 1.44 | 1.65 |
| Ss unaffected by target problem | .84 | .96 | 1.50 |
|  | Number of Affective Responses | | |
| Ss affected by target problem | 3.18 | 3.44 | 4.41 |
| Ss unaffected by target problem | 1.58 | 2.72 | 3.19 |

more engaged; they were more sympathetic to the information presented and they reacted with greater emotion.

The results in Table 5.3 demonstrate that viewers affected by news stories are more emotionally aroused by the news and are more likely to yield than viewers unaffected by these stories. However, it is reasonable to expect that the impact of yielding and affect on viewers' political judgments may vary according to their personal predicament. In particular, research in persuasion suggests that counterarguing/yielding exerts a greater impact on attitude change when the audience is personally involved. When the stakes are high, people appear to examine the message more carefully and to be especially influenced by the results of that examination (Chaiken, 1980; Petty and Cacioppo, 1984).

With regard to viewer's likelihood of naming the target problem as the most important facing the country, we assessed the degree to which the mediating effects of yielding and affect depended on their personal predicament. Because the level of yielding and affect varied significantly across the three treatments, we analyzed each treatment separately.[11] The results are presented in Table 5.4.

Consistent with the findings from experiments 1 and 2, these results provide little support for the counterarguing hypothesis. First, among viewers unaffected by the target problem, counterarguing (actually yielding) did not affect the likelihood of including the target problem in their list of the three most important problems facing the country. Whether or not these viewers yielded to news stories had little to do with

**TABLE 5.4**
**Determinants of Problem Importance: Experiment 3**

| | Treatment | | |
|---|---|---|---|
| | *Civil Rights* | *Unemployment* | *Social Security* |
| Effects of counterarguing: unaffected viewers | −.16 (.63) | .60 (.91) | 1.23 (1.21) |
| Effects of counterarguing: difference between affected and unaffected viewers | .89 (.75) | .03 (.90) | −.05 (1.37) |
| Effects of affect: unaffected viewers | .55 (.41) | .65 (.47) | .41 (.52) |
| Effects of affect: difference between affected and unaffected viewers | −.34 (.23) | −.40 (.28) | −.27 (.31) |
| N | 33 | 39 | 32 |

NOTE: Equations estimated by logit.

the likelihood that they would regard the target problem as one of the country's most important. Second, our prediction that the impact of yielding would be significantly strengthened among viewers personally affected by the news was supported in only one instance. Yielding to news coverage of civil rights was somewhat more influential in predicting viewers' spontaneous references to civil rights as a national problem among blacks than among whites. This difference, however, did not meet conventional levels of statistical significance ($p < .15$). When applied to news coverage of unemployment and social security, the differential mediation hypothesis failed completely—the effects of yielding were no different from the unemployed and employed, from the elderly and the young.

The results were somewhat more encouraging for the affect hypothesis, again consistent with the returns from experiments 1 and 2. Participants' readiness to name the target problem as one of the nation's most important was dependent upon the number of affects the news stories provoked. This was true for all three treatments among viewers unaffected by the news. In only the unemployment and civil rights treatments, however, did this effect approach statistical significance ($p < .10$). To our suprise, we also found evidence that affect played a *weaker* mediating role among viewers affected by the target problem. In assessing the importance of civil rights, blacks were influenced *less* by their emotional responses to news of civil rights than whites ($p < .10$).

Similarly, in assessing the importance of unemployment, the unemployed were moved *less* by emotion than were the employed (p < .10). A similar, but statistically unreliable difference appeared between elderly and young viewers shown news about social security.

## EXPERIMENT 4

Viewers are influenced not only by the amount, but also by the kind of attention network news pays to national problems. In Experiment 4 we examined whether stories that lead off the broadcast are especially effective in setting the public agenda.

We focus on the lead story because by the networks' own standards, it represents the day's most important news (Gans, 1981). In addition, based on a longitudinal analysis of national surveys, we knew that lead story coverage of national problems exerted a significantly stronger impact on public concern than ordinary coverage (see Behr and Iyengar, 1985).

Experiment 4 was conducted in August 1983 and included four experimental conditions. Each consisted of a 30-minute newscast, complete with commercials. Participants were informed that they were to watch a newscast selected at random from those broadcast during the previous month. In two of the conditions participants watched a story on significant increases in drug smuggling into the United States, whereas participants in the two remaining conditions saw a news story detailing the declining quality of American public schools. Half of the subjects—those viewing the story on drugs—saw it as the lead story, whereas the rest saw it in the middle of the newscast. The stories were identical except for the customary introduction associated with the lead story ("Good evening. This is the CBS Evening News, etc."), which was deleted when the story was shown in the middle of the newscast. An identical arrangement prevailed for coverage of education. Thus, experiment 4 enabled us to test the lead story hypothesis twice, once for illegal drugs and once for public education. Given that in each instance participants were exposed to exactly the same information, it could be determined whether or not the editorial decision to place one story at the beginning of the broadcast (by itself) affects viewers' political priorities.

As in experiment 3, participants were questioned immediately after they watched the newscast. Their responses provided mixed support to the lead story hypothesis. On the one hand, the story describing governmental attempts to halt the flow of illegal drugs was substantially more influential in the lead position than when it appeared in the middle of the newscast. When the story began the news, the illegal drug problem was rated a more important national problem ($p < .02$) and was more often named as one of the three most important problems facing the nation ($p < .05$). On the other hand, although the story recounting the difficulties facing the public schools was also more influential in the lead position, these differences were minute.

Following the logic developed in our analysis of experiment 3, we should find in experiment 4 a pattern of results for counterarguing, source credibility, and affect that match the results for agenda-setting. To the extent that counterarguing mediates the obtained effects of lead story coverage, we should find less counterarguing to the same story when it appears in the lead position than when it appears in the middle of the news. Similarly, if source credibility or affect mediate the occasional effects of lead story coverage, evaluations of credibility should be more favorable, and the level of affect should be higher, when coverage takes the form of the lead story.

None of these implications is borne out by the evidence. As shown in Table 5.5, the number of counterarguments was slightly lower in response to lead stories than to identical stories appearing in the middle of the newscast, but the difference was trivial. The differences in the number of affects and viewers' assessments of source credibility were also nonsignificant. Lead stories do not elicit fewer counterarguments, do not provoke more emotions, and have no effect on viewers' assessments of source credibility.

These results mean that the strengthening of the agenda-setting effect brought on by placing a news story in the lead position cannot be explained by the counterarguing hypothesis, the source credibility hypothesis, or by the affect hypothesis. The special power of lead stories must be due to other processes.

Although the boosting of the agenda-setting effect under conditions of lead story coverage cannot be explained by counterarguing, credibility, or affect, the priorities viewers attach to illegal drugs and public education should still be related to the amount of counterarguing provoked by the news coverage, the strength of viewers' emotional reactions, and by their assessments of source credibility. We thus estimated the effects of counterarguing, affect, and credibility on participants' importance ratings (using OLS) and spontaneous mentions (using logit). Preliminary analysis showed that the impact of the mediators differed significantly depending upon the type of news coverage. Consequently we estimated the effects of affect, source credibility, and counterarguing separately for lead story and middle story conditions. These results are presented in Table 5.6.[12]

TABLE 5.5
Counterarguing, Source Credibility, and Affect
by Position of News Story: Experiment 4

|  | *Lead Story Coverage* | *Middle Story Coverage* |
|---|---|---|
| Number of counterarguments | .21 | .39 |
| Number of affects | 1.35 | 1.26 |
| Source credibility | 3.93 | 4.18 |
| N | 57 | 57 |

As Table 5.6 suggests, counterarguing, credibility, and affect all played a mediating role in participants' composite ratings and spontaneous mentions. Fewer counterarguments, more favorable assessments of credibility, and stronger emotional arousal all contributed to agenda-setting. But—and this is the noteworthy feature of the results—this is so *only* when the story appears in the middle of the newscast. Among viewers who saw the key story in the middle of the broadcast, the less they argued, the more credibility they ascribed to the networks, and the more emotions they felt, the more importance they gave the target problem. Among viewers in the lead story conditions, in contrast, counterarguing, credibility, and affect did not mediate agenda-setting at all. The differences between lead and middle story conditions in the effects of counterarguing and source credibility were statistically significant ($p < .05$).

## CONCLUSION

Our chapter sought to set out and test among several psychological explanations for agenda-setting. We have focused on agenda-setting by television news in particular, because the evidence is overwhelming that citizens' views of national problems are shaped substantially by stories that come flickering onto their television screens. From the four experiments examined here, the following conclusions can be made: by paying attention to some problems at the expense of others, television news alters the public's sense of national priorities (experiments 1 and 2); television coverage of a particular problem tends to be more powerful among viewers personally affected by the problem (experiment 3); and finally, stories tend to be especially influential when they begin the broadcast (experiment 4). Our intent has been to try to explain

**TABLE 5.6**
**Determinants of Problem Importance: Experiment 4**

| Predictor | Lead Story Coverage | Middle Story Coverage |
|---|---|---|
| | *Composite Ratings (OLS Estimation)* | |
| Counterarguing | −.25 | −1.25 |
| | (.37) | (.51) |
| Source credibility | −.36 | .50 |
| | (.34) | (.31) |
| Affect | .17 | .46 |
| | (.32) | (.55) |
| N = 104 | | |
| | *Spontaneous Mentions (Logit Estimation)* | |
| Counterarguing | −.31 | −.33 |
| | (.49) | (.52) |
| Source credibility | −.21 | .45 |
| | (.60) | (.33) |
| Affect | .00 | .50 |
| | (.11) | (.49) |
| N = 114 | | |

each of these results in terms of three general hypotheses, each providing a different account of the psychological underpinnings of agenda-setting: the counterarguing hypothesis, which implies that television news is powerful because it presents information viewers find compelling; the affect hypothesis, which implies that television news is powerful because it evokes strong emotions; and the credibility hypothesis, which implies that television news is powerful because viewers regard the news as authoritative.

Of the three hypotheses, counterarguing fared the poorest. Support for counterarguing appeared only sporadically across our various tests: on one measure of importance (and marginally at that) but not the other in experiments 1 and 2; in response to news coverage of Social Security (marginally) but not coverage of civil rights and unemployment in experiment 3; not at all in tests of the special power of lead stories; and for only one of the two indicators when we assessed the agenda-setting effects of stories appearing in the middle of the newscast. All in all, these results constitute an erratic record for the hypothesis. As such, they are somewhat unsettling, as they imply that the effects of television news are mediated to a limited degree by careful deliberation on the viewer's part.

The evidence was more promising for the affect hypothesis. We found support for it in one of two measures in experiments 1 and 2; consistently for each of the three problems examined in experiment 3; and for both measures (though only marginally) in tests of agenda-setting by nonlead stories. The hypothesis failed in only one instance—it did not account for the special power of lead stories. Overall, the results suggest that television news owes some of its effectiveness to its ability to evoke emotion. This is important, for television more so than any other medium plays upon the audience's emotions. According to Reuven Frank, former president of NBC News, "The highest power of television journalism is not in the transmission of information, but in the transmission of experience" (quoted in Epstein, 1973: 242). In transmitting experience, television news evokes anger, fear, sympathy, pride, and more. As it does so, it shapes powerfully the public's understanding of political affairs.

Our evidence was strongest in support for the source credibility hypothesis. With a single exception—the lead story effect—all tests confirmed the mediating role of credibility. Viewers who regarded the networks as impartial and accurate sources of information were more influenced by the news than those with less faith in ABC, NBC, or CBS.

Americans, of course, differ in the credibility they grant network news. And, as our results demonstrate, these differences matter. Thus, it is highly significant that most Americans in fact trust television news. By a wide margin, Americans believe that television—not newspapers, radio, or magazines—provides the most intelligent, complete, and impartial news coverage (Bower, 1983). As Americans have welcomed Rather, Brokaw, and Jennings into their homes, they have made themselves vulnerable to a powerful influence.

Why does credibility matter so much? Our suspicion is that credibility separates viewers who pay attention to the news from those who do not. Viewers who grant considerable credibility to the networks are open to agenda-setting because they notice what the networks are saying. Those who grant the networks little credibility remove themselves from the networks' influences by turning their attention elsewhere.

This interpretation, which emphasizes selective attention, suggests that agenda-setting effects may be one manifestation of a general tendency in judgment. Extensive experimental evidence indicates that people generally are swayed by evidence that is distinguished primarily by its momentary salience. Salient evidence is accorded importance far in excess of its inferential value; logically consequential but perceptually innocuous evidence is discounted (for reviews of this research, see Taylor and Fiske, 1978; McArthur, 1981).

The analogy with agenda-setting is very close. As in experimental studies of salience, television newscasts direct viewers to consider some features of public life and to ignore others. As in research on salience, viewers' recall of information seems to have little to do with shifts in their political beliefs (Fiske et al., 1982; Iyengar et al., 1982). And finally, though the case is not completely settled, most accounts of salience effects point to the importance of selective attention (Fiske and Taylor, 1984).

The emphasis on selective attention is consistent with our findings on agenda-setting, the importance of credibility as a mediator of agenda-setting, and even the importance of affect, because one version of the affect hypothesis treats the significant consequence of emotional arousal to be the directing of attention. A selective attention interpretation is also consistent with perhaps our most intriguing result—the special power of lead stories. We have found that lead stories are particularly influential in shaping viewers' priorities. Their distinctiveness cannot be accounted for by their capacity to diminish counterarguing or to evoke more emotions because they do neither. And finally, lead stories seem to override or supercede "natural" processes of mediation. The results suggest that lead stories may owe their advantage to their special ability to command attention. Put differently, placing a story in the middle of the news may be tantamount to not broadcasting it at all.

In closing, we should emphasize that we consider our results and interpretations of them as tentative. Our experiments were not designed first and foremost to test among alternative theories of mediation. Their primary objective was to establish the basic agenda-setting phenomenon and explore conditions that might enhance or undermine it. Furthermore, the measures we developed to represent counterarguing, credibility, and affect are unproven and surely could be improved. And finally, our results are uneven. This chapter is intended only as an opening exploration into the murky psychological processes that underlie media political influence.

This is an important beginning, however, because research of this sort gets at the normative issues raised by television agenda-setting. Is the power of the networks to determine public thinking an occasion for applause or concern? The answer is unclear. To provide reasonable answers requires moving in two directions simultaneously: outside the networks, to assess how faithfully television news represents reality; and "inside" viewers, to ask how capably people deal with the flow of news. This chapter has addressed the second issue. Although subsequent research may well revise them, our conclusions are somewhat unsettling. They suggest that as citizens try to make sense of public affairs, they are captured by salience and are prisoners of their emotions.

# NOTES

1. After learning what we could about our participants' perceptions of our purpose, we then gently revealed our real purpose. We told them that we had altered the newscasts and described how and why we had done so, and tried to convey the indispensability of their participation to our understanding of the political effects of television news. Subjects who indicated keen interest in our work were sent copies of our data. This "debriefing" is an essential part of our experiments. As a general matter, our procedures adhere scrupulously to the American Psychological Association's guidelines governing experimental research.

2. The four questions were as follows: (1) "Shown below is a list of issues that have faced the nation in recent years. How important do you think each is?" The response options were "extremely important," "very important," "important," "not so important," and "not important at all." (2) "How much do you care about each?" ("very much," "a lot," "some," "a little," "not at all"). (3) "How much do you think people in government should worry about each?" ("very much," "a lot," "some," "a little" "not at all"). (4) "Compared with how you feel about other public issues, how strong are your feelings on this issue?" ("extremely strong," "very strong," "fairly strong," "not very strong").

3. The reliability of the composite index can be gauged by Cronbach's alpha, a measure of internal consistency. In all four experiments, the obtained value of alpha exceeded .70.

4. The thought listing procedure was worded as follows: "Now we want to know what you remember and what you felt about some of the stories you saw. Three of the stories are described on following pages. (Note: only one or two were relevant to our purposes.) For each story we have provided two boxes. Please fill in the boxes as follows. In the top box (What The Story Was About) please jot down information the story provided. In the bottom box (How You Felt About The Story) please list any thoughts, feelings, and reactions you had while you watched each of these stories. Here we do not want you tell us about the story itself, rather to give your feelings and reactions. Don't bother about grammar or writing in complete sentences."

5. The question was worded thus: "Some people think that television news programs report accurately and objectively on the important events that happen in the world. Suppose these people are at point one on the scale below. Other people think television news programs report on only certain kinds of events and that the reporting gives a biased and distorted picture of the world. Suppose these people are at the other end of the scale at point seven. And, of course, some people have opinions that fall somewhere in-between the two extremes. Where would you place yourself on this scale?"

6. The affect battery was worded thus: "In this section we are interested in the emotions you felt while viewing the news stories. Each of the stories you wrote about is listed below again. Along with each is a list of six feelings. Think back to how you felt when you saw the story. Then write 'yes' or 'no' in the space next to each of the feelings listed depending on whether the story made you feel that way."

7. Pooling assumes that susceptibility to the networks' agenda stems from common psychological processes. Its great attraction is the reliable estimates produced by a larger sample. In pooling across problems we are by no means suggesting that all individuals hold similar beliefs about the importance of national problems. Some will be primarily concerned with defense, others with unemployment. Because we assess *changes* in the

importance participants accorded the target problem over the course of the experiment, our analysis takes these differences into account. Finally, we did estimate the impact of counterarguing, credibility, and affect within each of the four treatments and found no marked differences.

8. We ignore the composite ratings here because black and elderly participants rated civil rights and Social Security, respectively, to be so important as to preclude any effects stemming from news coverage. The maximum problem importance rating is 20. Blacks shown no news of civil rights rated it at 18.9; elderly participants shown no news coverage of Social Security rated it at 18.0.

9. The interactive effects of personal experience and news coverage on viewers' political judgments are, in fact, a good deal more complex than our treatment here would suggest (for a more detailed account, see Iyengar and Kinder, 1985a).

10. In this experiment we neglected to include the question on source credibility. In addition, given the nature of the design, yielding thoughts in response to the key news stories were far more frequent than counterarguments. Our measure of counterarguing is therefore the number of yielding responses minus the number of counterarguments.

11. We estimated an equation (using logit) in which participants' spontaneous mentions were predicted from the number of yielding responses they made, the number of affects, participants' personal predicament, an interaction term between personal predicament and the number of affects. The coefficients for the number of yields and affects gauge the impact of these mediators among participants unaffected by the target problem. The interaction term coefficients indicate the extent to which the mediating effects of yielding and affect are different among participants personally affected by the target problem.

In contrast to experiments 1 and 2, here we need not rely on two-stage logit, for we tested and rejected the hypothesis of reciprocal effects between the spontaneous mentions on the one hand, and affect and yielding on the other. That is, when the former were treated as endogenous predictors of the latter, the coefficients were not statistically significant. These analyses are available from the authors.

12. Once again, we tested for the possibility of feedback between counterarguing, credibility, and affect on the one hand, and problem importance on the other. Using two-stage regression and two-stage logit analysis, we were unable to detect any such effects. These results are available from the authors.

# REFERENCES

ABELSON, R. P., D. R. KINDER, M. D. PETERS, and S. T. FISKE (1982) "Affective and semantic components in political person perception." Journal of Personality and Social Psychology 42: 619-630.

BEHR, R. and S. IYENGAR (1985) "Television news, real-world cues, and changes in the public agenda." Public Opinion Quarterly 49: 38-57.

BOWER, R. T. (1983) No title. Presented at the Annual Meeting of the American Association for Public Opinion Research, Buckhill Falls, Pennsylvania.

CHAIKEN, S. (1980) "Heuristic vs. systematic information processing and the use of source vs. message cues in persuasion." Journal of Personality and Social Psychology 39: 352-366.

CLARKE, M. (1984) "A role for arousal in the link between feeling states, judgments, and behavior," in M. Clarke and S. Fiske (eds.) Affect and Cognition: The Seventeenth Annual Symposium on Cognition. Hillsdale, NJ: Lawrence Erlbaum.

COMSTOCK, G. (1980) Television in America. Beverly Hills, CA: Sage.

EPSTEIN, E. (1973) News from Nowhere. New York: Random House.

ERBRING, L., E. GOLDENBERG, and A. MILLER (1980) "Front-page news and real-world cues: a new look at agenda-setting by the media." American Journal of Political Science 24: 16-49.

FISKE, S. T. and S. E. TAYLOR (1984) Social Cognition. Reading, MA: Addison-Wesley.

FISKE, S. T., D. A. KENNY, and E. TAYLOR (1982) "Structural models for the mediation of salience effects on attribution." Journal of Experimental Social Psychology 18: 105-127.

GANS, H. (1981) Deciding What's News. New York: Random House.

IYENGAR, S. and D. R. KINDER (1985a) Media and Mind: Television News and Public Opinion.

———(1985b) "More than meets the eye: television news, priming, and public evaluations of the president," in G. Comstock (ed.) Public Communication and Behavior. New York: Academic.

IYENGAR, S., M. D. PETERS, and D. R. KINDER (1982) "Experimental demonstrations of the not-so-minimal consequences of television news programs." American Political Science Review 81: 848-858.

IYENGAR, S., D. R. KINDER, M. D. PETERS, and J. KROSNICK (1984) "The evening news and presidential evaluations." Journal of Personality and Social Psychology 46: 778-787.

JOHNSTON, J. (1972) Econometric Methods. New York: McGraw-Hill.

KAHNEMAN, D., P. SLOVIC, and A. TVERSKY (1983) Judgment Under Uncertainty. New York: Cambridge University Press.

KINDER, D. R. and D. O. SEARS (1985) "Public opinion and political action," in G. Lindzey and E. Aronson (eds.) Handbook of Social Psychology. Reading, MA: Addison-Wesley.

KLAPPER, J. (1960) The Effects of Mass Communication. New York: Free Press.

LIPPMANN, W. (1922/1947) Public Opinion. New York: Harcourt, Brace, Jovanovich. (Originally published 1922)

MacKUEN, M. and S. COOMBS (1981) More Than News: Media Power in Public Affairs. Beverly Hills, CA: Sage.

MARKUS, G. (1970) Analyzing Panel Data. Beverly Hills, CA: Sage.

McARTHUR, L. Z. (1981) "What grabs you? The role of attention in impression formation and causal attributions," in E. Higgins et al. (eds.) Social Cognition: The Ontario Symposium. Hillsdale, NJ: Lawrence Erlbaum.

McGUIRE, W. J. (1981) "Theoretical foundations of campaign," in R. E. Rice and W. J. Paisley (eds.) Public Communication Campaigns. Beverly Hills, CA: Sage.

NEUMAN, R. (1976) "Patterns of recall among television news viewers." Public Opinions Quarterly 40: 115-123.

NISBETT, R. and L. ROSS (1980) Human Inference: Strategies and Shortcomings of Social Judgment. Englewood Cliffs, NJ: Prentice-Hall.

ORNE, T. (1962) "On the social psychology of the psychology experiment." American Psychologist 17: 776-783.

PETTY, R. and J. CACIOPPO (1984) "The effects of involvement on reponses to argument quantity and quality: central and peripheral routes to persuasion." Journal of Personality and Social Psychology 46: 69-81.

———(1981) Attitudes and Persuasion: Classic and Contemporary Approaches. Dubuque: William Brown.

PETTY, R., T. BROCK, and R. OSTROM (1982) "Historical foundations of the cognitive response approach to attitudes and persuasion," in Petty et al., (eds.) Cognitive Responses in Persuasion. Hillsdale, NJ: Lawrence Erlbaum.

TAYLOR, S. E. and S. T. FISKE (1978) "Salience, attention, and attribution: top of the head phenomena," in L. Berkowitz (ed.) Advances in Experimental Social Psychology, Vol. 11. New York: Academic.

ZAJONC, R. (1984) "The interaction of affect and cognition," in K. Scherer and P. Ekman (eds.) Approaches to Emotion. Hillsdale, NJ: Lawrence Erlbaum.

———(1979) "Feeling and thinking: preferences need no inferences." Presented at the annual meeting of the American Psychological Association.

Chapter 6

# COGNITIONS LEADING TO PERSONAL AND POLITICAL BEHAVIORS
## The Case of Crime

Tom R. Tyler
Paul J. Lavrakas

SINCE THE 1960s, social scientists have conducted a number of studies directed toward understanding the nature of citizen beliefs about the social problems of crime and violence and citizen behavioral responses to these problems. This interest is reflected in studies based on public opinion polls (Furstenberg, 1971; Marans et al., 1976), government-sponsored surveys of crime victims and nonvictims (Biderman et al., 1967; Ennis, 1967; Garofalo, 1977; Lavrakas et al., 1980; Scarr et al., 1972; Skogan, 1977; Skogan and Maxfield, 1981; Sparks et al., 1977), and other studies based on interviews with the victims of crimes (LeJeune and Alex, 1973; Rainwater, 1966; Symonds, 1975; Tyler, 1978; 1980). This research focus is the result of the widespread belief among social scientists and policymakers that crime is a major concern among members of the public and that it has a significant influence upon public behavior, the general quality of life in local communities, and the quality of life in the nation as a whole.

This chapter examines behavioral responses to crime and explores their cognitive antecedents, differentiating between possible "preventive" responses that citizens might take in reacting to crime and examining the cognitive distinctions underlying these separate responses.

## BEHAVIORAL RESPONSES TO CRIME

Several researchers have proposed categorizations for differentiating among various behavioral responses to crime. These include distinctions between "public-minded" and "private-minded" behaviors (Schneider and Schneider, 1978); "avoidance" and "mobilization" behavior (Furstenberg, 1972); and "crime-prevention" and "victimization-prevention" behavior (Kidder and Cohn, 1979). Each of these categorization schemes develops from differentiating among various motivational states that lead citizens to engage in different types of behavioral responses to crime. Although theoretically reasonable, these distinctions have not, in practice, reliably differentiated various behavioral responses to crime (Lavrakas, 1981b; Lavrakas and Lewis, 1980).

An alternative approach to classifying behavioral responses has been empirical, examining the actual relationship of various behavioral responses within natural settings. Based on a number of such studies (Lavrakas et al., 1980; Lavrakas and Lewis, 1980; Lavrakas and Herz, 1982; Lavrakas, 1982; Lavrakas, 1985) a reliable set of behavioral categories has been developed. This set of categories divides behaviors into three types: personal protection behaviors; household protection behaviors; and neighborhood/community anticrime responses.

Personal anticrime responses include all behaviors used by citizens to protect their own person. Although such behaviors clearly include the purchase of self-defense aids and other active self-defense strategies, the most pervasive personal anticrime response used by citizens is that of restricting one's own behavior (e.g., not going out alone at night, avoiding certain places, driving to nearby destinations rather than walking, etc.). Thus, behavioral restrictions are the prototype of personal anticrime responses (Lavrakas, 1982), with moving out of a neighborhood being one of the most extreme variations.

Household anticrime responses include all behaviors and strategies used by citizens to prevent illegal entry into their homes. Most of these specific responses come under the rubric of "access control" (Lavrakas, 1981a), and include responses aimed at creating physical barriers to would-be intruders (e.g., double-cylinder deadbolt locks, window bars, alarm systems, etc.), and those that strive to create a psychological barrier by giving a home a lived-in appearance (e.g., the use of timers on indoor lights and radios, stopping newspaper and mail deliveries, having one's grass mowed and sidewalks shoveled during vacations, and getting a "house-sitter" when away).

Finally, neighborhood/community anticrime responses include behaviors and strategies that strive to prevent crime from occurring in some specific geographical area by reducing criminal opportunities or by attacking the supposed "root causes" of crime. Those responses aimed at reducing the opportunity a would-be criminal has to successfully complete a victimization within some given locale range from passive responses (e.g., WhistleSTOP and Blockwatch programs) to quite active responses (e.g., citizen patrols and escort programs). Those responses directed at the root causes of crime may include citizen participation in employment, educational, and recreational programs, most often directed at youth.

The neighborhood/community responses that citizens engage in need not be directed toward one's own neighborhood. They can also include broader-scale political responses to crime. Such responses can involve efforts to improve the workings of the criminal justice system, support for "law and order" candidates and harsher crime control policies, or efforts to change the nature of society.

In theory, citizens could engage in all three types of anticrime behavior, in any combination of behaviors, or they could do nothing in response to the problem of crime. There is evidence, however, that citizens tend to engage primarily in personal protective behaviors, with some accompanying home protection responses, or in home protection responses and some neighborhood- or community-based responses (Lavrakas et al., 1980). In other words, the various types of behavioral response to crime are relatively independent of each other.

This separation is particularly true in the case of personal protective responses to crime and neighborhood/community responses. These tend to be "quite different, and mostly independent anti-crime responses" (Lavrakas et al., 1980: 191). Because citizens' groups often encourage the use of anticrime measures for the home, there is a weak positive relationship between home protection and neighborhood/community protection. Similarly, because those who strive for personal protection often retreat to their homes for safety, there is a weak positive correlation between some home protection measures and some personal protection measures. This does not extend, however, to the relationship between community participation and personal protection. In fact, research suggests that citizens tend to participate in neighborhood- or community-wide programs due to "public-minded" or "civic" motives that are related to social class or to general participation in groups, rather than to any special concerns about personal crime risks.

## CRIME-RELATED BELIEFS

It is important to consider which beliefs about crime might lead to each type of behavioral response outlined. Our efforts to understand public beliefs about crime are aided by a conceptual distinction first introduced by Furstenberg (1971) and supported by subsequent research on beliefs about crime. He noted that citizen reactions to crime could occur on two levels—personal and social. On the personal level citizens were concerned about their own vulnerability to victimization—being the victim of a crime. Such concern typically has been labeled "fear of crime" and separated into two distinct, but related, aspects: a cognitive estimate of estimated future risk and an affective "worry" about victimization (Baumer, 1980; Fowler and Mangione, 1974).

On the social level, crime risk concerns reflect a belief that either in the neighborhood, city, or at the national level, crime and violence are problems that need to be controlled or reduced.

Studies of public opinion consistently have found that both fear of crime and concerns about crime as a social problem are high. Large proportions of the public—especially city dwellers—express fear of personal crime victimization (Skogan, 1981), and many Americans also view crime as an important social problem requiring a local (neighborhood or city) or national response (Furstenberg, 1971: Garofalo, 1977).

Although there is widespread public concern about crime on both the personal and social levels, one important finding of the literature on crime-related beliefs is that these two types of concern are often orthogonal or unrelated. In other words, those with low levels of personal fear of crime are often as concerned about crime as a social problem as are those with high levels of fear and vice versa.

In an examination of citizen views about crime conducted in Baltimore, Furstenberg (1971) found that fear of crime and concern about crime as a social problem were distinct. More recently, Tyler (1980) found that judgments of personal crime risk were not related to judgments of the frequency of crime in samples of citizens in Chicago, Los Angeles, Philadelphia, and San Francisco. Similarly, Gordon et al. (1980) found that estimates of the risk of rape among women were not related to estimates of the number of rapes occurring. Furthermore, this separation of personal and social judgments is not confined to beliefs about crime. Tyler and Cook (1984) have shown that beliefs about personal risk and about the seriousness of social problems are distinct across a range of social and natural risks.

Although contrary to expectation, the separation of beliefs about the problem of crime into personal and social components is consistent with the finding of recent research on social cognition that people separate their personal and general views about the world. Individuals often do not draw implications about how a particular individual—whether themselves or someone else—will behave from general knowledge about the frequency of behaviors in the population (Borgida and Brekke, 1981). Particularly striking is that individuals do not draw implications from their own estimates of population frequency or base rate (Lyon and Slovic, 1976; Tyler, 1980).

There is also evidence for the separation of personal and social-level beliefs about crime and citizen beliefs about why crime occurs. Kidder and Cohn (1979), distinguishing between the two types of causal judgments (person-based and society-based), suggest that citizens will blame crime on either criminals or underlying social conditions. Tyler and Rasinski (1983) found that causal judgments on the personal and societal levels were unrelated—citizens blaming crime on social conditions did not draw the personal-level conclusion that criminals or victims were not to blame for crime, nor did those who blamed criminals and victims not blame social conditions. Instead, the two types of judgment were independent.

The independence of personal and societal-level judgments has also been found in studies other than those about crime. For example, Kluegel and Smith (1978), examining beliefs about opportunity, status, and achievement, found that views about oneself and views about the general state of society were distinct, and Major (1982) found that women's views about the general existence of discrimination in women's wages were not related to personal judgments about the adequacy of their own pay.

Although it might initially seem strange that citizens would separate their personal and social judgments, in fact this separation illustrates the interplay of two basic psychological motivations that guide the formation of personal beliefs: the desire to have correct beliefs about the world and the desire to preserve personally comforting illusions about oneself and the environment (Brickman, 1972).

To the extent that individuals are motivated to have accurate beliefs about risks such as crime, or about the nature of society more generally, they should rely upon their knowledge about the general nature of social problems such as crime. This is the case because crime victimization is a low-probability, high-consequence event—an event that has major consequences when it occurs, but does not happen very often to any particular person. Consequently, citizens are unlikely to have enough personal crime experience with which to form accurate knowledge about personal risks. As a result, citizens should rely on their general knowledge of the world. On the other hand, to rely on others, citizens would have to see others and their experiences as germane to their own situation. This requires an acceptance of a sense of similarity to others that violates important protective cognitions about personal uniqueness.

Recent research in social psychology suggests that people generally exaggerate their uniqueness, seeing themselves as more unique than is actually the case (Funder, 1980). In particular, people exaggerate their abilities to perform tasks and avoid risks that might befall others (Einhorn and Hogarth, 1978). Research has shown that drivers exaggerate their abilities relative to other drivers (Slovic et al., 1977; Svenson, 1981), and that people generally exaggerate their health (Larwood, 1978) and intelligence (Wylie, 1979). Also people unrealistically discount the likelihood that negative events will happen to them (Perloff, 1983; Weinstein, 1980), thinking that they will in some way avoid the misfortunes that befall others. In the area of crime, for example, people have been found to have an "illusion of invulnerability" that blinds them to their own crime risks (LeJeune and Alex, 1973). For example, when asked to assess their chances of becoming robbery and burglary victims in their own neighborhoods, compared to the chances of their neighbors, 75 percent of respondents who felt that their chances differed from their neighbors viewed themselves as less likely to be victimized than their neighbors (Lavrakas, Bennett, and Maier, 1983).

The separation of oneself from others represents a generally adaptive response to environmental risks (Taylor, 1982) and may also have positive effects on mental health (Alloy and Abramson, 1980, 1982). At the same time, however, to the extent that people exaggerate their uniqueness, they will not draw appropriate personal conclusions from information about general risks or general social problems. Hence they will adapt to hazards less effectively than would be possible.

The main conclusion drawn from this examination of the crime literature is that people do make a separation of the self and others. As previously suggested, people also segregate their behavioral responses to crime, and their beliefs about crime. In each case the segregation is along a similar dimension: personal versus social levels of response.

## THE INFLUENCE OF BELIEFS ON BEHAVIORS

A wide variety of studies have suggested that fear of crime motivates avoidance, that is, personal protection behaviors (see Dubow et al., 1978; Lavrakas, 1982; Tyler, 1980). At the same time, fear has not been found to lead citizens to join anticrime groups (Dubow and Podolefsky,

1982; Kidder, 1978; Lavrakas and Herz, 1982; Lewis et al., 1979; Podolefsky and DuBow, 1980), nor does it lead to support for punitive public policies (Sears et al., 1980; Tyler and Weber, 1982), opposition to gun control (Tyler and Lavrakas, 1983) or negative evaluations of local government (Tyler, 1978).

The finding that fear of crime does not have political implications is similar to the conclusion of several recent studies that personal experiences and concerns have limited political impact (Barnes et al., 1979; Brody and Sniderman, 1977; Cook, 1979; Sears et al., 1980; Schlozman and Verba, 1979).

In contrast to fear, concern about crime as a social problem has been found to influence neighborhood group-based activities. As Lavrakas et al. (1980: 160) suggest, "Concern about crime as a neighborhood social problem appears to provide the stronger impetus for citizen participation (in neighborhood groups)." In other words, it is "public-minded" motivations that lead to groups membership and group activity, not concerns about personal risk-avoidance. Similarly, Tyler (1978) found that local government evaluations were affected by judgments of the seriousness of the crime problem, and Tyler and Lavrakas (1983) found that community-level concerns governed support or opposition to gun control. More generally, Kinder and Kiewiet (1981) have suggested that political responses flow from the societal level. On the other hand, general judgments of rate or seriousness of crime do not influence personal protection behaviors (Tyler, 1980).

These failures of influence suggest strongly that there are two levels of response to thinking about, and acting in response to the crime problem. In both cases people separate general and personal levels of response to crime, and the influence of beliefs upon behaviors occurs within levels. This separation is not total, as both levels of belief influence home protection behavior.

## EXPERIENCE AND CRIME-RELATED BELIEFS

The final issue we wish to address is the origin of each type of belief in citizens' direct and indirect experiences with crime.

In considering the origin of crime-related beliefs, past research has emphasized the role of personal victimization in the formation of citizen beliefs about crime (Dubow et al., 1978). Although it is natural to focus on the influence of direct victimization experience on crime-related beliefs and behaviors, social psychologists have noted that direct experiences are only one of two potential influences on such judgments and behaviors. The other potential influence is socially transmitted information about crime acquired through social networks and the mass media. Social psychologists have argued that beliefs about the environment—such as crime risk judgments or estimates of the rate of crime—are determined through the integration of personal and socially transmitted experiences (Campbell, 1961; Ross, 1977; Tyler, 1980).

There are two types of indirect experience that might be relied upon in forming risk judgments—informal social contacts with neighbors, family, or friends, and mass media exposure to crime through television, radio, newspapers, and so on. Both reflect the aggregation of experiences with crime across people (Tyler, 1980, 1984) and, hence, provide information of greater potential value in risk assessment than the experience of any particular individual. Recent efforts at increasing crime awareness have utilized both of these types of indirect experience. One approach has been to develop neighborhood or community-based social networks to spread information about crime (Lavrakas, Rosenbaum, and Kaminski, 1983). Another has been mass media campaigns, such as the recent national effort to "take a bite out of crime" (Mendelsohn et al., 1981a, 1981b).

Considering direct personal victimization experience, it generally has been found that personal experience with crime influences fear of crime (DuBow et al., 1978; Lavrakas, 1982; Skogan and Maxfield, 1981; Tyler, 1980). On the other hand, victimization has not been found to be linked to estimates of the crime rate (Tyler, 1980), or to beliefs about the seriousness of the crime problem (Furstenberg, 1971).

In the case of indirect experiences with crime, the results are more complex. That evidence suggests that the two types of indirect experience have not been equally potent in influencing fear of crime. Studies of social networks suggest that increasing informal social communications about crime can influence personal fears (Skogan and Maxfield, 1981; Tyler, 1980). Evaluations of mass media campaigns, on the other hand, suggest that they have only a weak impact on personal fears. For example, Mendelsohn et al. (1981) found that only 13 percent of respondents indicated attitude change as a result of a national media campaign.

The finding that campaigns that focus on the development of social networks are effective—whereas mass media campaigns are less so—parallels the findings of crime victimization surveys and indirect experience. Several recent studies of crime victimization have found that in forming risk judgments citizens are influenced primarily by experiences conveyed through social networks, not by media reports of crime (Skogan and Maxfield, 1981; Tyler, 1978, 1980). In other words, in forming personal risk estimates in natural settings people utilize only one of the two types of indirect experience potentially available to them, relying on social communication, but generally ignoring the mass media.

The suggestion that people ignore the mass media may initially seem implausible, as it is commonly believed that media reports of crime are important in maintaining public fears. Certainly, the volume of crime reported in the media is quite high (Gordon and Heath, 1981; Graber, 1977). Nonetheless, recent studies suggest that media reports about crime are not an important influence on personal fears. Instead, personal fear is generated primarily by personal experiences with crime and experiences within one's social network.

Much evidence supports the conclusion that media reports of crime have little influence upon fear of crime. A survey of residents of Los Angeles (Tyler, 1978, 1980) and of residents of San Francisco, Philadelphia, and Chicago (Skogan and Maxfield, 1981; Tyler, 1980) drew similar conclusions—no relationship was found between the number of mass media crime reports recalled and fear of crime. Those who were aware of more crimes reported in the media were not more afraid of being victimized by crime. Instead, fear of crime was determined by personal victimization experience and knowledge of the experiences of friends, relatives, and neighbors.

Additionally, studies examining the relationship between the amount of television watched and fear of crime suggest that, when background differences associated with heavy television viewing are controlled for, those who view more television are not more afraid of crime victimization (Doob and MacDonald, 1979; Hughes, 1980).

Overall, therefore, recent studies on media influence suggest that the mass media do not influence personal fears about crime. This finding is consistent with that of research in other areas. Mass media campaigns to alert citizens to social risks have had limited success in altering smoking and other health-related attitudes (Mendelsohn et al., 1981a; Warner, 1977), seat-belt use (Robertson 1975; Robertson et al., 1974), and contraceptive use (Udry et al., 1972). These same types of personal judgments and behaviors have, however, been found to be influenced by social communications from friends, family, and neighbors (Antonovsky and Anson, 1976; Fhaner and Hare, 1973; Kunreuther, 1978). Although personal risk judgments are influenced by these informal social communications as well as by personal experiences, mass media reports appear to exert little influence upon them.

With general concern about the crime problem, however, the influence of media reports is quite different. On the general level research generally has suggested a major media influence. Several studies have found, for example, that judgments of the rate of crime are influenced by the media (Doob and MacDonald, 1979; Skogan and Maxfield, 1981; Tyler, 1980), and the media have also been found to influence beliefs about who the victims and perpetrators of crime generally are (Doob and MacDonald, 1979). More generally, the media is widely credited with an important role in spreading general information about the world (Roberts and Bachen, 1981). Similar influences on general judgments have been found when the experiences of friends, neighbors, and relatives are considered.

The conclusion that mass media reports of crime have an impact on general, but not personal, judgments is consistent with another recent finding about media effects. Heath (1984; Heath and Petraitis, 1984) examined the effect of newspaper reading on crime judgments and found that the amount of crime presented in the newspapers their respondents read was related to their fear of crime in areas outside their neighborhood (for example downtown areas), but not to neighborhood fears. In this work the media were found to influence personal fears, but only personal fears about remote areas with which subjects have little personal experience. In the case of personal neighborhood fears, no media effects were found.

## A MODEL OF CITIZENS' RESPONSES TO CRIME

The findings presented support a two-tiered model of citizen responses to crime. Basic to the model are the conceptual distinctions made among behaviors directed at personal protection, household protection, and community crime prevention. These three types of behavior were found generally to be distinct responses to the problem of crime, especially in the case of personal protection behavior and community crime prevention. The model supported by the data discussed in this review is shown in Figure 6.1. It includes the beliefs and experiences that are antecedent to the three types of behavior outlined. The key distinction is between personal and social levels of analysis. This distinction is maintained at the experience, belief, and behavior stages.

What is most striking about the model is that, at the belief and behavior stages, the two levels of the model are distinct and the influence of the previous stage occurs primarily within level. There is little

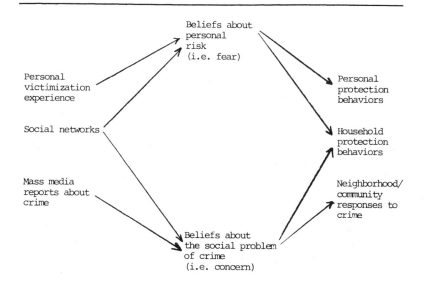

Figure 6.1   The Antecedents of Behavioral Responses to Crime

evidence of influence across levels at either the belief or behavior stages, with the exception of joint influences on household protection behaviors.

In his classic discussion of political thinking, Lane (1962) suggested that citizens "morselize" their experience, failing to build from their experiences to larger conclusions about the political and social system. These findings support the suggestion that citizens are not drawing social or political implications from their own experiences and fears. Instead, they are reacting to those experiences and fears in personal ways, by altering their own behaviors to reduce the risk of crime victimization.

It also is striking that citizens do not utilize their views about the world in general to form personal risk estimates. Instead, they segregate their personal and social judgments and behaviors. It is not a new finding that people separate out their personal lives and resist the impact of societal level events on them. In their classic study of soldiers during World War II, Shils and Janowitz (1948) suggested that soldiers' beliefs and behaviors were not influenced by the larger course of the war as long as their personal world and their primary social networks remained intact. Here too citizens' personal worlds—the world of their friends, family, neighbors, and themselves—is separate from the general world surrounding it.

It is important to examine why the two-tiered reaction to crime that has been outlined might occur. One possibility is that the psychological benefits of perceived uniqueness compensate for the lessened adaptive capability that results from holding such erroneous views. In other words, although citizens may adapt less effectively to crime because they see themselves as unique and, as a result, do not draw personal conclusions from general beliefs or mass media experiences, this loss in adaptive effectiveness may be compensated for by other psychological benefits.

Ultimately an understanding of the pattern of media effects outlined in this chapter requires a theory of cognitive processes that would tell us how media events are organized and stored in memory, as well as how that information is retrieved from memory and utilized in making judgments and determining the type and level of behavior to engage in (see Berkowitz, 1984). It is to the development of such a theory that much of the work in this volume is directed. The purpose of this chapter is not to present such a cognitive theory of media effects, but to outline the pattern of media impact that such a theory will be required to explain.

Finally, it should be noted that although the model presented in Figure 6.1 is a description of the general relationship between personal and societal beliefs and behaviors, it is no doubt true that there are circumstances under which people do draw personal implications from social information and circumstances under which people's general beliefs are influenced by their personal experiences and beliefs (Tyler and Cook, 1984). One example is the influence of such concerns on household protection behavior. Future research might profitably be directed toward the specification of the conditions under which each of these types of crossover effect occurs.

## REFERENCES

ALLOY, L. B. and L. Y. ABRAMSON (1982) "Learned helplessness, depression, and the illusion of control." Journal of Personality and Social Psychology 42: 1114-1126.
———(1980) "The cognitive component of human helplessness and depression: a critical analysis," in J. Garber and M.E.P. Seligman (eds.) Human Helplessness: Theory and Applications. New York: Academic.

ANTONOVSKY, A. and O. ANSON (1976) "Factors related to preventive health behaviors," in J. W. Cullen et al. (eds.) Cancer: The Behavioral Dimensions. Washington, DC: National Cancer Institute.

BARNES, S. H., B. G. FARAH, and F. HEUNKS (1979) "Personal dissatisfaction," in S. H. Barnes et al. (eds.) Political Action. Beverly Hills, CA: Sage.

BAUMER, T. L. (1980) "Research of fear of crime in the United States." Victimology 3: 254-264.

BERKOWITZ, L. (1984) "Some effects of thoughts on anti- and prosocial influences of media events: a cognitive-neoassociation analysis." Psychological Bulletin 95: 410-427.

BIDERMAN, A. D., L. A. JOHNSON, J. McINTYRE, and A. WEIR (1967) Report on a pilot study in the District of Columbia on Victimization and Attitudes Toward Law Enforcement. Washington, DC: President's Commission on Law Enforcement and the Administration of Justice.

BORGIDA, E. and N. BREKKE (1981) "The base-rate fallacy in attribution and prediction," in J. H. Harvey et al. (eds.) New Directions in Attribution Research (vol. 3). Hillsdale NJ: Lawrence Erlbaum.

BRICKMAN, P. (1972) "Rational and nonrational elements in reactions to disconfirmations of performance expectancies." Journal of Experimental Social Psychology 8: 112-123.

BRODY, R. A. and P. M. SNIDERMAN (1977) "From life space to polling place: the relevance of personal concerns for voting behavior." British Journal of Political Science 7: 337-360.

CAMPBELL, D. T. (1961) "Conformity in psychology's theories of acquired behavioral dispositions," in L. Berg and B. Bass (eds.) Conformity and Deviation. New York: Harper.

COOK, F. L. (1979) Who Should Be Helped? Public Support for Social Services. Beverly Hills, CA: Sage.

DOOB, A. N. and G. E. MacDONALD (1979) "Television viewing and the fear of victimization." Journal of Personality and Social Psychology 37: 170-179.

DUBOW, F. and A. PODOLEFSKY (1982) "Citizen participation in community crime prevention." Human Organization 41: 307-314.

DUBOW, F., E. McCABE, and G. KAPLAN (1978) "Reactions to crime: a critical review of the literature." Unpublished manuscript, Center for Urban Affairs and Policy Research, Northwestern University.

EINHORN, H. J. and R. M. HOGARTH (1978) "Confidence in judgment: persistence of the illusion of validity." Psychological Review 85: 395-416.

ENNIS, P. H. (1967) Crime Victimization in the United States. Washington, DC: President's Commission on Law Enforcement and the Administration of Justice.

FHANER, G. and M. HARE (1973) "Seat-belts: factors influencing their use." Accident Analysis and Prevention 5: 27-43.

FOWLER, F. J. and T. W. MANGIONE (1974) "The nature of fear." Unpublished manuscript, Survey Research Center, University of Massachusetts at Boston.

FUNDER, D. C. (1980) "On seeing ourselves as others see us: self-other agreement and discrepancy in personality ratings." Journal of Personality 48: 473-493.

FURSTENBERG, F. F. (1971) "Public reaction to crime in the streets." American Scholar 40: 601-610.

GAROFALO, J. (1977) Public Opinion About Crime. Washington, DC: U.S. Department of Justice, Law Enforcement Assistance Administration.

GORDON, M. T. and L. HEATH (1981) "The news business, crime and fear," in D. A. Lewis (ed.) Reactions to Crime. Beverly Hills, CA: Sage.

GORDON, M. T., S. RIGER, R. K. LeBAILLY, and L. HEATH (1980) "Crime, women, and the quality of urban life." Journal of Women in Culture and Society 5: 144-160.

GRABER, D. (1977) "Ideological components in the perceptions of crime and crime news." Presented at the annual meeting of the Society for the Study of Social Problems, Chicago, Illinois.

HEATH, L. (1984) "Impact of newspaper crime reports on fear of crime: multimethodological investigation." Journal of Personality and Social Psychology 47: 263-276.

HEATH, L. and J. PETRAITIS (1984) "Television viewing and fear of crime: where is a mean world?" Unpublished manuscript, Loyola University.

HUGHES, M. (1980) "The fruits of cultivation analysis: reexamination of some effects of television viewing." Public Opinion Quarterly 44: 287-302.

KIDDER, L. H. and E. S. COHN (1979) "Public views of crime and crime prevention," in I. H. Frieze et al. (eds.) New Approaches to Social Problems. San Francisco: Jossey-Bass.

KIDDER, R. L. (1978) "Community crime prevention: the two faces of delegalization." Unpublished manuscript, Center for Urban Affairs and Policy Research, Northwestern University.

KINDER, D. R. and R. KIEWIET (1981) Sociotropic politics: the American case. British Journal of Political Science, 11: 129-161.

KLUEGEL, J. R. and E. SMITH (1978) "Evaluations of social inequality: attribution, experiences and symbolic perceptions." Presented at the annual meeting of the American Psychological Association.

KUNREUTHER, H. (1978) Disaster Insurance Protection. New York: John Wiley.

LARWOOD, L. (1978) "Swine flu: a field study of self-serving biases." Journal of Applied Social Psychology 18: 283-289.

LAVRAKAS, P. J. (1985) "Citizen self-help and neighborhood crime prevention," in L. Curtis (ed.) American Violence and Public Policy. New Haven: Yale University Press.

———(1982) "Fear of crime and behavioral restrictions in urban and suburban neighborhoods." Population and Environment 5: 242-264.

———(1981a) "Household response to burglary," in D. A. Lewis (ed.) Reactions to Crime. Beverly Hills, CA: Sage.

———(1981b) Factors Related to Citizen Involvement in Anti-Crime Measures: An Executive Summary. Washington, DC: Government Printing Office.

———and E. J. HERZ (1982) "Citizen participation and neighborhood crime prevention." Criminology 20: 479-498.

LAVRAKAS, P. J. and D. A. LEWIS (1980) "The conceptualization and measurement of citizen crime prevention behaviors." Journal of Research in Crime and Delinquency 17: 254-272.

LAVRAKAS, P. J., D. P. ROSENBAUM, and F. KAMINSKI (1983) "Transmitting information about crime and crime prevention to citizens." Journal of Police Science and Administration 11: 463-473.

LAVRAKAS, P. J., S. BENNETT, and R. MAIER (1983) "Community crime control." Unpublished manuscript, Center for Urban Affairs and Policy Research, Northwestern University.

LAVRAKAS, P. J., E. HERZ, and G. SALEM (1981) "Community organizations, citizen participation, and neighborhood crime prevention." Presented at the meeting of the American Psychological Association, Los Angeles.

LAVRAKAS, P. J., J. NORMOYLE, W. G. SKOGAN, E. HERZ, G. SALEM, and D. A. LEWIS (1980) "Factors related to citizen involvement in personal, household, and neighborhood anti-crime measures." Unpublished manuscript, Center for Urban Affairs and Policy Research, Northwestern University.

LeJEUNE, R. and N. ALEX (1973) "On being mugged: the event and its aftermath." Urban Life and Culture 2: 259-287.

LEWIS, D. V., R. SZOC, G. SALEM, and R. LEVIN (1979) "Crime and community: understanding fear of crime in urban America." Unpublished manuscript, Center for Urban Affairs and Policy Research, Northwestern University.

LYON, D. and P. SLOVIC (1976) "Dominance of accuracy information and neglect of base-rates in probability estimation." Acta Psychological 40: 287-298.

MAJOR, B. (1982, June) "Individual differences in what is seen as fair." Presented at the Nags Head Conference on Psychological Aspects of Justice, Kill Devil Hills, North Carolina.

MARANS, R. W., S. NELSON, S. NEWMAN, W. ROGERS, and O. WORDEN (1976) "Public perceptions of the quality of life in metropolitan Detroit examined in I.S.R. study." I.S.R. Newsletter (Winter): 4-5.

MENDELSOHN, H., G. J. O'KEEFE, J. LIN, H. T. SPETNAGEL, C. VENGLER, D. WILSON, M. O. WIRTH, and K. NASH (1981a) "Public communications and the prevention of crime." Presented at the meeting of the Midwestern Association of Public Opinion Research, Chicago.

———(1981b) Public Communications and the Prevention of Crime: Strategies for Control (vol. 1—A narrative report). Center for Mass Communications, University of Denver.

PERLOFF, L. S. (1983) "Perceptions of vulnerability to victimization." Journal of Social Issues 39: 41-62.

PODOLEFSKY, A. and F. DUBOW (1980) "Strategies for community crime prevention: collective responses to crime in urban America." Unpublished manuscript, Center for Urban Affairs and Policy Research, Northwestern University.

RAINWATER, L. (1966) "Fear and the house-as-haven in the lower class." Journal of the American Institute of Planners. 32: 23-31.

ROBERTSON, L. S. (1975) "The great seat-belt campaign flop." Journal of Communication 26: 41-45.

———A. B. KELLEY, B. O'NEILL, C. W. WIXON, R. S. EISWIRTH, and W. HADDON (1974) "A controlled study of the effects of television messages on safety belt use." American Journal of Public Health 64: 1071-1080.

ROSS, L. (1977) "The intuitive psychologist and his shortcomings," in L. Berkowitz (ed.) Advances in Experimental Social Psychology (vol. 10). New York: Academic.

SCARR, H. A., J. L. PINSKY, and D. S. WYATT (1972) Patterns of burglary (Part 1). Washington, DC: National Institute of Justice.

SCHLOZMAN, K. L. and S. VERBA (1979) Injury to Insult: Unemployment, Class, and Political Response. Cambridge, MA: Harvard University Press.

SCHNEIDER, A. L. and P. R. SCHNEIDER (1978) Private and Public-Minded Citizen Responses to a Neighborhood-Based Crime Prevention Strategy. Eugene, OR: Institute for Policy Analysis.

SEARS, D. O., R. R. LAU, T. R. TYLER, and H. M. ALLEN, Jr. (1980) "Self-interest vs. symbolic politics in policy attitudes and Presidential voting." American Political Science Review 74: 670-684.

SHILS, E. A. and M. JANOWITZ (1948) "Cohesion and disintegration in the Wehrmacht in World War II." Public Opinion Quarterly 12: 280-315.

SKOGAN, W. G. (1981) "Fear of crime in America." Testimony before the Subcommittee on Crime, Judiciary Committee, U.S. House of Representatives.

———(1977) "Public policy and fear of crime in large American cities," in J. A. Gardiner (ed.) Public Law and Public Policy. New York: Praeger.

———and M. G. MAXFIELD (1981) Coping with Crime. Beverly Hills, CA: Sage.

SLOVIC, P., B. FISCHHOFF, and S. LICHTENSTEIN (1977) "Accident probabilities and seat-belt usage: A psychological perspective." Accident Analysis and Prevention 10: 281-295.

SPARKS, R. F., H. G. GLENN, and D. J. DODD (1977) Surveying Victims. London: John Wiley.

SVENSON, O. (1981) "Are we all less risky and more skillful than our fellow drivers?" Acta Psychologica 47: 143-148.

SYMONDS, M. (1975) "Victims of violence: psychological effects and aftereffects." American Journal of Psychoanalysis 35: 19-26.

TAYLOR, S. E. (1982) "Adjusting to threatening events: a theory of cognitive adaptation." Katz-Newcomb Lecture, University of Michigan.

TYLER, T. R. (1984) "Assessing the risk of crime victimization: the intergration of personal victimization experience and socially transmitted information." Journal of Social Issues 40: 27-38.

———(1980) "The impact of directly and indirectly experienced events: the origin of crime-related judgments and behaviors." Journal of Personality and Social Psychology 39: 13-28.

———(1978) "Drawing inferences from experiences: the effect of crime victimization experiences upon crime-related attitudes and behaviors." Unpublished dissertation, University of California, Los Angeles.

———and F. L. COOK (1984) "The mass media and judgments of risk: distinguishing impact on personal and societal level judgments." Journal of Personality and Social Psychology 47: 693-708.

TYLER, T. R. and P. LAVRAKAS (1983) "Support for gun control: the influence of personal, sociotropic, and ideological concerns." Journal of Applied Social Psychology 13: 392-405.

TYLER, T. R. and K. RASINSKI (1983) "Explaining political events and problems: the relationship between personal and environmental causality." Micropolitics 2: 401-422.

TYLER, T. R. and R. WEBER (1982) "Support for the death penalty: instrumental response to crime or symbolic attitude?" Law and Society Review 17: 21-45.

UDRY, R. J., L. T. CLARK, C. L. CHASE, and M. LEVY (1972) "Can mass media advertising increase contraceptive use?" Family Planning Perspectives 4: 37-44.

WARNER, K. E. (1977) "The effects of anti-smoking campaigns on cigarette consumption." American Journal of Public Health 67: 645-650.

WEINSTEIN, N. D. (1980) "Unrealistic optimism about future life events." Journal of Personality and Social Psychology 39: 806-820.

WYLIE, R. C. (1979) The Self-Concept. Vol. 2: Theory and Research on Selected Topics. Lincoln: University of Nebraska Press.

Chapter 7

# FINDING THE UNEXPECTED
## Cognitive Bonding in
## a Political Campaign

Klaus Schoenbach
David H. Weaver

THERE ARE A number of conflicting theories about the influence of
mass communication on beliefs and attitudes during political campaigns. In the past decade or so, more evidence has been mustered to
support the commonsense notion that media use can influence political
beliefs—the qualities we attribute to political objects such as politicians,
political groups, institutions, issues, and concepts. There is substantial
evidence that media can make voters aware of the major issues of an
election campaign (and concerned about them) and the images of
various candidates and political parties (Becker et al., 1975; Weaver et
al., 1981).

But although there are longitudinal and experimental studies that
support the influence of mass media exposure on cognitions or beliefs,
there is less agreement on the relationships between media exposure and
attitudes, and between beliefs and attitudes. The traditional hierarchy of
effects as described by Lavidge and Steiner (1961) argues that beliefs
change before attitudes do. But there is evidence to support the opposite
view—that attitudes can influence perceptual sensitivity, which in turn
leads to the strengthening of certain beliefs (Erbring et al., 1980).

These conflicting findings may be at least partially explained by
methodological problems, the specific historical context of the studies,
or by the nature of the stage within the communication process under
study. At this point, it seems safe to conclude only that the ordering of

media effects may vary at different points in time and in different situations, although there does tend to be evidence of stronger and more consistent media effects on cognitions than on attitudes and opinions (Becker et al., 1975; Weaver, 1984).

The data we report in this chapter allow for the possibility of differing influences between communication exposure, political attitudes, and political beliefs at different stages of a political campaign. The relationships between exposure, attitudes, and beliefs are examined during the precampaign period, climax of the campaign, and post-election period. The differing levels of voters' motivation to follow the campaign are also measured and controlled for as contingent conditions likely to affect the relationships between exposure, attitudes, and beliefs. The measure of motivation used in this study is need for orientation (Weaver, 1980), a combination of relevance of information and uncertainty about it that has proved useful for discriminating communication effects in several agenda-setting studies in the United States.

Some of these studies suggest that those voters with the highest levels of need for orientation (greatest relevance and most uncertainty) are the most susceptible to the influence of communication, at least late in a campaign (McCombs and Weaver, 1973; Weaver et al., 1975; Weaver, 1977; and Weaver et al., 1981). But these studies are mostly set in highly prominent elections, and most of them employ aggregate (group) measures of public agendas rather than individual measures of issue concerns. Other agenda-setting studies using individual-level measures have found *less* interested voters showing stronger agenda-setting effects than the more interested—for instance, McLeod et al. (1974) in their study of potential Madison, Wisconsin, voters in the 1972 U.S. presidential election. But, in this study, the more undecided younger voters showed stronger effects than the less undecided, suggesting that those with a moderate need for orientation (low interest and high uncertainty) were most affected. Likewise, Iyengar et al. (1983) found in two experiments with television news agendas using individual-level measures that the more involved and attentive persons were *less* affected by TV news agendas than were the less attentive.

These studies just cited suggest that one cannot always assume a positive relationship between the motive of need for orientation and media agenda-setting effects. There appear to be situations in which less interest (if not less uncertainty) predicts greater agenda-setting effects. Why would this be so? Perhaps those less interested in a particular campaign know less about the candidates and the issues, discuss them less with others, and therefore have less knowledge or less definite priorities of their own with which to counter the priorities of the media to which they are exposed. On the other hand, perhaps *groups* of highly interested and uncertain voters are more likely to be concerned about and discussing those issues covered most heavily by the media, even if their individual rankings of such issues don't match the media rankings very well.

The study reported in this chapter builds on an earlier panel study of West German voters during the first direct elections to the European Parliament in 1979 (Quarles and Schoenbach, 1982; Schoenbach and Quarles, 1983). In that study, path analyses were used to investigate the causal linkages between three seemingly different components of the voters' relations to the European election campaign:

(1) a campaign-relevant attitude—the one toward the idea of a European Community;

(2) the awareness of European matters as important issues in Germany; and

(3) the exposure to a number of campaign channels.

For three different stages of the election campaign, the purpose of the Quarles and Schoenbach study was to determine which one of the three variables influenced which one of the others with what time lag. Surprisingly, their analysis revealed that there were almost no causal linkages over time. Instead, they found reciprocal relationships between communication exposure, attitude toward the European Community, and the belief that European politics is an issue *within* each of the campaign stages. Particularly during the period of most intense campaign activity, the three variables formed a coherent system of interdependencies but dissolved immediately after election day.

Quarles and Schoenbach interpreted these findings as a "crystallization" or "bonding" effect of the campaign as a whole. Lazarsfeld et al. (1944) found in their classic election study that one major outcome of the campaign was to harmonize voters' party identification, candidate images, and vote intention—a process the researchers called "crystallization." They could demonstrate that the variables to be harmonized mainly crystallized around party identification as the most stable component of the voters' cognitive systems. Quarles and Schoenbach found a very similar role for the attitude toward European integration. It obviously served as a nucleus of crystallization processes. "Bonding" is another expression for this effect used by Dennis et al. (1979). These authors argue that during the 1976 presidential election campaign the relationships between candidates' images and issue differences, on the one hand, and voting intentions, on the other, were gradually being strengthened. So, the elements of the relationships under study became more and more consistent.

In the study reported here, we analyze the influence of subjectively felt need for orientation on "cognitive bonding" during the 1979 European Parliamentary election. We explore if and how differing levels of interest and uncertainty during the European Parliamentary campaign affect the relationships between exposure to communication, attitude toward the European Community, and the belief that European politics is an issue among West German voters. Do those voters with higher levels of need for orientation have attitudes and beliefs that are largely independent of each other and of their communication exposure, or do they demonstrate more cognitive bonding than those with lower levels of need for orientation?

## THEORETICAL BACKGROUND

In terms of psychological theories of motivation, the idea of a need for orientation is derived primarily from cognitive utilitarian theories (McGuire, 1974), which provide an explanation for one of three basic media audience orientations identified by Blumler (1979) in his discussion of the role of theory in uses and gratifications research: cognitive, diversion, and personal identity. Utilitarian theories of motivation also depict the individual person as viewing the outside world, and communications from it, as a valuable source of relevant information.

Even though cognitive utilitarian theories of motivation are only one of 16 kinds of theories of cognitive and affective motivation identified by McGuire (1974), the utilitarian theories seem especially applicable to political information seeking and media effects because these theories emphasize the role of information in problem solving.

Based on utilitarian-oriented theory (e.g., Tolman, 1932; Jones and Gerard, 1967) and research (e.g., Westley and Barrow, 1959; Chaffee and McLeod, 1973), McCombs and Weaver (1973) defined political "need for orientation" in terms of two lower-order (less abstract) concepts: political relevance and political uncertainty.

Because the news media (newspapers and television in particular) permeate nearly every aspect of American life and are readily available to most citizens, the third major factor suggested by these previous studies of information seeking (degree of effort required to receive the message) was considered a constant, although it can be argued that newspapers and other printed media require more physical and mental effort to use than do television and radio.

In the typology illustrated in Figure 7.1, high relevance and high uncertainty combine to produce high need for orientation, but both high relevance and low uncertainty and low relevance and high uncertainty produce a moderate level of need for orientation. And finally, low relevance and low uncertainty result in a low need for orientation. There is still an argument to be made that the two moderate need for orientation conditions are different qualitatively, if not quantitatively. But to this point, no tests have been done to see if the two moderate need for orientation conditions relate differently to media uses and media effects.

Although levels of relevance and uncertainty could be considered separate predictors of political information seeking and media effects, there are theoretical and methodological advantages to combining both concepts into a single hypothetical construct labeled as need for orientation. By combining uncertainty (the perceived existence of a gap or problem) with relevance (the perceived importance of the problem), one is tapping the major dimensions of many utilitarian theories of motivation in a single fairly abstract construct that may be applied to a wide variety of settings. And methodologically, it is easier and more parsimonious to use only one variable to partition a sample to observe media use-media effects relationships.

## DATA COLLECTION

The data used in this study are the same as those used by Quarles and Schoenbach (1982), hour-long personal interviews conducted three times in April, June, and July of 1979 with a representative panel of the West German electorate. This panel was part of an international comparative multimethod study assessing the role of the mass media in the first direct elections to the European Parliament (Blumler, 1983)—a not particularly powerful institution that has more of a symbolic value in the European Community. The first panel wave began in April 1979—shortly before the beginning of the election campaign in Germany on May 1. A representative sample of 813 West Germans 18 years and older was interviewed. The second wave was fielded on June 1 and

Uncertainty

|  |  | Low | High |
|---|---|---|---|
| Relevance | Low | Low Need for Orientation (Group III) ("Informed") * | Moderate Need for Orientation (Group II) ("Uninterested") * |
|  | High | Moderate Need for Orientation (Group II) | High Need for Orientation (Group I) ("Curious") * |

*See measurement section in text.

**Figure 7.1   Need for Orientation Typology**

finished June 9—one day before the election in Germany, with 578 panel members still in the sample. The third wave started one week after election day, on June 18, and was completed July 5. The 459 persons interviewed in all three waves constitute the panel used in this study. A comparison between these and those who were interviewed only once or twice showed no significant difference in age, sex, education, political participation, or attitudes toward the European Community (Schoenbach, 1983: 153ff).

**MEASUREMENT**

As in the previous study, the exogenous variables of our analysis are education and political participation. Education was measured by the highest educational degree the respondent achieved. Political participation was assessed by a nine-step Guttman scale: the lower end of the scale was determined by rejecting the statement, "I always cast my vote in elections." In West Germany, this form of political behavior is mainly ritualistic and does not express any particular participation or interest in politics. The top score of our scale was indicated by agreement with, "I am actively involved in a political party, a political club, or association."[1]

The indicators for political beliefs and attitudes were selected according to Fishbein's and Ajzen's (1975) definitions. They define "attitude" as "a learned predisposition to respond in a consistently favorable or unfavorable manner with respect to a given object" (p. 6).

Our measure for political attitude was the voters' evaluation of the European Community. Improving this evaluation was one of the major goals of the campaign. The measure in this study is slightly different from the one Quarles and Schoenbach used in 1982. It consists only of the answer to the following question:

> In general, do you think that West Germany's membership in the European Community is a good thing, a bad thing, or neither good nor bad?

Respondents replying "good" got one point, whereas all the others scored zero points.

According to Fishbein and Ajzen (1975), "beliefs" are perceived associations between objects and their attributes. These perceptions are defined as value-free in principle.[2] A political belief we considered to be related to the above-mentioned attitude was the *perceived* salience of European political issues. Respondents were asked to name objects they perceived to have a specific attribute (the most important issues with which *other people* are concerned). The open-ended question for this purpose read:

> What are the most important issues politicians and the population of the Federal Republic of Germany are dealing with at the time being?

Whenever a respondent mentioned an issue concerning European politics, he or she got a score of one on our variable.

Both European identification and perceived salience of European problems could either have influenced the exposure to, or been influenced by, campaign communication. Unlike some of the other countries participating in the election, West Germany was almost entirely focused on the *European* aspect of the event. All the campaign materials in West Germany—such as ads, leaflets, and posters—unanimously stressed the necessity of a faster European integration. Also, unlike in other countries, the importance of the European elections in Germany was not controversial (see Blumler, 1983).

Posters, leaflets, and ads in the press are still important communication channels of election campaigns in Europe. To determine the respondents' use of campaign communication, we constructed an index using the answers to three questions. Interviewees were asked whether they had seen campaign posters, campaign material sent to their homes (leaflets and brochures), or at least one ad in a newspaper or news magazine. Thus, depending on how many of these campaign channels the respondent had used, he or she could get up to three points.

All three variables were measured three times—before the election campaign, shortly before, and shortly after election day.

## NEED FOR ORIENTATION

This major contingent condition of our study was measured in two steps using our first panel wave: (1) Respondents were asked:

What about the issues that are important for Europe as a whole: Do you think that you are sufficiently informed about these issues or not sufficiently informed?

Those who answered "sufficiently informed" (202, or 44 percent of our sample) were called "the informed" and assigned the label "low need for orientation" because they did not express any uncertainty about the European issues. (2) Those who replied "not sufficient" or "it depends" are the ones in our analysis with a high level of uncertainty. But they can be split into two different subgroups—respondents who did not care about their low level of knowledge or who were not interested in more information, and voters who were interested enough in European issues to plan specific activities in order to overcome their ignorance. The following question allowing us to differentiate between these two groups was posed to all *not* considering themselves as sufficiently informed:

"What would you do to learn more about these issues?"

Respondents who answered "nothing" or "don't know" were called "the uninterested" (95, or 21 percent of our sample); those who mentioned at least one specific measure to combat their ignorance (for instance, reading books or asking experts) were called "the curious" (162, or 35 percent of all respondents).

In other words, those persons who expressed uncertainty about European issues and who considered such issues relevant enough to seek additional information were those with the highest level of need for orientation (the curious). Those who expressed uncertainty, but not interest in seeking additional information, were considered to have a moderate level of need for orientation (the uninterested). And those who expressed no uncertainty were considered to have a low level of need for orientation (the informed).[3] (See Figure 7.1)

## DATA ANALYSIS

Path analysis was employed to test the feasibility of alternative causal models, as was done in the earlier study by Quarles and Schoenbach (1982). To establish causal priorities *between* different panel waves is no problem in our study, but what happens *within* each of the three stages of the campaign—what are the causal directions of the relationships there between communication exposure and belief, exposure and attitude, and belief and attitude? To test all the possible causal combinations of these three variables, nine different models had to be constructed for each of the three panel waves. This had to happen three times because of the three different levels of need for orientation we are using in this study. So, in all, a total of 81 causal models had to be tested.

In order to decide which of the models revealed plausible causal priorities, we used the algorithm of PATHEVAL. PATHEVAL was designed by Watt to evaluate the structure of causal models. Watt (1979: 8) describes his test procedure as follows:

> The basic assumption of linearity in causal models allows one to compute the total effect of one variable on another by just adding the path values for all the different paths by which they are coordinated. When one has done this, the result is an estimate of the zero-order correlation, based on the assumptions of the causal diagram, and the estimates of the structural coefficients. If the structure of the relationships among variables is accurately represented by the causal diagram, this value should correspond to the observed zero-order correlation. Values which are substantively different from the observed values indicate that the structure of the causal model is not supported by the observed data.

In other words, discrepancies between original and regenerated correlation coefficients identify models that are implausible. For each model, Watt's test produces a summary statistic showing the goodness of fit of the causal structure.

## FINDINGS

Similar to the results of the Quarles and Schoenbach study (1982), all 81 different models of causal relationships *within* the three campaign stages proved to be plausible, thus showing again that significant paths between two variables at a time can be interpreted as reciprocal. The path model for all respondents is, in spite of a slight change in its variables (see above), almost identical with the one Quarles and Schoenbach obtained in 1982 (see Figure 7.2). They described this model as showing "very little evidence for the idea that communication, beliefs and attitudes are distinct entities capable of producing changes at later points in time independently of the other elements of the cognitive system." (Quarles and Schoenbach, 1982: 8). There are some interesting processes *within* the stages of the campaign, however. Before the election campaign, there is a slight mutual dependency of attitude and belief (.14). This dependency becomes somewhat stronger at the height of the campaign (.16) and includes the extent of exposure to communication. After the election, this more consistent cognitive system vanishes completely.

Figures 7.3, 7.4, and 7.5 show what happens to this "bonding and dissolution" process if we differentiate voters according to the level of subjectively felt need for orientation at the beginning of the election campaign. We can see an interesting contrast between the low need for orientation group (Figure 7.4) and the moderate need for orientation group (Figure 7.3). Only in the moderate group respondents does the hypothesized cognitive bonding at the end of the campaign take place (see Figure 7.3).

*The "uninterested."* These respondents considering themselves to be ignorant about European issues and not planning to do anything about it show a fairly strong consistency of their perceived salience of European politics, their attitude toward the European Community, and their exposure to campaign communication shortly before election day.

In other words, the probability that at the end of the campaign a person considers European politics an important topic, evaluates the

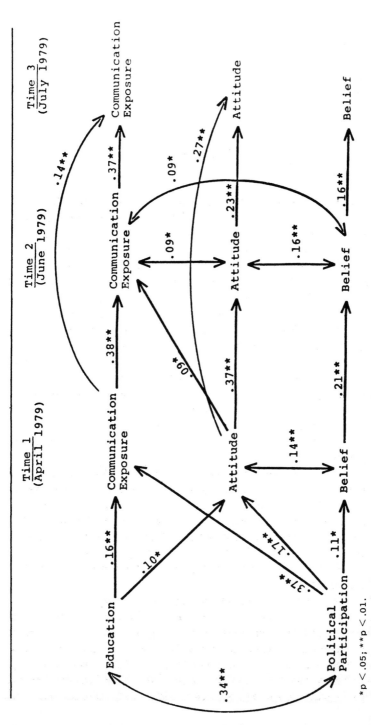

Figure 7.2 Path Analysis Results for All Voters (Significant Path Coefficients) (n = 459)

*p < .05; **p < .01.

European Community in a positive way, and uses more campaign materials is considerably higher in the uninterested group than in the rest of our panel respondents. And the bonding of the uninterested voters is mainly due to the variation in their perceived salience of European politics, which shows no significant autocorrelation over time. This salience changes freely and probably becomes easily associated with the attitude toward the Community and the campaign communication behavior.

*The Informed.* The low need for orientation group also contains some hints of a consistent cognitive system (see Figure 7.4). We find bonding of the attitude and the belief, but it already exists at the beginning of the campaign (.15). The campaign itself does not change anything about it, only the period *after* election day dissolves it. In general, "low need for orientation" people have the most static cognitive system. The autocorrelations in this group are particularly high, indicating that there is less change over time than in other groups. Surprisingly, these autocorrelations showing the resistance of the "informed" against change are even greater in the campaign period than after the election.

*The Curious.* Our third group, the curious persons with a high need for orientation, yields a completely different picture. This group is never bonded, not even in separate parts of their cognitive system (see Figure 7.5). This is due partly to their stable communication behavior and attitude toward the European Community expressed in high autocorrelations. But even their more changeable beliefs regarding the importance of European political issues are not associated with the other two components (political attitudes and exposure to campaign communication). In this subgroup, however, we find evidence for time-lag effects of the elements of our model on each other. A positive attitude at time 1 leads to more communication exposure at time 2 (.16) and to a greater salience of European issues at time 3 (.27). Moreover, a higher salience of European issues before the start of the campaign decreases the exposure to campaign material at time 2 (–.18), meaning that the few people who considered European politics as important even before the campaign started obviously became disappointed (or satisfied that they had enough information) and reduced their information activities. This is not terribly surprising, because "curious" voters with strong awareness of European issues must have noticed that the campaign exaggerated the importance of European politics considerably. Compared to the two other groups, their communication behavior is most strongly determined by their education and political participation, indicating that they could hardly be overwhelmed by the "environment of messages" (Savage, 1981) of the election.

*(text continues on page 172)*

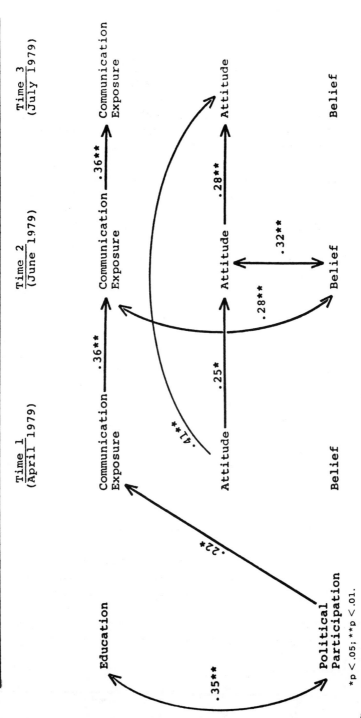

Figure 7.3 Path Analysis for "Uninterested" Voters (n = 95)

*p < .05; **p < .01.

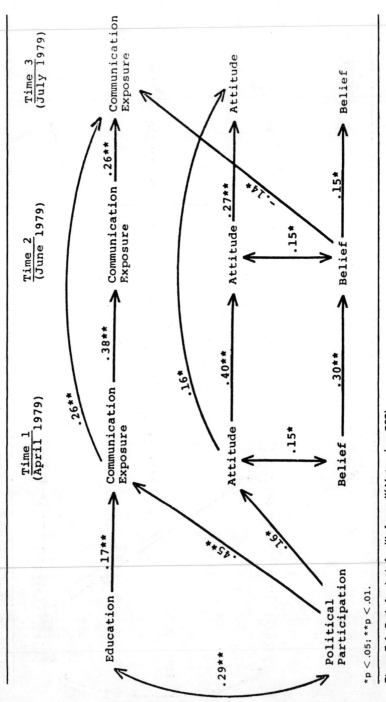

Figure 7.4 Path Analysis for "Informed" Voters (n = 202)

*p < .05; **p < .01.

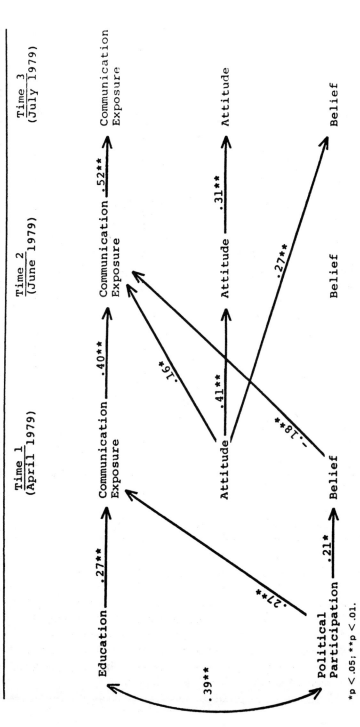

Figure 7.5  Path Analysis Results for "Curious" Voters (n = 162)

*p < .05; **p < .01.

## CONCLUSIONS

This study reveals an important modification of Quarles and Shoenbach's (1982) finding that one effect of a political campaign is "cognitive bonding," an increase of the consistency of different cognitive elements. After a partitioning of all respondents according to their need for orientation, only the most ignorant and uninterested group of voters showed cognitive bonding to a significant extent. The two other investigated groups—people who consider themselves informed and those who feel they are ignorant but who want to do something about it, are not pushed toward a more consistent cognitive system by the European campaign. The informed are hardly influenced at all, and the curious reveal some time-lagged effects due to preexisting attitudes and beliefs.

Bonding, it seems, is a surprise effect of this campaign. Voters who did not care about their cognitions were bonded most easily. They apparently were overwhelmed by the abundance and the omnipresence of campaign communication material providing them with information that they were not ready and willing to resist. As soon as this abundant information was missing—after the campaign—their cognitive system broke apart as quickly as it was constructed.

Quite different patterns existed for those voters who claimed to be informed (those with little uncertainty). They were fairly unimpressed by what was happening during the campaign. They held strong opinions that could not be changed much during a short period of time. The curious voters, on the other hand, were affected more easily, but in a different way. Compared to the uninterested with whom they shared uncertainty but not lack of interest, the curious voters showed effects over time not caused by communication behavior (at least not by the communication exposure measured in our study) but rather by preexisting attitudes and beliefs. They were not greatly influenced by the many pieces of information surrounding them, but rather designed their communication behavior carefully according to their attitudes and beliefs.

These results suggest the necessity of a different approach to explaining the effects of political campaigns. Schoenbach (1984), in his proposal for a "dynamic-transactional" model of media impact, points out that it may be wrong to look for *the* "dominant paradigm" of media effects. There seem to be different conditions under which different models provide the best possible explanation, rendering it rather pointless to push either the stimulus-response approach or the uses and gratifications model as the only way to describe the process of media effects. Either model can be fruitful in a specific situation. In most situations, however, combinations of *both* approaches are the most promising idea to explain effects.

In our study, we demonstrate that there are differential campaign effects depending on the amount of need for orientation voters feel in such a campaign. As in previous studies, the concept of need for orientation reveals considerable power as a contingent condition. In our case, however, as opposed to earlier studies mentioned above, it does not only specify *quantitative* differences in voters' susceptibility to the message of a campaign, but also indicates *qualitative* differences in *what* is happening. Uncertainty about the issues of the campaign combined with interest in being informed produces effect mechanisms that might best be explained by a motivational approach such as the uses-and-gratifications model. These voters show some selective exposure to communication in order to satisfy their needs.

The impact of a campaign on voters both uncertain and uninterested, on the other hand, looks more like a direct "trap" effect. The uninterested group does not care and therefore gets "trapped" in a highly communicative situation that leads to increased bonding of their cognitive systems. As soon as this situation is over, however, the short-lived nature of the impact of a campaign becomes evident.

This finding is not identical, but similar, to the results of agenda-setting studies by McLeod et al. (1974) and by Iyengar et al. (1983) mentioned earlier. Both studies found that more interested persons were *less* prone to agenda-setting effects. McLeod and his colleagues explain this finding by postulating that the less interested bring less structured personal agendas to the campaign and therefore are more susceptible to media influence. Iyengar and his colleagues employ a similar line of reasoning—that more interested media users tend to have more elaborate and strongly held judgments about public affairs, even though they assimilate and retain a greater amount of news than the less interested. Iyengar et al. (1983) also find that those viewers who are less able or willing to counterargue with a news presentation are more susceptible to agenda-setting effects, and counterarguing is significantly higher among the more interested and attentive viewers and among those with more political knowledge. In short, Iyengar and his associates conclude that media effects appear to be mediated not by the information that viewers recall, but rather by the covert evaluations triggered by the news presentations.

These findings are reasonably consistent with ours and they have important consequences for the design of political campaigns. Those who feel ignorant or uncertain obviously are the natural target group of a campaign, but one subgroup of these persons is particularly open to be affected—those who are not highly interested or attentive. In low-key campaigns especially, such as the one for the European Parliament where not very much is at stake, this group is most likely to be affected both cognitively and attitudinally because of a lack of critical information processing. Without the interest and knowledge to counterargue internally, a paradox is created: the *less relevant* the campaign is (the less people want to know about it) and the *more information* it produces, the greater its effects, at least in the short run.

# NOTES

1. The other items read (scores in parentheses) as follows:

"I stay informed about political events." (2)

"I often talk about politics with other people." (3)

"There are some political issues about which I have a strong opinion that I stand for publicly." (4)

"There are some political issues about which I look for information particularly thoroughly." (5)

"Occasionally, I attend speeches, discussions, and meetings about political issues." (6)

"Before the last national election or in other election campaigns I stood up for a political party or a candidate." (7)

This Guttman scale has a coefficient of reproducibility of .84.

2. See also the distinction Hovland et al. (1953: 7) make between "opinions" and "facts" (both are perceptions but the latter are easier to verify), on the one hand, and "attitudes," on the other ("responses which are oriented toward approaching or avoiding a given object, person, group, or symbol").

3. In previous studies employing need for orientation (see especially Weaver, 1980: 364-365), the measure has had four distinct categories: (1) low uncertainty-low relevance, (2) low uncertainty-high relevance, (3) high uncertainty-low relevance, and (4) high uncertainty-high relevance. Our measure in this study combines the first two categories into one (the informed voters, or those who feel little uncertainty) because these persons were not asked what they would do to learn more about European issues (our measure of relevance for those who expressed uncertainty) and because a separate analysis with another measure of relevance (willingness to sacrifice for another European country with economic difficulties) showed no differences in patterns of relationships between those who would sacrifice (n = 88) and those who would not (n = 114), as compared to all low uncertainty voters (the informed, n = 202). In other words, the level of relevance of European issues made no difference in patterns of relationships between communication exposure, attitudes, and beliefs for those with low uncertainty about these issues, but

relevance did make a difference for those with high uncertainty (the uninterested and the curious). Thus we report path analysis results for only three subgroups of voters in this study—the informed (low uncertainty), the uninterested (high uncertainty-low relevance), and the curious (high uncertainty-high relevance). (See Figure 7.1.)

# REFERENCES

AJZEN, I. and M. FISHBEIN (1980) Understanding Attitudes and Predicting Social Behavior. Englewood Cliffs, NJ: Prentice-Hall.

ATKIN, C. (1973) "Instrumental utilities and information seeking," in P. Clarke (ed.) New Models for Mass Communication Research. Beverly Hills, CA: Sage.

BECKER, L., J. McLEOD, and M. McCOMBS (1975) "The development of political cognitions," in S. Chaffe (ed.) Political Communication: Issues and Strategies for Research. Beverly Hills, CA : Sage.

BERLYNE, D. E. (1960) Conflict, Arousal and Curiousity. New York, McGraw-Hill.

BLUMLER, J. G. (1983) (ed.) Communicating to Voters: Television in the First European Parliamentary Elections. Beverly Hills, CA: Sage.

———(1979) "The role of theory in uses and gratification studies." Communication Research 6: 9-36.

CHAFFEE, S. H. and J. M. McLEOD (1973) "Individual vs. social predictors of information seeking." Journalism Quarterly 50: 237-245.

DENNIS, J., S. H. CHAFFEE, and S. Y. CHOE (1979) "Impact on partisan, image and issue voting," in S. Kraus (ed.) The Great Debates: Carter vs. Ford, 1976. Bloomington, IN: Indiana University Press.

ERBRING, L., E. GOLDENBERG, and A. MILLER (1980) "Front-page news and real-world cues: a new look at agenda-setting by the media." American Journal of Political Science 24: 16-49.

FISHBEIN, M. and I. AJZEN (1975) Belief, Attitude, Intention and Behavior. Reading, MA: Addison-Wesley.

FRUEH, W. and K. SCHOENBACH (1982) "Der dynamisch-transaktionale ansatz." Publizistik 27: 74-88.

HAWKINS, C. K. and J. T. LANZETTA (1965) "Uncertainty, importance and arousal as determinants of pre-decisional information search." Psychological Reports 17: 791-800.

HOVLAND, C. I., I. L. JANIS, and H. H. KELLEY (1953) Communication and Persuasion. New Haven, CT: Yale University Press.

IYENGAR, S., M. PETERS, and M. KINDER (1983) "Experimental demonstrations of the 'not-so-minimal' consequences of television news programs," in E. Wartella and D. C. Whitney (eds.) Mass Communication Review Yearbook (vol. 4). Beverly Hills, CA: Sage.

JONES, E. E. and H. B. GERARD (1967) Foundations of Social Psychology. New York: John Wiley.

LAVIDGE, R. J. and G. A. STEINER (1961) "A model for predictive measurements of advertising effectiveness." Journal of Marketing 25: 59-62.

LAZARSFELD, P. F., B. BERELSON, and H. GAUDET (1944) The People's Choice. New York: Columbia University Press.

McCOMBS, M. and D. WEAVER (1973) "Voters' need for orientation and use of mass communication." Presented to the annual conference of the International Communication Association, Montreal.

McGUIRE, W. J. (1974) "Psychological motives and communication gratification," in J. G. Blumler and E. Katz (eds.) The Uses of Mass Communications: Current Perspectives on Gratifications Research. Beverly Hills, CA: Sage.

McLEOD, J. M., L. BECKER, and J. BYRNES (1974) "Another look at the agenda-setting function of the press." Communication Research 1: 131-166.

QUARLES, R. C. and K. SCHOENBACH (1982) "Cognitive systems during political campaigns: bonding and dissolution." Presented to the Theory and Methodology Division, Association for Education in Journalism, Athens, Ohio.

SAVAGE, R. L. (1981) "From selective distortion through minimal effects to media election: four decades of media/voting research." Political Communication Review 6: 1-12.

SCHOENBACH, K. (1984, May) "The dynamic-transactional approach: a new paradigm of media effects." Presented at the 34th Annual Conference of the International Communication Association, San Francisco.

———(1983) Das unterschaetzte Medium: Politische Wirkungen von Presse und Fernsehen in Vergleich. Munich: Saur.

———and R. C. QUARLES (1983) "Kognitive harmonisierung im Wahlkampf." Rundfunk und Fersehen 31: 101-110.

TOLMAN, E. C. (1932) Purposive Behavior in Animals and Men. East Norwalk, CT: Appleton-Century-Crofts.

WATT, J. (1979) "Evaluating causal models." Presented to the Association for Education in Journalism, Houston.

WEAVER, D. (1984) "Media agenda-setting and public opinion: Is there a link?" in R. Bostrom (ed.) Communication Yearbook 8. Beverly Hills, CA: Sage.

———(1980) "Audience need for orientation and media effects." Communication Research 7: 361-376.

———(1977) "Political issues and voter need for orientation," in D. Shaw and M. McCombs (eds.) The Emergence of American Political Issues. St. Paul: West.

———D. GRABER, M. McCOMBS, and C. EYAL (1981) Media Agenda-Setting in a Presidential Election: Issues, Images, and Interest. New York: Praeger.

WEAVER, D., M. McCOMBS, and C. SPELLMAN (1975) "Watergate and the media: a case study of agenda-setting." American Politics Quarterly 3: 458-472.

WESTLEY, B. and L. BARROW (1959) "An investigation of news seeking behavior." Journalism Quarterly 36: 431-438.

Chapter 8

# PERSONAL RELEVANCE AND CAMPAIGN INFORMATION SEEKING
## A Cognitive
## Response-Based Approach

Richard M. Perloff

STUDENTS OF political behavior have long been interested in understanding what motivates individuals to think about politics. Democratic theory assumes that the public must be capable of conceptualizing political issues at some basic level; and consequently theorists have sought to discover the variables that motivate more systematic or "reasoned" political thinking (Downs, 1957; Converse, 1964, 1975).

Much of the research on political cognition has been guided by social psychological theories of attitude change. The earliest works on political thinking—such as those of Lane (1962) or Campbell et al. (1960)—were heavily influenced by affective or motivational approaches to attitude, such as those of Adorno et al. (1950), Smith et al. (1956), Festinger (1957), and even Freud (1959). However, as the field has become more cognitive and increasingly has emphasized the mental structure of voters' political attitudes (e.g., Feldman and Conover, 1984), these theories have proved to be inadequate. Newer, more cognitive theories of persuasion and attitude change are required if we are to understand

AUTHOR'S NOTE: I appreciate the assistance provided by Donna Rouner, Jack Suvak, Pam Kalis, and Therese Killen at various stages of this project. The study reported in this chapter was funded in part by a grant from the Graduate School at Cleveland State University.

the subtle influences of motivation on the development of political beliefs, attitudes, and behaviors.

One approach that appears initially promising is the cognitive response model of persuasion (Perloff and Brock, 1980; Petty and Cacioppo, 1981; Petty et al., 1981). According to this view, individuals actively respond to persuasive messages, counterarguing with those with which they disagree and elaborating favorably upon those with which they agree. As cognitive response studies have consistently shown, messages change attitudes when they contain arguments that elicit favorable cognitive responses, and they inhibit attitude change when the arguments evoke unfavorable mental reactions.

Recently, Petty and Cacioppo (1981) applied the cognitive response approach to information processing, arguing that there are two routes to attitude change: a central route, in which information is processed deeply and systematically; and a peripheral path, which is characterized by relatively effortless cognitive processing. Petty and Cacioppo argued that an important determinant of which route individuals use to process persuasive messages is their motivational state.

According to the cognitive response model, when people perceive that an issue is highly involving or highly relevant to them personally, they should process information deeply and systematically, or via "the central route." In other words, when individuals believe that an issue bears directly on their own lives, they will be motivated to devote the time and mental energy that is required to formulate a cogent position on the issue. Even if individuals initially disagree with the position being advocated, they may change their minds about the issue, provided the message contains enough compelling arguments to convince them that it is in their self-interest to adopt the advocated position.

On the other hand, when individuals perceive that an issue is of little personal consequence, they should adopt a more peripheral processing strategy. Under circumstances where individuals perceive that the issue has little bearing on their own lives, they should lack the motivation to systematically process message arguments. Instead, they should focus on such easily processed cues as the credibility or speaking style of the source, or they should focus on such well-learned scripts as "Faster speakers are more believable," or "Expert sources know what they're talking about." A number of recent laboratory studies have supported the cognitive response model (Chaiken, 1980; Petty and Cacioppo, 1984; Petty et al., 1981). These findings are generally consistent with research on social perception which has found that people process information more deeply and systematically when they perceive that it is personally relevant (Greenwald, 1980; Rogers et al., 1977).

These findings have interesting implications for research on political persuasion inasmuch as they concretely suggest how motivations can influence the processing of political messages. Based in part on cognitive response research, Perloff (1984) recently proposed a cognitive processing model of political involvement. According to this view, voters should process political information more deeply and perhaps systematically when they perceive that issues are personally relevant, whereas they should adopt a more short-circuited processing strategy under conditions of low personal relevance. In his 1984 paper, Perloff suggested additional implications for political persuasion and proposed a number of other effects that personal relevance might exert on political cognitions and behavior.

The purpose of this chapter is to take a first empirical stab at these issues and to outline some theoretical implications that follow from the data-collecting effort. The study reported in this chapter is designed with two purposes in mind. The study is designed, first, to shed light on the nature of the issues that voters perceive to be personally relevant.[1] Although personal relevance has been manipulated in the laboratory, it has received only limited attention in field studies of political communication. Those studies that have focused on the personal relevance of political issues have tended to equate personal relevance (or personal involvement) with extremity of initial attitude (Sherif and Hovland, 1961; Sherif et al., 1965). However, this may not always be true, and one of the purposes of this chapter is to take a look at which political issues people find personally relevant in the real world, and why.

Second, this study seeks to test for the first time a model of political cognition and political information seeking that is based in part on cognitive response research (Perloff, 1984). Based on this view, one might reasonably expect that when voters perceive that issues bear directly on their own lives, they will believe that their own interest will be best served by actively following the campaign in the political media. By the same logic, one might expect that when voters perceive issues to be relevant to them personally, they will be more motivated to formulate topic-relevant and policy-based thoughts about the candidates. Given the difficulty of adequately assessing cognitive processes in political surveys, this study will not focus directly on political information processing, although processing implications will be discussed where appropriate.

Finally, this chapter will theorize about several possible interrelationships between the cognitive response approach and the literature on self-interested political behavior. Cognitive response-based models of message processing and persuasion emphasize the effects of personal relevance, yet this too has been a focus of research on self-interest and symbolic politics (see Kiewet, 1981; Sears et al., 1980). In the past, these two research areas generally have been regarded as separate and unrelated approaches to the study of attitudes and persuasion. However, there are a number of interesting intersections between the cognitive response approach and the literature on self-interested behavior that merit scholarly attention.

The findings reported in this chapter are based on a survey of residents of Cleveland, Ohio, and its surrounding suburbs conducted during the 1984 Ohio presidential primary campaign. The first section of the chapter will explore the issues that respondents perceived to be personally relevant, and why; the second portion of the chapter will discuss the relationships between personal issue concerns and both political cognitions and campaign information-seeking behavior. The final portion of the chapter will relate the cognitive approach (Perloff, 1984) on which this study is based to the larger literature on self-interested political behavior.

## THE PERSONAL RELEVANCE OF POLITICAL ISSUES

### METHOD

A computer-generated random digit dialing procedure provided a list of all possible telephone numbers for residents of Cuyahoga County, Ohio (Cleveland and its surrounding suburbs). Student interviewers contacted respondents by phone to arrange a time for a 45-minute in-person interview. A total of 141 Cuyahoga County, Ohio, residents participated in the study.

*Measures.* Personal relevance was assessed by asking respondents to indicate to what extent each of 14 campaign issues affected them personally. The issues, which were selected through extensive pretesting, included inflation, income tax cuts, the size of the federal deficit, unemployment rates, economic recovery in northeast Ohio, social security, U. S. policy in Central America and the Chances for arms reduction talks between the United States and Soviet Union. Responses ranged from "affects me personally not at all" (1) to "affects me personally a lot" (7).

Liberalism-conservatism, party affiliation, and strength of party affiliation were assessed by several standard ISR/CPS questions. In order to determine whether perceiving political issues as personally relevant could be separated from extremity of political attitudes, it was necessary also to devise measures of attitude extremity. The liberal-conservative scale was transformed from a measure of direction of political attitudes to a measure of extremity of political attitudes by changing the scores assigned to the various responses. When the scale was used as a measure of extremity of attitudes, respondents received a score of either a very conservative response (originally a 7) or a very liberal response (originally a 1), and so forth.

Measurement of the extremity of attitudes toward the presidential candidates was based on responses to the SRC/CPS feeling thermometer question. Thermometer measures were included for each of the four major presidential candidates who appeared on the ballot in the 1984 Ohio primary: Gary Hart, Jesse Jackson, and Walter Mondale, who competed for the Democratic nomination, and Ronald Reagan, who was uncontested for the Republican nomination. Responses to the thermometer scales were scored so that both an extremely positive response, such as 100, and an extremely negative attitude, such as a 0, received a score of 50. The next responses, a 99 and a 1, were recorded as 49; a 2 and 98 received a 48, and so forth to 50, which was recorded as 0.

## RESULTS

Before discussing the results, it is useful to describe briefly the demographics of the sample. The average age of respondents was 43 years old. The sample was almost entirely (95 percent) white; 60 percent of the respondents were male and 40 percent were female. An income of under $10,000 per year was reported by 20 percent; 24 percent reported that they earned between $10,000 and $20,000, 34.7 percent earned between $21,000 and $35,000, 15 percent indicated that their salary was between $35,000 and $50,000, and 6 percent reported an income above $50,000. Finally, 45 percent of the sample identified themselves as Democrats, 27 percent considered themselves Republicans, and 28 percent said that they were Independents. This closely reflects national statistics on political party affiliation (Gallup Poll, 1984).

In order to discover the types of political issues that voters perceived to be personally relevant, a factor analysis was performed on respondent's personal self-relevance scores. A principal components analysis was performed using varimax rotation. Only items that loaded at or above .6 were used in further analyses. Two items were therefore

**TABLE 8.1**
**Varimax Rotated Factor Loadings of Principal Component**
**Analysis of Personal Relevance of Political Issues**

| Item | Type of Personal Relevance | | | |
|---|---|---|---|---|
| | *Factor 1* | *Factor 2* | *Factor 3* | *Factor 4* |
| U.S. policy in Central America | .84 | −.07 | .06 | .28 |
| U.S. policy in Middle East | .88 | .02 | −.02 | .16 |
| Chances for nuclear arms reduction talks | .72 | .25 | .19 | −.01 |
| Amount of money allocated to national defense | .69 | .27 | .22 | −.12 |
| Inflation rates | .32 | .74 | .09 | .09 |
| Personal income taxes | .02 | .88 | .02 | .06 |
| Interest rates | .07 | .77 | .14 | .10 |
| Amount of money allocated to Social Security | .04 | .19 | .84 | −.10 |
| Funding for Health and Human Services | .27 | .07 | .72 | .24 |
| Opportunities for minorities | .09 | −.01 | .62 | .28 |
| Unemployment rates | .10 | .10 | .23 | .83 |
| Economic recovery | .13 | .35 | .01 | .73 |
| Percentage of common variance | 33.7 | 13.5 | 10.9 | 8.7 |

NOTE: Factor 1 = personal relevance of foreign affairs; factor 2 = personal relevance of economic issues; factor 3 = personal relevance of social services; factor 4 = personal relevance of unemployment. Items that did not load at .60 or above on a factor were deleted from this table; n = 134; n in tables reflects missing data.

deleted—U. S. crime rates and the size of the federal deficit. Four factors emerged, accounting for 66.8 percent of the variance (see Table 8.1).

The first factor, perceived self-relevance of foreign affairs, accounted for the most variance (33.7 percent). Four items loaded on this factor, reflecting personal concern about United States policy in Central America, U. S. policy in the Middle East, the chances for nuclear arms reduction talks between the United States and the Soviet Union, and the amount of money allocated to national defense.

The second factor, perceived self-relevance of general economic issues, represented respondents' perceptions that inflation, amount of personal income taxes, and interest rates affected them personally. Perceived self-relevance of social services, the third factor, reflected personal concern about social security, the amount of money allocated to health and human services, and opportunities for blacks and other minorities. Finally, perceived self-relevance of unemployment reflected respondents' beliefs that they were affected personally by unemployment rates and by economic recovery in northeast Ohio.

None of the four personal relevance factors were significantly associated with having either extremely positive or extremely negative attitudes toward the four presidential candidates, or with extremity of political attitudes (having extremely liberal or extremely conservative attitudes). Thus, contrary to what social judgment theorists generally have argued, individuals can perceive that political issues affect them personally and fall at varying points on the political spectrum.

## THE MEANING OF PERSONAL RELEVANCE

What does it mean to believe that foreign affairs, economic issues, social services, and unemployment are personally relevant? Two different interpretations are suggested by previous research (e.g., Sears et al., 1980; Bobo, 1983). Voters' personal concerns may have their roots in self-interest or the belief that issues affect their short-term material, economic, or physical well-being (Sears et al., 1980); or in ideology. Ideology is used loosely here to refer to somewhat enduring political predispositions, global issue concerns, values, and affective responses to salient symbols.[2] In the context of the present study, an individual might perceive that social services are personally relevant for self-interested reasons if he or she receives money from Medicare or Social Security; on the other hand, a voter could be personally concerned about social services for ideological reasons, believing that budget cuts in human service programs are unfair and unjust or that the government is spending too much money on wasteful social programs. Or a voter might perceive that unemployment was personally relevant for self-interested reasons if he or she was currently laid off; more ideologically based concerns would be apparent if the individual made reference to a traditional liberal dissatisfaction with federal spending priorities or to humanitarian values that included compassion for the unemployed in northeast Ohio. A self-interested concern about foreign affairs would reflect worries about relatives or friends in Central America or the Middle East (Lau et al.,1978) or about the prospect of a draft or a war that would affect the respondent or his or her family in the short term. A more global and ideologically based concern would be reflected in statements about America's image abroad, or the need for peace in a nuclear age or in more abstract conceptions of the role of the United States in international affairs.

Two strategies were employed to determine whether these factors reflected predominantly self-interested or more global, ideological concerns. First, Pearson product moment correlations were computed between the summed items that loaded on each factor and both demographic and ideological measures. Second, a convenience sample of 23 additional respondents was interviewed in-depth to determine why voters perceived the four sets of issues to be personally relevant. These individuals were approached, for the most part, in shopping malls and were asked to indicate how personally relevant they believed issues from each of the factors were, and why. Two coders classified their responses as to whether they reflected self-interest, global ideological concerns, or both. The convenience sample was roughly comparable to the random sample with respect to demographic characteristics.

The responses of both the convenience and the random samples suggested that two of the factors clearly reflected self-interested concerns, whereas the other two were more ideological. Personal concern about economic issues was the most self-interested factor. It was not significantly associated with liberalism-conservatism, party identification, or the strength of party affiliation. At the same time, middle-aged respondents perceived economic issues to be more personally relevant than did older or younger individuals $[F(2,131) = 4.62, p < .01]$. Middle-aged consumers can probably more easily afford durable consumer goods (such as a car or a house), the prices of which are influenced by inflation and interest rates. In addition, when we asked our convenience sample why they felt that they were (or were not) affected by economic issues, 95 percent gave self-interested reasons (i.e., affects cost of living for them and their families).

Personal concern about unemployment also seemed to have a stronger basis in perceived self-interest than in ideology. The dynamics underlying personal concern about unemployment were somewhat more complicated, however. Among randomly sampled respondents, perceiving unemployment as personally relevant was significantly, if modestly, associated with being more liberal $(r = -.21, p < .01)$ and with being a strong rather than a weak Democrat $[t(53) = 2.11, p < .04]$. Although this suggests that personal concern about unemployment has its roots in ideology, there are compelling reasons to believe that it has a stronger basis in self-interest.

Although concern about unemployment in the random sample did not vary as a function of income, younger and middle-aged respondents perceived unemployment to be more relevant personally than did older individuals, who are less likely to have or to be seeking steady jobs $[F(2,131) = 15.10, p < .0001]$. Indeed, age accounted for more variance in personal concern about unemployment than it did for any of the other three factors. Moreover, when convenience sample respondents were asked why they felt that they were or were not affected by unemployment and the recovery in northeast Ohio, 70 percent replied in self-interested terms (e.g., "I may be looking for a job around here").

In contrast, perceiving that foreign affairs is personally relevant seemed to reflect more global ideological concerns. Greater personal concern about foreign affairs was associated with liberalism ($r = -.29$, p $< .001$) and with being a stronger rather than a weaker Republican [$t(31)$ = 2.22, p $< .03$]. Thus, voters along both ends of the political spectrum perceived that foreign affairs was relevant to them personally. Moreover, 70 percent of our convenience sample respondents replied in ideological terms when they were asked why they believed that foreign affairs was or was not personally relevant (e.g., "It bothers me that America has that kind of image"). Interestingly, there were no income, education, or age differences in concern about foreign affairs.

Finally, personal concern about social services seemed to be based primarily, but not exclusively, on ideological concerns. Democrats were more likely than Republicans to report that they were personally concerned about social services [$t(86) = 2.02$, p $< .03$]. In addition, it is difficult to explain on grounds other than ideology why this almost entirely white sample would be personally concerned about opportunities for blacks and other minorities. On the other hand, the convenience sample tended to split evenly on whether they perceived that social services were relevant for ideological or more self-interested reasons.[3]

The existence of four different types of personal issue concerns complicates predictions about the relationships between perceiving that issues are personally relevant and the processing of political information. A cognitive response-based approach to political information processing assigns central importance to perceived self-relevance, but as we have seen, in actual political settings issues can be perceived as personally relevant for self-interested or ideological reasons. A careful reading of cognitive response research suggests that self-relevance more closely corresponds to self-interest; indeed, the underlying theoretical assumption is that when individuals perceive that an issue will affect their own lives directly, they will believe that it is in their own self-interest to centrally process the arguments contained in the persuasive message. Based on this logic, it is suggested that only perceiving economic issues and unemployment as personally relevant should be associated with the quantity and quality of political cognitions and with the seeking of campaign information. On the other hand, it is more difficult to derive clear predictions about the relationships between the two more global, ideologically based concerns and the criterion variables. In the next section, we shall explore the relationships between all four personal issue concerns and both respondents' political cognitions and their information-seeking behavior.

## RELATIONSHIPS WITH POLITICAL COGNITIONS AND CAMPAIGN INFORMATION SEEKING

### SAMPLE

It was not feasible to ask open-ended questions of all the respondents; thus, 29 members of the sample were arbitrarily selected for more in-depth interviews. In addition, in order to increase the pool of open-ended response data, students were instructed to randomly select an individual who lived on their block and ask them both the closed-ended and open-ended questions; 30 individuals were interviewed in this manner and subsequent analyses indicated that they did not differ with the randomly sampled respondents on key demographic criteria. Altogether, 59 respondents were asked both open-ended and closed-ended questions.

### MEASURES

*Open-ended responses.* Three open-ended questions assessed voters' cognitions about the presidential candidates. Respondents were asked first to indicate if they planned to vote for one of the three Democratic presidential candidates, and why. The second question asked participants who they thought they would vote for in the general election, and why. The third set of questions, adapted from Weaver et al. (1983), instructed respondents to imagine that their friends had been away from the country for a while and asked them to describe the candidates and their issue positions. All three questions were followed up by probes. Two coders independently coded responses and agreed on whether it focused on one of the four issues, on a general aspect of the candidate's personality or image, or on the political party of the candidate. Two coders independently coded responses and agreed on the number of cognitions 93 percent of the time and on the type of cognitions 91 percent of the time.

Responses that concerned economic issues, unemployment, social services, or foreign affairs were classified as to whether they (1) focused on specific policy aspects of the issue; (2) referred to the issue in very general terms; (3) reflected group or self-interested responses; or (4) focused on relevant image attributes. Policy-oriented responses consisted of identifying the candidate's specific position on the issue or differentiating his position from another candidate's. For example, a policy-oriented response on economic issues would involve mentioning Reagan's supply-side position on economic recovery, whereas a policy-oriented response on foreign affairs would identify Hart's support of the nuclear freeze. In contrast, when a respondent said that Hart would bring more jobs to Ohio or that Reagan had improved the economy, these were coded as general issue responses. Personal or group-based self-interested responses were based on the respondent's perception that the candidate's position would adversely affect the self or that the candidate supported or opposed a large social group with which the respondent identified. An example of a group-based response on unemployment was "Hart understands the working man" or "Reagan helped put me out of a job"; on social services, it was exemplified by "Mondale promises to help older people" (like the respondent).

*Quantity of cognitions.* According to Perloff's political processing model, respondents who are most concerned about economic matters should give more economically based evaluations of the candidates than individuals least concerned about economic issues; analagously, one would also expect that respondents who are personally concerned about unemployment would be more likely than their less concerned counterparts cite unemployment and jobs as factors in their evaluations of the candidates.

The dependent variable for this analysis was the quantity of topic-relevant thoughts about the candidates that respondents were able to supply. This was assessed by calculating the proportion of responses that concerned the relevant issue divided by the total number of responses to the three open-ended questions.

*Policy-related cognitions.* If self-interest motivates respondents to develop an informed position on the topic, voters who are most concerned about an issue should be more likely to identify the candidates' specific policies on the issue than those who are least concerned about the issue. The dependent variable was the proportion of responses to the three open-ended questions that focused on the policy aspects of the issue.

*Statistics.* To compare the responses of individuals who perceived an issue to be highly relevant personally with those of persons who perceived the issue to be of little consequence, t-tests were conducted. Scores on the four perceived self-relevance factors were trichotomized. Thus, respondents whose scores on a factor ranked in the highest third were compared with individuals whose scores were in the lowest third.

## MEASURES OF INFORMATION SEEKING

A series of closed-ended questions tapped respondents' campaign information-seeking behavior. The questions tapped the following variables: interest in the 1984 election campaign, interpersonal discussion of the campaign, exposure to television and newspaper stories about national government and the presidential campaign, and attention to newspaper coverage of national government and the presidential campaign. Four gratifications sought from the campaign were also discussed: following the campaign to find out where the candidates stood on the issues, to learn about the weak points of the candidates, to see what the candidates were like as people, and to get into the excitement of the race. Effort expended in gaining information about the campaign from mass media was also assessed (see Rouner, 1983).

## AUXILIARY QUESTIONS

If perceiving that issues are personally relevant motivates more serious attention to campaign issues, one might expect that voters would be more psychologically involved in the election campaign when they perceive that issues will affect them personally. Therefore, several measures of involvement were included (e.g., Kaid, 1981; McLeod et al., 1979).

Psychological involvement in the 1984 election was measured by three sets of questions. Two seven-point scales tapped concern about the election. Respondents were asked how much they cared about the outcome of the 1984 election and how much the outcome of the election mattered to them. The second measure of involvement was conceptually similar to those developed by Krugman (1967). Respondents were instructed to ask themselves how closely they believed "me" was to the 1984 election on a 100-point scale where the election was located at 100.

(Individuals were also asked to indicate how close the 1984 election was to "issue emphasis.") Finally, if the perception that issues affect one personally causes voters to become ego-involved in an election campaign, there should be a significant correlation between perceived self-relevance of issues and the belief that one's *own* life would change if a Democrat or Ronald Reagan were elected president in 1984. These beliefs were assessed on a seven-point scale.

Four additional questions tapped behavioral involvement in the campaign (e.g., Milbraith and Goel, 1977). Respondents were asked how frequently they had engaged in four political activities during the primary campaign. These activities consisted of having passed out leaflets or campaign materials, wearing campaign buttons or displaying a bumper sticker, attending a political rally or dinner, or trying to influence someone else's voting decision. These questions were adapted from the SRC/CPS National Election Study questionnaire.

Pearson product-moment correlations were then computed between these four personal issue concerns and the various measures of involvement.

## RESULTS

### POLITICAL COGNITIONS

Only one of the four personal concerns was associated with having more topic-relevant (issue-specific) cognitions. Individuals who perceived that unemployment was highly personally relevant more frequently cited unemployment and jobs as factors in their evaluations of the candidates than did respondents least concerned about unemployment [$t(36) = 1.79$, $p < .05$]. In the light of these findings, it seemed reasonable to confine tests of the nature of respondents' policy-related cognitions as well as any auxilliary analyses to personal concern about unemployment.

Before discussing the findings on policy-related cognitions, it is useful to describe the results of several supplementary analyses of respondents' unemployment-related cognitions and attitudes. Among individuals most concerned about unemployment, the more they disagreed with Reagan's position on job programs the less they liked him ($r = -.55$, $p < .025$).[4] Among individuals least concerned about unemployment, a significantly lower and nonsignificant correlation was obtained (p = −.33, n.s.). There were no significant relationships between sharing views on job programs with the other candidates and holding positive attitudes toward them.) A subsequent analysis was conducted to determine whether proportion of unemployment-related cognitions mediated the relationship between sharing Reagan's views on the issue of federal jobs programs and attitude toward Reagan. However, there was no evidence that proportion of unemployment-related cognitions mediated the relationship between these two variables.

In addition, respondents who were most concerned about unemployment were not significantly more likely to cite the candidates' specific policies on unemployment or the revitalization of the Ohio economy as factors in their evaluation of the candidates. Thus, respondents who considered themselves Democrats did not say that they preferred one Democratic candidate over another because he had a more cogent plan to reduce unemployment or to stimulate economic recovery in northern Ohio, or to restrict Japanese imports. Instead, respondents who were personally concerned about unemployment tended to base their evaluations on rather general assessments of the candidates' positions on the issues ("Hart promises jobs"), on the perception that the candidate was on the side of larger social groups with which they seemed to identify (e.g., "Mondale will do the best job for the worker"; "Reagan's against the working guy"), or on image attributes ("Hart has charisma").

## CAMPAIGN INFORMATION SEEKING

The analyses of campaign communication provided little evidence that self-interested concerns about unemployment and economic issues were associated with more active seeking of campaign information (see Table 8.2).

In contrast, personal concern about foreign affairs was significantly associated with most of the measures of campaign interest and information seeking (e.g., exhibiting interest in the campaign, discussing campaign with other people, and with attention to the campaign in newspapers).

The same pattern emerged in the correlations between personal issue concerns and involvement in the primary campaign. Perceiving that economic issues or unemployment were personally relevant was not significantly associated with psychological or behavioral involvement in the election campaign. Personal concern about social services was not

TABLE 8.2
Zero-Order Correlations Between Personal Relevance of
Political Issues and Measures of Information Seeking
and Mass Media Use

| | Type of Personal Relevance | | | |
|---|---|---|---|---|
| Item | Foreign Affairs | Economic Issues | Social Services | Unemployment |
| Campaign interest | .34*** | .09 | .04 | .10 |
| Interpersonal discussion | .17* | −.07 | .13 | −.02 |
| Frequency of exposure to politics in newspapers | .15 | .12 | −.05 | .04 |
| Frequency of exposure to campaign in newspapers | .17* | −.02 | .09 | .03 |
| Attention to politics in newspaper | .24** | .10 | .04 | .00 |
| Attention to campaign in newspaper | .30*** | .09 | .13 | .07 |
| Frequency of national news exposure (TV) | .01 | .01 | −.02 | −.08 |
| Seeking information on candidate stands | .23** | .24** | .09 | .14 |
| Seeking information about candidates as people | .14 | .28*** | .11 | .08 |
| Seeking information on candidate weaknesses | .25** | .08 | .05 | .02 |
| Seeking excitement | .18 | −.03 | .08 | .06 |
| Effort in following campaign | .27*** | .11 | .07 | .08 |

NOTE: n = 134.
*p < 05; **p < 01; ***p < 001.

significantly correlated with the various measures of political involvement. In contrast, there were significant correlations between personal
concern about foreign affairs and caring about the outcome of the 1984
election, believing that it mattered who won the election, perceiving that
the election was "close to" the self and to issues, and with believing that
one's own life would change if either a Democrat or Ronald Reagan won
the election (see Table 8.3). Although the correlations were only modest,
the pattern was remarkably consistent.

## DISCUSSION

The starting point for this investigation was the laboratory research
on personal relevance. The results indicate that personal relevance takes

TABLE 8.3<br>
**Zero-Order Correlations Between Personal Relevance<br>
of Political Issues and Campaign Involvement**

| | Type of Personal Relevance | | | |
|---|---|---|---|---|
| *Item* | *Foreign Affairs* | *Economic Issues* | *Social Services* | *Unemployment* |
| Perceived closeness of election to self | .35*** | .07 | .07 | . .06 |
| Perceived closeness of election to issues | .23** | −.04 | −.06 | −.06 |
| Life change if Reagan reelected | .27*** | 13 | .12 | .14 |
| Life change if Democrat elected | .26** | .11 | .08 | .07 |
| Caring about '84 election | .37*** | .18* | .17* | .10 |
| Outcome of election matters | .30*** | .14 | .12 | .10 |
| Frequency of attending rallies | .26** | −.17* | .06 | −.02 |
| Frequency of wearing political insignia | .20** | −.21** | −.03 | .10 |
| Frequency of passing leaflets out | .09 | −.29*** | −.03 | −.02 |
| Frequency of trying to sway others' votes | .19* | −.10 | .13 | .19* |

NOTE: n = 134.
*p < 05; **p < 01; ***p < .001.

on different forms and more complex meanings in the real world than it does in the laboratory studies of personal relevance. People perceive that political issues affect them for two different types of reasons. Some issues are perceived as personally relevant primarily because they affect one's own material well-being (economic matters and unemployment), whereas other issues (foreign affairs and social services) seem to be relevant for more global, ideological reasons. These results (coupled with subsequent findings) definitely suggest that self-interested and ideologically based self-relevance are very different aspects of voters' political psychology.

None of the personal relevance factors were significantly associated with having either extremely positive or negative attitudes toward the four presidential candidates or with extremity of political attitudes. Thus, contrary to what social judgment theorists have generally maintained, individuals can perceive that political issues are highly relevant personally and fall at varying ends of the political spectrum.

Several other findings were also noteworthy. The federal deficit, which undoubtedly exerts an indirect impact on respondents' lives, did not load with other economic items. In addition, only a few of the demographic variables were associated with personal concern about political issues. This points up the importance of measuring self-relevance subjectively—by asking voters which issues they considered to affect them personally—rather than making assumptions about what they find important.

The existence of both self-interested and more global ideologically based concerns required that we take a closer look at the predictions that were generally derived from cognitive response research. A careful reading of the cognitive response studies suggested that personal relevance actually referred to perceived self-interest in a political communication context. Therefore, based on Perloff's (1984) cognitive response-based model, it could only clearly be predicted that personal concern about economic issues and unemployment would be associated with the pattern of respondents' political cognitions and information-seeking behavior. The results provided only limited support for these predictions.

Respondents who perceived economic issues as personally relevant were not significantly more likely than their least concerned counterparts to possess more economically related cognitions—that is, to evaluate the candidates in terms of where they stood on the economy. On the other hand, respondents who were most concerned about unemployment were more likely than their least concerned counterparts to cite unemployment and jobs as factors in their evaluations of the candidates. In addition, there was some evidence of "issue-based thinking" among a small sample of respondents who were most concerned about unemployment. The more that these individuals disagreed with Reagan's position on job programs, the less they liked him. At the same time, respondents who were most concerned about unemployment did not cite the candidates' specific policies on unemployment or concrete aspects of their plans for economic recovery as factors in their evaluations of the candidates.

Instead, respondents based their evaluations on general assessments of whether the candidate would or would not reduce unemployment or on their perception that the candidates were "good for" or "bad for" working people (or on relevant image attributes). It appears that respondents who were most personally concerned about these issues— particularly unemployment—adopted what might be called a self-interested processing strategy: They gave some thought as to whether the candidate would be beneficial to their own interests or to those of the larger group with which they identified, but they were not motivated to evaluate the candidates' specific positions on the issue or to actively seek out information from the mass media.

Nevertheless, these findings should be taken with caution. Voters typically are not as motivated to process campaign information in the primary as in the general election, and image information tends to dominate mass media coverage of the primary campaign (Patterson, 1980). Therefore, it would be useful to test the study's hypotheses in a general election campaign when voters are more motivated to process political messages and when candidates are somewhat more likely to clearly communicate their positions on the issues. In the final section of the chapter, conditions that might facilitate such processing are discussed.

At the same time, the present findings have strongly suggested that abstract ideologically based personal concerns play an important role in the seeking of political information. In a somewhat similar vein, Weatherford (1983) recently found that the most frequent followers of national news give more weight to abstract conceptions of overall business conditions, whereas infrequent media users place more emphasis on salient personal concerns. Why, in the present study, did personal concern about foreign affairs play such an important role in voters' political information seeking? One reason derives from the prominent position that foreign affairs occupied in national politics over the past several years. The death of American Marines in Lebanon, the United States's invasion of Grenada, and the escalating nuclear arms were the subject of considerable public debate. Thus, individuals concerned about foreign affairs may have been particularly likely to find themselves drawn into the political process and concerned about the election campaign. Alternatively, both concern about foreign affairs and political information seeking may have been caused by a third variable: long-standing interest in politics.

The data do not allow us to say which of these interpretations best account for the results. Nor, unfortunately, do the findings suggest why concern about foreign affairs was associated with more active information seeking, but not with the nature of respondent's political cognitions, whereas concern about unemployment showed the opposite pattern. One can only speculate that when individuals are concerned about unemployment they process information in a very narrow and parochial way. They evaluate a candidate partly on the basis of their beliefs as to whether his or her election will help or hurt their own interests; in the primary, at least, self-interest does not motivate a more systematic search of campaign information. In contrast, when individuals are concerned about more global foreign policy issues they process information in a more diffuse and "outward" fashion. When they evaluate a candidate, they do not focus in depth on his or her foreign policy positions, but on a variety of issues and attributes—yet concern about foreign affairs may motivate these voters to search the environment outside of themselves, for they report that they frequently use campaign media and that they are psychologically involved in the election campaign.

Yet, despite these interpretive difficulties and in spite of the limitations imposed by correlational analyses, the results have interesting implications, especially in light of recent research on ideology and symbolic politics (e.g., Sears et al., 1980). As noted above, the present findings provide a mixed picture of the relationships between self-interest and the pattern of respondents' political cognitions and their information-seeking behavior. In contrast, the data are quite consistent with the view that global, ideological concerns may underlie much of voters' political information-seeking behavior.

In the final section of this chapter, I will briefly review research that suggests several conditions under which self-interest *can* influence political behavior, and I will seek to integrate this line of research with the cognitive response model of persuasion. The focus of this discussion will be on the implications of cognitive response research for the processing and effects of persuasive political messages.

## SELF-INTEREST, SYMBOLIC POLITICS, AND COGNITIVE RESPONSES

In a series of intriguing studies, Sears and his colleagues have shown that ideologically based "symbolic" predispositions predict policy attitudes and voting behavior better than self-interest (Sears et al., 1980; Kinder and Kiewet, 1979; Lau et al., 1978). The picture is somewhat complicated, however, by evidence that self-interest will influence political behavior when voters perceive that the outcome of the election will have a particularly *strong and immediate* impact on their pocketbooks (e.g., Sears & Citrin, 1982) or their children's safety (e.g., Allen and Sears, 1979). Private needs and personal economic problems may also influence policy attitudes when voters attribute responsibility for these problems to the government (Brody and Sniderman, 1977; Feldman, 1982; see also Sears and Lau, 1983). Another condition under which self-interest may affect political behavior has been suggested recently by Bobo (1983). Bobo has argued that when self-interest is more broadly conceptualized so as to reflect individuals' long-term interest as members of a social group, it will significantly predict political attitudes and behavior.

From an information processing perspective, it is important to understand the cognitive processes that mediate the effects of self-interest on political behavior under these conditions. Cognitive response research suggests that under these conditions of self-interest, information should be processed more deeply or centrally; it should be linked up with a large number of elements in the individual's schema in a meaningful and functional way. Cognitive response analyses, as well as other approaches, should be useful in further elucidating these mediating processes. The cognitive response approach may also be useful in this context for it suggests the types of persuasive messages that should be maximally effective under high and low self-interest.

Applied to political persuasion, the cognitive response approach suggests that when individuals are high in such perceived self-interest, and are therefore motivated to deeply process message arguments, political advertisements will be most likely to change attitudes if they contain cogent arguments, compelling evidence, and other types of "issue appeals." A campaign based on images and visual appeals would be too superficial to sway self-interested voters. On the other hand, these more affective strategies would be very effective with voters who are low in perceived self-interest inasmuch as they lack the motivation to deeply process message arguments. Appeals that might be of particular impact on these voters would make use of classical conditioning, refer to subjective norms (through a list of media endorsements), or make statements that link the candidate or issue with positively valenced stimuli (such as political parties or influential leaders).

Although there have been no tests of these predictions in an actual electoral setting, existing studies of political communication provide indirect support for this cognitive response view (for a review, see Perloff, 1984). Moreover, preliminary evidence from a recent study of a Cleveland-area issue campaign provide some—albeit qualitative—support for this cognitive response model. In May, 1984, Cuyahoga County voters were asked to approve a property tax increase to finance a domed sports arena. The issue generated considerable interest among voters, and analyses of voters' open-ended reasons for supporting or opposing the dome revealed that individuals had a large and diverse number of thoughts about the issue.

Preliminary analyses suggested that there was little evidence that the quantity or complexity of cognitive responses was associated with standard indices of self-interest. Unfortunately, the questionnaire did not measure self-interest in the broader sense that Bobo (1983) has advocated. However, it seems plausible that one reason that respondents appeared to process the issue so deeply may have been that they perceived that it affected their long-term self-interest as Clevelanders. Unfortunately, advocates of the property tax to finance the dome adopted a slick and somewhat simple-minded advertising strategy that relied on visuals, endorsements, and simple appeals emphasizing "Jobs for Cleveland." Partly as a result of the opposition's issue-based campaign, in which they emphasized the cost and fairness of the tax, the property tax was defeated by a two-to-one margin.

It is interesting to speculate whether individuals will process political information differently, depending on the nature of their self-interest. One wonders whether voters might be more inclined to engage in a more active and systematic information search when their self-interest is long term rather than short term and concerns a social group to which they belong rather than their own private needs. The urgent demands that immediate personal problems, such as unemployment, inflation, and cuts in Medicare, place on individuals may make it difficult for them to engage in anything other than a short-circuited information search. On the other hand, when long-term rather than short-term interests are at stake and it is the social group, rather than the self, that is the victim (or beneficiary), individuals may be more able and motivated to process campaign information both deeply and systematically. According to this view, Hispanic voters (to take one example) may be more likely to carefully evaluate candidates' positions vis-à-vis the Hispanic community when they perceive that the campaign will bear on the long-term interests of Hispanic citizens rather than their own short-term personal needs. The impact of such personal concerns on the processing of persuasive political messages remains an interesting issue for future studies of political communication.

## NOTES

1. Researchers define issue involvement as the extent to which the issue is personally relevant or intrinsically important to the individual (Petty and Cacioppo, 1979, 1981). This chapter uses the term personal relevance rather than involvement for two reasons. First, it is the extent to which an issue is personally relevant that is manipulated in laboratory studies. Secondly, political involvement is a more general construct that has never been consistently defined or operationalized (see Kaid, 1981) possibly because it consists of several very different dimensions (Fiske and Kinder, 1981).

2. It is important to note that respondents could have ideologically based concerns and possess either sophisticated or unsophisticated ideological belief system, as Converse (1964) or Conover and Feldman (1984) might assess them.

3. Other samples, particularly those containing many older individuals, might very well perceive social services to be relevant for more self-interested reasons (see Iyengar and Kinder's chapter in this volume).

4. Expert judges—professors specializing in political communication—were asked to indicate where they believed the four candidates stood on five issues, including government aid to the unemployed, that were probed elsewhere in the survey. Judges ranked the candidates on five-point Likert scales; subsequent analyses revealed high agreement among judges on the candidates' positions on the issues (r = .98; see Perloff et al., (1984). The measure of agreement with the candidate reported in this section of the chapter was constructed by subtracting the respondent's own position on the issue from his or her perception of the candidate's position. Liking of the candidate was assessed by the feeling thermometer.

# REFERENCES

ADORNO, T. W., E. FRENKEL-BRUNSWIK, D. J. LEVINSON, and R. N. SANFORD (1950) The Authoritarian Personality. New York: Harper.

ALLEN, H. M., Jr. and D. O. SEARS (1979) "Against them or for me: community impact evaluations," pp. 171-175 in L. Datta and R. Perloff (eds.) Improving Evaluations. Beverly Hills, CA: Sage.

BOBO, L. (1983) "Whites' opposition to busing: symbolic racism or realistic group conflict?" Journal of Personality and Social Psychology 45: 1196-1210.

BRODY, R. A. and P. M. SNIDERMAN (1977) "From life space to polling place: the relevance of personal concerns for voting behavior." British Journal of Political Science 7: 337-360.

CAMPBELL, A., P. E. CONVERSE, W. E. MILLER, and D. E. STOKES (1960) The American Voter. New York: John Wiley.

CHAIKEN, S. (1980). "Heuristic versus systematic information processing and the use of source versus message cues in persuasion." Journal of Personality and Social Psychology 39: 752-766.

CONOVER, P. J. and S. FELDMAN (1984) "How people organize the political world: a schematic model." American Journal of Political Science 28: 95-126.

CONVERSE, P. E. (1975) "Public opinion and voting behavior," pp. 75-170 in F. I. Greenstein and N. W. Polsby (eds.) Handbook of Political Science (vol. 4). Reading, MA: Addison-Wesley.

———(1964) "The nature of belief systems in mass publics," in D. E. Apter (ed.) Ideology and Discontent. New York: Free Press.

DOWNS, A. (1957) An Economic Theory of Democracy. New York: Free Press.

FELDMAN, S. (1982) "Economic self-interest and political behavior." American Journal of Political Science 26: 446-466.

FESTINGER, L. (1957) A Theory of Cognitive Dissonance. Evanston, IL: Row, Peterson.

FISHBEIN, M. and I. AJZEN (1975) Beliefs, Attitude, Intention and Behavior: An Introduction to Theory and Research. Reading, MA: Addison-Wesley.

FISKE, S. and D. R. KINDER (1981) "Involvement, expertise and schema use: Evidence from political cognition," pp. 131-140 in N. Cantor and J. R. Kihlstrom (eds.) Personality, Cognition and Social Interaction. Hillsdale, NJ: Lawrence Erlbaum.

FREUD, S. (1959) Beyond the Pleasure Principle. New York: Bantam.

The Gallup Poll: (1984) Public Opinion 1983. Wilmington DE: Scholarly Resources.

GREENWALD, A. G. (1980) "The totalitarian ego: fabrication and revision of personal history." American Psychologist 35: 603-618.

KAID, L. L. (1981) "Political advertising," in D. D. Nimmo and K. R. Sanders (eds.) Handbook of Political Communication. Beverly Hills, CA: Sage.

KIEWIET, L. R. (1981) "Policy-oriented voting in response to economic issues." American Political Science Review 75: 448-459.

KINDER, D. R. and L. R. KIEWIET (1979) "Economic grievances and political behavior: The role of personal discontent in collective judgments in congressional voting." American Journal of Political Science 23: 495-527.

KRAUS, S. (1979) [ed.] The Great Debates; Carter vs. Ford 1976. Bloomington: Indiana University Press.

KRUGMAN, H. (1967) "The measurement of advertising involvement." Public Opinion Quarterly 30: 583-596.

LANE, R. E. (1962) Political Ideology: Why the Common Man Believes What He Does. New York: Free Press.

LAU, R. R., T. A. BROWN, and D. O. SEARS (1978) "Self-interest and civilians' attitudes toward the war in Vietnam." Public Opinion Quarterly 42: 464-483.

McLEOD, J. M., C. R. BYBEE, and J. A. DURALL (1979) "Equivalence of informed political participation: the 1976 presidential debates as a source of influence." Communication Research 6: 463-487.

MILBRAITH, L. W. and M. L. GOEL (1977) Political Participation: How and Why Do People Get Involved in Politics. Chicago: Rand McNally.

PATTERSON, T.E. (1980) The Mass Media Election: How Americans Choose Their President. New York: Praeger.

PERLOFF, R. M. (1984) "Political involvement: a critique and a process-oriented reformulation." Critical Studies in Mass Communication 1: 146-160.

———and T.C. BROCK (1980) " 'And thinking makes it so': Cognitive responses to persuasion," pp. 63-99 in M. Roloff and B. R. Miller (eds.) Persuasion: New Directions in Theory and Research. Beverly Hills, CA: Sage.

PERLOFF, R. M., D. ROUNER, and J. SUVAK (1984) "A reexamination of issues and images in the 1984 Ohio Primary." Presented at the annual convention of the Midwestern Association of Public Opinion Research, Chicago.

PETTY, R. E. and J. T. CACIOPPO (1984) "The effects of involvement on responses to argument quantity and quality: central and peripheral routes to persuasion." Journal of Personality and Social Psychology 46: 69-81.

———(1981) Attitudes and Persuasion: Classic and Contemporary Approaches. Dubuque, IA: William Brown.

———(1979) "Issue involvement can increase or decrease persuasion by enhancing message-relevant cognitive responses." Journal of Personality and Social Psychology 37: 1915-1926.

———and R. GOLDMAN (1981) "Personal involvement as a determinant of argument-based persuasion." Journal of Personality and Social Psychology 47: 847-855.

PETTY, R. E., T. M. OSTROM, and T. C. BROCK (1981) (eds.) Cognitive Responses to Persuasion. Hillsdale, NJ: Lawrence Erlbaum.

ROBINSON, M. and M. SHEEHAN (1983) Over the Wire and on TV. New York: Russell Sage.

ROGERS, T. B., N. A. KUIPER, and W. S. KIRKER (1977) "Self-reference and the encoding of personal information." Journal of Personality and Social Psychology 35: 677-688.

ROUNER, D. L. (1983) "Individual and environmental determinants of television viewing behavior." Ph. D. dissertation, University of Wisconsin.

SEARS, D. O. and J. CITRIN (1982) Tax Revolt: Something for Nothing in California. Cambridge: Harvard University Press.

SEARS, D. O. and R. R. LAU (1983) "Inducing apparently self-interested political preferences." American Journal of Political Science 27:223-252.

SEARS, D. O., C. P. HENSLER, and L. K. SPEER (1979) "Whites' opposition to 'busing': Self-interest or symbolic politics." American Political Science Review 73: 369-384.

SEARS, D. O., R. R. LAU, T. R. TYLER, and H. M. ALLEN Jr. (1980) "Self-interest vs. symbolic politics in policy attitudes and presidential voting." American Political Science Review 74: 670-684.

SHERIF, C. W., M. SHERIF, and R. E. NEBERGALL (1965) Attitude and Attitude Change. Philadelphia: Saunders.

SHERIF, M. and C. I. HOVLAND (1961) Social Judgment: Assimilation and Contrast Effects in Communication and Attitude Change. New Haven: Yale University Press.

SMITH, M. B., J. BRUNER, and R. WHITE (1956) Opinions and Personality. New York: John Wiley.

WEATHERFORD, M. S. (1983) "Judging politicians' management of the economy: the role of the media." American Politics Quarterly 11: 31-48.

WEAVER, D. H., D. A. GRAYER, M. E. McCOMBS, and C. H. EYAL (1981) Media Agenda-Setting in a Presidential Election: Issues, Images, and Interest. New York: Praeger.

Chapter 9


# MOTIVATION AND POLITICAL
# INFORMATION PROCESSING
## Extending the Gratifications Approach


Gina M. Garramone


ONE NEEDN'T scour the literature on political communication to uncover many allusions to the importance of audience motives in determining media effects. For example, what Americans extract from our most celebrated form of political communication—the presidential debate—depends on what they are looking for. Katz and Feldman (1962) concluded that the 1960 Nixon-Kennedy debates changed few opinions on the campaign issues because people were more interested in such matters as personality and presentational style. Yet Sears and Chaffee (1979) found evidence of some important learning of political information from the 1976 Carter-Ford debates for that minority of voters who are called "issue-oriented." The story is the same for other motives and other mass-mediated political messages: What you seek influences what you get.

Less prevalent in the political communication literature, however, are explications of the *process* by which motives influence media effects. The role of motives in determining the effects of political information has been most thoroughly investigated by communication researchers operating from a uses and gratifications perspective. The gratifications perspective holds that "audience members must be viewed as active processors rather than passive receivers of media messages" (McLeod and Becker, 1981: 71). This chapter will review political gratifications research with a critical eye, suggesting that gratifications researchers have ignored a basic premise of their approach by slighting the study of information processing per se. A conceptual model of the relationship between motives and political information processing is developed to provide a framework for recent research in the area. New data are presented illustrating some of the relationships outlined in the model.

## CRITIQUE OF POLITICAL GRATIFICATIONS RESEARCH

The shortcomings of gratifications research as an approach to political information processing derive from the limited scope of both the questions addressed and the methods used. In terms of the questions addressed, gratifications researchers have failed to consider many of the potential impacts of motives on political information processing. Gratifications research has narrowly focused on the relationship of motives to the acquisition or selection of political information, rather than considering their relationship to political information processing in a broader sense. The impact of motives on the processing (i.e., encoding, storing, decoding) of political information has been virtually ignored, as has the influence of motives on the utilization of political information in candidate evaluation, vote decision making processes, interpersonal discussions, and so forth.

Even in their investigation of the acquisition of political information, gratifications researchers have tended to focus on broad categories of motives for selecting media sources, rather than exploring the role of more specific motives in the selection of specific types of political information. Thus, the research reveals that an informational motive is related to newspaper exposure, rather than specifying the type of information sought and its consequential impact on the specific type of political content attended to. Although some effort has been made to differentiate more specific motives (e.g., motives to learn candidate issue stands versus motives to learn candidate personal qualities), little effort has been made to relate such motives to specific content. Political content does vary across media, and the audience may therefore use medium as an efficient surrogate for selecting particular content. But content also varies within a medium (e.g., news stories versus editorials) and even within messages (e.g., audio versus video channel content), so research might address how the audience selects content at a more detailed level.

The focus of gratifications research on the acquisition of political information has inhibited the investigation of the *interaction* of motives and message characteristics. By primarily treating exposure as a dependent variable, rather than controlling for it, gratifications researchers have failed to determine how motives and message characteristics interact to influence attention to, encoding, and utilization of political information.

The customary methodology of gratifications research is suboptimal, in both design and measurement, for the study of information processing. Most political gratifications research has utilized survey methodology, which offers the advantage of natural exposure conditions. But as is common in survey methodology, the generalizability is accompanied by a lack of control and valid measurement of internal processes. Attempts to measure the acquisition of political information have been limited to self-reports of exposure and attention. Little attempt has been made to measure processing per se, although several techniques might be adapted from studies of social cognition (e.g., cognitive response— Petty et al., 1980; processing tracing—Payne et al., 1978). Many techniques for measuring processing, however, would require that gratifications researchers move from the field into the laboratory.

Approaches to measuring *motives* have also been limited by survey methodology. Most gratifications studies have relied upon audience self-reports of motives (e.g., McLeod et al., 1983; Becker, 1976). Other researchers have made inferences about audience motives by measuring some separate, yet related variable or variables. For example, in the research of Kline et al. (1974) on uses of family planning information, motives were inferred from variables such as age and sex. Another strategy is to manipulate the motives of the subjects (Garramone, 1983). Although numerous problems beset the manipulation of motives in the laboratory, the control afforded is functional when the objective is to explore information processing. Finally, questions regarding motives and political information processing are best approached with multiple methodological tools, including survey and experimental methodology and the variety of methods of measuring and manipulating audience motives.

## A CONCEPTUAL APPROACH TO MOTIVATION AND POLITICAL INFORMATION PROCESSING

Although the uses and gratifications perspective holds that audience members are active processors rather than passive receivers of media messages, gratifications researchers have given little attention to information processing per se. To better recognize the omissions of gratifications research, it is useful to explicate the potential influences of motivation on the processing of political media messages. A conceptual approach will be offered for this purpose in the next section. The four components of this approach—information acquisition and processing, cognitive schemata, motives, and message attributes—will be discussed in that order.

*Information acquisition* involves exposure and attention processes. It encompasses the degree and direction of information selection. Included in the acquisition component are extent of exposure and attention to the media and political content within the media, and the specific media and content selected. Acquisition includes all information selection behavior, such as differential attention to the audio versus video component within a political commercial message. *Processing* involves the encoding, storing, and decoding of information. This includes the number and specificity of concepts used to process information. For example, some persons may use many concepts when encoding a political message; others may use few. Similarly, some persons may encode political information into broad, abstract concepts (e.g., conservative), whereas others may encode the same information into specific, concrete attributes (e.g., voted against food stamps).

Recent psychological research indicates that information processing is strongly influenced by *cognitive schemata* (Wyer et al., 1982; see Lau's chapter, this volume). Schema theories have been tested repeatedly and substantiated experimentally for nonpolitical information (Cantor, 1981; Schank and Abelson, 1977) and are now being applied successfully to political thinking (Lau, 1984; Kinder and Fiske, 1981; Graber, 1984).

To illustrate the potential impact of schemata on political information processing, consider a schema for a politician's personality. A political person schema would contain abstract personality trait concepts (e.g., untrustworthy). Such a schema would then be expected to direct acquisition processes toward that information perceived as relevant to such concepts (e.g., the candidate's body gestures and appearance).

Cognitive schemata are expected to have a direct impact on information processing. *Motives*, in turn, should influence information processing indirectly via their impact on schema activation. Higgins and King (1981) outlined four recent information processing approaches addressing the question of *which* schemata are used to process any particular piece of information. One approach has focused on the effects of goals or motives on the encoding of information (Cohen and Ebbesen, 1979; Jeffery and Mischel, 1979; Wyer et al., 1982; Zajonc, 1960; White and Carlston, 1983; Hennigan et al, 1982). When people approach information with the intention of using it to attain a particular goal, an appropriate schema is activated, or "tuned in." For example, a motive to attend to political information to form an impression of the candidate's personality may activate a schema containing abstract personality traits.

What motives activate schemata for political information processing? All the motives identified by gratifications researchers as relevant to political communication may influence schema choice. Thus, motives to form an impression of candidate personal qualities, learn candidate issue stands, acquire information for political discussion, enjoy the excitement of an election and satisfy personal identity motives may each activate a particular type of schema. To predict how these political motives may influence schema activation and subsequent information processing, one may look to research investigating nonpolitical motives and schema activation.

For example, two motives for attending to political messages—to form an impression of candidate personal qualities and to learn candidate issue positions—are similar to the impression formation and recall motives that Ebbesen, Cohen, and associates (Ebbesen et al., 1975, 1977; Cohen and Ebbesen, 1979) found resulted in different information processing behavior. Recall-motivated persons remembered more details from a videotape of an actor than did impression-motivated persons.[1] In addition, although mean trait ratings under the two motive conditions were similar, they were more highly correlated under impression-motive conditions than under recall-motive conditions. Moreover, the pattern of intercorrelations among trait ratings by impression-motivated persons was similar to the pattern of independent judges' estimates of trait cooccurrences. Thus, impression-motivated persons were less likely to base their inferences of the actor's traits on different aspects of his or her behavior and more likely to base these judgments on their prior assumptions about how traits are interrelated (i.e., their implicit personality theories).

Ebbesen and his associates attributed their results to the different schemata activated by the two motives. The recall motive activated a schema that facilitated the encoding of detailed information. The impression motive activated a person schema of general attributes, which fostered reliance on assumed trait interrelationships when making personality judgments. Based on these findings, one might predict that a motivation to learn candidate issue stands would activate a schema of rather concrete and specific issue-relevant attributes and their interrelationships (e.g., the knowledge that specific political parties and specific candidates tend to hold certain positions on such issues as defense spending, welfare spending, taxes, etc.). Consequently, one might also predict that issue-motivated persons would attend to, encode, and recall more issue information from political messages than would impression-motivated persons. Impression-motivated persons, on the other hand, should be more likely than the issue-motivated to base their inferences of the candidate's traits on assumptions about how traits are interrelated.

Additionally, individuals attend to and encode the selected aspects of information that are particularly relevant to their goals, and if information channels are perceived to differ in the amount of such information they contain, perhaps persons will differentially attend to channels based on their motivations. Although issue information is primarily contained in the audio component of a televised political message, personality information is present in both the audio and video components. The candidate's facial expressions, body postures, and motions are all video-contained information relevant to personality judgments. Thus, one would predict that persons attending to a political message to form a personality impression would pay more attention to the *video* channel and encode more visual information than would those attending to learn issue stands.

Other studies of social cognition are also relevant. In his theory of cognitive tuning, Zajonc (1960) proposed that persons will "tune in" different information depending upon whether they anticipate *transmitting* or *receiving* a communication. His research found that persons who anticipated transmitting information were much more specific in their responses than persons who anticipated only receiving information. Anticipated transmitting might correspond to anticipated political discussion. One might predict, therefore, that the schemata of persons anticipating later discussion of a political message would include more specific attributes than would the schema of those not anticipating such discussion.

One can also speculate about the nature of the schema that are activated by excitement motives. Seeking excitement from political information may activiate schemata centered on contest or conflict concepts, such as win/lose, thrust and parry. Consequently, a candidate's statement in a debate might be encoded as a "point" in his or her favor, rather than as an elucidation of a policy position. Indirect evidence for the impact of motives on political schemata use has been uncovered by Graber (1984) in her intensive analysis of news processing behavior. She found that choice of a particular schema for processing news depended in part on the individual's interest and "current information needs." Furthermore, interest spurred by a specific goal, such as the need to become informed about candidates just before an election, resulted in greater learning than when interest was unfocused.

In addition to motives, *message attributes* may influence schema choice. The other approaches to schema selection outlined by Higgins and King (1981) relate to stimulus (e.g. message) characteristics rather than to motivational factors. One approach has been to consider the effects of the match between the characteristics of the stimulus information and the content of a particular schema (Cantor and Mischel, 1977). For example, Graber (1984) reported that viewers found it easiest to match schemata to news stories when the stories conformed closely to their expectations. Another approach is to consider the effects of the relative accessibility of different schemata that could be used to characterize the information (Higgins et al., 1977). For example, content of the first part of a message may activate schemata that are used in subsequent processing. Thus if the concept "liberal" is stressed in the first part of a political message, it becomes more accessible and the likelihood of later information being encoded in terms of this concept is increased. Similarly, if the content of a political message emphasizes general, abstract attributes (e.g., pro-business) this may increase the likelihood that the audience encodes the message in general, rather than more specific (e.g., voted to give tax breaks to large corporations) attributes. A final approach is to consider the information-processing effects of drawing attention to different characteristics of the stimulus information (Taylor and Fiske, 1978). For example, messages presented via a multi-channel medium such as television may accentuate one channel over another. Dramatic visuals might draw attention to the video channel while diverting attention from the audio channel. Because visual content tends to stimulate visual encoding (Rossiter and Percy, 1980), messages in which the visual content is dominant may facilitate iconic rather than verbal encoding.

The evidence that message attributes influence schema activation yields some predictions regarding how various types of political messages might be processed. For example, issue and image commercials differ in both their content and their presentational style.[2] For example, image commercials tend to use more complex video techniques (e.g., montage) and tend to feature settings or behaviors of dramatic interest in (e.g., candidate's small children playing in the foreground, candidate sitting on the front porch with a coffee mug). The prominence of visual information in image commercials should be related to greater attention to and encoding of the visual component of the commercial. Although information in issue political commercials tends to be very specific (e.g., "As mayor, I intend to make jobs for San Diegans top priority."), the information in image commercials tends to be more general (e.g., "He's the right man for a tough job."). Viewers should, therefore, use more general attributes when they process image than when they process issue commercials. Graber's (1984) research supports this prediction: When news stories included clear generalizations, people tended to process the information in more abstract terms.

In summary, although the gratifications perspective falls within the transactional model of mass communication effects, gratifications researchers have given little attention to the interaction of motivation and political message attributes. Schema activation and subsequent political information processing behavior may depend upon both attributes of the message and the audience member's motivation for attending to the message.

## EMPIRICAL INVESTIGATIONS

The conceptual approach outlined in the previous section will serve as a framework for my recent research investigating the role of motives in political information processing. A detailed description of this research is provided, as well as a reinterpretation of previously reported research.

### MOTIVES AND PROCESSING

Experimental research was conducted by the author to explore the influence of two political motives—to form an impression of candidate personal qualities and to learn candidate issue stands—on the processing of a political commercial (Garramone, 1983). To activate the corresponding schemata, subjects were instructed to attend to a political commercial either "to learn where the candidate stands on issues" or "to form an impression of the candidate's personality." All subjects then viewed a five-minute political commercial. After viewing the commercial, they completed a brief questionnaire. Subjects indicated on 7-point scales how much attention they paid to what they *heard* and what they *saw*. *Issue knowledge* was measured by an additive index formed from ten true-false issue items. *Video recall* was indicated by an index formed from ten true-false items regarding the video portion of the commercial.

Subjects were also asked to rate the candidate on a 7-point scale for ten personality traits.

As predicted, issue-motivated persons recalled more issue information than did impression-motivated persons. Although the impression-motivated reported paying greater attention to the video component of the commercial than did the issue-motivated, the difference between motive conditions for the video recall measure failed to reach significance.[3] The intercorrelations among trait ratings indicated that, contrary to the model prediction, the issue-motivated were more likely than the impression-motivated to base their judgments of the candidate on assumptions about how traits are interrelated.

The experimental manipulation of motives facilitates the study of information processing, but invites questions of generalizability. To bolster the external validity of the experimental findings, a second study was conducted using survey methodology (Garramone, 1984). Interviews were conducted with a random telephone sample of 367 mid-Michigan voters during the final week of the 1982 gubernatorial campaign.

Respondents were asked what information they could recall from the candidates' commercials. Responses were recorded verbatim by the interviewer. Each specific response was coded in terms of two factors. The first factor, video versus audio recall, was coded in the following manner: recall responses that could be conceived of as *visual* in nature were coded as video, whereas all others were classified as audio. For the second factor, image versus issue recall, responses concerning issues or a candidate's stand on issues were coded as issue. Comments regarding the candidate's personal orientation, campaign activities featured, or comments regarding the nature of the commercial itself were coded as image. Motives were measured, rather than manipulated, by asking respondents to evaluate several "reasons some people have given for why they pay attention to the campaign for governor." The issue and impression motive items were worded: "To see how the candidates stand on the issues" and "To judge the personal qualities of the candidates," respectively. The survey findings indicated that there was a significant relationship between extent of issue motives and issue recall and between extent of impression formation motives and video channel recall.

Research pertinent to the anticipated political discussion motive has also been conducted recently. Experimental findings reported by McLeod and Becker (1981) are consistent with the hypothesis that schemata activated by persons anticipating political discussions differ from those activated by persons not anticipating discussion. Motives were manipulated by informing subjects that the experiment in which they would be involved would include a "test on what you know about the current situation in Pakistan," or that they would be required to write an essay "explaining your opinion on giving foreign aid to Pakistan." Subjects then waited in a lounge area containing public affairs and entertainment periodicals and their behavior was observed through a one-way mirror. Although the test group used the public affairs media somewhat more than did the essay group, the essay group wrote lengthier essays and used more distinct pieces of information than did the test group. However, no group differences emerged on the objective knowledge measure. Thus, the lengthier essays cannot be attributed merely to greater knowledge regarding the Pakistani situation. If the essay condition is interpreted to correspond to "anticipated discussion," and the test condition to "no anticipated discussion," the essay results are consistent with the prediction that voters are likely to use more specific political terms when they anticipate participation in a political discussion.

Some previously unreported data from a pilot study conducted by the author provides a more direct test of the impact of anticipated discussion on schema activation. The results indicated that subjects asked to discuss political commercials with another individual did not use more characteristics to describe the candidate than students in the no discussion condition. As expected, however, the discussion group described the candidate with more words per characteristic than did the no discussion group [t (78) = 1.70, p < .05]. These studies suggest that a need to discuss politics motivates voters to describe candidates and issues more specifically and extensively.

## MOTIVES AND MESSAGE ATTRIBUTES

To investigate the interaction of motives and message attributes, the author conducted an experiment exploring the effects on information processing, vote intention, and candidate image of two types of motives (learning candidate issue stands versus forming an impression of the candidate's personal qualities) and two types of political commercials (issue versus image). A total of 120 students were randomly assigned to one of four experimental conditions. In each condition, subjects were told that they would be watching two commercials for a political candidate. For the *issue motivation* condition, subjects were instructed to watch the political commercials "to try to learn where the candidate stands on issues." For the *image motivation* condition, subjects were instructed to watch the commercials "to learn the candidate's personal qualities." In the *issue commercial* condition, subjects watched two issue-oriented commercials for the candidate, and in the *image commercial* condition, subjects watched two image-oriented commercials.

Commercials were designated as issue or image based on the prominence of the visual information and the use of general attributes. Both of the issue commercials portrayed the candidate explaining, in detail, his issue stands to constituents who had been affected by his policies. The first image commercial used a montage format showing the candidate engaged in various activities (e.g., at meetings, parades, jogging) and featuring such voice-over comments as "not too busy to listen to the people" and "Roger Hedgecock cares." The second image commercial featured the candidate and his family thanking campaign volunteers for their efforts. The candidate and his wife were sitting on the front porch of their home, while their young children played in the foreground.

Following exposure to the commercials, subjects were asked to "write down everything you recall from the commercials." Subjects' responses were coded with the sentence serving as the unit of analysis. Use of general attributes in information processing was indicated by the word-to-sentence ratio because general attributes tend to be represented with fewer words than do more specific attributes (e.g., "family man" versus "has a wife and two little boys"; "athletic" versus "shown jogging through the park"). Visual processing was measured by the proportion of sentences referring to content present only in the video component of the commercials. Candidate image was ascertained by asking subjects to rate the candidate on ten personality traits. Intention to vote was measured by asking subjects how likely they would be to vote for the candidate if he were to run for office in their city.

The results indicate that issue commercials resulted in greater intention to vote for the candidate than did image commercials (Table 9.1), but that this relationship held only for issue-motivated persons [Figure 9.1; $F(1,116) = 4.29$, $p < .05$]. Motivation and commercial type had no main or interaction effects on candidate image. Both manipulated variables, however, had the predicted main effects on the use of general attributes in information processing. Persons motivated to learn the candidate's personal qualities and those exposed to the image-oriented commercials displayed a greater tendency to process with general attributes than those motivated to learn issue stands, or those exposed to issue-oriented commercials, respectively. No interaction emerged for processing with general attributes.

TABLE 9.1
**TABLE 9.1**
**Mean Scores of Criterion and Information Processing**
**Variables by Motivation and Commercial Type**

|  | *Motivation* | | | *Commercial Type* | | |
|---|---|---|---|---|---|---|
|  | *Issue* | *Image* | *t* | *Issue* | *Image* | *t* |
| Intention to vote | 4.30 | 4.43 | .69 | 4.57 | 4.17 | 2.07* |
| Candidate image | 46.15 | 44.60 | 1.52 | 45.93 | 44.82 | 1.10 |
| General attributes | .09 | .11 | 3.38* | .08 | .11 | 3.79* |
| Visual | .28 | .32 | 1.32 | .22 | .37 | 4.44* |

NOTE: N = 120.
*p < .05

As predicted, persons exposed to the image-oriented commercials engaged in more visual processing than did those exposed to the issue-oriented commercials (Table 9.1), but this relationship emerged only for those persons seeking information about the candidate's personal qualities [Figure 9.2; $F(1,116) = 8.75$, $p < .01$]. The influence of motivation on visual processing was in the predicted direction, but was not significant. Motivation, commercial type, and visual processing significantly interacted in their relationship with candidate image (Figure 9.3). The amount of visual processing had less impact on candidate image ratings when motivation and commercial type matched (e.g., issue motivation and issue commercial) than when motivation and commercial type did not match (incremental $r^2 = .05$, $p < .01$). When they did not match, the more visual processing that subjects engaged in, the more positively they rated the candidate's image. These findings suggest that the amount of visual processing may be especially likely to influence candidate ratings when viewers seek a particular type of television content, but encounter a different kind.

## THEORETICAL IMPLICATIONS AND DIRECTIONS FOR FUTURE RESEARCH

### SUMMARY

The recent research extending the gratifications approach in political communication to include information processing per se has demonstrat-

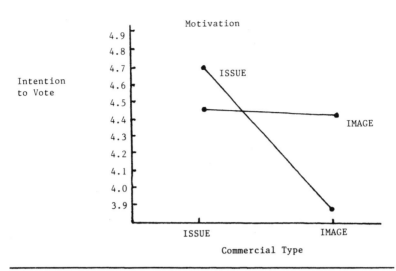

**Figure 9.1  Two-Way Interaction Between Motivation and Commercial Type for Intention to Vote**

ed the usefulness of melding the two research perspectives. Although gratifications research has enlightened us regarding the impact of motives on the acquisition of political information, it has done less to unravel the effects of motives on other components of political information processing. The studies reported in this chapter shed some light on the issues in mind. The results of the first experiment demonstrated that subjects motivated to learn where the candidates stood on issues recalled more issue information than did subjects instructed to form an impression of the candidate's personality (impression-motivated subjects). Impression-motivated individuals in turn reported that they paid greater attention to the video component of the commercial. The results of a survey corroborated these findings; there were significant relationships between extent of issue motive and issue recall and between impression formation motives and video channel recall. At the same time, the results of a third study revealed that another motivation—the motive to discuss politics—led subjects to describe candidates more specifically and extensively.

The final experiment examined the effects of motives and message attributes on information processing and voting intention. The results indicated that issue commercials increased the intention to vote for the candidate more than did image commercials, but only for issue-

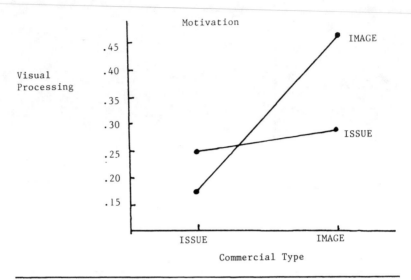

**Figure 9.2  Two-Way Interaction Between Motivation and Commercial Type for Visual Processing**

motivated individuals. Similarly, exposure to the image-oriented advertisements led to more visual processing than did exposure to issue-oriented commercials, but only among individuals seeking information about the candidate's personal qualities.

Taken together, this research supports the contention that "what you seek influences what you get." The voter, therefore, is still pictured as active and somewhat obstinate. But the nature and breadth of voter activity is clarified by the recent findings. The voter is active not only in selecting political messages to attend to, but in encoding and using those messages. Active processing is not limited to voters seeking "objective" issue information, but instead includes those with a variety of motives. Finally, the voter appears quite active even in processing information presented via a "low involvement" medium such as television. Furthermore, viewers can be active, yet focus on visual—as well as issue—information.

**DIRECTIONS FOR FUTURE RESEARCH**

These preliminary findings have some important implications for political communication. Although research indicates that political

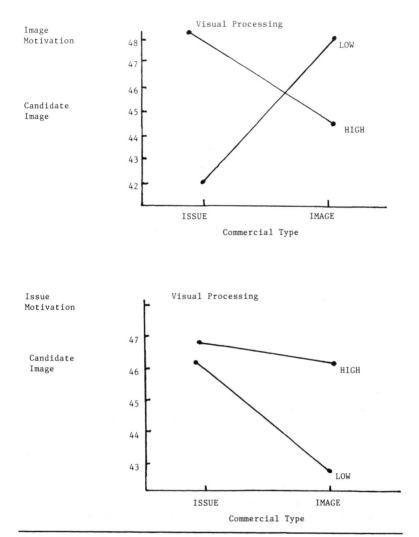

**Figure 9.3  Three-Way Interaction Between Motivation, Commercial Type, and Visual Processing**

schemata tend to be basically stable over time (Lau, 1984), the motives that influence schema choice may or may not be so stable. Young people do learn certain motives for using the mass media that may continue to influence their political information processing throughout their lifetimes. For example, Chaffee et al. (1973) found that youngsters in families that encourage free and argumentative discussion of social and political topics are more likely to use television for informational purposes, whereas children in families that discourage such discussion and seek close control of youngsters' behavior tend to use television more for entertainment. If youngsters from these two types of families do indeed differ in their motivations for using television, they may consequently differ in their processing of television information.

However, the specific uses that people want to make of political information also vary over time. In their analyses of the 1976 presidential election, Weaver et al. (1981) found voters highly interested in the personal characteristics of the candidates throughout the campaign period. Shortly before the election date, however, the voters appeared to become highly interested in issue positions of the candidates. If such a change in motives leads to the use of different schemata, then political information provided at the end of a campaign may be processed somewhat differently than political information provided at the beginning of a campaign. Political information processing might be facilitated if political leaders and journalists learned to match their messages to the processing proclivities of their audiences at that point in time (Graber, 1984).

Additional motives for attending to political information should also be explored—specifically the motivation to attend because of the excitement or drama involved. Kelley (1962) argues that the Kennedy-Nixon debates were sought out by many viewers because of the inherent entertainment value they offered. Blumler (1969) found that producers of a series of election campaign analysis programs in Britain made a deliberate attempt to attract and hold an audience for their program by increasing its entertainment value. The schemata activated by such an excitement motive should be investigated, as well as their impact on political information processing. Second, additional schemata and information processing variables should be explored. For example, the occurrence of self-references in information processing, sometimes used to indicate involvement, may result from the activation of the self-schema. The contribution of personal identity motives to self-schema activation might be investigated, as well as the processing consequences of such activation.

# NOTES

1. Other research, however, indicates that people told to remember details about another person may actually remember *less* than people who are merely forming an impression of that person (Srull, 1981, 1983; Wyer and Gordon, 1982).

2. The designation of "issue" versus "image" commercials is not made in ignorance of the literature indicating that candidate issue stands and images are often perceived as inseparable (Kraus and Smith, 1962; Hart, 1982). Rather, the labels are used to distinguish commercials that tend to fall at opposite ends of a continuum in terms of the amount or prominence of several attributes (e.g., type of language used, production techniques, etc.).

3. The failure of the video recall comparison to reach significance was attributed to the very low reliability of the index.

# REFERENCES

BECKER, L. B. (1976) "Two tests of media gratifications: Watergate and 1974 elections." Journalism Quarterly 53: 26-31.

BLUMLER, J.G. (1969) "Producers attitudes towards television coverage of an election campaign: a case study." Sociological Review Monographs 13: 85-115.

CANTOR, N. (1981) "A cognitive-social approach to personality," in N. Cantor and J. F. Kihlstrom (eds.) Personality, Cognition, and Social Interaction. Hillsdale, NJ: Lawrence Erlbaum.

———and W. MISCHEL (1977) "Traits as prototypes: effects on recognition memory." Journal of Personality and Social Psychology 35: 38-48.

CHAFEE, S. H., J. M. McCLOUD, and D. WACKMAN (1973) "Family communication patterns and adolescent political participation," in J. Dennis (ed.) Socialization to Politics: A Reader. New York: John Wiley.

COHEN, C. E. and E. B. EBBESEN (1979) "Observational goals and schema activation: a theoretical framework for behavioral perception." Journal of Experimental Social Psychology 15: 305-329.

EBBESEN, E. B., C. E. COHEN, and R. B. ALLEN (1977) "Encoding the processing of person information: behavior scanning and semantic memory." Unpublished manuscript, University of California, San Diego.

EBBESEN, E. B., C. E. COHEN, and J. L. LANE (1975) "Encoding and construction processes in person perception." Presented at the American Psychological Association Convention, Chicago.

GARRAMONE, G. M. (1984) "Audience motivation effects: more evidence." Communication Research 11: 79-96.

———(1983) "Issue versus image orientation and effects of political advertising." Communication Research 10: 59-76.

GRABER, D. (1984) Processing the News: How People Tame the Information Tide. New York: Longman.

HART, R. P. (1982) "A commentary on popular assumptions about political communication." Human Communication Research 8: 366-379.

HENNIGAN, K. M., T. D. COOK, and C. L. GRUDER (1982) "Cognitive tuning set, source credibility, and the temporal persistence of attitude change." Journal of Personality and Social Psychology 42: 412-425.

HIGGINS, E. T. and G. KING (1981) "Accessibility of social constructs: information-processing consequences of individual and contextual variables," in N. Cantor and J. F. Kihlstrom (eds.) Personality, Cognition, and Social Interaction. Hillsdale, NJ: Lawrence Erlbaum.

HIGGINS, E. T., W. S. RHOLES, and C. R. JONES (1977) "Category accessibility and impression formation." Journal of Experimental Social Psychology 13: 141-154.

JEFFERY, K. M. and W. MISCHEL (1979) "Effects of purpose on the organization and recall of information in person perception." Journal of Personality 47: 397-419.

KATZ, E. and J. FELDMAN (1962) "The debates in the light of research: a survey of surveys," in S. Kraus (ed.) The Great Debates. Bloomington: Indiana University Press.

KELLEY, S. (1962) "Campaign debates: some facts and issues." Public Opinion Quarterly 26: 351-366.

KLINE, F. G., P. V. MILLER, and A. J. MORRISON (1974) "Adolescents and family planning information: an exploration of audience needs and media effects," in J. G. BLUMLER and E. KATZ (eds.) The Uses of Mass Communication: Current Perspectives on Gratifications Research. Beverly Hills, CA: Sage.

KRAUS, S. and R. G. SMITH (1962) "Issues and images," in S. Kraus (ed.) The Great Debates. Bloomington: Indiana University Press.

LAU, R. R. (1984, May) "Political schemas, candidate evaluations, and voting behavior." Paper presented to the 19th Annual Carnegie Symposium on Cognition, Carnegie-Mellon University, Pittsburgh.

McLEOD, J. M. and L. B. BECKER (1981) The uses and gratifications approach," in D. Nimmo and K. R. Sanders (eds.) Handbook of Political Communication. Beverly Hills, CA: Sage.

McLEOD, J. M., C. R. BYBEE, and J. A. DURALL (1983) "Evaluating media performance by gratifications sought and received." Journalism Quarterly 59: 3-12.

———(1979) "Equivalence of informed participation: the 1976 presidential debates as a source of influence." Communication Research 6: 463-487.

PAYNE, J. W., M. L. BRAUNSTEIN, and J. S. CARROLL (1978) "Exploring predecisional behavior: an alternative approach to decision research." Organizational Behavior and Human Performance 22: 17-44.

PETTY, R., T. OSTROM, and T. BROCK (1980) Cognitive Responses in Persuasive Communication: A Text in Attitude Change. New York: McGraw-Hill.

ROSSITER, J. R. and L. PERCY (1980) "Attitude change through visual imagery in advertising." Journal of Advertising 9: 10-16.

SCHANK, R. and R. P. ABELSON (1977) Scripts, Plans, Goals, and Understanding: An Inquiry into Human Knowledge Structures. Hillsdale, NJ: Lawrence Erlbaum.

SEARS, D. O. and S. H. CHAFFEE (1979) "Uses and effects of the 1976 debates: An overview of empirical studies," in S. Kraus (ed.) The Great Debates: Carter vs. Ford, 1976. Bloomington: Indiana University Press.

SRULL, T. K. (1983) "Organizational and retrieval processes in person memory: an examination of processing objectives, presentation format, and the possible role of self-generated retrieval cues." Journal of Personality and Social Psychology 44: 1157-1170.

———(1981) "Person memory: some tests of associative storage and retrieval models." Journal of Experimental Social Psychology 7: 440-462.

TAYLOR, S. E. and S. T. FISKE (1978) "Salience, attention, and attribution: top of the head phenomena," in L. Berkowitz (ed.) Advances in Experimental Social Psychology (Vol. 11). New York: Academic.

WEAVER, D. H., D. A. GRABER, M. E. McCOMBS, and C. H. EYAL (1981) Media Agenda-Setting in a Presidential Election: Issues, Images and Interest. New York: Praeger.

WHITE, J. D. and D. E. CARLSTON (1983) "Consequences of schemata for attention, impressions, and recall in complex social interactions." Journal of Personality and Social Psychology 45: 538-549.

WYER, R. S. and S. E. GORDON (1982) "The recall of information about persons and groups." Journal of Experimental Social Psychology 18: 128-164.

WYER, R. S., T. K. SRULL, S. E. GORDON, and J. HARTWICK (1982) "Effects of processing objectives on the recall of prose material." Journal of Personality and Social Psychology 43: 674-688.

ZAJONC, R. B. (1960) "The process of cognitive tuning in communication." Journal of Abnormal and Social Psychology 61: 159-167.

# PART III

## MACRO IMPLICATIONS

Chapter 10

# PATTERNS OF POLITICAL COGNITION
## An Exploration of the Public Mind

W. Russell Neuman
Ann C. Fryling

THE TRADITIONAL paradigm for research on mass political behavior focuses on the distribution of political power and influence—most notably the demographic correlates of opinion and political participation. Several classic studies of American voting, for example, follow this paradigm, including those by Berelson et al. (1954) and Campbell et al. (1960, 1966).

The cognitive perspective in the study of political behavior, in contrast, focuses not so much on how the public aligns itself on prominent political questions but rather on how such issues are conceptualized and organized in individuals' minds. Cognitive researchers, for example, are particularly concerned with how an issue might come to be defined as politically salient in the first place or how two mutually contradictory beliefs might both be endorsed enthusiastically by the same individuals. The work of Lasswell (1930), Lane (1962), McCloskey et al., (1960), and Converse (1964) exemplifies this perspective.

The dividing line between traditional public opinion research and the cognitive perspective is not distinct. But perhaps the most critical distinction between the two could be outlined as follows. In the traditional paradigm, opinion is taken as a given and the demographic correlates are defined as problematic. Studies, for example, will focus on what types of people support a particular candidate or issue. In the traditional survey, the don't-know and no-opinion responses fall into residual categories or drop completely from sight. In the cognitive perspective, however, the opinion itself is seen as problematic. A no-opinion response to a survey question is not seen as measurement error but rather a meaningful response worthy of further attention. In fact, the cognitive analyst may well puzzle over the remarkable fact that the harried housewife and the retired heavy equipment operator actually do have opinions about foreign aid and debt policy. Work by Simon (1957) and Downs (1957) on the practical costs of acquiring and organizing political information, and by Olson (1965) on the trade-offs in deciding to participate actively in political affairs, have influenced this line of scholarship.

Both traditional and cognitive work on public opinion analyze trends, but each does so differently. The former traces trends in the direction of support for well-known policy or a prominent candidate whereas the latter focuses on the processes by which issues and candidates rise to public consciousness in the first place. Thus, the study of agenda-setting, or changes in cognitive structure or underlying political symbolism, tend to reflect the cognitive perspective. Examples of provocative work along these lines might include Downs (1972), Smith (1980), and Gamson and Lasch (1983).

There is a natural complementarity of cross-checking strengths and biases between traditional and cognitive research designs. Cognitive research, especially as it emphasizes depth interviews and the close analysis of the natural language of political discourse, can be used to validate the results of large-scale, closed-ended surveys. The frequently cited (but less often followed) guidelines of Campbell and Fiske's classic article on convergent validity (1959) stress the importance of tempering conclusions from data on attitudes and behavior until confirming results from other measurement approaches have been demonstrated. It is an important lesson.

The focus of this chapter is on the blurred borderline between individual and aggregated opinion. Our highly industrialized and centralized society requires a clear-cut "public opinion," an acknowledged will of the majority. Understandably, the system will not tolerate a collective "don't know" at the time of a critical election. Indeed, most of us have become quite accustomed to well-publicized polls, market indicators, and elections that present a falsely concrete image of the public will for all to observe. Our point, however, is that this public opinion whole is very much more than a simple sum of its parts.

We will rely primarily on two extended examples of cognitive research: one based on individual level cognitions and the other on aggregate cognitive processes. The first is the widely acknowledged trend in American public opinion toward political cynicism and alienation. An analysis of the variety of styles of political cognition that underlies this trend helps to put the phenomenon in perspective. The second example focuses on the widely researched agenda-setting function of the mass media—"the ability to effect cognitive change among individuals" (McCombs and Shaw, 1972: 1). In this case, the cognitive perspective draws attention to the diversity of the audience for mass communication and the fact that the process of public agenda building varies for different types of issues.

## STYLES OF POLITICAL COGNITION: THE CASE OF POLITICAL ALIENATION AND ALLEGIANCE

One of the most central findings of cognitively oriented research on political attitudes is the recognition of the spectacular diversity in individuals' interpretations of the meaning of political issues. Any two strongly-agree responses to the same survey item may well be based on entirely divergent patterns of thought. Take, for example, the issue of political alienation. The percentage of Americans who report that "the government in Washington can be trusted to do what is right" "most of the time" or "always" declined steadily from 76 percent in 1964 to 25 percent in 1980 (Miller, 1983). Few trends in public opinion have been so dramatic, especially concerning such potentially fundamental beliefs about our central political institutions. Political scientists, as a result, hastened to examine the data closely and try to understand the origins of such a dramatic shift of public perceptions. Did this trend represent a significant threat to the viability of the political system? The first researchers to explore these trends drew on the traditional paradigm and concluded that indeed it did. Arthur Miller and his colleagues at the University of Michigan, for example, expressed grave concern (Miller, 1974, Miller et al., 1976). They analyzed indicators of distrust including such statements as "the government is pretty much run by a few big interests looking out for themselves," and "most of the people running the government don't seem to know what they are doing." They found that agreement with such items was clearly tied to policy dissatisfaction. More important, they argued, it is unlikely that solutions more acceptable to the total population will be found because of an increasing polarization of issue beliefs. It appears to be a problem of policy paralysis. A move to the left or right in an administration's social policy would significantly further alienate those on the other side of the ideological spectrum, yet both those on the left and on the right are strongly dissatisfied with the status quo. It would appear to be a potentially dangerous catch-22.

Research in the cognitive tradition, however, suggests that Miller may have exaggerated the problem. Jack Citrin, for example, with his colleagues at the University of California, Berkeley conducted an in-depth analysis of political cynicism in the mass electorate. He argues that the apparent cynicism may reflect more of an emerging zeitgeist of antipolitical rhetoric and a fashionable and ritualistic criticism of politicians and political institutions. He notes:

> To agree verbally that many people "running the government" are corrupt, incompetent or untrustworthy is like shouting "kill the umpire" at a baseball game. Bloodthirsty rhetoric threatens neither the life expectancy of umpires nor the future of the national pastime [1974: 978].

The key issue to emerge from the Miller-Citrin debate is the cognitive significance of political cynicism. Clearly, more and more Americans from almost every demographic and political stratum have been using a more cynically oriented form of political discourse. But what do these words mean to those who use them?

Other research has indicated that the broad movement of the Index of Political Trust in aggregate is actually a confluence of smaller, more particular shifts of beliefs and attitudes. Hensler, for example, demonstrated the importance of clarifying the distinction between local and national government. Some individuals pay particular attention to local politics while practically ignoring national and international events (Hensler, 1971). So, for some, the phrase "the people running the government" translates without a second thought into the imagery of the mayor and the board of alderman rather than national political institutions. Other methodological analyses revealed that the cynicism items that Miller and the Michigan researchers used reflect a complex multi-dimensionality (Balch, 1974). Citrin (1975) pointed out the importance of separating out dissatisfaction with current political incumbents from a more fundamental alienation from the political system itself. Such phrases as "the government" and "the current administration" blur together in the minds of many respondents if careful distinctions are not made. Accordingly, Citrin and his associates developed a more systemically oriented index of political alienation-allegiance.

More recently, Miller has found evidence that these political measures are tapping concerns with the health of the economy as well as the health of the polity (1983). This suggests a point Converse had made somewhat earlier in his studies of political beliefs and cognitive structure. He observed that the cognitive perspective of a substantial stratum of the citizenry leads to a fairly straightforward equation between current economic well-being and "good" politics. He labeled it the "Nature of the Times" perspective (1964).

Furthermore, the expression of political alienation may be a self-conscious rationalization for political inactivity. Thus, some respondents may find the statement that all politicians are untrustworthy as a convenient justification for not voting. Yet for others, increased dissatisfaction may reflect a trend in the opposite direction, that is, a politicization and an increasing sense that political policies affect their own personal well-being. This may well be especially true for women, blacks, and other minorities throughout this period. Perhaps Miller's work would have been strengthened by drawing more heavily on the cognitive tradition, which attempts to sort out these factors (see Lane, 1969; Schwartz, 1973).

Depth interview research demonstrates that an aggregated index of political alienation does indeed mask important differences in how political issues are being conceptualized by the mass polity. In the following transcriptions, taken from depth interviews conducted in California in the early 1970s, respondents with almost identical scores on a survey index of political alienation-allegiance are compared.

These two individuals do not represent particularly extreme cases. They live in adjoining middle-class neighborhoods near Oakland, California, and both are Republicans.

The first man is a retired cabinetmaker and had some high school education. The second is a car salesman; he had some college education. On a series of alienation-allegiance questions the cabinetmaker selected the allegiant reponse without a single exception, almost as if it were a test in which he proudly identified the "right" answer. His lack of complaints about the political system seems to be more of a reflection of his cognitive style and disinclination to make negative remarks about anything, than any particular appreciation for the American brand of democracy or a satisfaction with social trends or particular policies.

The car salesman, on the other hand, ticks off a number of recent events and even compares the American political system to various brands of European socialism. His allegiance appears to be at least partially grounded in a thoughtful and comprehensive evaluation of political structure and current political policies in the light of his own political beliefs and values. In traditional public opinion research these two individuals would simply be equated as having the same "attitude." But as the transcripts reveal, such measures miss significant differences in cognitive organization—differences that could prove to be critically important in the ultimate link between attitude and behavior.

The cabinetmaker:

Q: Now let's start by your telling me what things about America today you are well satisfied with.

A: Everything. I'm not dissatisfied with anything! No.

Q: Could you be more specific? Could you give me some examples of things you are satisfied with?

A: Just nothing that I could complain about. So . . . if there's nothing I can complain about why I must be satisfied with everything. I have no bones to pick about anything. Nothing to say.

Q: Is there anything at all about life in America today with which you're not satisfied?

A: No, I'm satisfied with everything in America today. Well, no.

Q: Even little things?

A: Little things—sure.

Q: You're satisfied with little things?

A: Sure. I haven't got a gripe against anything. I'm well satisfied! I'm just well satisfied.

Q: My goodness! That's unusual . . .

A: Yeah. I couldn't . . . can't think of a thing. No. I just get along good with everybody and there's no gripes. Well, if I'd been robbed or had some robberies or things like that I wouldn't be as satisfied with that but I've never been robbed, nobody's bothered me ever so until that time I'll be satisfied—that's all.

Q: What or who do you think is responsible for your satisfaction? Everything being so . . . ?

A: Everything and everybody. I don't know. I just haven't any gripes against nothing.

Q: Would you say that government and the way it operates has something to do with the fact that you're satisfied with life?

A: Well, there's nothing I can do about it—so if it's good, bad or indifferent—I just don't complain about it. I don't complain about the President. I don't complain about anybody.

Q: Is that because you think you have to accept it?

A: Naturally. What can I do about it. There's nothing I can do about it. I'm just a person, you know.

Q: We would like to hear about any complaints you might have.

A: No. I have no complaints. None whatsoever. I've never complained to anybody ever. They might complain to me and I might say, "Well, maybe so." You know. But I wouldn't agree with them but that's their opinion and I just . . . well, I can't say "You're right," because I don't know. So that's the way it goes. And I can't say, "You're wrong," because I don't know.

The car salesman:

Q: First I would like to start with your telling me the things about America that you are well satisfied with.
A: Specific things?
Q: Yes.
A: Now this is always hard to volunteer information.
Q: Think about it.
A: That's right. Think of things that I am dissatisfied with would be next. Well, I am satisfied that in spite of inflation, business is progressing—that we are attempting to . . . a program with the world. That our involvement in Vietnam seems to be coming to an agreeable or acceptable close. Although I rather doubt that this area of the world will become trouble free, but I think that our role is going to be more acceptable to everybody.
Q: Okay. Like you mentioned the world economic situation and monetary problems—who or what do you think is responsible for the fact that they are getting better?
A: Well, I think that the administration that we have today is more concerned—with a responsibility toward working people. The reason is that you have to have a healthy business climate to have a healthy employment. This is prime concern of big business always, and without big business we could not have any healthy working situation. Unless we became a totally socialistic country which hasn't proven to be feasible for other countries on a grand national scale. I am thinking of Sweden in particular. Britain is a combination kind of a medium situation between the two. And we seem to be approaching Britain's status as a socialist government.
Q: But you think it is due to the present administration?
A: No. The present administration is slowing this. I happen to be against involvement in our government. I am against big federal government, and more for anything that can be done on a local level, right down to the city backing it up. I would rather have the county do it than the federal government. The closer it is to the people that are involved— the more concern will be taken with having it—a program which really serves the people, and not serves a lot of bureaucratic procedures.
Q: Is this something that you think about a lot, or . . . ?
A: No, this is just a general philosophy that I have always had.

The depth interview materials demonstrate the dramatic divergence of cognitive styles that, by the nature of survey research, become aggregated and interpreted as the same "public opinion." A different approach to question wording in measuring alienation-allegiance, perhaps one based on specific policy preferences, may well have painted a different picture of these two respondents. Thus, drawing on Campbell and Fiske's model, one would want to see evidence of increased alienation from a diverse compendium of indicators before concluding that such a trend was, indeed, what it first appeared to be.

There will, no doubt, continue to be a tension between the kinds of insights drawn from the rich data of natural political language in a small, limited sample and the aggregated patterns from larger, systematic surveys, but it should be a constructive tension. Work at the aggregate level can speak to the issue of congitive styles. Our case in point is research on the agenda-setting function of mass media.

## MASS MEDIA AND AGENDA-SETTING

The research reviewed above on individual differences in the character of political alienation runs contrary to a fundamental element of modern political life—the fact that almost everyone gets their political information from the same common sources, the mass media. The original work of McCombs and Shaw (1972) on media agenda-setting focused on the hypothesis that although the media, strictly speaking, may not tell the public what to think, they may influence what the public thinks about—that is, set the public agenda. They interpreted a correlation between the rank order of media coverage of political issues and the corresponding public opinion ranking of the importance of those issues as supporting the agenda-setting hypothesis. Actually, there are four possible patterns that might be evident in a study of agenda-setting as outlined in Figure 10.1. The correlation McCombs and Shaw found could have resulted from some combination of patterns 1, 2, or 3. The question of which pattern is dominant is critical to understanding how political ideas are conceptualized in mass electoral politics.

Initial findings from the Media Agenda Project, in which we are currently involved, provide some surprising answers. The project has integrated a content analysis of media coverage of ten prominent political issues with national public opinion time-series data collected by the Gallup Organization. The public opinion data set consists of references to those issues named in response to the question: "What do you think is the most important problem facing this country today?" The data and technique of analysis are described in more detail in the Appendix.

It was with some irony, then, that we reviewed the time-series data for these ten issues and found evidence of every pattern except consistent

## I MEDIA AGENDA SETTING

## II PUBLIC OPINION CUES

## III INTERACTIVE FEEDBACK

## IV INDEPENDENCE – NO RELATIONSHIP

MEDIA          PUBLIC OPINION

Figure 10.1 Agenda-Setting: Possible Causal Patterns

media agenda-setting. By far, the most dominant pattern was Interactive Feedback. It characterized the causal pattern for the issues of drug abuse, energy, inflation, pollution, race relations, and Watergate. The rise of issue salience in public opinion was consistently ahead of the media in the case of Poverty and Vietnam. For the issues of Crime and Unemployment, issue saliences varied independently in the media and public opinion.

Figure 10.2 presents the over-time curves for media and public attention to energy issues for the period 1972-1980. The energy curves illustrate the characteristic interaction effect between media coverage and public concern. The two are clearly linked; the time-series correlation is .85. But a close analysis of the curves indicates that public opinion lagged behind media through the 1973-1975 period and led the media from 1977 to 1980. There are also several disjunctures indicating that an upsurge in public concern does not always correspond to an equivalent increase in media coverage. The Arab oil embargo of the winter of 1973-1974, on the one hand, was a dramatic, clear-cut and universally perceived crisis. The media led public opinion, but the responses to the crisis by the media and the public were almost identical. The vagaries of gasoline supply; fluctuations in prices and demand for gas, heating, oil and natural gas; and President Carter's energy policy initiatives, on the other hand, were more complex and less clear-cut events. At times, the public seemed to respond more quickly to economic pressures connected to energy costs, or to continue expressing high levels of concern with heating costs after the newness and newsworthiness of the issue had caused it to drop from the pages of the newspaper. The energy crisis is an interesting example because, as Miller et al. (1979) have demonstrated, the public is as likely to respond to real-world cues as to media cues in interpreting the political salience of economic events.

Figure 10.3 demonstrates an interesting case in which public concern runs ahead of media coverage. The war in Vietnam, perhaps the dominant story of the decade, commanded the attention of the media and the concern of the public.[1] Both the media and the public followed the build-up and wind-down of the war, but in both cases the public seemed to move one step ahead of the media. Perhaps the public recognized the global significance of the involvement of American troops in a land war in Asia before the reporters who were concentrating on the details of Vietnamese politics and American military strategy. Perhaps also the public tired of thinking about Vietnam and turned their attention to other matters at the first indication the war was slowly winding to a close. That would explain the 1969-1973 period. Figure 10.3 makes clear, however, that the media were responding to the immediacy of

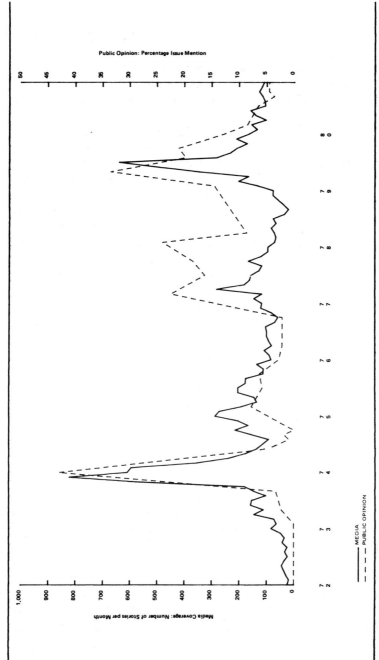

**Figure 10.2   Political Salience of the Energy Crisis: Interaction Between Media Coverage and Public Opinion**

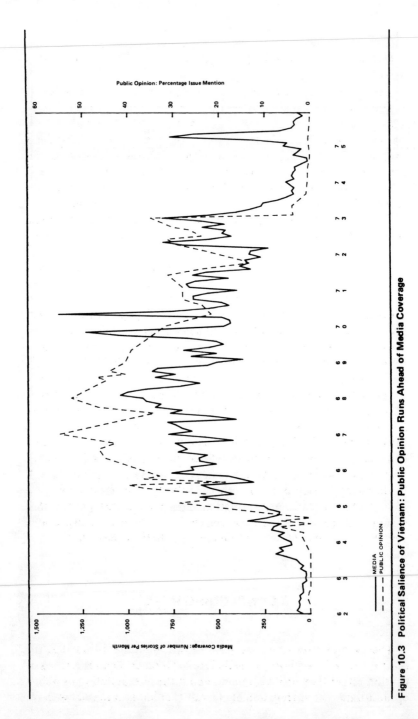

**Figure 10.3   Political Salience of Vietnam: Public Opinion Runs Ahead of Media Coverage**

individual military, political, and diplomatic events, whereas the public was responding to the broader, aggregate issue of American involvement in Vietnam.

Finally, Figure 10.4 illustrates the fascinating case of media and public attention to unemployment—two statistically independent curves. Clearly, both the media and the public responded to the postwar unemployment crises of World War II in the mid-1940s and Vietnam in the mid-1970s. The character of the response, however, is quite different, especially in the 1970s. During this period, all of the variations in unemployment rates, and the various policy initiatives responding to it, generated quite different patterns for the media and the public.

The data do not demonstrate that the media never play an agenda-setting role. Sometimes they do; quite often they do not. What the data do demonstrate (and why we felt it important to integrate these findings into this discussion of political cognition) is that the public appears to organize its conceptualization of public issues around broadly defined concerns. There is a natural and critically important disjuncture between the way the media organize their news stories and the way average citizens organize their political attitudes. The media immediately respond to policy statements and the latest unemployment figure from the Labor Department. The public moves more slowly and with more inertia and, in most cases, responds only to the broad contours of the policy debate and real-world events. The public is capable of ignoring media coverage or expressing more concern than media coverage might otherwise justify. These examples demonstrate that linkages between media coverage and public opinion over time can be very complex. We find no evidence of the postulated knee-jerk public response to media cues that dominates the agenda-setting literature. If further work by ourselves and others confirms these initial findings, it could lead to a significant reformation of the agenda-setting thesis. It is, we argue, evidence that even research entirely dependent on aggregated data can contribute to our understanding of political cognition.

## A CONCLUDING NOTE

The examples on which we have drawn are quite diverse but the central theme is, we hope, nonetheless convergent. Ours is a word of caution rather than disillusionment about the interpretation of public opinion data. The aggregation of individual opinions into what we have

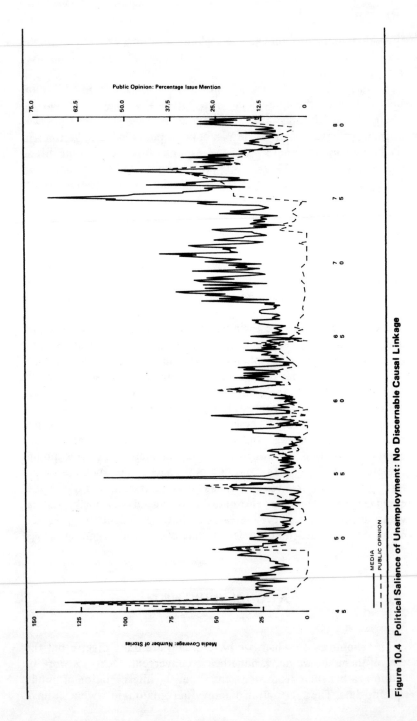

**Figure 10.4 Political Salience of Unemployment: No Discernable Causal Linkage**

come to call public opinion inevitably leads, in some degree, to the adding of apples and oranges. Any two supporters of a particular policy position might well have entirely divergent rationales for their political beliefs. Individuals, even though they are entirely dependent on the news media for information on foreign events, may nevertheless persist in organizing their conceptions of these events in ways quite different from the journalistic community reporting them.

The tension between individual-level political cognitions and aggregated public opinion does allow some middle ground. We can (to push the analogy to its limit) learn to aggregate the apples with apples and the oranges with oranges. But to do that, we must be able to identify persisting patterns of political cognition, and employ an appropriate array of methodological approaches to study them.

Lippmann's *Public Opinion* was published just as sample surveys were beginning to emerge as a research tool in 1922. It is still frequently read and cited by modern scholars. His sensitivity to the issue of political cognition, especially his imagery of the "world outside and the pictures in our heads" and his discussion of political stereotypes and the role of the press in affecting public opinion remains as provocative as ever. His analysis was not based on surveys but drew on a broad array of clinical, experimental, anecdotal, and historical materials and an informal content analysis of the media. His diverse methods allowed him to capture a number of the subtleties of linkage between the media and the public mind and, in turn, between public opinion and public policy. The tools of measurement developed since then allow us to be more precise and systematic and that is indeed important. But such precision should not lull us into a false sense of security in having captured a full measure of public opinion. We might keep in mind a central insight of his book— the individual mind processes information in subtle and complex ways and the "public opinion" of the polity as a whole is correspondingly rich, complex, and diverse.

## APPENDIX

The time-series data reported here were integrated from four sources: the Gallup Poll for public opinion, the *New York Times Index,* the *Readers' Guide to Periodical Literature,* and the Vanderbilt Archives index for media issue coverage trends. The data cover the period 1945 to 1980. For the public opinion data, respondents were asked straightforwardly: "What do you think is the most important problem facing this country today?" The responses were transcribed and coded by the Gallup Organization. The data set includes all issues mentioned by at least one percent of the respondents at some point during the time period. The current analyses focus on ten prominent and persistent issues.

The media data consist of the number of stories in each issue area reported during each month of the time interval. The media coding staff was extensively trained and carefully supervised. Intercoder reliability tests were conducted and, in all cases, the correlation coefficients were greater than .90. The *New York Times Index* was used as an indicator of newspaper content. The *Times* was selected because of its widely acknowledged reputation as a source of record, and the fact that reporters and editors from other newspapers, as well as the wire services, have been known to follow the lead of the *Times* closely (Crouse, 1972: 84).

Because of the broad diversity of magazines available to the American public, no single magazine could serve as a meaningful indicator. As a result, thirty magazines were chosen from six broad categories: (1) news (including, for example, *Time, Newsweek*), (2) mass appeal (*Readers' Digest, Life, Look*), (3) commentary (*Atlantic, New Republic*), (4) business (*Business Week, Fortune*), (5) science (*Scientific American*), and (6) women's magazines (*McCall's, Ladies' Home Journal*). As with the *New York Times* and television, the number of stories presented for each issue area was counted for each month.

Television became an increasingly important source of news for the American public during the 1960s and 1970s (Bower, 1973: 100), so television news coverage was integrated into the data set. Using the synopses of the individual news programs published by the Vanderbilt Archives, the number of stories in each issue area included on the CBS Evening News broadcasts were coded. The television data were only available for the period starting with 1972.[2]

The issue areas and their time periods are as follows:

| | | | |
|---|---|---|---|
| Crime | (1966-1980) | Poverty | (1964-1980) |
| Drug problems | (1966-1975) | Racial problems | (1954-1980) |
| Energy | (1972-1980) | Unemployment | (1945-1980) |
| Inflation | (1945-1980) | Vietnam | (1962-1975) |
| Pollution | (1968-1980) | Watergate | (1972-1976) |

A perusal of the media and public opinion graphs and Direct Granger Causality were used to assess the agenda-setting functions of the media. Direct Granger Causality is a statistical technique designed for the analysis of time-series data. It is similar to a system of regression equations but uses past values of the variables predict present values of the variables. In the two variables case there would be two equations:

$$Y = \alpha \text{ past } Y + \beta \text{ past } X$$
$$X = \sigma \text{ past } X + \gamma \text{ past } Y$$

From these equations, four tests are run to see if $\beta$ and/or $\gamma$ are significant. If neither is significant, then X and Y are independent. If both are significant, then there is feedback in the model (i.e., X ↔ Y). If $\beta$ is significant and $\gamma$ is not, then X is said to lead, or Granger Cause Y (i.e., X → Y). If $\gamma$ is significant and $\beta$ is not, then Y is said to lead, or Granger Cause X (i.e., Y → X). For further information on Direct Granger Causality Methodology, see Freeman (1982).

The Media Agenda Project is being conducted jointly at MIT and Princeton and involves the collaboration of Professor James R. Beniger (Beniger et al., 1984).

## NOTES

1. It should be noted that the amount of media coverage (indicated on the left scale in Figures 10.2, 10.3, and 10.4) varies quite a bit among the three issues we examined. Vietnam received twice as much coverage as the energy crisis and ten times as much as unemployment at comparable peak periods. The public response to each, however, was roughly the same, peaking with 40 percent to 55 percent of the public nominating the issue as one of the most important problems.

2. In order to assure that the addition of television stories in 1972 did not affect the results, the analysis was done three different ways: first, only the newspaper and magazine figures were added together; second, the newspaper, magazine, and television figures were added together assuming that there were no television stories prior to 1972; and third, all media were added together and the average number of TV stories covered for each issue was used for the months prior to 1972. In all cases, the results of the Granger analyses were in the same direction.

## REFERENCES

BALCH, G. (1974) "Multiple indicators in survey research: the concept 'sense of political efficacy.' " Political Methodology 1: 1-44.

BENIGER, J. R., W. R. NEUMAN, and A. D. FRYLING (1984, May) "National problems, media coverage and opinion policy change." Presented at the Association of Public Opinion Research Meetings, Delavan, WI.

BERELSON, B. R., P. F. LAZARSFELD, and W. N. McPHEE (1954) Voting. Chicago: University of Chicago Press.

BOWER, R. T. (1973) Television and the Public. New York: Holt, Rinehart & Winston.

CAMPBELL, A., P. E. CONVERSE, W. E. MILLER, and D. E. STOKES (1966) Elections and the Political Order. New York: John Wiley.

———(1960) The American Voter. New York: John Wiley.

CAMPBELL, D. T. and D. W. FISKE (1959) "Convergent and discriminant validation by the multitrait-multimethod matrix." Psychological Bulletin 56 (March): 81-105.

CITRIN, J. (1974) "Comment: the political relevance of trust in government." American Political Science Review 68: 973-988.

———H. McCLOSKEY, J. M. SHANKS, and P. M. SNIDERMAN (1975) "Personal and political sources of political alientation." British Journal of Political Sciences 5: 1-31.

CONVERSE, P. E. (1964) "The nature of belief systems in mass politics," pp. 202-261 in D. E. Apter (ed.) Ideology and Discontent. New York: Free Press.

CROUSE, T. (1972) The Boys on the Bus. New York: Random House.

DOWNS, A. (1972) "Up and down with ecology—the 'issue-attention cycle.' " Public Interest 28: 38-50.

———(1957) An Economic Theory of Democracy. New York: Harper & Row.

FREEMAN, J. R. (1983) "Granger causality and the times series analyses of political relationships." American Journal of Political Science 27: 327-358.

GAMSON, W. and K. LASCH (1983) "The political culture of social welfare policy," in S. E. Spiro and E. Yaar-Yuchtman (eds.) Evaluating the Welfare State. New York: Academic.

HENSLER, C. P. (1971) "The structure of orientations toward government." Presented to the American Political Science Association Meeting, Chicago.

KRAUS, S. and D. DAVIS (1976) The Effects of Mass Communication on Political Behavior. University Park: Pennsylvania State University Press.

LANE, R. E. (1962) Political Ideology. New York: Free Press.

LASSWELL, H. (1930) Psychopathology and Politics. Chicago: University of Chicago Press.

LIPPMANN, W. (1922/1947) Public Opinion. New York: Free Press. (originally published 1922)

McCLOSKEY, H., P. J. HOFFMAN, and R. O'HARA (1960) "Issue conflict and consensus among party leaders and followers." American Political Science Review 54: 406-429.

McCOMBS, M. and D. SHAW (1972) "The agenda-setting function of the mass media." Public Opinion Quarterly 36: 176-187.

MILLER, A. (1983) "Is confidence rebounding?" Public Opinion 6: 16-20.

———(1974) Political issues and trust in government: 1964-1970." American Political Science Review 68: 951-972.

———E. GOLDENBERG, and L. ERBRING (1979) "Type-set politics." American Political Science Review 73: 67-84.

MILLER, A., W. E. MILLER, A. RAINE, and T. A. BROWN (1976) "A majority party in disarray." American Political Science Review 70: 753-778.

OLSON, M., Jr. (1965) The Logic of Collective Action. Cambridge, MA: Harvard University Press.

SCHWARTZ, D. (1973) Political Alienation and Political Behavior. Hawthorne, NY: Aldine.

SIMON, H. A. (1957) Administrative Behavior. New York: Free Press.

SMITH, T. W. (1980) "America's most important problem—a trend analysis." Public Opinion Quarterly 44: 164-180.

Chapter 11


# LEARNING ABOUT POLITICS
# FROM THE MEDIA
## A Comparative Study of
## Sweden and the United States

Arthur H. Miller
Kent Asp

CITIZENS IN contemporary societies are exposed to a constant flow of information through various channels of mass communication. Television, newspapers, magazines, and radio routinely link millions of people with many aspects of social reality beyond the reach of their personal experience. Indeed, in some areas of life, our *only* experience of events and reality is mediated, either by the mass media or through informal interpersonal networks.

In the political realm especially, our dependence on the news media is virtually complete. We rarely, if ever, witness political events, decisions, or actions firsthand. Research regarding the role and effectiveness of the mass media in educating and informing the public is, therefore, important for understanding voter rationality and political behavior in democratic systems.

Despite earlier conclusions of "minimal effects" (Klapper, 1960), research on the educational capacity of the mass media has increased recently. Some of this work has focused on the informational content of the message, arguing that the public cannot be knowledgeable if the media present little substantive information (e.g., Graber, 1976; Asp, 1980). Others have investigated the question of agenda-setting or what the citizen learns about public affairs from the media (for reviews of pertinent findings see Erbring et al., 1980; McCombs and Shaw, 1972,

1976; Palmgreen and Clarke, 1977). Yet a third set of studies explores the relationship between media usage and the level of information that the citizen has about public affairs (e.g., Clarke and Freden, 1978; Miller and MacKuen, 1979; Robinson, 1972), or knowledge gaps that may be related to media content and use (for an excellent review, see Gaziano, 1983).

Despite promising results, research on the information effects of the media remains inconclusive. For example, Robinson (1967, 1972) has argued that it would be naive to expect public information levels to be raised through mass media efforts. On the other hand, Gaziano (1983) points to numerous studies purporting to show a relationship between media usage and the level of political knowledge held by the public. However, this work often fails to differentiate effects that are attributable to the medium rather than to the audience. It is unclear, for example, whether the reliance measures used by previous studies are indicators of basic social-psychological differences between people, or varying degrees of exposure to different media (Robinson 1975, 1976; Becker and Whitney, 1980; O'Keefe, 1980; McDonald, 1983).

Our exploration of public learning about politics from the mass media responds to some of these limitations in earlier research by conceptualizing information processing as an interaction between the characteristics of the medium and those of the audience. We reject the direct effects model postulated by some earlier media research (e.g., Hyman and Sheatsley, 1947; Berelson et al., 1954) because it fails to consider varying audience sensitivities to different news topics. Likewise, we disagree with the uses and gratifications approach as it places too much emphasis on motivations for media usage.

Unlike this earlier research, our theoretical description of the process by which people learn about politics from the mass media is heavily influenced by contemporary work in cognitive psychology. This work suggests that beyond the content of the message or any influence unique to the particular medium (e.g., newspaper versus television) the cognitive organization of the receiver is a factor in the amount of political information that the citizen abstracts and retains from the media, an argument that is elaborated upon below.

## A COMPARATIVE FRAMEWORK

In addition, we believe that it is theoretically important to consider the possible impact that cultural and institutional factors may have on learning from the mass media. Very little research has been concerned with assessing how social and political structural variables influence both the type of information conveyed by the media and the impact that the media has on mass political attitudes. For example, research criticizing U.S. television news for shallow coverage frequently mentions the disruption of commercials or the entertainment aspect of news reporting as limiting the quality of the information conveyed (Patterson and McClure, 1976; Robinson, 1976). Yet it is difficult to test empirically these arguments based on data from the United States alone, as all three national networks are commercially operated and use a similar format for news presentation. One approach to answering such questions, therefore, is to examine the impact of the media in different cultures where the economic, social, or political structure of the media vary in ways that are theoretically relevant.

Comparing Sweden and the United States, for example, makes good sense because they differ in terms of certain cultural and political features relevant to theories of media effects. Most notable among these differences are the relative importance of political parties and the seriousness accorded to the political process.

Swedish politics are characterized by a strong multiparty system (five major parties) that has remained relatively stable for 50 years and a unicameral parliament in which, unlike many other European countries, the prime minister is only slightly more salient than the leaders of the opposition parties. Swedish electoral campaigns are traditionally very sober, almost dull affairs in which the combatants have a down-to-earth, factual, calm discussion of specific issues, avoiding unnecessary attention via attacks on personalities (Holmberg, 1978).

The United States, in contrast, has witnessed a steady decline during the past two decades in the strength of its two political parties, along with a simultaneous reduction in party loyalty among the electorate. At the same time, the role of candidates, and their personalities have become increasingly important in national politics. Issues receive scant attention by comparison; and the hoopla of national party conventions in the United States epitomizes an entertainment aspect of politics that is unheard of in Sweden.

Such political differences as these are also apparent in the features that distinguish the media of the two countries. Despite the "independent" status of some Swedish newspapers, including the prestigious *Dagens Nyheter,* a majority of the Swedish newspapers declare allegiance to one or another party (see Gustafsson and Hadenius, 1976, for a summary discussion of the party press in Sweden). The political affiliations of various newspapers, as well as government subsidies to help maintain newspapers, are historically established and widely accepted throughout Sweden. The party orientation of a newspaper is clearly projected in editorials and through the greater amount of coverage given to the newspaper's endorsed party, but it is much less evident in regular news reporting.

Unlike newspapers, television news and campaign coverage in Sweden is free of obvious partisan linkage. The two television channels are operated by publicly controlled corporations intent on applying nonpartisan factuality and equal-time guidelines to the coverage of electoral campaigns and political news more generally. Television presentation of daily news in Sweden is again a more staid undertaking than in the United States, although there is some concern about presenting the news in ways that will stimulate public interest.

Newspapers in the United States are not openly affiliated with any particular political party. They may on occasion print editorial endorsements of particular candidates, and many of them may be classified as having a liberal or conservative orientation in their editorials and reporting styles; nevertheless, the stated goal of newspapers and the popular perception of television news is one of objective, nonpartisan reporting of news events.

Although the U.S. press has often been praised for its attempted objective reporting and its watchdog role in American politics, it has also been criticized for superficial coverage of politics. Both the print media and television have been accused of concentrating on the personalities and "horse race" aspects of politics rather than dealing with the substantive issues. Moreover, television news and political programs have been described as providing more entertainment than information.

Given these structural and style differences in the mass media of the two countries, it would seem reasonable to hypothesize that the information function of the media will be stronger in Sweden than in the United States. The total absence of commercials on Swedish television, the continual provision of in-depth discussions of issues and the greater emphasis on serious news reporting, all suggest that we should expect a stronger impact of television on political learning in Sweden than is found in the United States. On the other hand, because newspapers are more clearly associated with a particular party in Sweden than in the United States, we might expect that the medium would have more of a reinforcing effect in the former country but impart more information in the latter.

In brief, we may hypothesize that the extent of learning about politics from the mass media is influenced by a combination of factors including the type of medium attended to, the psychological orientation of the receiver, and constraints in the cultural environment. Before we can turn to an examination of how these factors interact to influence learning about politics, we need to operationalize the concept of political knowledge.

## MEASURING POLITICAL KNOWLEDGE

Some earlier studies have narrowly defined being "informed" or "knowledgeable" about politics as knowing specific facts, such as the names of prominent politicians, or as the ability to quote sections from government documents; for example, the country's constitution (see Graber, 1980; or Gaziano, 1983, for a review of this research). However, in our estimation, being able to recite government statistics or knowing how long various office holders serve hardly conveys a comprehension of major political issues or a knowledge of party and candidate differences.

Our approach to the concept of political knowledge is quite different. We argue that, regardless of specific content, the verbalization of salient reasons for preferring or opposing political alternatives is a strong indicator of possessing information about public affairs.[1] That is, the sheer number of substantive comments that survey respondents make when asked in an open-ended manner to evaluate political parties can provide a useful measure of how well informed people are about politics.

Answering open-ended questions requires the verbalization and structuring of a position in one's own words. The researcher provides no response alternatives; it is the respondent who determines both the substantive framework and how much or how little will be said. Research on cognitive psychology demonstrates that the person who can recall more about a topic has usually spent more time thinking about it in the past, has a richer store of information about the subject, and an organized cognitive framework that is available for readily processing additional, related information that may be encountered in the future (Taylor and Crocker, 1978). The number of responses given in answer to open-ended questions thus gives a direct measure of the amount of knowledge in memory and an indirect measure of how that knowledge is cognitively organized (Fiske et al., 1983).

The obvious advantage of employing this approach is cross-cultural comparability of measurement.[2] The disadvantage is that a measure of political knowledge based on the number of statements made when evaluating political parties provides no way of controlling for either the accuracy or sophistication of the comments. The measure does reflect diversity of knowledge about political parties, however, as the same substantive comment (for example, mentioning a specific policy position taken by the party) is counted only once no matter how many times it is repeated. A respondent making more than one comment about the parties has thus mentioned a diverse set of reasons for their evaluation of the parties including various issues, past performance or future promises, groups associated with the parties, characteristics of the party leaders, political ideology, and a host of other topics.

Despite the superiority of a measure based on open-ended questions, we validate our results by using two additional structured measures of information holding that reflect the accuracy and the breadth of a respondent's political knowledge.[3] Although the structured measures tap a different type of political knowledge—one based more on recognition and recall, rather than on the active information searching required for responses to open-ended questions—we expect all three indicators to be correlated and, therefore, to provide a useful validity check on the analysis results.

## THE EFFECT OF MEDIA
## USAGE ON INFORMATION LEVEL

Does frequent use of the mass media increase one's knowledge about politics? Are newspapers or television more effective as a means of informing the public? Given that television presentations are thought to be more staid in Sweden, and that Swedish television is without the disruption of commercials, is television a more potent source of political information in Sweden than in the United States? Do people who have cognitively richer political schemas pay more attention to the media and learn more than aschematics? These are some of the questions we sought to answer with our various measures of political knowledge. The specific data we employ come from the American National Election Survey of 1976 and the 1979 Swedish Election Study.[4]

The independent variables we chose are based on frequency of media usage rather than media reliance. A major controversy has developed in the mass communications literature regarding the difference between exposure and reliance or dependency measures (e.g., Miller and Reese, 1982; McDonald, 1983; McLeod et al., 1983). Our position is that reliance and dependency measures confound two separable factors:

frequency of contact with or exposure to information in the media, and a personal preference for one medium over another. The former is a behavioral indicator; the latter is a statement about self assessment—I am the type of person who probably depends more on such-and-such a medium. No doubt even exposure measures reflect some influence of the psychological self-image assessment but it should be far less than is true for reliance measures (this point is suggested by McLeod et al., 1983).

As we were interested in separating analytically the influence of the medium from the cognitive sensitivity of the audience, we selected frequency of exposure to newspapers and television news as the independent variables of primary importance for testing our hypotheses.[5] We also included a measure of exposure to special TV programs about the election campaign.[6] Theoretically, if the viewer's interest in politics interacts with exposure to the medium to determine the level of political knowledge gained from the media, we would hypothesize that people should learn more from special political programs than from the regularly scheduled news. Such a finding would suggest that the lack of knowledge gained from TV news found by some previous research is not dependent on the characteristics of the medium but results from an interaction of media and audience factors.

Given the previous research findings, we were not surprised to discover that newspaper reading had a greater impact than television viewing on the level of political information (see, for example, Clarke and Fredin, 1978; McClure and Patterson, 1976; Miller and MacKuen, 1979). In both Sweden and the United States, newspaper reading was more strongly associated with all three measures of information holding than was watching television news (see Table 11.1). Such a discovery confirms once more the "great uniformity of findings regarding the superiority of newspapers over television in conveying political information" (McLeod et al., 1983). Nevertheless, watching televised campaign programs was significantly associated with greater knowledge about political parties and issues, thus demonstrating that at least some types of television programs convey more than an inconsequential degree of political information.

One of the most surprising findings of Table 11.1 derives from a comparison of the effects that media usage has on information holding in Sweden and the United States. Virtually all of the comparable correlations between media exposure and information level, regardless of measure used, are higher for the United States. Most notable are the differences evident for the party evaluation measures. The other two dependent variables produce much smaller differences but nonetheless generally run in the same direction. These results imply that the more

**TABLE 11.1**
**Relation Between Frequency of Media Usage
and Information Holding**

| | Sweden | | | United States | | |
|---|---|---|---|---|---|---|
| | Party Evaluation[a] | DK on Issues[b] | Party Policies[c] | Party Evaluation[a] | DK on Issues[b] | Party Policies[c] |
| Zero-Order Correlations | | | | | | |
| Newspaper | .29 | .32 | .25 | .44 | .39 | .32 |
| TV news | .02 | .15 | .07 | .12 | .10 | .09 |
| TV programs | .13 | .20 | .17 | .27 | .23 | .21 |
| Multiple R | .36 | .39 | .30 | .45 | .47 | .39 |
| Regression Coefficients[d] | | | | | | |
| Newspaper | .12 | .13 | .11 | .19 | .17 | .13 |
| TV news | .01 | .10 | .01 | .04 | .06 | .04 |
| TV programs | .07 | .06 | .09 | .13 | .11 | .10 |
| Multiple R | .49 | .48 | .34 | .52 | .51 | .43 |

a. Number of substantive comments given to open-ended questions asking what respondent likes/dislikes about each political party.
b. Number of don't-knows given in response to a series of survey questions about issues.
c. Accuracy with which respondent could match party position with policy alternatives.
d. Standardized regression coefficients representing the impact of media usage on information holding after removing the effects of education, political interest, and strength of party identification. The multiple R is for the entire equation including education, interest, and party identification.

serious approach to newscasting on Swedish television does not alone ensure that the public will gain a high level of political knowledge from the medium. Other factors apparently enter into the equation.

The lower correlations for Sweden in Table 11.1 in fact suggest that Swedes are less reliant than Americans on the mass media for their political information. This conclusion is made even more evident with a closer examination of information level by frequency of media usage in the two countries. Before turning to this comparison it is instructive to note that the aggregate level of political knowledge in the two countries was exactly the same—the average number of open-ended comments made about each party was 1.57 in both countries. A comparison of information level by frequency of media usage reveals how the media in the two countries help produce this overall similarity in the level of political knowledge. Whereas low-frequency media users in Sweden have more information about political parties than their American counterparts, the most frequent media users in the United States are substantially better informed than the comparable group in Sweden. Figures 11.1-11.3 reflect this pattern of differences between the two countries. Evidently, low media users in Sweden, unlike those in the United States, are utilizing sources other than the mass media for political information—most likely originating from direct involvement with partisan organizational activities.

The most frequent media users in the two countries diverge quite sharply in their relative levels of information. In the United States frequent media users are better informed than would be expected from a linear extension of the information levels among lower-frequency media users (see Figures 11.1-11.3). In Sweden, however, information holding is lower than expected among the regular media users relative to the less frequent users. The divergence in information level among frequent media users in the two countries can be explained by drawing upon recent work in cognitive social psychology.

## POLITICAL SCHEMAS AND INFORMATION PROCESSING

The most relevant concept from this work is the notion of schema, which helps us understand how people organize their thoughts about the world (for a review of the relevant literature see Taylor and Crocker, 1981). Every day the average citizen is confronted with information from the media and other sources on a multitude of topics, including politics. People are more attentive to some of these items than to others. They take in information on those items to which they attend, storing it in a form that is readily accessible for use in the interpretation of similar events or topics in the future.

A person who has a rich political schema, or party schema, for example, would be more attentive to political news and would have a framework into which any new piece of political information could be incorporated (Hamilton, 1981). Available political news would, therefore, be more meaningful for them; they would more readily recall the new information and relate it to other pieces of previously stored political information. In addition, previous research suggests that people with richer schemas (labeled political experts or sophisticates) can be expected to be more interested and involved in politics, as well as more likely to follow political news (Fiske et al., 1983).

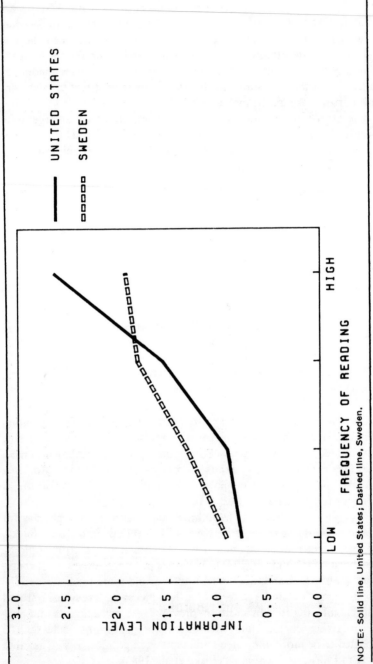

NOTE: Solid line, United States; Dashed line, Sweden.

Figure 11.1  Information About Parties by Frequency of Newspaper Reading

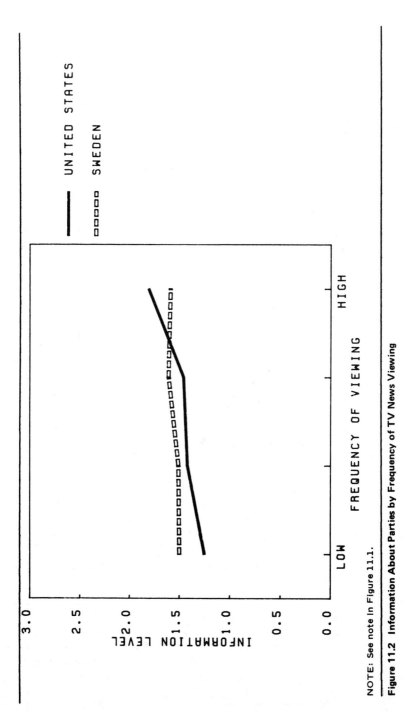

NOTE: See note in Figure 11.1.

Figure 11.2  Information About Parties by Frequency of TV News Viewing

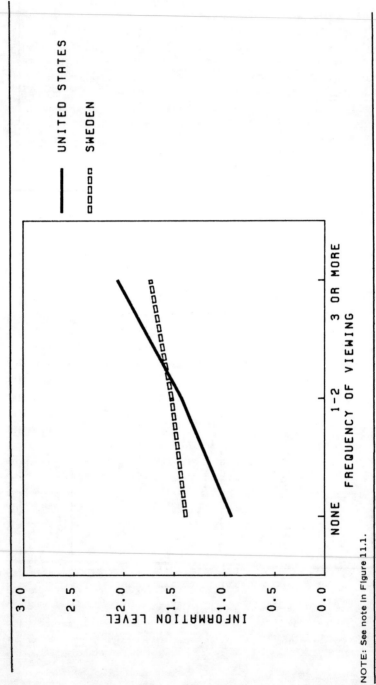

NOTE: See note in Figure 11.1.

Figure 11.3  Information About Parties by Frequency of Viewing TV Campaign Programs

There is no agreed-upon battery of survey questions for measuring directly the richness of political schemas. Nevertheless, social and political variables such as education, interest in politics, and strength of party identification should indicate indirectly the extent to which the citizen has developed a rich cognitive framework about politics, which in turn will influence how they react to political information. Education is important for the obvious reason that it provides, in a formal setting, a basic understanding of the political system, in turn giving incoming media information greater relevance and meaning. By teaching approaches to problem solving, formal education also provides intellectual tools and norms that promote media usage and information seeking. Similarly, political interest and strength of party identification can also be viewed as indirect measures of cognitive richness and the ability to process efficiently incoming political information and meaningfully apply it. These characteristics should not only affect media usage habits in the two countries but they should influence the extent of learning about politics from the mass media as well.

## COGNITIVE RICHNESS AND MEDIA USAGE

The relationship between education and newspaper usage is substantially different for Sweden and the United States (see Table 11.2). Level of formal education is a major determinant of newspaper reading about politics in the United States. As predicted, the better-educated respondents in the United States were considerably more likely to read about politics than were the less well educated. In Sweden, the differences in frequency of reading about politics across levels of education ran in the same direction but they were nearly insignificant. It appears from these data that the usage of newspapers for political information may be less elitist in character in Sweden than in the United States, especially because slightly over 60 percent of the Swedish respondents fell into the lowest education category.

The stronger impact of education on higher rates of newspaper reading in the United States appears to be partially offset by involvement with the political parties in Sweden. The correlation between strength of attachment to political parties and frequency of reading about politics is twice as strong in Sweden as in the United States (see Table 11.2). The difference in the size of the correlation is probably a reflection of the relationship between the political parties and the press

**TABLE 11.2**

**Frequency of Reading About Politics in Newspapers, Television News Viewing, and Viewing Elections Programs by Education, Political Interest, and Party Identification**

| Frequency | Education | | | Political Interest | | Party Identification | | |
|---|---|---|---|---|---|---|---|---|
| | Low | Medium | High | Low | High | None | Weak | Strong |
| **Sweden 1979** | | | | | | | | |
| Newspaper reading | | | | | | | | |
| Low | 53[a] | 52 | 24 | 77 | 11 | 71 | 52 | 37 |
| High | 21 | 18 | 31 | 9 | 59 | 13 | 18 | 33 |
| (N) | (1729) | (586) | (329) | (1199) | (341) | (215) | (534) | (867) |
| | | r = .10 | | r = .52 | | | r = .23 | |
| Watching TV news | | | | | | | | |
| Low | 22 | 34 | 34 | 29 | 21 | 37 | 30 | 18 |
| High | 58 | 40 | 39 | 45 | 61 | 40 | 48 | 61 |
| | | r = −.19 | | r = .15 | | | r = .16 | |
| Viewing election shows | | | | | | | | |
| Low | 18 | 20 | 20 | 26 | 11 | 33 | 19 | 12 |
| High | 46 | 38 | 36 | 30 | 64 | 30 | 38 | 55 |
| | | r = −.07 | | r = .26 | | | r = .21 | |

*United States 1976*

| | | | | | | | | |
|---|---|---|---|---|---|---|---|---|
| **Newspaper reading** | | | | | | | | |
| Low | 58 | 39 | 18 | 71 | 11 | 52 | 37 | 24 |
| High | 14 | 21 | 44 | 3 | 59 | 16 | 25 | 37 |
| (N) | (374) | (1881) | (828) | (723) | (901) | (372) | (938) | (561) |
| | | r = -.07 | | r = .25 | | | r = .12 | |
| **Watching TV news** | | | | | | | | |
| Low | 16 | 24 | 25 | 36 | 14 | 24 | 24 | 15 |
| High | 61 | 52 | 52 | 36 | 71 | 46 | 52 | 64 |
| | | r = -.07 | | r = .25 | | | r = .11 | |
| **Viewing election shows** | | | | | | | | |
| Low | 26 | 20 | 10 | 35 | 7 | 24 | 19 | 12 |
| High | 47 | 42 | 51 | 24 | 65 | 34 | 42 | 61 |
| | | r = .09 | | r = .35 | | | r = .12 | |

a. Table entries are column percentages. In each case the middle category of the frequency of exposure measure has been deleted for parsimony of presentation. That percentage can be calculated by adding the low plus high percentage and subtracting from 100.

b. For parsimony of presentation the category of partisan leaners has been excluded from the table. This group generally compares very closely with the weak partisans.

in Sweden. It seems reasonable to expect that strong party identifiers will read about politics in a newspaper more frequently because they recognize it as expressing their partisan orientation. Given that strong party identifiers (those most likely to read about politics) constituted 36 percent of the Swedish population but only 23 percent of the United States sample, partisan politics must play a more important role in stimulating newspaper usage for political learning in Sweden than in the United States.

Not surprisingly, those most interested in politics were highly motivated to seek out political information from newspapers in both countries.[7] Only a small proportion of those expressing a low level of interest in public affairs used newspapers regularly to learn about politics (see Table 11.2).

Television news was clearly preferred over newspapers as a source of political information among the less well educated, and to a certain extent, by those with relatively little interest in politics (see Table 11.2). In both countries, about six of every ten less well-educated respondents reported watching TV news virtually every day. Given that a majority of these people rarely follow politics in the newspaper, television news was obviously an important source of political information for them. Although better educated people likewise watched television news with a fairly high degree of regularity, they also frequently read about politics in newspapers and were thus less reliant on television for their political information.

In both countries those least interested in politics were also more likely to use television than newspapers for learning about politics. They rarely read about politics but nearly half of them were regular viewers of television news. This relatively high frequency of news viewing among the least interested results in much lower correlations than were found with newspaper reading. Clearly, watching television news to learn about politics requires less self-motivation and personal effort than seeking political information by reading newspapers. But a cognitive explanation is also very relevant for the greater television usage among the less educated and least interested: These people are less involved in politics and are more likely to be attracted by the vivid or colorful type of information conveyed by television news.

Turning to television viewing of campaign programs, however, we again find a larger impact of political interest, and in Sweden, strength of party identification (see Table 11.2). Watching interviews of party leaders or presidential debates is a more selective activity than watching the nightly news. The less well-educated, the least politically motivated, and nonpartisan respondents showed less sustained interest in watching campaign programs than in viewing the daily news. The result of this selective viewing was that the campaign program audience in both countries was better educated and more interested in politics than the ordinary TV news audience.

In general, the data analysis demonstrates that the overall pattern of media usage among various groups is the same in Sweden and in the United States. Television news and televised campaign programs especially appear to be used to the same degree by similar groups in both countries. But there is one important difference between the two countries that focuses on the role of the daily newspaper. The relationship between newspaper reading about politics and formal education is much stronger in the United States than in Sweden.

## NEWSPAPER EFFECTS AND AUDIENCE SENSITIVITY

Regular newspaper readers in Sweden, for example, were predominantly strong partisan identifiers; in the United States they were disproportionately better educated. These characteristics apparently reflect varying audience sensitivity to learning about politics from different mass media sources.[8] For example, increased education level appears to amplify the effect of newspaper usage on knowledge about politics—note the larger regression coefficients for newspapers in Table 11.3 among college as compared with grade-school educated respondents. A similar pattern of coefficients is also found by level of political interest. Better educated and politically interested people presumably come to the newspaper with cognitive skills and a richer political schema that prepare them to more readily incorporate political information into their cognitive framework.

Newspapers have less of an impact, on the other hand, among strong partisan identifiers—the heavy newspaper users in Sweden—than they do among weak identifiers. Contrary to what was hypothesized, strong partisan attachment failed to increase the importance of learning about parties through the mass media. No doubt strong partisans have various direct, organizational avenues for obtaining information about the parties and thus may be more knowledgeable about the party system and less reliant on the media for their information about partisan politics. These expectations appear to be fulfilled in the United States where the average number of open-ended comments made about the parties were .95, 1.51, and 2.08 for nonidentifiers, weak, and strong

**TABLE 11.3**

**Regression Coefficients Predicting Information Holding About Parties by Education, Political Interest, and Strength of Party Identification**

| | Sweden Education | | | United States Education | | |
|---|---|---|---|---|---|---|
| | Low | Medium | High | Low | Medium | High |
| Newspaper | .25 | .34 | .40 | .17 | .32 | .38 |
| TV news | .06 | .02 | −.13 | .15 | .12 | .08 |
| TV programs | .14 | .07 | −.03 | .34 | .26 | .21 |
| Multiple R | .34 | .32 | .35 | .41 | .38 | .40 |

| | Sweden Political Interest | | United States Political Interest | |
|---|---|---|---|---|
| | Low | High | Low | High |
| Newspaper | .18 | .29 | .22 | .32 |
| TV news | .07 | .02 | .08 | .06 |
| TV programs | .13 | .09 | .25 | .14 |
| Multiple R | .27 | .31 | .33 | .37 |

| | Sweden Strength Party ID | | | United States Strength Party ID | | |
|---|---|---|---|---|---|---|
| | None | Weak | Strong | None | Weak | Strong |
| Newspaper | .32 | .38 | .34 | .36 | .41 | .35 |
| TV news | .12 | .01 | −.13 | .14 | .06 | .09 |
| TV programs | .04 | .16 | .08 | .25 | .25 | .12 |
| Multiple R | .33 | .38 | .36 | .39 | .42 | .35 |

partisans, respectively. But, despite the higher level of political knowledge found for strong identifiers, the United States coefficients in Table 11.3 reveal the lowest media effects for this group, implying a weaker linkage between information level and media usage for them than for other less partisan groups. Among the Swedes, as expected, media effects were also somewhat lower for the strongest party identifiers. Surprisingly, however, strong partisans in Sweden were not significantly better informed about the parties than were weaker identifiers— the average number of comments made about the parties were 1.29, 1.53, and 1.58 for nonidentifiers, weak, and strong partisans, respectively.[9]

Cognitive psychology provides two closely related explanations for the relatively low level of information evident among strong identifiers in Sweden and the weaker impact of media usage on political knowledge among strong partisans in both countries. The first comes from work on schemas and the notion of biased assimilation (Fiske and Taylor, 1984: 149). Strong partisans may be very sensitive to news about their own party but they may fail to retain information about other parties because it is less relevant to their cognitive orientation. In response to open-ended questions, strong identifiers in both countries did in fact make more comments about their own party than about opposing parties. If our measure of information holding focused only on knowledge about one's own party, we would find a larger media effect among strong partisans relative to those with a weaker identification. But our concern here is with knowledge of political parties in general. In this case, having a very strong party identification appears to limit general political learning by inducing biased assimilation. Given that a larger percentage of Swedes than Americans were strong partisans, there is, in the aggregate, a greater degree of biased assimilation in Sweden. Because strong party identifiers are also the heavy newspaper users in Sweden, biased assimilation helps to explain the Figure 11.1 discrepancy in level of information among frequent newspaper readers in the two countries.

A closely related but alternative explanation is suggested by recent work on the connection between affect and cognitions (Zajonc, 1980). Zajonc argues that affect and cognitions are processed largely independently. Under some circumstances affective and cognitive processes may proceed in parallel without influencing each other. One implication of this work is that individuals who feel very strongly about something may make statements that express their emotions very clearly but suggest only a limited amount of information and cognitive processing. Party identification may be such a basic aspect of the political self-concept for strong partisans that they devote little active processing time to thinking about what it means to be a member of a particular party unless that attachment is challenged (Markus and Sentis, 1980). On the whole, this research suggests that very strong identifiers might give a limited set of responses when they are asked what they like and dislike about various parties. Indeed, strong partisans—particularly in Sweden—have a tendency to exhibit intensity of affect in their response by saying they dislike "everything" about all the other parties.

Although this response may indicate strong emotions, it gets treated by our measure of political knowledge as only one response. According to theories of cognitive psychology, however, a schematic person—one who has a rich and highly structured framework for encoding and interpreting information—may "chunk" that information in a highly efficient way. A person with an impoverished schema, on the other hand, may morselize the stream of information or see politics as a series of unconnected events (Tesser, 1978; Lane, 1956). In some instances, therefore, the brief statement, "I like everything about my party and dislike everything about the other parties" may reflect a high degree of chunking or efficient information processing. Of course, such a categorical response to the parties may likewise result in biased information processing that limits the encoding and assimilation of new information about either one's own party or the opposition parties. Whatever the explanation, the net result is that strong identifiers in Sweden appear to be less well informed than expected—again helping to explain the Figure 11.1 discrepancy between the level of information for the frequent newspaper readers of the two countries.

## TELEVISION EFFECTS AND AUDIENCE SENSITIVITY

An examination of television effects on information holding reveals the same pattern of relationships across varying levels of party identification as was found for newspaper reading—stronger effects among the weaker identifiers. But a substantially different pattern of relationships emerge by level of education and political interest. Frequent viewing of TV news and campaign programs has more effect on increasing political knowledge among the lower educated and least interested respondents than among the better educated and more interested (see Table 11.3). Although the correlations between television news viewing and information level about politics is not significant for the total population, in both countries TV news is a critical source of public affairs information among the less well educated and less interested who make little use of newspapers.

The more substantial impact of televised campaign programs relative to the effect of TV news suggests a possible explanation for the minimal effects associated with the news coverage. The evening news deals with a variety of events occurring during the day, not simply political events. Viewers come to the news, therefore, with a general cognitive orientation, whereas when they watch campaign programs, it is with the specific intention of learning about politics. In short, they have been cognitively primed and their political schemas have been activated by knowing about the topic of the program in advance. Cognitively, therefore, individuals may be more responsive to the content of campaign programs and subsequently learn more from them than from the news.

A further implication of this audience sensitivity explanation is that the heightened impact of TV news among the lower educated may occur because they view the news with greater attentiveness and purpose because they rarely have newspapers as an alternative information source. In part this also helps to explain why television has a greater impact among the less well educated in the United States compared with Sweden (see regression coefficients by education level in Table 11.3). The less well educated in Sweden were somewhat more likely than their United States counterparts to read newspapers or obtain partisan information from organizations such as the political parties or labor unions. In addition, the relatively greater impact of TV found for the United States may arise because television news coverage there employs a more vivid and lively style of presentation. As Fiske and Taylor (1984: 194) point out, vividly presented information "serves mainly to catch the attention of people who are uninvolved."

In summary, newspapers and television in the United States have a somewhat greater impact on the citizen's level of political information than in Sweden. Americans who rarely use the mass media for information about politics are relatively uninformed compared to their Swedish counterparts. Alternative sources of political information are apparently available to Swedes, whereas Americans fall back on the readily accessible, vivid, but more superficial information conveyed by television.

Beyond this important difference the analysis reveals substantially similar media effects in the two countries. The significance of audience sensitivity is suggested by both the Swedish and American data. Media usage apparently interacts with the cognitive sensitivity of the audience to affect political learning. Higher education, for example, promotes learning from newspapers in both societies, whereas strength of party identification reduces it. Television, on the other hand, had a relatively more potent effect on political knowledge among the less well educated, particularly in the United States. Television news should not be written off as uninformative as it is clearly an important source of political learning among the lesser educated in both Sweden and the United States.

## CONCLUSION

At the outset of this report we suggested that media usage and the effects of mass communication on political learning could be expected to differ in Sweden and the United States. Nevertheless, substantial cross-cultural similarity was found in media usage patterns and the importance of the media for political learning.

Active use of the media to follow public affairs contributes significantly to the citizen's political knowledge in both societies even after controlling for various motivational and cognitive factors including education, political interest, and strength of partisan attachment. This is not a "hypodermic" effect, however. Rather, audience sensitivity and media usage interact to amplify the effect of the media on the information level among certain subgroups.

A broader theoretical understanding of both the power and limits of the mass media to influence political attitudes and knowledge must incorporate a psychological theory of information processing. Without an explication of information processing at the individual level the audience becomes a black box in the study of media effects. Notions of schematic information processing provide a conceptual framework for interpreting and explaining many of the significant findings in media research.

The interpretations and conclusions suggested by the concept of schematic information processing differ substantially from the motivational interpretations derived from the uses and gratification approach. Rather than needs that must be gratified, the relative use of various media can be explained on the basis of the cognitive richness of the audience, differences in attention to vivid information, and the relevance of the information to the prior expectations and political schema of the audience. The cognitive approach also raises concerns about reliance measures. People may tell us that they rely more on TV for their political information because it is a more vivid medium, but that does not necessarily mean they gain most of their political knowledge from television. People frequently make errors when asked to report on their own behaviors or decision-making processes. To accurately understand the impact of information processing on learning about politics we must separate those cognitive and motivational factors from the inherent properties of the medium. Reliance measures fail to do this.

Differences in the format and presentation of television news in Sweden and the United States, when coupled with the common finding of weak effects on political learning, also provides further insight into television as a medium. Despite the absence of commercials in Sweden, television news generally is not a potent source of political information. This suggests that either there are fewer differences between Swedish and United States news presentation style than popularly thought, or that television is not a good medium for conveying political information. Perhaps the fleeting nature of television's message prevents the audience from learning much. Alternatively, perhaps the general audience is cognitively less attentive to political information transmitted via the TV news than through newspapers or special campaign programs. Whatever the explanation, the analysis suggests the simplicity underlying research claiming that TV news does not inform the public because it is superficial and mainly entertaining. There are clearly alternative explanations that also should be considered.

Moreover, television news is very important for lesser-educated citizens. Without TV they would surely be less well informed. The problem, of course, for those who rely upon television news as their sole source of political information, is the quality of the news content conveyed by the medium. We have not examined the quality of political knowledge associated with media usage only the quantity; thus we cannot speak to the relative merits of the informal content of television news and campaign programs versus that of newspapers.

A critical element of democratic systems is an informed citizenry. The relatively lower impact of television on how well informed the public is, therefore, argues for the maintenance of a healthy, competitive newspaper industry in both countries. Despite widespread TV news viewing, newspapers remain the most potent medium for informing the public. The extent of learning from various media sources, however, depends on three elements: the characteristics of the medium, factors in the social environment, and the cognitive structuring of the audience. To understand more fully the limits on the extent to which citizens can learn about politics from the mass media, all three of these elements must be considered by future researchers.

## NOTES

1. This approach is similar to the message discrimination concept discussed in Clarke and Kline (1974) and Palmgreen et al. (1974). Previous applications of this measure of information holding can be found in Clarke and Fredin (1978) and Miller and MacKuen (1979).

2. The survey questions used were identical in both countries. Respondents were asked to explain in their own words what they liked and disliked about each major party. As many as five positive and five negative comments per party were coded for each respondent. Although Sweden has five political parties and the United States has only two, comparability was obtained by dividing the number of comments made by the number of parties in each country. The final measure indicates the number of comments made per party and can be interpreted as the amount of information held about political parties in general, rather than knowledge about a particular party.

3. Accuracy of knowledge about political parties was measured by whether or not the respondent could correctly match a party and its policy alternative on particular substan-

tive topics. Respondents' breadth of political knowledge was operationalized as the ability to state policy preferences over a wide range of policy areas. An index was created showing the number of items to which a respondent gave a substantive answer rather than saying "don't know." Although the actual questions used to construct these structured measures of information holding are not identical in both surveys, they can validate the *pattern* of relationships found with the open-ended measures.

4. The 1979 Swedish Election Study conducted by the University of Gothenburg was based on personal interviews during October and November. The 1850 respondents were selected with probability sampling methods to represent the eligible electorate throughout Sweden.

The 1976 American National Election Survey was conducted by the University of Michigan, Institute for Social Research. The study employed personal interviews with a cross-sectional sample of the eligible electorate 18 years old and older (N = 2248) immediately before and after the presidential election of that year.

5. The survey questions used to measure frequency of newspaper reading about politics were as follows:

*Sweden:* How often do you read articles on politics in the daily newspaper? (responses: never, sometimes, often, every day).

The Trichotomy used in Table 11.2 combines never and sometimes in the low category.

*United States:* Some people don't have time to read the entire daily newspaper. I'm going to read you a list of different kinds of stories in the news. Just tell me if you read them frequently, sometimes, rarely, or never. How often do you read stories about national politics?

The lower category in Table 11.2 is formed by combining responses of rarely and never.

The survey questions used to measure the frequency of TV news viewing were as follows:

*Sweden:* How often do you see the evening news (Rapport/Aktuellt). Response categories were: 6-7, 3-5, 1-2 days per week, less often, or never.

*United States, 1976:* How often do you watch national news broadcasts in the early evening (frequently, sometimes, rarely, or never)?

Frequency of watching the news was collapsed as follows in Table 11.2:

*Sweden:* Low, 2 or fewer days per week; medium, 3-5 days; high, every day.

*United States:* Low, rarely or never; medium, sometimes; high, frequently.

6. In addition to the national news, television presents a variety of special campaign-related programs that potentially act as another source of political information. During the last three weeks of the 1979 Swedish election campaign, for example, five television programs presenting interviews with the leaders of Sweden's five political parties were broadcast. Similarly, in 1976, the U.S. television networks carried a series of four debates between the presidential and vice-presidential candidates of that year.

The frequency distributions for watching the Swedish party leader interviews and the U.S. presidential debates were nearly identical. In both countries more than 80 percent watched at least one of the programs.

The frequency of viewing election programs was collapsed for the analysis in Table 11.2. The low category indicated that none of the programs had been watched, medium referred to 1 or 2, and high meant 3 or more.

7. Unlike education and strength of party identification, the measure of political interest was not exactly the same in both the Swedish and American surveys. The United States question refers to following what goes on in government and public affairs, whereas the Swedish question asks only about interest in politics.

## REFERENCES

ASP, K. (1983) "The struggle for the agenda: party agenda, media agenda, and voter agenda in the 1979 Swedish election campaign." Communication Research 3: 333-355.
———(1980) "Mass media as molders of opinion and suppliers of information: a study of extraparliamentary action in Sweden," in G. Wilhoit and H. deBock (eds.) Mass Communication Review Yearbook (vol. 1). Beverly Hills, CA: Sage.
BECKER, L. B. and D. C. WHITNEY (1980) "Effects of media dependencies on audience assessment of government." Communication Research 7: 95-120.
BERELSON, B., P. F. LAZARSFELD, and W. McPHEE (1954) Voting. New York: Duell, Sloan and Pearce.
CLARKE, P. and E. FREDIN (1978) "Newspaper, television and political reasoning." Public Opinion Quarterly 42: 143-160.
CLARKE, P. and G. KLINE (1974) "Media effects reconsidered: some new strategies for communication research." Communication Research 1: 224-240.
ERBRING, L., E. GOLDENBERG, and A. H. MILLER (1980) "Front-page news and real world cues: another look at agenda-setting by the media." American Journal of Political Science 24: 16-49.
FISKE, S. T. and S. E. TAYLOR (1984) Social Cognition. Reading, MA: Addison-Wesley.
FISKE, S. T., D. R. KINDER, and W. M. LARTER (1983) "The novice and the expert: knowledge based strategies in political cognition." Journal of Experimental Social Psychology 19: 381-400.
GAZIANO, C. (1983) "The knowledge gap: an analytical review of media effects." Communication Research 10: 447-486.
GRABER, D. (1980) Mass Media and American Politics. Washington, DC: Congressional Quarterly Press.
———(1976) "Press and TV as opinion resources in presidential campaigns." Public Opinion Quarterly 40: 285-303.
GUSTAFSSON, K. E. and S. HADENIUS (1976) Swedish Press Policy. Stockholm: The Swedish Institute.
HAMILTON, D. L. (1981) "Cognitive representations of persons," in E. T. Higgins et al. (eds.) Social Cognition. Hillsdale, NJ: Lawrence Erlbaum.
HOLMBERG, S. (1978) "Pressen och karnkraften." Statsvetenskaplig Tidskrift 4: 211.
HYMAN, H. H. and P. B. SHEATSLEY (1947) "Some reasons why information campaigns fail." Public Opinion Quarterly 11: 412-423.
KLAPPER, J. (1960) The Effects of Mass Communication. New York: Free Press.
LANE, R. (1956) Political Ideology. New Haven, CT: Yale University Press.

MARKUS, H. and K. SENTIS (1980) "The self in social information processing," in J. Suls (ed.) Social Psychological Perspectives on the Self. Hillsdale, NJ: Lawrence Erlbaum.

McCLURE, R. D. and T. E. PATTERSON (1976) "Print vs. network news." Journal of Communication 26: 23-28.

McCOMBS, M. E. and D. SHAW (1976) "Structuring the unseen environment." Journal of Communication 26: 18-22.

———(1972) "The agenda-setting function of mass media." Public Opinion Quarterly 35: 176-187.

McDONALD, D. (1983) "Investigating assumptions of media dependency research." Communication Research 10: 508-528.

McLEOD, J. M., C. J. GLYNN, and D. A. McDONALD (1983) "Issues and images: the influence of media reliance in voting decisions." Communication Research 10: 37-58.

MILLER, A. H. and M. MacKUEN (1979) "Learning about the candidates: the 1976 presidential debates." Public Opinion Quarterly 43: 326-346.

MILLER, M. M. and S. D. REESE (1982) "Media dependency as interaction: Effects of exposure and reliance on political activity and efficacy." Communication Research 9: 227-248.

O'KEEFE, G. (1980) "Political malaise and reliance on media." Journalism Quarterly 57: 122-128.

PALMGREEN, P. C. and P. CLARKE (1977) "Agenda-setting with local and national issues." Communication Research 4: 435-452.

PATTERSON, T. E. and R. D. McCLURE (1976) The Unseeing Eye. New York: Putnam.

ROBINSON, J. (1967). "World affairs information and mass media exposure." Journalism Quarterly 44: 23-31.

ROBINSON, P. (1972) "Mass communication and information diffusion," pp. 71-93 in F. G. Kline and P. J. Tichenor (eds.) Current Perspectives in Mass Communications Research. Beverly Hills, CA: Sage.

ROBINSON, M. J. (1976) "Public affairs television and the growth of political malaise." American Political Science Review 70: 409-432.

———(1975) "American political legitimacy in an era of electronic journalism," in D. Cater and R. Adler (eds.) Television As a Social Force. New York: Praeger.

TAYLOR, S. E. and J. CROCKER (1981) "Schematic bases of social information processing," in E. T. Higgins et al. (eds.) Social Cognition. Hillsdale, NJ: Lawrence Erlbaum.

———(1978) "Salience, attention and attribution: top of the head phenomena," in L. Berkowitz (ed.) Advances in Experimental Social Psychology (vol. 11). New York: Academic.

TESSER, A. (1978) "Self-generated attitude change," in L. Berkowitz (ed.) Advances in Experimental Social Psychology (vol. 11). New York: Academic Press.

ZAJONC, R. (1980) "Feeling and thinking: preferences need no inferences." American Psychologist 35: 151-175.

# Chapter 12

# INTEGRATIVE COMPLEXITY
# OF POLICY REASONING

## Philip E. Tetlock

OBSERVERS OF THE political scene lavish attention on the opinions that high-level policymakers express on issues of the day. All this attention is not, of course, surprising. The opinions policymakers express are often taken as clues to future decisions with potential national and international consequences (Graber, 1976). It is perhaps surprising, however, that observers devote relatively little attention to *how* policymakers appear to think—to the styles of reasoning they use in explaining and justifying their views to others. Do policymakers, for instance, see solutions to problems as essentially simple (all considerations pointing to the one conclusion) or complex (competing values must be weighed against each other)? Are policymakers tolerant or intolerant of alternative ways of looking at issues? Do policymakers deduce positions from general principles or reason inductively from specific experiences and cases?

Much can be learned about both policymakers and the world in which they operate from careful examination of their styles of political reasoning. Much can also be revealed from careful examination of variables in the real world that covary with styles of political reasoning. Substantial individual differences exist in styles of reasoning (Putnam,

AUTHOR'S NOTE: Preparation of this chapter was assisted by the Institute on Global Conflict and Cooperation and by the Survey Research Center at the University of California, Berkeley. Correspondence concerning this chapter should be sent to Philip E. Tetlock, Department of Psychology, 3210 Tolman Hall, University of California, Berkeley, CA 94720.

1971; Tetlock, 1984a). Significant relationships exist, moreover, between these individual differences and political attitudes and policy stands. Styles of reasoning also vary as a function of situational variables, including political role (Tetlock, 1981a; Tetlock et al., 1984), the issues under discussion (Tetlock, 1984c; Tetlock et al., forthcoming), and levels of stress and threat (Staw et al., 1981; Suedfeld and Tetlock, 1977).

This chapter describes a series of studies that explore both individual difference and situational correlates of styles of political reasoning in primarily "elite" samples (e.g., United States senators, Supreme Court justices, British parliamentarians). The chapter is divided into two sections. The first section describes the stylistic dimension of reasoning on which my own work has focused: conceptual or integrative complexity. A brief review of integrative complexity theory is also provided. The second section describes empirical work that probes relationships between integrative complexity and a variety of attitudinal, personality, and situational variables. It is argued that a comprehensive explanation of the findings must draw on a number of theoretical traditions, including personality theories, role theories, and theories of cognitive processing under uncertainty and value conflict. Finally, the discussion concludes by discussing directions that future research on the integrative complexity of political elites might take, emphasizing the need for work on how the mass media communicate (and sometimes distort) debates among political elites to the general public.

## THEORETICAL BACKGROUND

Integrative complexity theory was originally developed to explain individual differences in the complexity of the cognitive rules people use to analyze incoming information and to make decisions (Harvey et al., 1961; Schroder et al., 1967). The theory focused on two cognitive stylistic variables, differentiation and integration. Differentiation refers to the number of dimensions of a problem that are taken into account in evaluating or interpreting events. For instance, a politician might analyze policy options in an undifferentiated way by placing options into one of two value-laden categories: the "good socialist policies" that promote redistribution of wealth and the "bad capitalist policies" that preserve or exacerbate inequality. A highly differentiated approach would recognize that different policies can have many, often contradictory, effects that cannot be readily classified on a single evaluative dimension of judgment—for example, effects on the gross national product, the government deficit, interest rates, inflation, unemployment, the balance of trade, and a host of other economic and political variables. Integration refers to the development of complex connections among differentiated characteristics. (Differentiation is thus a prerequisite for integration.) The complexity of integration depends on whether the decision maker perceives the differentiated characteristics as operating in isolation (low integration), in first-order or simple interactions (the effects of A on B depend on levels of C, moderate integration), or in multiple, contingent patterns (high integration).

Advocates of the early trait view of integrative complexity (or conceptual complexity as it was then known) relied heavily on the semiprojective Paragraph Completion Test for assessing individual differences in cognitive functioning. Subjects were presented with sentence stems (e.g., Rules . . . , When I am criticized . . .) and asked to complete each stem and to write at least one additional sentence. Trained coders rated subjects' responses on a 7-point scale designed to measure the integrative complexity of subjects' thinking in the topic area. Scores of 1 reflected low differentiation; scores of 3 reflected moderate to high differentiation, but low integration; scores of 5 reflected moderate to high differentiation and moderate integration; and scores of 7 reflected high differentiation and high integration (development of complex comparison rules to integrate differentiated perspectives). Scores of 2, 4, and 6 represented transition points between adjacent levels.

Two points concerning the integrative complexity coding system deserve mention here. First, with adequate training (two to three weeks), coders can rate verbal responses for integrative complexity with high levels of reliability (Pearson product-moment correlations between .85 and .95). Second, the complexity coding system focuses on the cognitive *structure,* not the *content,* of expressed beliefs and is not biased for or against any particular philosophy. One can be simple or complex in the advocacy of a wide range of political positions.

Early laboratory research using the Paragraph Completion Test showed that systematic individual differences do, indeed, exist in integrative complexity. The test demonstrated predictive power in a variety of experimental contexts, including Inter-Nation Simulations of crisis decision making (Driver, 1965; Schroder et al., 1967; Streufert and Streufert, 1978), studies of bargaining and negotiation behavior (Pruitt and Lewis, 1975; Streufert and Streufert, 1978), and studies of attitude change (Crano and Schroder, 1967; Streufert and Fromkin, 1972). Relative to integratively simple subjects, subjects classified as integratively complex utilized a broader range of information in forming impressions of others and in making decisions, were more tolerant of dissonant or incongruent information, and were more likely to be successful in achieving mutually beneficial compromise agreements in bargaining games.

Such empirical successes notwithstanding, it became clear by the late 1960s that a static trait model of integrative complexity was inadequate. Integrative complexity of cognitive functioning at a given time was not just a function of stable dispositional variables; several experiments indicated that situational factors also influenced integrative complexity (Driver, 1965; Schroder et al., 1967). Some environments were much more conducive to complex information processing than were others. Schroder et al. (1967) and Streufert and Streufert (1978) explicitly recognized this point in their "interactionist theories" of integrative complexity—theories stipulating that, (1) moderate levels of threat, time pressure, and information load are most likely to promote integratively complex styles of thinking; and (2) individual differences in integrative complexity determine how people react to changing levels of these environmental variables.

Another critical development in the evolution of integrative complexity theory and research occurred in the mid-1970s. Prior to that time, research on the integrative complexity construct was primarily limited to experimental studies that examined the interactive effects of dispositional integrative complexity (assessed by the Paragraph Completion Test) and situational variables (environmental stressors) on subjects' selection of "low-involvement" response options (endorsing attitudes or making decisions with no important consequences for subjects' own futures or those of others). The external validity limitations of such studies are well known (see Janis and Mann, 1977; Tetlock, 1983d). In an innovative study of revolutionary leaders, Suedfeld and Rank (1976) showed that, unlike other measures of cognitive style that are linked to specific paper-and-pencil tests (e.g., the Dogmatism or Tolerance of Ambiguity scales, the Embedded Figures Test), the integrative complexity coding system is not tied to the coding of only Paragraph Completion Test responses. They also found that integrative complexity was a powerful predictor of which revolutionary leaders were and were not successful in retaining power after the success of their revolutionary movements.

Since then, a large number of studies have used the integrative complexity coding system to analyze a broad range of archival documents and to test an even broader range of hypotheses (Levi and Tetlock, 1980; Raphael, 1982; Suedfeld and Tetlock, 1977; Suedfeld et al., 1977; Tetlock, 1979, 1981a, 1981b, 1983a, 1983b, 1984a; Tetlock et al., 1984; Tetlock et al., forthcoming). These novel methodological applications of the coding system have enormously expanded the data base of integrative complexity theory. The coding system has been used to analyze diplomatic communications during major international crises, transcripts of Japanese cabinet meetings prior to the decision to attack the United States in 1941, pre- and postelection speeches of American presidents in the twentieth century, confidential interviews with members of the British House of Commons, American and Soviet foreign policy statements in the post-World War II era, and magazine editorials. The "nomological network" (Cronbach and Meehl, 1955) surrounding the integrative complexity construct has expanded to include not only individual difference predictions, but a wide array of hypotheses concerning situational determinants of complex information processing that even the later "interactionist" theories of integrative complexity had not anticipated (e.g., hypotheses concerning the effects of role demands, accountability, groupthink, and value conflict on integrative complexity of functioning). Indeed, as we shall see, the very identity of integrative complexity as a purely cognitive construct has been challenged.

In brief, data generation has in this case outpaced theory generation (a situation similar in some respects to the state of the cognitive dissonance literature in 1960s). In the next section, we examine some of the major findings that have emerged from the new wave of political psychology research on integrative complexity and propose explanatory principles for organizing and interpreting these findings.

## SOME MAJOR RECENT FINDINGS

Lewin's classic formula, Behavior = f (Person, Environment), summarizes a good deal of what has been learned about determinants of integrative complexity in the last twenty years. Today, we know that integrative complexity possesses some attributes of a relatively stable individual difference variable (moderate consistency across time, situations, and issues) and some attributes of a relatively context-specific variable (predictable variation as a function of situational and issue variables). Although much remains to be learned, we have also made some progress in delineating boundary conditions for when it is more or less useful to think of integrative complexity as an individual-difference versus context-specific variable. In short, our understanding of integrative complexity has itself become much more integratively complex.

The research on individual differences in integrative complexity among political leaders has largely focused on the relationships between political ideology and integrative complexity. The key question has been whether persons who differ in ideological orientation (e.g., isolationists versus internationalists, liberals versus conservatives) also differ in the complexity of their styles of reasoning about policy issues. To be sure, systematic ideology-complexity relationships do exist. However, the observed relationships have proven to be much more complex—contingent on situational and issue variables—than traditional trait analyses of links between cognitive style and ideology suggested. Although some main effects exist, the integrative complexity of political leaders' statements appears to be an interactive product of at least three categories of variables: ideological orientation, issue domain, and political role.

## INTEGRATIVE COMPLEXITY AND ISOLATIONISM IN THE EARLY POSTWAR PERIOD

Tetlock (1981b) carried out the first of what was to be a series of studies of individual differences among United States senators in the integrative complexity of their policy statements. The primary goal of the study was to test hypotheses derived from McClosky's (1967) classic study of personality correlates of isolationist foregin policy sentiment in the American public. On the basis of three national surveys in the 1950s, in which a large battery of personality and attitude scales were administered, McClosky concluded that isolationists differed from nonisolationists on a variety of dimensions. Isolationists—particularly "jingoistic" ones who sought to insulate the United States from the rest of the world by overwhelming superiority of force—were more intolerant of ambiguity, closed to new experiences, prone to dichotomous (good-bad) forms of thinking, and likely to possess strong positive affect toward in-groups (patriotic Americans) and strong negative affect toward out-groups (foreigners, Communists). McClosky argued that psychodynamic processes similar to those hypothesized to underlie the authoritarian personality (Adorno et al., 1950) influenced the content and structure of isolationist belief systems. For instance, he proposed that the rigidly chauvinistic overtones in isolationism represented means of coping with severe inner conflicts and feelings of inferiority.

Tetlock (1981b) tested the generalizability of McClosky's psychological portrait of the isolationist to senators who held office in the 82nd Congress (1951-1952). Speeches of senators were subjected to both integrative complexity coding and a complementary coding technique—evaluative assertion analysis—for measuring the intensity of speakers' attitudes toward ingroup and outgroup symbols (see Osgood et al., 1956). Tetlock used the coding techniques to analyze randomly selected passages from foreign policy speeches of senators who had been classified, on the basis of Guttman scaling of their foreign policy voting patterns, as isolationist, ambivalent isolationist, and internationalist. The results strongly suppported McClosky's analysis. Isolationists were much less integratively complex than nonisolationists. Relative to nonisolationists, isolationists also evaluated outgroups more negatively and in-groups more positively. Ambivalent isolationists fell between these two groups. Discriminant analysis indicated that the content analytic indicators were powerful joint predictors of isolationist orientation. One highly discriminant function emerged that accounted for 41 percent of the total variation and permitted correct classification of 66 percent of the senators into the isolationist, ambivalent, and nonisolationist categories, against a chance accuracy rate of 37 percent.

McClosky thus appears to have been correct: Isolationist sentiment in the early post-World War II period—among both elites and followers—seems to have been a posture of belligerency in international affairs, one that had "more to do with hostility against foreign nations and disavowal for the well-being of others than with the considered assessment of the risks arising from foreign entanglements (McClosky, 1967: 104). The isolationist relies heavily upon "dichotomous thought processes, that lack breadth of perspective and that seek to exclude whatever is different, distant, or unfamiliar" (p. 107).

**INTEGRATIVE COMPLEXITY AND
GENERAL POLITICAL ORIENTATION**

A second study explored the relationships between integrative complexity and overall liberalism-conservatism of senators' voting records in the 94th Congress (Tetlock, 1983b). This study was designed to test two viewpoints that have dominated speculation on links between cognitive style and ideology, viewpoints that I label as the rigidity-of-the-right and ideologue hypotheses. The rigidity-of-the-right hypothesis derives from the well-known work on the authoritarian personality.

Authoritarian personality theory traces a cluster of beliefs—including political-economic conservatism, ethnocentrism, and cynicism and pessimism about human nature—to deeply rooted psychodynamic conflicts that, in turn, can be traced to the early parent-child relationship. The theory leads us to expect that persons who advocate right-wing (authoritarian) political causes will be especially likely to think about events in rigid, dichotomous, and affectively charged ways (see Stone, 1980; Wilson, 1973).

Critics were, however, quick to note the insensitivity of the above argument to "authoritarianism of the left" (Rokeach, 1956; Shils, 1958). An alternative view—the ideologue hypothesis—asserts that, although advocates of left-wing and right-wing political causes take dramatically different positions on many policy issues, they display very similar styles of reasoning about these issues. Differences in the content of left-wing and right-wing belief systems should not be allowed to obscure fundamental similarities in how ideologues organize and process political information. True believers (regardless of their cause) are held to be more dogmatic, intolerant of ambiguity, and integratively simple than their moderate counterparts who have resisted the absolutist doctrines of the left and right.

Tetlock (1983b) attempted to test the rigidity-of-the-right and ideologue hypotheses by coding the integrative complexity of randomly selected passages drawn from speeches of senators with extremely liberal, moderate, and extremely conservative voting records. He found that senators with conservative voting records in the 94th Congress made less integratively complex policy statements ($M = 1.79$) than their moderate ($M = 2.51$) or liberal ($M = 2.38$) colleagues. This finding remained significant after controlling for a number of potential confounding variables, including political party affiliation, education, age, years of service in the Senate, and types of issues discussed.

These results converge impressively with previous work on nonelite samples, work that indicates that right-wing respondents score more highly than moderate and left-wing respondents on self-report measures of dogmatism, intolerance of ambiguity, and cognitive simplicity (see Stone, 1980; Wilson, 1973, for reviews). Nonetheless, two problems complicate interpretation of the results. The first problem stems from relying on public statements for inferring the cognitive styles of senators. Public policy statements may shed more light on how senators seek to influence other political actors (colleagues, the executive branch of government, the press) than on how senators actually think about policy issues. In short, conservatives may differ from moderates and liberals in *rhetorical* style, not *cognitive* style.

The second problem stems from the limited ideological range of positions represented in the United States Senate. A defender of the ideologue hypothesis could argue that there were not enough representatives of the ideological left to provide a fair test of the hypothesis (i.e., there is no influential Socialist or Communist party in the United States).

To clarify these issues, Tetlock (1984a) and Tetlock et al. (1984, forthcoming) performed a series of additional studies of the complexity-ideology relationship.

## INTEGRATIVE COMPLEXITY IN THE BRITISH HOUSE OF COMMONS

Tetlock (1984a) reported a study that provided a stronger test of the complexity-ideology relationship than the earlier Tetlock (1983b) study of senators. The raw data consisted of confidential in-depth interviews that the political scientist Robert Putnam (1971) conducted with 93 members of the British House of Commons. There is good reason to believe that strategic political motives exerted much less influence on what the politicians said in this setting than in more public settings such as press conferences or in parliament (see Putnam, 1971, for relevant evidence). The politicians interviewed were willing on several occasions to criticize their own party and even themselves in the course of the discussions. In addition, the politicians examined in this study represented a wider variety of ideological positions than exists in the United States Senate. The parliamentarians included extreme socialists (who favored the nationalization of all major industries), moderate socialists (who favored limited public control of major industries), moderate conservatives (who favored limited denationalization of industry), and extreme conservatives (who opposed any government intervention in the economy).

Coders rated the integrative complexity of statements randomly drawn from the interviews with the parliamentarians (Tetlock, 1984a). The results revealed highly significant differences among the four ideological groups. Moderate socialists (M = 3.07) discussed issues in more integratively complex terms than extreme socialists (M = 2.17), moderate conservatives (M = 2.65), and extreme conservatives (M = 1.97). Moderate conservatives were more complex than extreme conservatives and extreme socialists. Extreme conservatives and socialists, the two groups most dissimilar in the content of their political beliefs, had the most similar levels of integrative complexity. These relationships between political ideology and integrative complexity remained highly significant after controlling for a variety of background variables as well as belief and attitudinal variables assessed in the Putnam research.

In addition to its relationship to political ideology, integrative complexity was correlated with a host of relevant cognitive stylistic variables assessed in the original Putnam (1971) research. From these correlations emerges a more detailed portrait of the integratively complex politician. The more integratively complex the politician, the more likely he or she was to: (a) deemphasize the differences between the major political parties; (b) be tolerant of opposing viewpoints; (c) think about issues in relatively nonideological terms; and (d) be unconcerned with assigning blame for societal problems. In short, integrative complexity was associated with a pragmatic, open-minded and non-partisan world view.

What interpretation should one attach to the links between political ideology and integrative complexity? At first glance, the data would appear to vindicate advocates of the ideologue hypothesis. When the confidential statements of politicians who represented a wide spectrum of ideological positions were analyzed, we found that extremists of the left and right were similar to each other in styles of reasoning, but different from individuals closer to the center of the political spectrum. The ideologue hypothesis, however, leaves important questions unanswered. Why does the point of maximum integrative complexity consistently appear to be displaced to the political left of center? Why, for instance, were both liberals and moderates more integratively complex than conservatives in the United States Senate? Why were moderate socialists more integratively complex than moderate conservatives in the British House of Commons? The ideologue hypothesis is not explanatory, but rather descriptive: It simply asserts that as one departs from an ill-defined political center or midpoint, one is increasingly prone to view issues in simple, dichotomous terms. What determines where this mysterious midpoint lies? Why are liberals and moderate socialists apparently closer to it than conservatives? Why was it necessary to go as "far out to the political left" as "radical socialists" to find a marked decline in the integrative complexity of thought? Advocates of the ideologue hypothesis need to offer defensible and explicit criteria for specifying the conditions that must be satisfied to test the hypothesis.

A more refined and sophisticated theoretical analysis is needed of the relationship between integrative complexity and political ideology, one that clarifies the social and cognitive processes that underlie the complexity-ideology relationship. The value pluralism model of ideological reasoning represents one attempt to fill this theoretical void. The value pluralism model can be summarized in the following two general sets of propositions: (1) Underlying all political ideologies are core or "terminal" values (Lane, 1973; Rokeach, 1973, 1979) that specify what the ultimate goals of public policy should be (e.g., economic efficiency, social equality, individual freedom, crime control, national security). Ideologies vary not only in the types of values to which they assign high priority (Rokeach, 1973), but also in the degree to which high priority values are acknowledged to be in some degree of tension or conflict with each other. In monistic ideologies high priority is attached to only one value or set of values that, it is claimed, are highly consistent with each other. In pluralistic ideologies, high priority is attached to values that, it is recognized, are in frequent, even intense, conflict with each other. Important values often point to contradictory policies (e.g., "I value social equality, but dislike paying for it through taxes," "I want to protect the environment, but don't want to slow economic growth"). (2) Advocates of the "most pluralistic" ideologies should exhibit the most integratively complex styles of reasoning. This prediction is based on Abelson's (1959, 1968) influential work on the strategies people use for resolving cognitive inconsistency in belief systems. Abelson maintained that, *whenever feasible,* people prefer modes of resolving cognitive inconsistency that are simple and require minimal mental effort. (People, in this view, are "cognitive misers"; Taylor and Fiske, 1984.) Simple modes of resolving inconsistency are feasible when the conflicting values activated by a policy choice are of very unequal strength. It is then easy to deny the less important value and to bolster the more important one, a process consistency theorists described as "spreading of alternatives."

By contrast, simple modes of inconsistency reduction are much less practical for advocates of pluralistic ideologies. When conflicting values are of approximately equal strength, denial of one value and bolstering of the other are much less plausible coping strategies (Abelson, 1959, 1968). People must turn to more effort-demanding strategies such as differentiation (e.g., distinguishing the impact of policies on conflicting values) and integration (developing rules or schemata for coping with trade-offs between important values). For instance, in domestic policy debates, liberals and social democrats are most committed to the often conflicting values of social equality and economic freedom (see Rokeach, 1973, 1979). They are therefore under the greatest psychological pressure to take into account the effects of policy proposals on both values as well as to develop guidelines or criteria for finding appropriate compromises between the two values (compromises that may, of course, have to take different forms in different economic and political circumstances).

To summarize, the value pluralism of an ideology determines both the frequency with which people experience cognitive inconsistency and the complexity of the strategies they rely upon to cope with inconsistency. A value pluralism analysis of the complexity-ideology relationship has several noteworthy advantages. It not only helps to explain existing data; it leads to a variety of novel and testable theoretical predictions—a number of which have subsequently been supported.

With respect to existing data, the value pluralism model is well positioned to explain why several studies have found that advocates of centrist and moderate left-wing causes tend to interpret issues in more integratively complex ways than do advocates of conservative causes. Evidence from survey studies of the general public and from content analyses of political writings suggests that advocates of centrist and moderate left-wing causes are more likely to hold at least partly contradictory values. They are likely to value both social equality and economic freedom, economic growth and environmental protection, deterring "Soviet expansion" and maintaining good working relations with that country, to oppose oppressive right-wing dictatorships and the radical guerilla movements that frequently emerge in opposition to them, and so forth. From this standpoint, the point of maximum integrative complexity is often displaced to the left of center because that is the point of maximum value pluralism, at least on many issues.

The value pluralism model also clarifies how far to the sociopolitical left or right one must go for integrative complexity to decline: to the point where conflict between core values begins to diminish sharply. For instance, in domestic policy debates, one would expect to—and actually does—find a sharp reduction in integrative complexity as one moves from moderate socialists (who, according to Rokeach, 1973, place nearly equal importance on freedom and equality) to extreme socialists (for whom concern for equality seems to dominate concern for individual economic rights). Similarly, one would expect to—and one does—find a reduction in integrative complexity as one moves from moderate socialists to moderate conservatives (for whom economic freedom is a dominant value) to extreme conservatives (for whom economic freedom is the overwhelmingly dominant value).

Although the value pluralism model can account for existing data on ideological "main effects" in integrative complexity, the model strongly implies that traditional trait analyses of the complexity-ideology relationship are of only limited usefulness. We should not assume that certain ideological groups will always be more integratively complex than other groups; rather, we should expect ideology-by-issue and ideology-by-situation interactions in the integrative complexity of styles of reasoning.

We turn now to these potential moderator variables of the complexity-ideology relationship.

## IDEOLOGY-BY-ISSUE INTERACTIONS IN INTEGRATIVE COMPLEXITY

One key determinant of the feasibility of simple modes of resolving value conflict is the degree to which the policy domain under discussion activates conflicting values of approximately equal strength. And value conflict may well be most intense in different issue domains for different ideological groups. For instance, American conservatives in the 1980s may experience their most intense value conflicts over such issues as defense spending (e.g., national security versus fiscal restraint or economic recovery) or compulsory military service (e.g., national security versus individual liberty). Liberals may experience their most intense value conflicts over such issues as redistributive income policies (e.g., equality versus economic efficiency or individual economic rights).

Two studies have revealed support for ideology-by-issue interaction predictions of the value pluralism model. In one study, Tetlock at al. (forthcoming) examined the relations between integrative complexity and political ideology among United States Supreme Court justices who served on the Court between 1946 and 1978. The study assessed the integrative complexity of opinions that each of 25 justices authored (or at least put their names on) as well as the overall liberalism-conservatism of each justice's voting record (Tate, 1981). Consistent with past work on senators, justices with liberal and moderate voting records exhibited more integratively complex styles of reasoning than did justices with conservative voting records. However, these relationships between integrative complexity and political ideology were more powerful on cases involving economic conflicts of interest (e.g., labor versus management, business versus government) than on cases involving civil liberties issues (e.g., due process and First Amendment questions). Tetlock et al. argue that civil liberties issues were more likely to activate shared elite values—common to both liberals and conservatives—such as constitutional protections for freedom of speech and press and due process of law (see McClosky and Brill, 1983). The competing ideological groups were less likely, therefore, to experience differential value conflict on these issues. By contrast, much less value consensus probably existed on the economic conflict of interest cases (see Chong et al., 1983). Good reasons exist, moreover, for suspecting value conflict in this policy domain to be more intense for liberals than for conservatives (a policy domain that frequently activates conflicts between private economic interests and public ones).

In a second study, Tetlock (1984c) obtained even more direct evidence for the hypothesized role of value conflict in promoting integratively complex thought. Two types of information were collected from a nonelite (college student) sample: (1) subjects' rank order evaluations of the importance of each of 18 terminal values from the Rokeach Value Survey (values included national security, natural beauty, economic prosperity, equality, and freedom); (2) subjects' support for six public policy positions and their thoughts on each issue (e.g., redistributive income policies, domestic CIA activities, defense spending). Each of the public policy issues had been selected on the basis of pretest scaling data indicating that the issue brought at least two values from the Rokeach Value Survey into conflict (e.g., the defense spending question was phrased in such a way as to activate tension between the values of national security and economic prosperity). On five of six issues, a significant trend was found for people to report more integratively complex thoughts to the degree the issue domain activated conflicting values that people held to be: (a) important in their value hierarchy; (b) close to equally important. This study provides the most direct evidence yet that the degree of value conflict between basic political values does indeed influence the complexity of thought in that domain.

## POLITICAL ROLES AND INTEGRATIVE COMPLEXITY

Intensity of value conflict is a major, but not the only possible determinant of the integrative complexity of people's reasoning about a policy domain. For instance, political roles appear to exert an important influence. Some roles seem to encourage integrative complexity; others, integrative simplicity.

A particularly powerful variable in this regard is the distinction between being "in power" (the policymaking role) and "out of power" (the opposition role). Governing a country—developing policies one actually expects to implement—is generally a more integratively complex task than opposing the government. The policymaking role inevitably requires making unpopular trade-off decisions (Katz and Kahn, 1978; Thurow, 1980) that, at least in democracies, must be justified to skeptical constituencies motivated to argue against positions one has taken (e.g., explaining to various interest groups why it was not possible to satisfy all of their conflicting demands). Integrative complexity is needed both at the level of private thought (to work out viable compromise policies that at least partly satisfy major constituencies) and at the level of public rhetoric (to develop cogent two-sided appeals that sensitize antagonized constituencies to the complexity of the policymaking role) (see McGuire, forthcoming; Tetlock, 1983a).

Far fewer pressures exist on opposition politicians to think or speak in integratively complex terms. The mass electorate possesses little knowledge of major policy issues and little motivation to think carefully about political messages or to defend the government (see Kinder and Sears, forthcoming; Sniderman and Tetlock, forthcoming). The essence of the opposition role is to rally anti-government sentiment—a goal that is most effectively achieved not by evenhanded "on the one hand" and "on the other" rhetoric, but rather by constructing easily understood (integratively simple) and memorable attacks on the government. In the opposition role, one is free to find fault, to focus selectively on the shortcomings of proposals advanced by those in power and on the advantages of one's own proposals.

Several studies support the claim that the policymaking role encourages integrative complexity. Suedfeld and Rank (1976), for instance, observed that revolutionary leaders (from several nations) made more integratively complex statements after coming to power than before coming to power. Perhaps even more telling, Suedfeld and Rank (1976) also found that revolutionary leaders who retained power in the postrevolutionary period were much more likely to display such upward shifts in integrative complexity than were leaders who failed to retain power. Tetlock (1981a) observed a similar upward shift in the integrative complexity of policy statements that American presidents issued during election campaigns and immediately after coming to power (post-inauguration). Most twentieth-century presidents apparently have believed that, although integratively simple rhetoric is useful for rallying popular support during elections, it is politically prudent to present issues in more integratively complex terms once they have assumed office. Tetlock et al. (forthcoming) have even found evidence for the "in-power"/"out-of-power" complexity shift among (life-tenured) justices of the United States Supreme Court. Judicial opinions for the majority (which thus have the force of law) tended to be more integratively complex than dissenting or minority opinions.

Transitions in political roles do not, however, affect all ideological groups equally. Tetlock et al. (1984) examined the integrative complexity of liberal, moderate, and conservative senators in five Congresses, three dominated by liberals and moderates (the 82nd, 94th, and 96th Congresses) and two dominated by conservatives (the 83rd and 97th Congresses). Tetlock et al. found that liberals and moderates were more integratively complex than conservatives in the Democrat-controlled 82nd, 94th, and 96th Congresses, replicating the earlier Tetlock (1983b) findings. However, when the political balance of power shifted in favor of conservatives (e.g., in 1953 and 1981 with Republicans gaining control of both the Senate and the presidency), the complexity-ideology relationship disappeared. No significant differences existed in integrative complexity as a function of political ideology. Interestingly, this pattern was due to *sharp declines* in the integrative complexity of liberals and moderates in the Republican-dominated Congresses, not to an increase in the integrative complexity of conservatives. Conservatives displayed much more traitlike stability in integrative complexity both within and across Congresses.

These findings suggest an important qualification to the value pluralism model's prediction of greater integrative complexity among liberals and moderates than among conservatives. Liberals and moderates may present issues in more integratively complex terms only when they are forced, so to speak, by their political role to confront the tensions between basic values inherent in their ideological outlooks. Conservatives, with their presumably more internally consistent value systems, are relatively unaffected by shifts in political role. There is less potential value conflict that they can be "forced" to confront.

It should also be noted that the archival evidence on links between political roles and integrative complexity is highly consistent with recent experimental evidence on the effects of accountability on complexity of reasoning. The policymaking role is, in a sense, one of high accountability. One can be called upon to justify what one has done by a variety of constituencies. One is, moreover, potentially accountable not only for the short-term consequences of one's policies, but for the (more unpredictable) long-term consequences as well. The opposition role is, in a sense, one of low accountability. One has the rhetorical freedom to focus single-mindedly on the flaws in the position of the other side. Experimental data suggest that the types of accountability created in policymaking roles are indeed likely to promote integratively complex reasoning by subjects on policy issues (see Tetlock, 1983a, 1983e, forthcoming). Accountability, especially to unknown or multiple constituencies, appears to encourage subjects to engage in "preemptive self-criticism"—an attempt to anticipate objections that might be raised to the policy stands they have taken.

## THE NEED FOR INTEGRATION IN INTEGRATIVE COMPLEXITY RESEARCH

The integrative complexity of a person's style of reasoning can be shaped by a wide range of variables—the personality of the perceiver, the issue domain under discussion, and the social and informational environment in which the discussion is taking place. Determinants of integrative complexity can be viewed from a correspondingly wide range of theoretical perspectives—psychodynamic theories of political belief systems, information processing theories of cognitive functioning under stress, the value pluralism model, and theories of impression management and role performance. The explanatory "ranges of convenience" of these different theoretical positions have yet to be clearly delineated.

It may prove useful to conclude this chapter by taking stock of what has been and what remains to be learned. Our knowledge of determinants of integrative complexity can be broken down into three broad categories—individual differences, issue domains, and the social and informational environment.

### INDIVIDUAL DIFFERENCES

Knowledge of the integrative complexity of a person's style of reasoning in one issue domain, role relationship, or situation permits substantially better than chance accuracy prediction of the integrative complexity of that person's style of reasoning in other issue domains, role relationships, or situations. Much descriptive and explanatory work, however, remains to be done. Better estimates using a wider range of data sources are needed of the degree of cross-issue, cross-role, and cross-situational stability and consistency of individual differences in integrative complexity. Careful conceptual and statistical analyses are needed of what is meant by such commonly used terms as "stability" and "consistency" of individual differences (see Lamiell, 1983). The underlying sources of individual differences in integrative complexity are also in need of clarification. What impact do psychodynamic processes, such as those suggested by Adorno et al. (1950), McClosky (1967), or Wilson (1973), have on integrative complexity and its relation to ideological positions such as isolationism or conservatism? What impact do early socialization experiences, including, but not limited to, child-rearing practices have on integrative complexity (see Harvey et al., 1961)? To what extent do individual differences in integrative complexity reflect differences in motivation to engage in complex thought (e.g., tolerance of ambiguity) as opposed to differences in ability to engage in complex thought? To what extent do individual differences in integrative complexity reflect "intrapsychic" processes (cognitive style, motivational conflicts) as opposed to impression management processes (attempts to create desired impression on others) (see Tetlock and Manstead, forthcoming)?

## ISSUE DOMAINS

Different issue domains elicit different levels of complexity of reasoning for different individuals. The value pluralism model identifies one key causal factor: issue domains "pull" greater complexity to the degree they activate important and conflicting values. Other processes are also undoubtedly at work. How knowledgeable is the person about the issue domain? (No one doubts that individuals well trained in a subject matter will have more integratively complex "cognitive maps" of that subject matter than will individuals who lack such training; see Axelrod, 1976.) Does "ego involvement" in a topic facilitate or inhibit integrative complexity? Or is the relationship curvilinear, with moderate levels of ego-involvement most conducive to complex reasoning?

## THE SOCIAL AND INFORMATIONAL ENVIRONMENT

Situational variables may influence integrative complexity by affecting people's motivation or ability to engage in complex thought. High levels of stress may, for example, affect ability to think in integratively complex terms. More common, though, I suspect, are situational variables that affect motivation to reason in integratively complex ways: pressures to conformity in small groups (Janis, 1982; Tetlock 1979), political roles (Tetlock, 1981a), demands for accountability (Levi and Tetlock, 1980; Tetlock, 1983a) and the like. These "motivational" variables may exert their influence through a number of mechanisms (e.g., by affecting people's perceptions of whether complex reasoning will facilitate attaining important goals, by affecting perceptions of the importance of the goals). Difficult questions also remain concerning the "locus" of the effects of many situational variables: Do they influence how people are thinking, what they are saying, or some combination of the two?

## A CLOSING COMMENT: THE MEDIA FILTER

Up to this point, the focus has been on the integrative complexity of what political elites actually say. The general public, however, lacks direct access to these elites; it relies on the mass media for insights into how presidents, senators, and Supreme Court justices think. Unfortunately, researchers have yet to examine the integrative complexity of media coverage of elite political controversies.

One important question concerns the degree to which various media simplify (perhaps oversimplify) political issues. The prevailing sentiment in both the academic and political worlds is that such simplification does indeed occur (see Gans, 1979; Patterson, 1980; Robinson and Sheehan, 1983). Representative Synar certainly expresses a concern of many in Congress when he complained of television, in particular, that "if you can't sell an issue in twenty seconds you can't use it. It only takes five seconds to say 'Your congressman is against prayer.' It takes me five minutes to explain why that's wrong. But television won't give me five minutes. Television demands that I boil everything down to a single sentence" (quoted in Easterbrook, 1984: 69).

Integrative complexity coding—which can be readily adapted to analyze television and newspaper coverage of issues as well as statements of political leaders—would appear an ideal tool for exploring this issue. The integrative complexity of policy statements of key decision makers can be compared directly to the integrative complexity of media reports and commentary on those same statements. A variety of hypotheses can be tested concerning the degree to which simplification will occur in different media and in different circumstances. Are some media (e.g., television) more prone to simplify than others (e.g., the press)? What media characteristics predict degree of simplification? Is the elite press less likely to simplify than the popular press? What role does political ideology play? Are conservative media more likely to simplify than their liberal and moderate counterparts (a parallel to data on political elites)? Or is a more complex prediction necessary? Do the media tend to simplify the positions of politicians with whom they disagree but to report faithfully the complexity of the positions of politicians with whom they feel sympathetic? What role does competition among media play in determining degree of simplification? Does competition exacerbate the trend to simplification (increasing the need to present issues in sharp, dichotomous terms that "grab" audience attention), or does it encourage more reflective, complex coverage (increasing the need to show sensitivity to the many facets of political controversies in order to forestall charges of biased or inept reporting)? Are state-controlled media (e.g., in Canada, Western Europe) more or less resistant to simplification pressures than their private enterprise counterparts? What impact do demands for judicial accountability such as libel suits have on the complexity of coverage? Finally, does the tendency to simplify vary as a function of stress or issue domain? Is simplification more likely in periods of crisis? Does simplification decline as journalists have opportunities to become more familiar with particular policy problems (learning effects)?

In brief, a host of factors—ideological, economic, legal, psychological—are likely to shape the complexity of media political coverage. The answers that ultimately unfold to these questions are, moreover, fraught with both theoretical and policy implications. From a theoretical viewpoint, integrative complexity research on the communications media will enrich our understanding of how institutional-systemic variables interact with psychological ones to shape how people think (psychologists always seem to need reminding that purely individualistic theories of cognition are inadequate). From a policy viewpoint, such research will enrich our understanding of how the media—the critical link between political elites and masses in democratic societies—structure the terms of debate on key issues of the day.

# REFERENCES

ABELSON, R. P. (1968) "Psychological implication," in R. P. Abelson et al. (eds.) Theories of Cognitive Consistency: A Sourcebook. Chicago: Rand McNally.

———(1959) "Modes of resolution of belief dilemmas." Journal of Conflict Resolution 3: 343-352.

ADORNO, T., E. FRENKEL-BRUNSWIK, D. LEVINSON, and N. SANFORD (1950) The Authoritarian Personality. New York: Harper.

AXELROD, R. (1976) Structure of Decision. Princeton, NJ: Princeton University Press.

CHONG, D., H. McCLOSKY, and J. ZELLER (1983) "Patterns of support for democratic and capitalist values in the United States." British Journal of Political Science 13: 401-440.

CRANO, W. and H. M. SCHRODER (1967) "Complexity of attitude structure and processes of conflict resolution." Journal of Personality and Social Psychology 5: 110-114.

CRONBACH, L. J. and P. MEEHL (1955) "Construct validity in psychological tests." Psychological Bulletin 52: 281-302.

DRIVER, M. J. (1965) "A Structural Analysis of Aggression, Stress and Personality in an Inter-Nation Simulation." Institute Paper 97. Lafayette, IN: Institute for Research in the Behavioral, Economic, and Management Sciences, Purdue University.

EASTERBROOK, G. (1984) "What's wrong with Congress?" The Atlantic 254: 57-84.

GANS, H. (1979) Deciding What's News: A Study of CBS Evening News, NBC Nightly News, Newsweek and Time. New York: Vintage.

GRABER, D. (1976) Verbal Behavior and Politics. Urbana: University of Illinois Press.

HARVEY, O. J., D. HUNT, and H. M. SCHRODER (1961) Conceptual Systems and Personality Organization. New York: John Wiley.

JANIS, I. L. (1982) Victims of Groupthink (2nd ed.). Boston: Houghton-Mifflin.

——— and L. MANN (1977). Decision Making. New York: Free Press.

KATZ, D. and R. L. KAHN (1978). The Social Psychology of Organizations (2nd ed.). New York: John Wiley.

KINDER, D. and D. O. SEARS (forthcoming) "Public opinion and political behavior," in G. Lindzey and E. Aronson (eds.) Handbook of Social Psychology (3rd ed.). Reading, MA: Addison-Wesley.

LAMIELL, J. T. (1983) "A case for an ideothetic psychology of personality: a conceptual and empirical foundation," in B. Maher (ed.) Advances in Experimental Personality Research (vol. 11). New York: Academic.

LANE, R. E. (1973) "Patterns of political belief," in J. N. Knutson (ed.) Handbook of Political Psychology. San Francisco: Jossey-Bass.

LEVI, A. and P. E. TETLOCK (1980) "A cognitive analysis of the Japanese decision to go to war." Journal of Conflict Resolution 24: 195-212.

McCLOSKY, H. (1967) "Personality and attitude correlates of foreign policy orientation," in J. M. Rosenau (ed.) Domestic Sources of Foreign Policy. New York: Free Press. Press.

——— and A. BRILL (1983) Dimensions of Tolerance: What Americans Believe About Civil Liberties. New York: Russell Sage.

OSGOOD, C. E., S. SAPORTA, and J. C. NUNNALLY (1956) "Evaluative assertion analysis." Litera 3: 47-102.

PATTERSON, T. E. (1980) The Mass Media Election: How Americans Choose Their President. New York: Praeger.

PRUITT, D. G. and S. A. LEWIS (1975) "Development of integrative solutions in bilateral negotiation." Journal of Personality and Social Psychology 31: 621-633.

PUTNAM, R. (1971) "Studying elite culture: the case of ideology." American Political Science Review 65: 651-681.

RAPHAEL, T. D. (1982) "Integrative complexity theory and forecasting international crises." Journal of Conflict Resolution 26: 423-450.

ROBINSON, M. and M. SHEEHAN (1983) Over the Wire and on Television. New York: Russell Sage.

ROKEACH, M. (1979) Understanding Human Values: Individual and Social. New York: Free Press.

————(1973) The Nature of Human Values. New York: Free Press.

————(1956) "Political and religious dogmatism: an alternative to the authoritarian personality." Psychological Monographs 70 (No. 18, Whole No. 425).

SCHRODER, H. M., M. J. DRIVER, and S. STREUFERT (1967). Human Information Processing. New York: Holt, Rinehart, & Winston.

SHILS, E. E. (1958) "Ideology and civility: on the politics of the intellectual." Sewanee Review 66: 950-980.

SNIDERMAN, P. M. and P. E. TETLOCK (forthcoming) "Public opinion and political ideology," in M. G. Hermann (ed.) Handbook of Political Psychology (vol. 2). San Francisco: Jossey-Bass.

STAW, B. M., L. E. SANDELANDS, and J. E. DUTTON (1981) "Threat-rigidity effects in organizational behavior: a traditional analysis." Administrative Science Quarterly 26: 501-524.

STONE, W. F. (1980) "The myth of left-wing authoritarianism." Political Psychology 2: 3-20.

STREUFERT, S. and W. FROMKIN (1972) "Complexity and social influence," in J. T. Tedeschi (ed.) Social Influence Processes. Chicago: Aldine.

STREUFERT, S. and S. STREUFERT (1978) Behavior in the Complex Environment. Washington, DC: Winston & Sons.

SUEDFELD, P. (1983) "Authoritarian leadership: a cognitive-interactionist view," in J. Held (ed.) The Cult of Power: Dictators in the Twentieth Century. New York: Columbia University Press.

————and A. D. RANK (1976) "Revolutionary leaders: long-term success as a function of changes in conceptual complexity." Journal of Personality and Social Psychology 34: 169-178.

SUEDFELD, P. and P. E. TETLOCK (1977) "Integrative complexity of communications in international crises." Journal of Conflict Resolution 21: 169-184.

————and C. RAMIREZ (1977) "War, peace, and integrative complexity: United Nations speeches on the Middle East problem." Journal of Conflict Resolution 21: 427-442.

TAYLOR, S. E. and S. T. FISKE (1984) Social Cognition. Reading, MA: Addison-Wesley.

TETLOCK, P. E. (1984a) "Cognitive style and political belief systems in the British House of Commons." Journal of Personality and Social Psychology 46: 365-375.

————(1984b) "A value pluralism model of ideological reasoning." Presented at the annual meeting of the American Psychological Association, Toronto, Canada.

————(1984c) "Accountability: the neglected social context of judgment and choice," in B. M. Staw and L. Cummings (eds.) Research in Organizational Behavior (vol. 7). Greenwich, CT: JAI Press.

————(1983a) "Accountability and complexity of thought." Journal of Personality and Social Psychology 45: 74-83.

————(1983b) "Cognitive style and political ideology." Journal of Personality and Social Psychology 45: 118-126.

————(1983c) "Policy-makers' images of international conflict." Journal of Social Issues 39: 67-86.

————(1983d) "Psychological research on foreign policy: a methodological overview," in L. Wheeler (ed.) Review of Personality and Social Psychology (vol. 4). Beverly Hills, CA: Sage.

———(1983e) "Accountability and perseverance of first impressions." Social Psychology Quarterly 46: 285-292.

———(1981a) "Pre- to post-election shifts in presidential rhetoric: Impression management or cognitive adjustment?" Journal of Personality and Social Psychology 41: 207-212.

———(1981b) "Personality and isolationism: Content analysis of senatorial speeches." Journal of Personality and Social Psychology 41: 737-743.

———(1979) "Identifying victims of groupthink from public statements of decision makers." Journal of Personality and Social Psychology 37: 1314-1324.

———and A.S.R. MANSTEAD (forthcoming) "Impression management versus intrapsychic explanations in social psychology: a useful dichotomy?" Psychological Review.

TETLOCK, P. E., J. BERNZWEIG, and J. L. GALLANT (forthcoming) "Supreme Court decision making: cognitive style as a predictor of ideological consistency of voting." Journal of Personality and Social Psychology.

TETLOCK, P. E., K. HANNUM, and P. MICHELETTI (1984) "Stability and change in senatorial debate: testing the cognitive versus rhetorical style hypotheses." Journal of Personality and Social Psychology 46: 621-631.

THUROW, L. C. (1980) The Zero-Sum Society: Distribution and the Possibilities for Economic Change. New York: Basic Books.

WILSON, G. D. (1973) The Psychology of Conservatism. New York: Academic.

# PART IV

## REAL-WORLD EFFECTS

Chapter 13

# THE STUDIES AND
# THE WORLD OUTSIDE

## Sidney Kraus

The greatest of all mysteries is what the voters think, feel and want today, what they will think and feel and want on election day, and what they can be induced to think and feel and want by argument, by exhortation, by threats and promises, and by the arts of manipulation and leadership [Speech by Walter Lippmann to the National Press Club, September 23, 1959; cited in Steel, 1981].

We know a good deal about media's impact on the social and political behavior of individuals. But although we know more and more about media effects we seem to know less about how individuals "take" the information they receive from other individuals and the mass media, how they *think* about it, change or accept it, and finally arrive at a conclusion that prompts their actions. In one sense, this is an odd state of affairs because for several decades we have had the theoretical underpinnings for such investigations.

Two pioneers, Lippmann (1922) in the study of public opinion and Schramm (1955) in the assessment of mass communication process and effects, provided insightful comments about information processing. Lippmann suggested that "the world outside [is different for each individual and forms] the pictures in our heads." Schramm proposed

AUTHOR'S NOTE: I wish to thank the John and Mary R. Markle Foundation for their generous support in the gathering of materials for this chapter and Richard Perloff and the authors of chapters in this book for their comments.

that "perception is the interpretive process through which we pass all the stimuli that we accept from our environment, and meaning is what comes out of this process—the 'picture in our heads.'"

Often, in social science research, we are unable to observe directly certain behaviors. As with the formation or holding of *attitudes*, we cannot directly observe the processing individuals *do* with the information they receive. Schramm noted that "we can't see meaning or observe perception. Everything we know about it [sic] has to be inferred backward from overt response and forward from stimulus."

Lippmann's and Schramm's observations suppose that an individual's perception of an event is influenced by (1) the social world as perceived by the individual, and (2) the information the individual received from a stimulus (e.g., mass media's rendition of an event).

Schramm's comments were offered three decades after Lippmann's seminal work on public opinion. Now, three decades after Schramm's comments, social scientists pursue the realms of perception and meaning from a variety of perspectives.

In this volume the perspectives taken by the researchers are as varied as are the disciplines with which they are associated. Some of the studies were the products of ongoing research. Most, however, were conceived of or modified, on the basis of a flow chart (constructed by the editors) that attempted to outline a series of questions about political information processing (see Schematic Model of Political Information Processing). Each study, however, attempts to shed some light on the answer to the question: "How do individuals process political information?" Further, it was intended that the collection of studies as a whole would offer some insight into the role of the mass media as they affect individual's information processing responses.

The question that may be asked about these studies is: To what extent do their findings reflect the real world in which the mass media and individuals function regularly? For example, do voters in presidential elections exhibit behaviors suggested by some of the studies? Do the mass media influence voters in ways that cause change and/or consistency in the cognitive processes of voters? What relationship can be demonstrated to be operant between mass media information and the processing of that information among individuals? Do the televised presidential debates, for example, prompt voters to process information differently than they process other kinds of political information? Does the information processing of reporters covering political events differ from the information processing of voter-viewers of the same events? Questions like these are not easy to answer. But, attempts to do so are necessary, especially given Schramm's observations about inference, and the changes that have and are occurring in the relationships among political actors, the media, and voters.

Some of these changes are evident from the comments of one political expert. After Richard Nixon won the presidency in 1968, his media manager, Roger Ailes, said, "This is the beginning of a whole new concept. This is it. This is the way they'll be elected forever. The next guys up will have to be performers" (quoted in McGinnis, 1969, and Diamond and Bates, 1984). Then came the "great communicator" and former film actor, President Ronald Reagan.

In 1983, Ailes suggested that "the TV public is very smart in the sense that somewhere, somehow, they make a judgment about the candidates they see. Anybody who claims he can figure out that process is full of it" (quoted in Diamond and Bates, 1984). He is not, perhaps, as eloquent as Lippmann; we persist, however, with the task "of figuring out that process," despite what may happen to our digestive systems.

## PURPOSE AND METHOD

This chapter reviews the studies in Parts I, II, and III, explicating their major findings with relevant research from other studies. Where appropriate, studies were submitted to a goodness of fit test with a wide range of experiential materials gathered in three presidential elections.

During the presidential primaries and general elections of 1976, 1980, and 1984 this writer was (on site) a participant-observer in or (on site) an observer of over 100 political events (debates, press conferences, rallies and protests, national party conventions, media preparations, etc.).

Notes and records from these events along with other materials (e.g., press releases, campaign notes, audio and video tapes of political newscasts and events, etc.) were collected. From these observations and materials a "real-world" explanation of the studies' findings (those included in previous chapters) were made as appropriate. A major concern was the applicability of a given study to media effects.

These analyses, then, include the writer's empirical political field experiences and previous research as interpreted and applied by him to the empirical studies in this volume, studies that the authors and readers may interpret differently. The review of the studies appears in the order indicated by the Schematic Model—ability to process; motivation to process; processing effects; and impact on polity.

## ABILITY TO PROCESS

Democratic theory (Kraus and Davis, 1981) assumes that voters are capable of comprehending, distilling, and making sense of political information—that they are able to adequately process the information they receive. The chapters reviewed in this section touch on three different aspects of the ability to process: the limits of voters' information-processing capacities (Herstein), individual differences in their political cognitive structure (Lau and Erber), and macro differences that stem from voters' educational and cultural backgrounds (Miller and Asp).

## HERSTEIN

Several models guide research in mass media effects (see Kraus and Davis, 1976). Today, the most dominant model of mass media effects is the transactional model, which assumes an interactive relationship between the media and their audience (see discussions of Neuman and Fryling, Garramone, and Miller and Asp; see also Bauer, 1964; Graber, 1984; and Kraus and Davis, 1976). Other models are used by political scientists and psychologists to help determine how voters decide to vote (e.g., Brody and Page, 1973; Campbell et al., 1960; Kelly and Mirer, 1974; Lazarsfeld et al., 1944).

In several field tests comparing his newly developed process model with other models of voting behavior, Herstein's ("Voter Thought Processes and Voting Theory") model fared quite well. Tests of his model in the 1978 Pennsylvania gubernatorial election correctly predicted 94 percent of the votes of those indicating a vote preference. In the 1980 Ohio primary the model predicted 69 percent of the voting intentions in the Spring, and in the Fall, correctly predicted 87 percent of those voters who expressed a preference.

An early experiment by Herstein found that "negative overall evaluations [of candidates] played an important role in voters' choices, emerging as the only perfect predictor of choice."

Two aspects of the Herstein model differ from many other such models. First, a provision is made for the voter's negative "gut" feelings about candidates. Second, the voter is assumed to compare non-negatively evaluated candidates on attribute dimensions rather than evaluating each candidate overall and then comparing. No further processing is done on a candidate given such an evaluation. Herstein related these two aspects of the process model to the impact that media may have on the voter. The media may determine salient topics; they may provide information for comparisons of candidates and their position on issues; and they may provide negative news about a candidate that is assessed by the voter as compelling.

Herstein's process model makes sense, especially when considered along with Iyengar and Kinder's discussion of agenda-setting effects of media on the saliency of issues, and Neuman and Fryling's study supporting the interactive (transactional) model of agenda-setting effects. What is needed, however, is an explication of how voting process models interrelate with media effects models, especially the transactional model.

## CANDIDATE FLUKES AND
## NEGATIVE VOTER REACTIONS

Herstein argues that most of the time voters vote for the candidate they really want. "The only danger," he cautions, "is that the media or some cognitive fluke [of the voter, the candidate, or both] will make relatively unimportant items salient at the time of [the voter's] decision."

Candidates' "flukes," clever remarks, gaffes, and general appearance in televised presidential debates have been salient features of press coverage late in elections, near the time of vote decision. Three examples (Kraus, 1984b) relate the "danger" that Herstein notes.

Richard Nixon, in the first debate of 1960, looked tired and drawn, and appeared to be ill. His makeup was applied by an adviser, not a professional. Kennedy appeared to be alert, fresh, and in command. Kennedy won.

Gerald Ford's comments (second debate of 1976) about Soviet domination in Eastern Europe prompted questioner Max Fankel to ask, "Did I understand you to say that the Russians are *not* using Eastern Europe as their sphere of influence?" Ford confirmed and Carter won.

Ronald Reagan's retort (second debate, 1980) "There you go again!" and Jimmy Carter's claim to have consulted his young daughter, Amy, on a foreign policy issue, prompted viewers and the press to record the debate in Reagan's favor.

The salient candidate fluke may be perceived by some voters as negative whereas it is ignored by others. The several erroneous comments on various topics and events made by President Reagan in his campaign and while in office prompted a congressman to make the remark about the "Teflon presidency" (see discussion of Lanzetta et al.). The press made that description salient among voters.

Herstein calls for more testing of his process model with other voting models. It may prove useful to include tests of media effects models that may account for the saliency of unimportant campaign items among voters.

## LAU AND ERBER

One major aspect of democratic theory posits that a free flow of information is necessary in order to create a more informed electorate, capable of making choices among candidates running for offices and deciding on issues confronting the body politic. In establishing this tenet, political theorists in the eighteenth century "argued that democracy is based on an educated and informed public which acts responsibly on what it knows" (Kraus and Davis, 1976).

Social and political scientists have, for some time, been concerned with the amount of knowledge voters have about political issues and candidates. Exposure to sources of information, then, becomes an integral part of assessing the amount of information held by voters. Voters' personal experiences and perceptions mediate their exposure to political stimuli.

In a review of studies about the relationship between exposure to political information and political participation Milbrath (1965; see also Milbrath and Goel, 1977) noted, among several patterns, that *"persons who lack education and sophistication about politics tend to shut-out political stimuli."*

Political sophistication may be measured by the amount and accuracy of the knowledge held by a voter; amount of issues on which a voter has opinions; knowledge of candidates' positions on issues; and whether or not the voter has an ideological framework. Milbrath argues that *"the more sophisticated a person's cognitions and beliefs about politics, the greater the likelihood of his participation in the political process"* (Milbrath, 1965). Political sophistication of the voter, then, is an important aspect of furthering democratic ideals.

Lau and Erber ("An Information Processing Perspective on Political Sophistication") departed from the traditional measurement of political sophistication by measuring it "in cognitive knowledge-based terms," with differing levels of conceptualization. They operationalized sophistication to include knowledge, performance, and interest. With this measure they examined the differences between experts and novices in their processing of information during the 1980 presidential election.

Lau and Erber concluded that more issues were used by experts than novices in evaluating candidates, and that "party identification and feelings were more important [in the experts' evaluations of candidates] than [in] those of novices." Pointing out that their "measure of political expertise overlaps substantially with any measure of overall media consumption," they suggest that experts rely primarily on newspapers for political information whereas television is the medium for novices.

Providing a new twist on Lazarsfeld et al.'s (1944) finding of *selective attention* and Brodbeck's (1959) speculation about Harry Stack Sullivan's *selective inattention*, Lau and Erber suggest that newspaper reading and television viewing provide different "information environments" that allow voters to attend to—or ignore—news reports. "*It is easier*" they claim, "*to turn the page of a newspaper than to get up and switch the station*" (italics mine). The political experts' use of a "newspaper environment" accounts, in part, for the "greater stability" of political views. Presumably, political novices with remote control television would show an increase in the stability of their political views.

Lau and Erber also suggest that "even if the visual and print media are more or less equal in their ability to set the agenda, if readers can more easily selectively choose what they see compared to news watchers then . . . agenda-setting might be a phenomenon limited chiefly to political novices." McLeod et al. (1974) have investigated the agenda-setting effect on voters with low interest. This reasearch needs to be extended to political novices.

Finally, Lau and Erber take the position that it is reasonable for voters to process political information in terms of personal or group interests; they have no objections when voters "evaluate candidates by personality factors." Though their position is supportable, evaluating candidates on the basis of their personality raises questions about democratic ideals. There is much evidence supporting the contention that the lack of interest in political matters, coupled with the large amount of television viewing, conditions many voters to make judgments about the image of the candidate. Also, candidates prepare themselves for television appearances, hoping to convey a positive image. In fact, presidential candidates with poor television performances do not fare well among the electorate (see discussions of Herstein; Lanzetta et al.; and Miller and Asp). given this evidence of television personality effects, do we really want to say that voters should continue to make such superficial evaluations?

## MILLER AND ASP

Since the early days of communication research, when studies began to incoporate social science investigative techniques, researchers have looked at how the mass media inform and educate citizens, promoting a sense of language, political socialization, nation building, and modernization of societies. Given our technological advances, it is all too easy to forget how important the media were (and remain) in the lives of citizens thoughout the world.

For Lerner's (1958) Turkish Grocer, "[Movies] were his avenue to the wider world of his dreams. It was in a movie that he had first glimpsed what a *real* grocery store would be like." Doob (1961) "found only one man [among a group of adult males in a small Nigerian village] who had any knowledge about world affairs, including some recent developments in the field of atomic warfare. To all the rest it seems the mass media had failed to communicate such information, but with him they have been successful, undoubtedly because he alone in the village had a radio." Yu (1963) quotes an Associated Press report about the experiences of an Indian scholar in a 1959 trip behind the Bamboo Curtain: "Even in a most backward and traditional [Chinese] village I saw a loudspeaker hidden in a treetop. You can escape the sun and the moon but you cannot escape the radio and the loudspeaker."

Our technological sophistication today has not altered the earlier importance of media in developing and maintaining various aspects of political and social processes. Miller and Asp ("Learning about Politics From the Media in Sweden and the United States") found that although there were media structural differences, and differences in partisan attachments to media between the two countries, there was "substantial cross-cultural similarity . . . in media usage patterns and the importance of the media for political learning."

Their findings on informational levels of Swedish and American citizens are especially noteworthy:

(1) In both countries, newspaper readers *retained more information* than television news viewers (see discussion of Lau and Erber).

(2) A more serious approach to television newscasting (Sweden) does not necessarily result in citizens' acquisition of greater knowledge.

(3) Swedish low-frequency media users hold more information about political parties than American counterparts, but among most frequent media users Americans are better informed than Swedes.

Miller and Asp point out that interpretations and conclusions from studies utilizing schematic information processing differ substantially from those incorporating "motivational interpretations derived from the uses and gratification approach" (see discussion of Garramone). They believe that measures of the relative use of the media can be explained by three considerations: (1) cognitive richness of the media audience; (2) variations in attention to vivid information; and (3) "relevance of the information to the prior expectations and political schema of the audience." But they caution that reliance measures fail to recognize the impact of information processing on learning about politics (see discussion of Perloff); it is necessary, they conclude, to "separate . . . cognitive and motivational factors from the inherent properties of the [mass] medium."

Miller and Asp's study presents several implications for other studies in this volume (see especially discussions of Garramone; Lau and Erber; Tyler and Lavrakas; Perloff; and Schoenbach and Weaver; see also O'Keefe, 1985).

## FOREIGN AND AMERICAN PRESS AND POLITICAL PROCESSES

Miller and Asp find five notable differences in media and politics between Sweden and the United States. First, in Sweden the political parties are important, whereas in the United States the strength of the parties have declined. Second, Sweden's Prime Minister is "only slightly more salient than the leaders of the opposition parties;" candidates' role and their personalities are of primary importance in U.S. national elections (see discussion of Lanzetta, et al). Third, U.S. political conventions have entertainment value whereas issues receive little attention. Both are not true of Sweden. Fourth, newspapers have linkages to parties in Sweden, although Swedish television news and coverage lacks purposeful partisanship. U.S. newspapers are not affiliated with political parties, and "the popular perception of television news is one of objective, non-partisan reporting of news events." Last, generally, the Swedish press is serious about political coverage of issues, whereas the press in the United States concerns itself largely with "horse-race" aspects of politics "rather than dealing with substantive issues" (see Katz and Feldman, 1962).

Observations of American and foreign political reporters and their coverage during the last three presidential campaigns confirm many of the structural and style differences outlined by Miller and Asp. A few examples from those campaigns are illustrative of some of Miller and Asp's observations.

Although the Swiss political and media systems vary somewhat from those of Sweden, interactions of this writer with two Swiss reporters suggest similarities of the press' role in both countries. Just before the beginning of the 1984 presidential debate between Walter Mondale and Ronald Reagan on the evening of October 21, two Swiss reporters approached this writer in the balcony of the Music Hall in Kansas City where selected credentialed members of the press were seated to observe the debate. One of the reporters was covering the debate for Swiss radio, the other for the *Swiss Weekly*. Displaying a copy of the October 15 issue of *Newsweek*, the print reporter asked why Americans are so concerned with who wins debates? (*Newsweek*'s cover displayed photos of Mondale and Reagan below the heading, "The [first] Debate—Who Won?") "Why," he asked, "are not presidential issues more important than presidential television personalities?" The other reporter commented that, by and large, European reporters "look more *seriously* at elections and issues than evidently American reporters do . . . at least in their published stories."

There's some truth to those comments. Results of interviews with American reporters covering the national parties' convention in 1984 revealed that the reportage of politics in America is often event-centered with a concentration on entertainment values, especially in the television medium. Responses in two of these interviews illustrate the observations.

Jim Fulton, a reporter for KDYL News Radio in Salt Lake City, Utah, filed about 14 stories of his own origination each day of the convention. When asked how he finds a story, Fulton replied, "You hang around. It's amazing what you pick up in the halls, and that's where you pick the stuff up. You don't get it off press releases." Sandy Lesko, a reporter for WJKW-TV in Cleveland, Ohio filed two stories per day. Her response to the question about finding a story: "We have them preplanned in advance. Before we even come to the convention we write out a list of ideas. . . . We're doing a piece on these elephants that they're renting out through [a] Talent Agency at the Republican convention. We have pictures of the elephant being pedicured at the Mall, and playing the harmonica."

These examples are typical of the kinds of stories sought, and what radio and television (and often print) disseminate during a campaign and particularly during conventions. Theodore White (1982) observed that, "Television at conventions focuses on the junction of events on the floor, snaring personalities, displaying the pageantry, switching now and then to the podium, where speakers ache for attention." Miller and Asp are correct when they state that "the hoopla of national party conventions in the United States epitomizes an entertainment aspect of politics which is unheard of in Sweden [for the matter, in most European countries]."

There is a puzzling element about Miller and Asp's (and this writer's) view of the dominance of media entertainment values and voter decision making on the basis of candidate images: The electorate relies less on political parties and there has been an increase in issue voting in the last two decades (see Nie et al., 1979).

Of particular note is Miller and Asp's conceptualization of information processing "as an interaction between the characteristics of the medium and those of the audience." This transactional approach is most descriptive of much of the current research on mass communication effects being conducted by social scientists today (see discussion of Herstein; Neuman and Fryling; Iyengar and Kinder).

## MOTIVATION TO PROCESS

Even if voters possess the ability to process political information, they may differ widely in the extent to which they are motivated to attend to and think about political communications. The chapters discussed in this section focus on three different dimensions of political motivation—interest and uncertainty (Schoenbach and Weaver), personal relevance (Perloff), and gratifications sought from mass media (Garramone).

## SCHOENBACH AND WEAVER

Every so often in social science research we are confronted with an unexpected result, a result that begs for explanation. For example, in communication research it is axiomatic that people with more exposure to communication (mass media and interpersonal discussion) on a given topic exhibit more knowledge than those who are less exposed to information on that topic; usually, there is a positive linear correlation between exposure and knowledge. But, in a study during a political campaign, it was revealed that exposure to the media's information about candidates and office holders was inversely (negatively) correlated with knowledge about them—the more exposure to the information, the less the respondents knew, and the less exposure to information the more the respondents knew (Kraus et al., 1974).

Again, we witness an unexpected and somewhat related finding, this time in the results of a study by Schoenbach and Weaver ("Finding the Unexpected: Cognitive Bonding in a Political Campaign"). In a secondary analysis of a panel of West German voters during the European Parliamentary Elections of 1979, the authors explored different levels of interest and uncertainty. They looked at how those variables affected the relationships among "exposure to communication, attitude toward the European Community, and the belief that European politics is an issue among the voters." They found that among "informed," "curious," and "uninterested" voters, only those in the latter group "[showed] a fairly strong consistency of their perceived salience of European politics, their attitude toward the community, and their exposure to campaign communication." The "informed" group exhibited some cognitive consistency with their attitude and belief; the "curious" group revealed no consistency whatsoever, "not even in separate parts of their cognitive system."

The major conclusion of the study suggests that voters, who initially consider themselves to be ignorant about political matters, are not concerned about the state of their knowledge, attitudes, and beliefs (political cognitions), and will, in all probability, consider the campaign at its conclusion as important and positive, having used more campaign materials than others (crystallization; bonding). Thus, Schoenbach and Weaver point to a paradox: "The *less relevant* the campaign is (the less people want to know about it) and the *more information* it produces, the greater its effects, at least in the short run" (see discussion of Perloff).

This "crazy quilt" pattern needs to be explored further as it has implications for major areas of communication and social science research—agenda-setting, information-seeking, uses and gratifications, cognition, and mass media effects in political campaigns, generally.

**INTEREST**

Of particular note is the question of motivation among the "un-interested" group (see discussion of Garramone). What accounts for this group's emergence during the campaign with high levels of campaign information usage? The researchers suggest that the "uninterested" voters "were not ready and willing to resist" the abundance of campaign communication that reached them. That explanation must be considered in light of cognitive and political campaign literature that suggests that very little effort is needed to block or avoid unwanted information (e.g., Berelson et al., 1954; Graber, 1984; Klapper, 1960; Lazarsfeld et al., 1944; Lachman et al., 1979).

Further, the authors claim that "as soon as this abundant information was missing—after the campaign—[the uninterested voter's] cognitive system broke apart as quickly as it was constructed." The image comes to mind of a beautiful balloon filled with air, not to be displayed, but to burst in the end.

One of the dominant psychological predispositions of individuals that accounts for learning from mass media sources is interest. Graber, who had collaborated with Weaver (the second author of the study being discussed) and others in an agenda-setting study during a presidential election in the United States suggests, "Usually, interest spurred by a specific goal, such as the need to become informed about candidates just before an election, results in a greater impetus to learning than occurs when interest is unfocused" (Graber, 1984; Weaver, 1977; Weaver et al., 1981).

**AN UNINTERESTED CASE**

This writer found only one remote case from experiential campaign materials that offers a small bit of explanation for the unexpected finding. An untypical Republican delegate (she prefers to remain annonymous) interviewed on the convention floor in 1984 gave this response to a question about her interest in the campaign and the convention:

> Who's interested? Not me and not the voters in my district. I'm tired, messed-up and hungry. I could care less. They're going to nominate

Reagan; we all know that, so why are we here? I wouldn't be here if I didn't have relatives in the area. *I didn't care at the beginning of this election, and I really don't care now. I've learned a lot, and I'll probably forget as much as I've learned when it's over. But, I guess it was worthwhile.* The voters don't give a hoot about all this anyway. Look at this bag. It's got more crap in it than the luggage I brought with me. . . . I expect to find nothing of interest from these television pushers [reporters interviewing delegates]: besides, I miss my soap operas [italics mine].

## PERLOFF

The Perloff study ("Personal Relevance, Political Cognition, and Campaign Information-Seeking") tested his previously developed model (Perloff, 1984) on cognitive processing of political involvement among a sample of Ohio voters in the 1984 presidential primary. Essentially he sought to determine whether or not voters' perceived self-interest motivates them to seek more information about those issues, ultimately affecting how deeply they process political information (see discussions of Garramone and Schoenbach and Weaver). As Perloff implies, his study is pitted against a conclusion in the earlier work of Sears et al. (1980)—ideology of the voter is a better predictor of voting behavior and political beliefs than is voter self-interest (for a completely different view see discussion of Herstein). The "debate" on self-interest versus ideology as predictors of voters' beliefs and their voting behavior was not resolved in the Perloff study. He did, however, provide correlational evidence for adopting a cognitive response-based approach to information-seeking, which incidentally, was not what Sears et al. (1980) investigated.

Perloff's findings provide a mixed picture of the relationships between self-interest and the pattern of respondents' political cognitions and their information-seeking behavior. Three factors, two of which Perloff alludes to, may be responsible for the mixed picture. First, the data were collected during a primary when voters are usually not as interested in thinking about politics as they are in the general election. Second, Perloff correctly points out that correlational analyses impose limitations—they suggest relationships, but of course do not show causation, or the influence that one variable may have on another. The reader should compare this study with Schoenbach and Weaver's "uninterested" voter, who evidently processed more information than the "curious" voter.

Third, the demographic makeup (income) of the sample may have been a mitigating factor in demonstrating the relationships between criterion measures and personal relevance measures. The sample's distribution of low versus higher income may have served to underestimate the effect that certain issues (social service, unemployment, economy) have on the motivation (relevancy) of low-income voters (see the discussion of Garramone).

Nevertheless, this study should encourage researchers to apply Perloff's personal relevancy model in their studies of mass communication effects during elections. Personal relevance is more complicated than assumed. Perloff demonstrates that there are important different effects between ideologically based and self-interested relevance. His findings also point to several interesting ways in which personal relevance may affect the processing of news and political advertising.

It may prove useful to compare the Perloff findings on personal relevance with polling data publicized during the Ohio primary. In any event, this study should be examined in light of several other important studies in this volume bearing on motivation, relevancy, and interest (see studies cited above; for example, compare Iyengar and Kinder with Perloff—personal relevance may impact differently on news, advertising, and other effects).

## GARRAMONE

Three and a half decades ago, Newcomb (1950) argued that "*any* motive, for a given individual at a given moment, may acquire any degree of intensity." He was suggesting that "even the most unusual and eccentric motives may become intense," such that it may be incomprehensible to others (see discussions of Perloff and Schoenbach and Weaver).

Garramone ("Motives and Political Information Processing: Extending the Gratifications Approach") concludes from her research that "what you seek influences what you get" (for different results see discussions of Perloff; Schoenbach and Weaver). She reviews four of her studies, combining the uses and gratifications research approach with political information processing, and suggests five major findings. First, subjects who were motivated to learn candidates' stands on issues from a political commercial recalled more issue information than those who were motivated to get an impression of candidates' personalities. Second, subjects motivated to get an impression of candidates' personalities paid greater attention to the video component of the commercial than those motivated to learn issues. Third, those who were motivated to discuss politics described candidates in specific and intensive terms. Fourth, when viewing issue commercials those subjects who were issue-motivated "increased their intention to vote for the candidate more than [image-motivated individuals]." Finally, the viewing of image-oriented advertisements led individuals who were motivated toward image reception to engage in more visual processing than issue-motivated individuals (see discussion of Lanzetta et al.).

Garramone claims that "gratifications researchers have given *little* attention to the interaction of motivation and political message attributes" (see discussion of Schoenbach and Weaver). Miller and Asp (Chapter 12), however, "disagree with the uses and gratifications approach [precisely because] it places too much emphasis on motivation for media use." They argue for a cognitive psychology approach that looks "beyond the content of the message or any influence unique to [a] particular medium" (see discussion of Perloff). They contend that the "cognitive organization of the receiver" is an important factor.

Both Garramone and Miller and Asp, however, view the transactional model of mass communication effects as a predominant model (see conclusion; see also discussions of Herstein; Iyengar and Kinder; and Neuman and Fryling). Neither Garramone's nor Miller and Asp's position vis-à-vis individual motives as predictors of mass communication effects on political behavior resolves the issue in favor of one or the other. One can find evidence supporting both positions.

Several distinctive differences between the two research efforts should be noted: the study by Miller and Asp was a cross-cultural investigation, Garramone's was conducted with Americans; Miller and Asp used survey methodology, whereas Garramone, for the most part, conducted experimental research; and the variables of the studies were, by and large, categorically and conceptually different. Another difference can be seen in the amount of information provided about the demographical make up of subjects and respondents and their attributes. Although both studies, well conceived and executed, are important in understanding political information processing, Garramone's motivational concept is so much a part of what we know about behavior from learning theory and persuasion research that it is difficult to dismiss.

## PROCESSING AND EFFECTS

Having reviewed the antecedents to political information processing, we can turn to the critical issues involved in the processing and effects of political messages. The relationship between political communication processes and effects has occupied mass communication researchers since the time of Lippmann and Lazarsfeld. The four chapters discussed below focus on agenda-setting both from a micro processing perspective (Iyengar and Kinder) and a more macro approach (Neuman and Fryling), on the processing of nonverbal cues (Lanzetta, Sullivan, Masters, and McHugo) and on the impact of media reports on crime (Tyler and Lavrakas).

## IYENGAR AND KINDER

In four complex experiments, Iyengar and Kinder tested some psychological explanations for the agenda-setting effect of television news with a sample of New Haven, Connecticut, residents. They found that (1) television news alters the public's sense of national priorities, (2) television coverage of a particular problem tends to be more powerful among viewers personally affected by the problem, and (3) reports tend to be especially influential when they begin the broadcast. Before discussing these findings it is important to review a methodological problem associated with agenda-setting research.

### THE ISSUE OF MEASURING ISSUES

Essentially, the agenda-setting *hypothesis*, as it is referred to in the communication discipline, suggests (for a defined period) a positive relationship between what the media report and the issues believed to be important by the public. Two reviews of this literature (Kraus and Davis, 1976; Kinder and Sears, 1985) point to several methodological problems. Of prime concern has been the issues of causation and effect. "Is there a direct influence from mass media political reports upon the perceptions and behaviors of voters attending those reports"(Kraus and Davis, 1976)? Apparently, the problem of measuring agenda-setting arises with the way in which questions are constructed to determine respondents' concerns about events and issues. Results of studies in which respondents are asked to rank or rate a list of issues (e.g., by indicating "which issue has been most important thus far?"; McLeod et al., 1974) tend to be different from those in which respondents are given open-ended questions (e.g., "What are you *most* concerned about these days? That is, regardless of what the politicians say, what are the two or three *main* things which you think the government *should* concentrate on doing something about?"; McCombs and Shaw, 1972).

These two ways of obtaining the importance of issues among respondents emanate from different conceptual frameworks. Ranking or rating issues "places the measurement of the dependent variable in the category of *perceived issue salience*, anchored in the interpersonal environment of the individual." Using open-ended questions to determine the important issues, "locates the dependent variable in the *individual issue salience* category" (Kraus and Davis, 1976).

The Iyengar and Kinder experiments utilized both forms of the question. Respondents, in one instance, were asked to *rate* the importance of each of four sets of national problems; in the other, "to *name* the three most important problems facing the nation" (italics mine). The ratings were added together and formed "a composite index of problem importance." Thus, they had two measures of *problem importance*—the index of rated responses and the open-ended responses.

The psychological mechanisms to assess whether television news moves viewers' perceptions of issue importance included *counterarguing* (coded responses to brief descriptions of television reports eliciting respondents' reactions recalled from their viewing); *source credibility* (respondents' ratings of objectivity and accuracy of television newscasts); and *affective arousal* (respondents were assigned a score representing the number of negative emotions aroused by viewing the television reports.

Although overall Iyengar and Kinder found that television news set the agenda for the viewers, once again the knotty problem of assessing issues was evident. News reports "stir up" the emotions of viewers, supporting the agenda-setting function of television news (consider a somewhat different finding that people learn more from candidates' political television commercials than they do from evening television newscasts; Patterson and McClure, 1976). Iyengar and Kinder found that "for every three affects [negative emotions aroused] elicited by news coverage of a particular problem, change in the composite importance ratings increased by nearly a full point." There were, however, no influences of affect "on change in the likelihood of mentioning the problem as one of the country's most important" (see their Table 5.2).

Also, although there was some "sporadic" support for counterarguing ("marginally" on spontaneous mentions) there was no support for counterarguing in the composite ratings. Only with source credibility were there consistent effects among composite ratings and spontaneous mentions.

Hence, in two of the three causation tests—between respondents' ratings of issues and spontaneous mentions on one hand, and the three measures (affect, counterarguing, and source credibility) on the other—we are again confronted with somewhat differing results that may have come about from the use of open-ended or rating responses. One must temper these comments by noting the striking impact of television news coverage on problem importance (Figure 13.1). Both the problem ratings and the volunteered mentions of problem importance increased from pre- to posttest on issues covered by television news.

Although this study makes a substantial contribution to the agenda-setting literature, and advances our understanding of issues measurement, it does not resolve the issue of measuring issues.

The authors' concerns over the generalizability of their study was effectively pursued; they were careful in the design and execution of their study, and they believe their "results do generalize to the natural setting."

## THE NEWS-GATHERING PROCESS

Most anyone who has traveled with media personnel, or has observed reporters while they prepare items for the next day's newspaper or the evening television news, will attest to the fact that a reporter's "nose for news" is combined with his or her sense of the public's receptivity to those news items. Although it is true that "media people must work in a transactional environment without knowing much about the audience with whom they are interacting" (Graber, 1984) they do have a sense of, a feel for, that information particular audiences want.

Reporters covering certain "beats" acquire an understanding of both the sources of news and those who would be receptive to that news. Gans (1979) notes that, "The only characteristic of the audience that the journalists do keep in mind is its receptivity of the news." Further, Gans confirms the transactional relationship between journalists and their audiences:

Journalists strike a bargain with their audiences . . . they want viewers and readers to pay attention to important news because "people should know

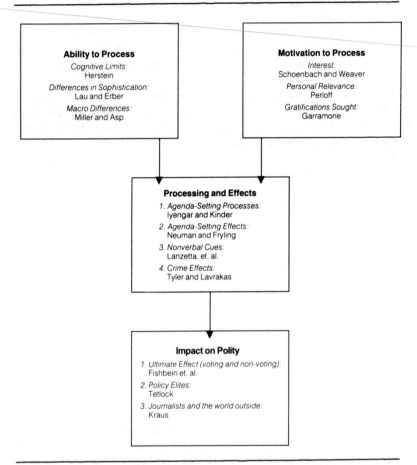

Figure 13.1   Schematic   Model   of   Political   Information   Processing   (Perloff   and
Kraus)

what is going on in the world"; in exchange they will supply interesting
stories to please them . . . [they] make a special effort to find stories that
will attract and then hold audience attention.

Reporters and correspondents exchange analyses of events, issues,
and personalities in the news, and discuss the public's and elite's reactions to their stories. In short, most seasoned reporters are uniquely
qualified for their news-gathering missions, and many of them are keen,
constant observers of the public mood (see discussion of Miller and
Asp).

It should not be unexpected, then, for Iyengar and Kinder to have found that television news "alters the public sense of national priorities." If their experiment and the above observations are not persuasive, the reader should review the television news reports, and the public's concern, in the 1960s. Did the events, broadcast nightly on television, reflect or cause the protests and marches aganist America's involvement in Vietnam? According to Neuman and Fryling's analysis the public set the agenda on Vietnam for the media, though both followed the "build-up and build-down" of the war.

Did television news coverage of the marches for blacks' access to voting booths, schools, and the like, change the public's priorities about civil rights? The agenda-setting function may be symbiotic; the public's beliefs and actions, and the media's portrayal of events may affect each others' priorities.

## ISSUE SALIENCY AND PERSONAL RELEVANCE

There's an old saying about what is important to the public, especially during elections: "Pocketbook issues, for the most part, will take precedence over other issues when people vote for candidates, or referendums." During the recessions of the 1970s, and the early part of this decade, bills and referendums to increase taxes and school levies failed one after another in most cities and suburbs. Most unemployed or laid-off workers are more concerned with getting back to work than they are with other issues. When viewing a television newscast segment about a plant or factory that may be built, reopened, or abandoned these individuals would most likely be highly interested, retain most of the segment, and enter into discussions about it with their peers. The relevance of the news item for them is obvious (see discussion of Perloff). Once again, it is to be expected that as Iyengar and Kinder found, "television coverage of a particular problem tends to be more powerful among viewers personally affected by the problem."

## DECIDING WHAT NEWS COMES FIRST

The results of the third and fourth experiments ("television coverage of a particular problem tends to be more powerful among viewers personally affected by the problem," and "stories tend to be especially influential when they begin the broadcast," respectively) confirm, for the most part, earlier experiments by Carl Hovland and his associates. Their studies suggest that in the order of presentation, what is presented first (primary) may be more persuasive than what is presented last (recency) given a certain set of conditions; especially when a "point [made by the communicator] is sympathetic to [the audience's] own" (see, e.g., Hovland, 1958).

It is important to note that the experimental stimuli in the Iyengar and Kinder study came from network television newscasts, not from local television. The "lead story" in local television depends more often upon the visual dimensions of the segment than the substance of it. Network news, however, tends to be issue-oriented as well as event-centered. Both local and network newscasts will at times display the same lead story, usually when a critical and salient event emerges (e.g., Watergate; Hinckley shooting President Reagan).

The selection process, however, is much the same for television news networks and local television stations. Lead stories are decided upon in an "assembly line" atmosphere of hectic preparation, "and virtually choose themselves most of the time," usually a few hours before the broadcast, though last-minute breaking news may influence news placement. Criteria for story selection in network television is fourfold: (1) *rank in governmental and other hierarchies;* (2) *impact on the nation and the national interest;* (3) *impact on large numbers of people;* and (4) *significance for the past and future"* (Gans, 1979).

It is particularly noteworthy to compare Gans's second criterion for story selection with the result in two of Iyengar and Kinder's experiments, that "television news alters the public's sense of national priorities."

## NEUMAN AND FRYLING

Much discussion has taken place in the past three decades about the influence of public opinion on issues and various institutions affecting society. Recently, the American Academy of Political and Social Science devoted an issue of its publication *(The Annals)* to the topic "Polling and the Democratic Consensus" (Martin, 1984). Repeatedly, social scientists commented on two aspects of opinion assessment. They noted the increase since the middle of this century of the use of quantification, computers, and polling as tools of the journalistic and political professions, and they found *a paucity of evidence about poll effects.*

Also, during this period, debate has continued on individual opinion versus collective or aggregated opinion in the assessment of concerns held by the American public. To some, the use of polls or aggregated data to assess the "mood" of the public suggests the notion of a "public mind"—an attempt to collect individual opinions, put them together, and conclude with a public "consensus." To others, the sum of the parts (individual opinions) does not necessarily equal the whole (consensus).

Neuman and Fryling ("Patterns of Political Cognition: An Exploration of the Public Mind") focus, they say, "on the blurred borderline between individual and aggregated opinion [since] our highly industrialized and centralized society requires a clear-cut 'public opinion,' an acknowledged will of the majority." They assert "that this public opinion whole is very much more than the simple sum of its parts." To support that assertion, Neuman and Fryling examined individual opinions and public opinion. First, they analyzed individual opinions with two in-depth interviews taken from a study of political cynicism in the American electorate in the early 1970s. They tentatively suggest that although in traditional public opinion research the two individuals would be "equated as having the same attitude ... [their responses reveal a ] dramatic divergence of cognitive styles which, by the nature of survey research, become aggregated and interpreted as the same 'public opinion.' "

In their second examination—public opinion—they begin by suggesting four possible causal patterns of agenda-setting; (1) media agenda-setting, (2) public opinion clues, (3) interactive feedback (between 1 and 2), and (4) independence (no relationship between 1 and 2). Using national public opinion data collected over a period of 35 years by the Gallup Organization, the authors, in a unique research design, compared the public's response to the question, "What do you think is the most important problem facing this country today?" with a content analysis of media's coverage of the prominent issues (see discussion of Iyengar and Kinder). They then took the results of the time-series data (for ten issues) and matched them to the four causal patterns of agenda-setting. They found "evidence of every pattern except consistent media agenda-setting [causal pattern #1]." The most dominant pattern was interactive feedback, the third pattern (see discussions about the transactional model in Garramone; Herstein; Iyengar and Kinder; Miller and Asp; and Schoenbach and Weaver).

Explaining these results, Neuman and Fryling make an important distinction between how the media organize their conception of events and how individuals do. Although individuals depend on media for much of their information, they process that information "in ways quite different from the journalist community" reporting that information.

Some examples of polling and the reporting of polls may prove useful considering Neuman and Fryling's research.

## POLLING AND REPORTING OF POLLS

It consistently has been reported (most recently on the CBS *Morning Show,* April 26, 1985) that after Walter Cronkite announced that "we must negotiate a pull-out from Vietnam," President Johnson was certain that Cronkite's comments would affect public opinion against his Vietnam policy. If there are still some skeptics who believe that the marches, protests, and the public opinion polls did not play a large part in Johnson's decision to finally pull out of Vietnam (see discussion of Iyengar and Kinder) they should be directed to a recent national poll that found "the [Vietnam] war . . . is even less popular today than when Saigon fell" (Clymer, 1985).

That poll, incidently, alters the downward trend that Americans lack trust in our government (Miller, 1983; a finding referred to by Neuman and Fryling prior to the Clymer's *New York Times* report). In response to the statement that Washington could be trusted to do the right thing all or most of the time, 47 percent agreed, up 22 points from the low of 25 percent in 1980 (a further testimonial to President Reagan; see discussion of Lanzetta et al.).

Evidently, the Clymer report was not a polling collaboration between two news organizations, or between the *New York Times* and a polling organization, which has been the case in the past. Although modern polling began as a press function to increase circulation, it has become a staple for the press and television. There are several "marriages" between pollsters and the media, and several "incestuous" relationships between mediums. For example, *Time* occasionally likes to use the research firm of Yankelovich, Skelly, and White, Inc.; *Newsweek* often commissions the Gallup Organization; ABC News has been wedded to the Louis Harris Organization, but has had romances with the *Washington Post*; CBS News and the *New York Times* have had a long relationship; and NBC News and the Associated Press gave birth to several surveys in presidential campaigns (for an excellent discussion of Watergate, the press, and polling see Lang and Lang, 1983).

Polls taken during the last three presidential elections prompted the phrase, "a volatile electorate" (Neuman and Fryling would have something to say about that description of the "voters' mind"). An example reported in a working paper on polling (Kraus, 1984a) is illustrative of such volatility. On October 11, 1976, *Time*, with the polling of Yankelovich and his associates, reported the following:

> What once looked like a Carter runaway has turned into one of the tightest presidential races in U.S. history. Making the present situation even more volatile, the Yankelovich study found 52 percent of the voters still have not firmed up their final voting plans . . . Said Pollster Daniel Yankelovich: "Our *Time* survey suggests that the race will seesaw back and forth until the very last minute, reflecting the voters' agonized and disappointed frame of mind."

The "seesaw situation" came from voters responses to the question, "If the election were held today, whom would you choose between Democrat Carter and Republican Ford?" *Time* displayed a table showing the percentages of voters supporting Ford and Carter using Yankelovich's polling during the period, March through September:

|           | *Ford* | *Carter* |
|-----------|--------|----------|
| March     | 46     | 38       |
| April     | 38     | 48       |
| August    | 40     | 46       |
| September | 43     | 43       |

On the first of November, the *Time*/Yankelovich team reported that their latest survey, conducted during the previous weekend, showed Carter moving ahead of Ford, 48 percent to 44 percent, with eight percent "not sure." In the article, however, they reported on two earlier surveys: a telephone survey conducted in October from the sixteenth to the nineteenth with 1578 registered voters, and "interviews held immediately after the [second] presidential debate with 608 voters—a cross section of the original nationwide sample."

The telephone survey revealed that Ford had now moved ahead of Carter by three percentage points, 45 to 42, with 13 percent of the voters undecided. Noting that two out of three people in the second survey had watched the debate, the article went on to report several findings about voter perceptions of the candidates' performance, and claimed that the debate evidently "helped many undecided voters to make up their minds about the candidates."

*Time* made several generalizations. They felt that "Carter's lead is quite volatile." Reporting on the final debate they suggested that, "One result . . . was to mend somewhat the public images of both candidates." Later they suggested that "each candidate's campaigning has done more to hurt his opponent's image than to improve his own standing with the voters." This latter assertion is difficult to comprehend as the reader is unable to determine how the data were grouped. Were Ford supporters separated from Carter's, or were all voters grouped together? It could be interpreted that Carter supporters criticized Ford (and vice versa), but responses were not matched with vote intention. One can only surmise that this was another of the many incidents in past years where the press failed to make poll results clear, misinterpreted the data, or made unwarranted generalizations. The volatility of the press in the reporting of volatile polls suggest that the tail was wagging the dog.

This real-world example supports Neuman and Fryling's finding of the interactive pattern of agenda-setting. A recent study, however, found that "media agenda-setting is indeed unidirectional—television news influences public concern and not vice versa" (Behr and Iyengar, 1985). Certainly, Neuman and Fryling's comments ring true (especially when considered along with the *Time* example): the organization of media presentations about the polls and events differ from the way in which individuals process information. In addition, their results further support the transactional model of mass communication effects as the dominant model (Bauer, 1964; Kraus and Davis, 1976; Graber, 1984).

Finally, it should be noted that the agenda-setting methodology in Neuman and Fryling does not resolve the problem of open-ended issues responses versus rating or ranking of issues (see discussion of Iyengar and Kinder).

## LANZETTA, SULLIVAN, MASTERS, AND McHUGO

Lanzetta et al. have suggested that the way in which candidates exhibit "expressive behavior" may determine whether or not they get elected. The authors of this innovative experimental study confirmed three hypotheses relating to a candidate's television image in a presidential election: (1) images vary among candidates; (2) television viewers' responses to the candidates' images vary and change according to a leader's political success; and (3) television images of candidates affect viewer's attitudes toward them. Further, the authors assert that reactions to political leaders, and support for them, are "a function of the emotions they elicit, and hence are not likely to be determined by party identification or issue evaluation." However, party identification does mediate nonverbal effects.

The reader should compare this study with a study by Friedman et al. (1980). Examining network television reporting in the 1976 presidential campaign, Friedman et al. found that "Cronkite, Brinkley and Reasoner were perceived as having a more positive facial expression when saying Carter's name than when saying Ford's name . . . Chancellor's expressions were more positive when referring to Ford, and for Walters the difference was slight." It appears that network anchorpeople's and candidates' expressive behaviors do not go unnoticed by voter-viewers. These findings are in keeping with a body of evidence on televised presidential debates demonstrating that image, as well as issue components of a candidate's television performance, affect voter-viewers' decisions (e.g., Kraus, 1962 and 1979).

## TELEVISED PRESIDENTIAL DEBATES AND CANDIDATE IMAGES

Research on the 1960 televised debates between John F. Kennedy and Richard M. Nixon found that what a candidate "looked like" apparently was more important to voters than what he said (Kraus, 1962). The 1976 debates, with Jimmy Carter and Gerald Ford, found voters reacting more to the candidates' issue positions than to their images. It was suggested that the debate between "Mr. Dull and Mr. Duller" forced viewers to pay attention to what was said; candidate images were too boring to be of consequence (Kraus, 1979).

Just prior to the 1980 Cleveland televised debate, both Ronald Reagan and Jimmy Carter devoted several days preparing for their appearances. Though Reagan had considerable public performance experience—radio sports announcer, film actor, television MC, union president, and governor—he was coached on style as well as substance. His now famous retort, "There you go again!" accompanied by a smile and a turn toward President Carter in the debate, was scripted by one of his aides who had studied tapes of Carter's performance. After the debate, several members of the audience in the Music Hall of the Cleveland Convention Center provided statements about the poor image of the president and the positive one of Reagan. Random interviews with reporters and Cleveland viewers of the debate confirmed those impressions; subsequent media reports echoed the general view of Reagan over Carter in image standings.

Although it was true that Carter's popularity had been declining in the polls (due to his "rose garden strategy," developed as a political response to the taking of American hostages in Iran) and that the economy was in poor shape, nevertheless, polls just prior to the Cleveland debate (a week before the election) indicated a close race between the two candidates. Reagan wanted that debate, and he won it, and probably the election, in part as a result of his image performance.

Before the Louisville debate in 1984, President Reagan was perceived by members of the press and the public as a "great communicator." Walter Mondale and his aides maintained that he would wage an issue campaign, pooh-poohing press admonishments of his "lackluster" image in public performances. Surprisingly, the tables were turned— President Reagan's performance lacked luster (his age arose as an issue) whereas Mondale's performance brought unexpected bonus points in image ratings.

In their second meeting before the cameras (Kansas City), Reagan was back to his old self, dispelled the age issue, and gained at least equal footing with Mondale.

## THE "TEFLON" IMAGE

Lanzetta et al. comment on the relationship of their findings to the image of President Reagan. They suggest that their findings on nonverbal cues may be the Teflon in the Teflon factor.

Throughout his campaigns for the presidency, and during his administration, candidate and President Reagan committed several errors of fact in speeches (some critics suggest errors in judgment as well) that the public evidently dismissed as unimportant (see discussion of Herstein). In a speech to farmers he did not know what *parity* meant. Often, Reagan would mix up the names and faces of political dignitaries. He claimed that the United States should concentrate on land-based missiles and not worry about submarines because they are not nuclear.

According to a 1982 private poll taken by Richard Wirthlin, Reagan's pollster, "only 38 percent of the respondents . . . felt that the President knew what he was doing." That low percentage did not hurt the President. U.S. Representative Pat Schroeder of Colorado stated that the presidency was coated with Teflon, "nothing negative ever seemed to stick to it, or him" (*Newsweek,* 1984: 38). President Reagan's ability to overcome negative perceptions of voters suggests that his overall positive image more than compensates for his substantive mistakes. A particular case in point was noted in that *Newsweek* review of the 1984 campaign:

> When [President Reagan] was working on his speech justifying the invasion of Grenada and the loss of American lives in Beirut, his man Deaver showed him the story about the wounded marine who—unable to speak—scrawled the motto "Semper Fi" on a pad and handed it to his general. "If you can read it without choking up," Deaver said "I'll let you keep it."
>
> Reagan tried and couldn't finish. "All right, give it back," Deaver said, but Reagan wouldn't; he kept the clipping, rehearsed it to 12 different groups till he could handle it and used it as the emotional coda to his speech. In the 24 hours thereafter, his approval rating for handling the crisis in Lebanon jumped 15 points.

There is much in the world outside to validate the findings of Lanzetta et al. Image makes a difference; the public processes emotional stimuli with emotional responses, perhaps even more than other cognitive stimuli.

## TYLER AND LAVRAKAS

Crime has been a major public concern, persisting for at least the last seven decades. Public opinion polls show that Americans, especially urban residents, fear for their safety and believe that crime is a significant national problem.

The public's concern notwithstanding, only three presidents since Herbert Hoover have strongly and systematically sought to combat crime. Calder (1982) notes that, "Not every president has vigorously exercised [the role of conservator-in-chief of the public order and safety]." He suggests that although Presidents Kennedy, Johnson, and Nixon "made the choice to conduct wars on crime, no doubt well-intentioned and partly successful, their ideological precommitments have substantially influenced the nature, direction and content of their policies." Calder concludes that good intentions aside, these presidents' crime programs were narrowly conceived and had little chance for measurable impact.

Development of a national policy to deal with crime is a complex undertaking (for integrative complexity and policymaker reasoning see discussion of Tetlock). According to Tyler and Lavrakas ("Distinguishing the Cognitions Leading to Personal and Political Behavior"), it is not likely that a national policy campaign aganist crime will filter down to the individual, such that he or she will adopt personal protection behaviors. They suggest that the processing of national crime messages may prompt the individual to believe that crime is a social problem requiring certain *household protection behaviors,* but evidently will not convince the individual to engage in *personal protection behaviors* (to attenuate these findings, see below, O'Keefe, 1985).

Reviewing the literature on behavioral responses to crime, Tyler and Lavrakas found that messages from two levels (personal and social) accounted for individual's cognitions about crime, and affected their behaviors. However, a model, developed as a result of their review, shows a distinction between the personal and social levels—experience, belief, and behavior occur differently on each level. They report "little evidence of influence across levels at either the belief or behavior stages, with exception of joint influences upon household behaviors." Although these findings pose serious implications for the effectiveness of a governmental policy attempting to ameliorate crime and bring about workable safety conditions for citizens, they must be considered along with media effects on crime prevention.

## MEDIA EFFECTS ON CRIME PREVENTION

Citing several studies about media effects and crime, Tyler and Lavrakas conclude: (1) mass media do not influence personal fears about crime; (2) judgments of the rate of crime are influenced by the mass media; and (3) amount of crime reported in newspapers correlated with readers' fear of crime in areas other than their neighborhoods. Several studies suggest either that the media have effects on individual and social behavior, or that public information campaigns have significant, salient effects on audiences (see Atkin, 1979; Chaffee, 1981; Douglas et al., 1970; Hanneman and McEwen, 1973; Maccoby and Solomon, 1981; McAlister et al., 1980; O'Keefe and Atwood, 1981; and see below, O'Keefe, 1985). As to Tyler and Lavrakas's second and third conclusion, the practice of reporting crime needs to be considered.

How do the media convey acts of crime to the public? Gans (1979) observed that "unique crime stories are sought after by journalists to the extent that a 'journalistic crime wave' may be established." Is there a relationship between the crime wave and the amount of news about crime? Jones (1976) contends that there ought to be a relationship. Gans (1979) replies to Jones with the suggestion that, "Even if journalists continue to emphasize dramatic crimes, they can 'tag' stories by reporting the rates for such crimes, thus providing a balance to the exaggeration that accompanies highlighting."

The *threat* of violent action and the *dangers* inherently involved in violent acts conveyed by the media ought to provide the motivation for individuals to adopt personal protection behaviors (see discussion of Garramone; for a discussion of fear/threat appeals and the mass media see Kraus et al., 1966; Leventhal, 1970; Rogers, 1975; Rogers and Mewborn, 1976). Media messages about crime fill the printed page and news broadcasting. Gans's comments on "highlighting" of crime notwithstanding, creating a realistic sense of danger may prove useful to promote remedial legislation and personal protection behaviors. A recent study (O'Keefe, 1985; not available when Tyler and Lavrakas completed their review) refutes several hypotheses and assumptions previously associated with the efficacy of national crime campaigns, and has particular relevance for this discussion.

Since October, 1979, the Advertising Council conducted a national campaign to promote crime prevention. Produced under the sponsorship of the Crime Prevention Coalition, televised public service announcements (PSAs), radio spots, and magazine and newspaper advertisements used an animated dog, "McGruff" (shades of "Smokey the Bear"?), with the theme, "Take a Bite Out of Crime" (Tyler and Lavrakas refer to the earlier study by Mendelsohn). The campaign was conducted in three phases: (1) suggesting tips about protecting homes and property; (2) urging audiences to observe and report suspected criminal behavior; and (3) organizing neighborhood and local groups to support community crime prevention activities.

O'Keefe (1985) examined the effects of the campaign with data collected from a national sample survey and a three-city panel survey. He found "that the campaign had marked influences on individuals' cognitions, attitudes, and behaviors regarding crime prevention." Specifically, he found that individuals exposed to the campaign knew more about crime prevention, more about how effective citizens' prevention efforts were, and were more confident about being able to protect themselves, than those not exposed to the campaign.

For the most part, O'Keefe's findings substantiate the model drawn by Tyler and Lavrakas. The difference between the two reports is in the assessment of television and its effects on personal protection behaviors and fear of crime in individuals' neighborhoods. O'Keefe (1985) offers somewhat of a contrast to the Tyler and Lavrakas implication about crime reported in newspapers and readers' fear of crime in areas *other than their own neighborhoods*. On this point O'Keefe's findings are impressive:

> The strongest relationships between McGruff exposure and behavioral changes occurred among the cooperative action-taking steps. . . . *Campaign exposure was significantly correlated with increases in "keeping a watch" outside one's home, reporting suspicious events to the police, and joining crime prevention groups or organizations"* [italics mine].

One could classify "keeping a watch" and "reporting" crimes as either personal protection behaviors or neighborhood protection behaviors. The operationalization of these terms presents a problem when aggregating findings among media and crime prevention studies.

O'Keefe (1985) concludes with an interesting observation about media effects on cognition: "Among the less threatened and at risk, the campaign appears to have done a better job of stimulating cognitive and attitudinal changes, along with some action-taking as well."

In another study O'Keefe (1984) found that

> the amount of time spent viewing televised crime entertainment programs was. . . unrelated to nearly all of the crime perceptions and attitudes examined. . . . However, the extent of attendance to crime related television news content was significantly associated with certain kinds of citizen orientations toward crime, notably including perceptions of neighborhood danger, perceived likelihood of being a victim of violent crime, and the extent of worry over being victimized.

The O'Keefe and Tyler and Lavrakas conclusions about the mass media and their effects on individuals' crime perceptions are variously supported by Tamborini et al. (1984). Tamborini et al. found that exposure to a television documentary on crime influenced "certain perceptions while leaving other associated judgments unaffected." However, Tamborini et al. provide evidence supporting the Tyler and Lavrakas model, especially the distinction between television effects on societal and personal levels. Tamborini et al. conclude the following:

> With regard to the societal versus personal-level distinction, the demonstration of an effect on general perceptions of crime and or fear for one's

mate (without influencing personal fear) supports the notion that information associated with societal-level judgments is segregated in processing and does not influence personal perceptions.

Tyler and Lavrakas call for a theory that accounts for how individuals organize and store information from media events in memory, and how they retrieve and utilize that information. Their review, however, suggests that such a theory may need to be developed separately for personal and social levels of influence. Tyler and Lavrakas offer one explanation for differential media effects on personal and societal levels. They suggest that "citizens may adapt less effectively to crime because they see themselves as unique;" they do not internalize mass media experiences, but instead "may be compensated by other psychological benefits." Tamborini et al., citing Einhorn and Hogarth (1978), offer another explanation: "An exaggeration of one's own ability to deal with the danger of crime may reduce the impact of information about threat to others on fear for one's own safety."

O'Keefe (1985) suggests that recent research on campaigns lacks consistent "conceptual or theroretical perspectives." He argues that it is critical for future investigations of campaigns to consider "contingencies under which different media messages result in different effects [at different times]."

It is also critical to resolve among studies the ambiguities involved in the classification of crime protection behaviors, and to provide a clarified rationale for why the media have differential effects on personal and societal levels.

Hotspur put it cogently when he said, ". . . out of this nettle danger, we pluck this flower, safety" (Shakespeare, *Henry IV*, I, II, 3).

## IMPACT ON POLITY

The final step in the political communication process is polity itself— both the voter and the larger policymaking sector. This section reviews research on the antecedents of voting behavior itself (Fishbein, Middlestadt, and Chung), the level of thinking among policy elites (Tetlock), and the interface between political information processing, journalism, and the world outside, as represented by this chapter.

## FISHBEIN, MIDDLESTADT, AND CHUNG

Upon first inspection of the Fishbein et al. study ("Predicting Participation and Choice Among First Time Voters in U.S. Partisan Elections") one might wonder why the study is included in a volume that purports to shed light on the mass media and political thought. The reader will not find a single word connected to the mass media (e.g., information, communication, etc.). Nor will the reader locate any hint of *how* voters process political information or *think* about politics. To Fishbein et al., those are "*external* variables that can influence [voting] behavior only indirectly" (italics mine). The direct influence on voting stems from the voter's intentions. Fishbein et al. believe "that behaviors under an individual's volitional control [e.g., voting] are predictable from a knowledge of a person's intention [when] viewed as a function of attitudes and subjective norms"—hence, Fishbein and his associates' *theory of reasoned action.* Fishbein et al. however, do not take into account internal processes because beliefs and norms are enough, according to the reasoned action theory.

It is precisely because the theory of reasoned action eliminates mass media reports, party identification, partisan attitudes, candidate images, and political issues as primary determinants of voting choice that the study is important for our consideration.

In some five studies in a seven-year period, Fishbein and other researchers have applied the theory of reasoned action to the study of voting choice. Their findings have resulted in a theory of voting behavior (Fishbein et al., 1980; Fishbein and Ajzen, 1981).

The present study consisted of 108 potential first-time voters (18- and 19-year old undergraduate students) who completed a questionnaire two weeks before the 1980 presidential election, and were interviewed for 10 minutes by telephone just after the election. The major conclusion of the study "is the finding that participation as well as [vote] choice can be accurately predicted from a knowledge of the potential voter's intention to engage in each of the alternatives available in the election in question" (see discussion of Lau and Erber).

### FROM LAZARSFELD TO FISHBEIN

The classical study of mass media's role in the 1940 presidential campaign (Lazarsfeld et al., 1944) found that over half the voters made up their minds in May and voted that way in November. In that study an index of political predisposition helped explain voting intentions. For four and a half decades since that precursory study a good deal of research on political participation and the role of the mass media has been conducted. Though social scientists have researched the spectrum from how voters perceive and use political information to how they make up their minds in elections, Fishbein and his associates have defined their research in a very precise, cogent, and limited manner. Their present research does not concern how voters arrive at their voting intentions. Nor is it concerned with any changes that may have occurred over time. Indeed, the two data collection points were separated by about two weeks—just before and after the election.

Fishbein and his colleagues, with well-constructed studies, have demonstrated much support for their theory of reasoned action. If the theory succeeds over time and serves as a predictor of behaviors in various social and political contexts, an important major contribution will have been made.

Communication researchers will want to investigate three questions:

(1) Do print readers evaluate candidates more on beliefs than do television viewers?

(2) Do novices evaluate more on norms than experts (see Lau and Erber)?

(3) Do those voters with high and low personal relevance differ in weights (see Perloff)?

## TETLOCK

Tetlock ("Integrative Complexity of Policy Reasoning") reviews the literature on integrative complexity with an emphasis on "*how* policymakers appear to think." He asks, for example, "Do policymakers . . . see solutions to problems as essentially simple (all considerations pointing to one conclusion) or complex (competing values must be weighed against each other)?"

His review shows that there are substantial differences among individuals in their styles of reasoning, and that situational variables may bring about different reasoning styles. Communication researchers, however, suggest another aspect of integrative complexity, one that may account for the ability of policymakers to see solutions to problems in simple or complex terms.

Hale and Delia (1976) argues that "the higher one's level of complexity, the greater his cognitive flexibility. . . . Those with more complex interpersonal construct systems . . . adopt with less strain a set to 'understand' why another behaves as he does and to take an integrative orientation in processing successful blocks of contradictory information rather than focusing upon the immediate salient information" (see also, Crockett et al., 1975; Delia et al., 1975; Mayo and Crockett, 1964; Press et al., 1975).

Tetlock concludes his chapter with a discussion of media and integrative complexity. Pointing out that "researchers have yet to examine the integrative complexity of media coverage of elite political controversies," Tetlock raises several important questions. Correctly noting that the media do simplify complicated issues, Tetlock asks the major question of "the degree to which various media simplify (perhaps oversimplify) political issues."

## COMPLEXITY VERSUS SIMPLICITY IN MEDIA REPORTS

Both politicians and journalists have been subjected to the criticism (more often by experts and elites) that they oversimplify complex issues in their discourses. This may be a function of their beliefs that in order to achieve their objectives (reaching voters, constituents, and news audiences), issues must be conveyed in cogent, easy-to-understand terms. At times, however—especially in the reporting of polling data—the press complicates instead of simplifying the essential part of the story (see discussion on Neuman and Fryling). Also, the structure of campaigns, congressional committee hearings, and media, because of space and time limitations, often require that discussions, reports, and messages be reduced from a larger body of information to a shorter, simpler version. Gans (1979) noted that "journalism is an empirical discipline but one which requires that its findings be presented as interestingly and in as few minutes and words as possible."

The journalists' views of the subject at hand, and the audience that is to be informed about it, is yet another aspect of complex and simple presentations. Complicated political issues (most public issues tend to be complex) are reported by journalists in codified ways, and retained by news audiences in even shorter codes. This state of affairs may not be ideal in creating a more informed public. Lippmann has suggested that "in view of the technical complexity of almost all great public questions, it [may not be] really possible any longer for the mass of voters to form significant public opinions" (quoted in Steel, 1981). Gans (1979), however, raises an important point about news and its relationship to lay and expert audiences. He suggests that experts want "explanatory-predictive news," whereas lay audiences "seem to prefer dramatic description." In his view, expert news does not necessarily add to our democratic process; if it did he would advocate abolishing "popular news."

Also, it can be argued that the voting public often makes its decision about candidates on the basis of personality (image factors) and not necessarily on substance (issues), complex or otherwise (see discussions of Lanzetta et al. and Miller and Asp).

Political experts and democratic theorists may find it a dolorous condition to accept the notion that political reasoning and policy-formation are not factors that affect voters' decision making. If that is the case, the mass media are at least providing a service to voters in its reduction of complex issues into simple explanations. If not, many changes in media structure and in the way messages are received by news audiences are needed. That, of course, would require substantial incentives for the media and news audiences.

## CONCLUSION

The group of studies in this volume are innovative and provocative. Representing a wide variety of disciplines in the social sciences, these researchers often display unique and different approaches to the study of political information processing of individuals and voters, and the role the media assume as they affect that processing. What they have discussed, what this writer has reviewed about their studies, and the experiential application made by this writer to their findings, represent a small but perhaps significant step in the scholarly understanding of how individuals process information.

As a final note, the reader may have been struck by the many references in this review to the transactional model of studying mass communication effects. At the conclusion of their volume on how the mass media affect political behavior, Kraus and Davis (1976) argue aganist the one-way communicator-dominated model in research designs, and for a two-way model, the transactional model. They cite Zimmerman and Bauer (1956), Davison (1959), and Bauer (1964), whose experiments and reviews offer a compelling argument for the transactional model:

(1) "Zimmerman and Bauer (1956) jarred our preconceptions of audience behavior by suggesting that audience members select new information with reference to their relationship to other future audiences."

(2) Davison (1959) argued that the audience "cannot be regarded as a lump of clay to be molded by the master propagandist. [The audience] *must get something from the manipulator if he is to get something from them. A bargain is involved"* (italics mine).

(3) Bauer (1964) insists that "the argument for using the transactional model for *scientific* purposes is that it opens the door more fully to exploring the intention and behavior of members of the audience and encourages inquiry into the influence of the audience on the communicator by specifically treating the process as a two-way passage."

This writer believes that the evidence supports the view that the transactional model is most productive in the quest to find mass media effects simply because it helps explain the behaviors of receivers as well as the media. He admits to that preference as a predisposition in reviewing the studies.

## REFERENCES

ATKIN, C. K. (1979) "Research evidence on mass mediated health communication campaigns," in D. Nimmo (ed.) Communication Yearbook 3. New Brunswick, NJ: International Communication Association.

BAUER, R. A. (1964) "The obstinate audience: the influence process from the point of view of social communication." American Psychologist 19: 319-328.

BEHR, R. and S. IYENGAR (1985) "Television news, real-world cues, and changes in the public agenda." Public Opinion Quarterly 49: 38-57.

BERELSON, B. R., P. F. LAZARSFELD, and W. N. McPHEE (1954) Voting. Chicago: University of Chicago Press.

BRODBECK, A. J. (1959) "The principles of permanence and change: electioneering and psychotherapy compared," pp. 414-436 in E. Burdick and A. J. Brodbeck (eds.) American Voting Behavior. Glencoe, IL: Free Press.

BRODY, R. A. and B. I. PAGE (1973) "Indifference, alienation and rational decision." Public Choice 15: 1-17.

CALDER, J. D. (1982) "Presidents and crime control: Kennedy, Johnson and Nixon and the influences of ideology." Presidential Studies Quarterly 4: 574-589.

CAMPBELL, A., P. E. CONVERSE, N. E. MILLER, and D. E. STOKES (1960) The American Voter. New York: John Wiley.

CHAFFEE, S. H. (1981) "Mass media in political campaign: an expanding role," in R. E. Rice and W. J. Paisley (eds.) Public Communication Campaigns. Beverly Hills, CA: Sage.

CLYMER, A. (1985) "What Americans think now." New York Times Magazine (March 11): 34.

CROCKETT, W. H., S. MAHOOD, and A. N. PRESS (1975) "Impressions of a speaker as a function of set to understand or to evaluate, of cognitive complexity, and of prior attitudes." Journal of Personality 43: 168-178.

DAVISON, W. P. (1959) "On the effect of communication." Public Opinion Quarterly 20: 238-248.

DELIA, J. C., W. H. CROCKETT, A. N. PRESS, and D. J. O'KEEFE (1975) "The dependency of interpersonal evaluations on context-relevant beliefs about the other." Speech Monographs 42: 10-19.

DIAMOND, E. and S. BATES (1984) The Spot: The Rise of National Advertising on Television. Cambridge: MIT Press.

DOOB, L. W. (1961) Communication In Africa: A Search for Boundaries. New Haven, CT: Yale University Press.

DOUGLAS, D. F., B. H. WESTLEY, and S. H. CHAFFEE (1970) "An information campaign that changed community attitudes." Journalism Quarterly. 47: 479-487.

EINHORN, H. J. and R. M. HOGARTH (1978) "Confidence in judgment: persistence of the illusion of validity." Psychological Review 85: 395-416.

FISHBEIN, M. (1980) "A theory of reasoned action: some applications and implications," in H. Howe and M. Pose (eds.) Nebraska Symposium on Motivation, 1978. Lincoln: University of Nebraska Press.

———and I. AJZEN (1981) "Attitudes and voting behavior: an application of the theory of reasoned action," pp. 253-313 in G. M. Stephenson and J. M. Davis (eds.) Progress in Applied Social Psychology (vol. 1). New York: John Wiley.

FRIEDMAN, H. S., T. J. MERTZ, and M. R. DiMATTEO (1980) "Perceived bias in the facial expressions of television news broadcasters." Journal of Communication 30: 103-111.

GANS, H. J. (1979) Deciding What's News. New York: Pantheon.

GRABER, D. (1984) Processing The News: How People Tame the Information Tide. New York: Longman.

HALE, C. and J. G. DELIA (1976) "Cognitive complexity and social perspective-taking." Communication Monographs 43: 195-203.

HANNEMAN, G. J. and W. I. McEWEN (1973) "Televised drug abuse appeals: a content analysis." Journalism Quarterly 50: 329-333.

HOVLAND, C. I. (1958) "The role of primacy and recency in persuasive communication," pp. 137-149 in E. E. Maccoby et al. (eds.) Readings in Social Psychology; (3rd ed.). New York: Holt, Rinehart & Winston.

JONES, T. E. (1976) "The press as monitor." Public Opinion Quarterly 40: 239-243.

KATZ, E. and J. J. FELDMAN (1962) "The debates in light of research: a survey of surveys," pp. 173-223 in S. Kraus (ed.) The Great Debates: Background, Perspective, Effects. Bloomington: Indiana University Press.

KELLY, S. Jr., and T. W. MIRER (1974) "The simple act of voting." American Political Science Review 61: 572-591.

KINDER, D. R. and D. O. SEARS (1985) "Public opinion and political action," in G. Lindzey and E. Aronson (eds.) Handbook of Social Psychology. Reading, MA: Addison-Wesley.

KLAPPER, J. (1960) The Effects of Mass Communication: An Analysis of Research on the Effectiveness and Limitations of Mass Media in Influencing the Opinions, Values, and Behavior of Their Audiences. New York: Free Press.

KRAUS, S. (1984a) "The volatility in reporting the volatile poll results in recent presidential elections: the tail that wags the dog." Presented at the International Society of Political Psychology, June 24-27, Toronto, Canada.

———(1984b) "Presidential Debates: Images and Issues." The Christian Science Monitor (October 4): 15.

———(1979) [ed.] The Great Debates; Carter vs. Ford 1976. Bloomington: Indiana University Press.

———(1962) [ed.] The Great Debates. Bloomington: Indiana University Press. (Reissued as Great Debates, 1960: Kennedy vs. Nixon [1977])

———and D. DAVIS (1981) "Political debates," in D. Nimmo and K. R. Sanders (eds.) Handbook of Political Communication. Beverly Hills, CA: Sage.

———(1976) The Effects of Mass Communication on Political Behavior. University Park: Penn State University Press.

———E. EL-ASSAL, and M. L. DeFLEUR (1966) "Fear threat appeals in mass communication: an apparent contradiction." Speech Monographs 33: 23-29.

KRAUS, S., T. MEYER, and M. SHELBY, Jr. (1974) "16 months after Chappaquiddick: effects of the Kennedy broadcast." Journalism Quarterly 51: 431-440.

LACHMAN, R., J. L. LACHMAN, and E. C. BUTTERFIELD (1979) Cognitive Psychology and Information Processing: An Introduction. Hillsdale, NJ: Lawrence Erlbaum.

LANG, G. E. and K. LANG (1983) The Battle for Public Opinion: The President, the Press, and the Poll During Watergate. New York: Columbia University Press.

LAZARSFELD, P., B. BERELSON, and H. GAUDET (1944) The People's Choice. New York: Columbia University Press.

LERNER, D. (1958) The Passing of Traditional Society: Modernizing the Middle East. New York: Free Press.

LEVENTHAL, H. (1970) "Findings and theory in the study of fear communication," in L. Berkowitz (ed.) Advances in Experimental Social Psychology (vol. 5.). New York: Academic.

LIPPMANN, W. (1922/1947) Public Opinion. New York: Macmillan. (originally published 1922)

MACCOBY, N. and D. S. SOLOMON (1981) "Heart disease prevention: community studies," in R. E. Rice and W. J. Paisley (eds.) Public Communication Campaign. Beverly Hills, CA: Sage.

MARTIN, J. L. (1984) [ed.] "Polling and the democratic consensus." The Annals of the American Academy of Political and Social Science 472: 1-208.

MAYO, C. W. and W. H. CROCKETT (1964) "Cognitive complexity and primacy-recency effects in impression formation." Journal of Abnormal and Social Psychology 68: 335-338.

McALISTER, A., P. PEKKA, K. KOSKELA, V. PALONEN, and N. MACCOBY (1980) "Mass communication and community organization for public health education." American Psychologist 35: 375-379.

McCOMBS, M. E. and D. L. SHAW (1972) "The agenda-setting function of mass media." Public Opinion Quarterly 36: 176-187.

McGINNIS, J. (1969) The Selling of the President, 1968. New York: Trident.

McLEOD, J. M., L. B. BECKER, and J. E. BYRNES (1974) "Another look at the agenda-setting function of the press." Communication Research 1: 131-166.

MILBRATH, L. W. and M. L. GOEL (1977) Political Participation: How and Why Do People Get Involved in Politics. Chicago: Rand McNally.

————(1965) Political Participation. Chicago: Rand McNally.

MILLER, A. (1983) "Is confidence rebounding?" Public Opinion 6: 16-20.

NEWCOMB, T. M. (1950) Social Psychology. New York: Dryden Press.

Newsweek (1984, November/December) Election Extra.

NIE, N. H., S. VERBA, and J. R. PETROCIK (1979) The Changing American Voter. Cambridge: Harvard University Press.

O'KEEFE, G. J. (1985) " 'Taking a bite out of crime': the impact of a public information campaign." Communication Research 12: 147-178.

————(1984) "Public views on crime: television exposure and media credibility," pp. 514-535 in R. Bostrom (ed.) Communication Yearbook 8. Beverly Hills, CA: Sage.

————and L. E. ATWOOD (1981) "Communication and election campaigns," in D. Nimmo and K. R. Sanders (eds.) Handbook of Political Communication. Beverly Hills, CA: Sage.

PATTERSON, T. E. and R. D. McCLURE (1976) The Unseeing Eye. New York: Thomas Crowell.

PERLOFF, R. M. (1984) "Political involvement: a critique and a process-oriented reformation." Critical Studies in Mass Communication 1: 146-160.

PRESS, A. N., W. H. CROCKETT, and J. G. DELIA (1975) "The effect of cognitive complexity and the perceivers set upon the organization of impressions." Journal of Personality and Social Psychology 32: 865-872.

ROGERS, R. W. (1975) "A protection motivation theory of fear appeals and attitude change." Journal of Psychology 91: 93-114.

————and C. R. MEWBORN (1976) "Fear appeals and attitude change: effects of a threat's noxiousness, probability of occurrence, and the efficacy of coping responses." Journal of Personality and Social Psychology 34: 54-61.

SCHRAMM, W. (1955) "Introductory note: the meaning of meaning," in W. Schramm (ed.) The Process and Effects of Mass Communication. Urbana: University of Illinois Press.

SEARS, D. O., R. R. LAU, T. R. TYLER, and H. M. ALLEN, Jr. (1980) "Self-interest vs. symbolic politics in policy attitudes and presidential voting." American Political Science Review 74: 670-684.

STEEL, R. (1981) Walter Lippmann and the American Century. New York: Vintage.

TAMBORINI, R., D. ZILLMAN, and J. BRYANT (1984) "Fear and victimization: exposure to television and perceptions of crime and fear," pp. 492-511 in R. Bostrom (ed.) Communication Yearbook 8. Beverly Hills, CA: Sage.

YU, F.T.C. (1963) "Communications and politics in communist China," pp. 259-297 in L. W. Pye (ed.) Communication and Political Development. Princeton: Princeton University Press.

WEAVER, D. H. (1977) "Political issues and voter need for orientation." pp. 107-119 in D. Shaw and M. E. McCombs (eds.) The Emergence of American Political Issues: The Agenda-Setting Function of the Press. St Paul: West.

————D. A. GRABER, M. E. McCOMBS, and C. H. EYAL (1981) Media Agenda-Setting in a Presidential Election: Issues, Images, and Interest. New York: Praeger.

WHITE, T. H. (1982) America in Search of Itself: The Making of the President 1956-1980. New York: Harper & Row.

ZIMMERMAN, C. and R. A. BAUER (1956) "The effects of an audience on what is remembered." Public Opinion Quarterly 20: 238-248.

# NAME INDEX

The symbol r appearing in a citation indicates that the name appears in a reference. The symbol n indicates names included in notes.

# ABOUT THE
# CONTRIBUTORS

KENT ASP is Lecturer at the Department of Political Science at the University of Gothenburg. He is currently engaged in the Swedish Election Research Program. His research has centered on mass media contents and mass media effects. He is coauthor (with Sören Holmberg) of *Kampen om kärnkraften. En bok om väljare, massmedier och folkomröstningen 1980 (The Struggle About the Nuclear Power. A book about voters, mass media and the 1980 Referendum).*

JEAN-KYUNG CHUNG received her B. A. from Sogang University in Korea in 1976 and her M.A. in psychology at the University of Illinois at Champaign-Urbana in 1980. She is currently teaching and doing research in Korea and completing her Ph.D. at Illinois.

RALPH ERBER is completing his graduate work in social psychology in the Department of Psychology at Carnegie-Mellon University. He received his B.A. in social science from the University of Mannheim in 1980. His research focuses on the role of affect in social information processing and political cognition.

MARTIN FISHBEIN received his B.A. from Reed College in 1957 and his Ph.D. (in psychology) from UCLA in 1961. Since that time he has been at the University of Illinois at Champaign-Urbana, where he is currently Professor of Psychology and Research Professor, Institute of Communications Research. He has been a Guggenheim fellow and twice has been a Visiting Scholar at the London School of Economics and Political Science. He was one of ten initial inductees in the American Marketing Association's Attitude Research Hall of Fame in 1981 and in the same year received the Phillip D. Converse Award for distinguished contributions to theory and science in marketing. In 1982 he received a NARM Special Recognition Award for his contribution to the development of market research in the recorded music industry. In addition to contributing over 50 articles to professional journals, he has authored or edited five books.

ANN C. FRYLING is a doctoral candidate in the Department of Political Science at the Massachusetts Institute of Technology and Visiting Lecturer in Communications at Tufts University. Her research and teaching interests include agenda-setting, media effects, Congress and the American political process, and political socialization.

GINA M. GARRAMONE is Assistant Professor in the Department of Advertising at Michigan State University. Her research interests include uses and effects of the media, information processing of media messages, and applications of new media technologies to political communication. She has published in *Public Opinion Quarterly, Human Communication Research, Communication Research, Journalism Quarterly, Communication Yearbook,* and *Journal of Broadcasting and Electronic Media.*

JOHN A. HERSTEIN, Jr., received his B.A. from the University of Nebraska and his M.S. and Ph.D. in psychology from Carnegie-Mellon University. From 1979 to 1981 he was a postdoctoral research associate at Ohio State University, studying person memory organization. He has taught in the political science department at the State University of New York at Stony Brook and is currently writing a book tentatively entitled *Political System Design and Simulation.*

SHANTO IYENGAR is Associate Professor of Political Science at the State University of New York at Stony Brook. He previously taught at Kansas State University and Yale University and has published widely in major academic journals.

DONALD R. KINDER is Associate Professor of Political Science and Psychology, and Associate Research Scientist at the Center for Political Studies, University of Michigan. He has also taught at Yale University and has published widely in major psychology and political science journals.

SIDNEY KRAUS is Professor and Chairman in the Department of Communication at Cleveland State University and Distinguished Visiting Professor of Communication at Ohio University. His Ph.D. is in communication research and radio and television from the University of Iowa (1959). Kraus was a Ford Fellow, received a Fulbright Award, and was the Chairman of the 1976 Presidential Debates Debriefing Conference in Washington, D.C. His 1962 publication on presidential debates was selected for inclusion in the White House Library. In 1977 he received the First Communicator of the Year Award from the Radio and Television Council of Greater Cleveland. He has attended all of the presidential debates since 1976 and was a credentialed observer of the Democratic and Republican conventions in 1984. The editor of two books on televised presidential debates, he coauthored *The Effects of Mass Communication on Political Behavior,* and has published widely in academic journals. Sidney Kraus is currently completing a book entitled *Presidential Debates and Public Policy.*

JOHN T. LANZETTA is Lincoln Filene Professor of Psychology at Dartmouth College. He received his B.S. in engineering physics from Lafayette College and his Ph.D. in psychology from the University of Rochester in 1952. He served as editor of the *Journal of Personality and Social Psychology* from 1970 to 1977 and is currently on the editorial board of the *European Journal of Experimental Social Psychology.*

RICHARD R. LAU is Associate Professor in the Department of Social Sciences at Carnegie-Mellon University. He received his Ph.D. in social psychology from UCLA in 1979. His research focuses on political cognitions and on the development of health beliefs and health behaviors.

PAUL J. LAVRAKAS is Associate Professor with the Medill School of Journalism and the Center for Urban Affairs and Policy Research at Northwestern University. He is also the Director of the Northwestern University Survey Laboratory. He received his Ph.D. in applied social psychology from Loyola University of Chicago in 1977. His research interests include citizens' reactions to crime and survey research methods. He has published a number of articles on fear of crime and citizens' protective responses to crime, and has evaluated several federally funded community anti-crime programs. He has been a consultant to the National Institute of Justice since 1978.

ROGER D. MASTERS is John Sloan Dickey Third Century Professor of Government at Dartmouth College. He received his Ph.D. at the

University of Chicago in 1961. He is chairman of the editorial board of the "Biology of Social Life" section of *Social Science Information* and has published over 90 scholarly articles and essays. He is the author of two books: *The Nation Is Burdened: American Foreign Policy in a Changing World* and *The Political Philosophy of Rousseau.*

GREGORY J. McHUGO received his Ph.D. in experimental psychology from Dartmouth College in 1979. He is currently Research Associate/ Visiting Assistant Professor of Psychology at Dartmouth. His publications and interest focus on psychophysiology and on the effects of politicians' expressive displays.

SUSAN E. MIDDLESTADT is Assistant Professor in the Department of Advertising at the University of Illinois at Champaign-Urbana. She received her A.B. from Bucknell University in 1972 and her Ph.D. in psychology from the University of California, Berkeley. Before joining the faculty of the University of Illinois in 1984, she was the Research Director of Attitude and Behavior Research, Inc. As a research consultant, she worked on various projects concerned with understanding and changing health, educational, political, and consumer behaviors.

ARTHUR H. MILLER is Professor of Political Science at the University of Iowa. He was previously Study Director of the University of Michigan American National Election Studies. He has written numerous journal articles on the effects of mass media on political behavior. In particular, his work has focused on agenda-setting, the media's impact on citizen confidence in government, and the role of presidential debates in electoral outcomes. His work on American elections has appeared in various professional journals in the U.S. and Europe. He is coauthor of *The American National Election Studies Data Sourcebook: 1952-1978.*

W. RUSSELL NEUMAN did his doctoral work in political sociology at the University of California, Berkeley, and taught at Yale University before joining the faculty at MIT in the Department of Political Science. He is co-director of the MIT Research Program on Communications Policy. His current research includes studies of agenda-setting, the acquisition of political knowledge, and the impact of new technologies on the economics of mass communications. His most recent study, *The Paradox of Mass Politics: Knowledge and Opinion in the American Electorate,* will be published by Harvard University Press.

RICHARD M. PERLOFF is Associate Professor of Communication at Cleveland State University. His research specialty is political persuasion. He has published articles in a number of communication and psychology books and journals. His work includes ". . . 'And Thinking Makes It So': Cognitive Responses to Persuasion" (with T. Brock), in *Persuasion: New Directions in Theory and Research* (Sage, 1980); "Sociocognitive biases in the Evaluation Process (with V. Padgett and T. Brock), in *Values, Ethics, and Standards in Program Evaluation* (Jossey-Bass, 1980); and "Political Involvement: A Critique and a Process-Oriented Reformulation," in *Critical Studies in Mass Communication* (1984). He received his Ph.D. in mass communications from the University of Wisconsin in 1978 and was an Ohio State University Postdoctoral Fellow in social psychology and mass communication in 1978-1979.

KLAUS SCHOENBACH is Professor of Communications at the Institute for Communications Research at the University of Munich in West Germany. His major teaching and research interests are in political communication, local communication, and content analysis. He received his Ph.D. from Johannes-Gutenberg University in Mainz in 1975 and since that time has written two books, one an empirical study of journalists' ethical behavior in West Germany and the other on the political effects of the press. He has also coedited a book on mass media and elections (with Winfried Schulz) and is the author of numerous articles and monographs. He has been a Visiting Professor at Cleveland State University and Indiana University.

DENIS G. SULLIVAN, Professor of Government at Dartmouth College since 1968, received his Ph.D. from Northwestern University in 1962. He has published widely on voting behavior and is the recipient of several grants, including a Ford Foundation grant to study the Democratic nominating convention and a Guggenheim Foundation research grant for study of the effects of facial displays on leadership status.

PHILIP E. TETLOCK received his Ph.D. from Yale University in 1979 and is currently Associate Professor of Psychology at the University of California, Berkeley. His research interests include social cognition, decision making, and impression management. He is the author of a number of articles in professional books and journals, including

"Psychological Research on Foreign Policy: A Methodological Overview," in L. Wheeler (ed.) *Review of Personality and Social Psychology* (vol. 4), 1983 (Sage Publications), and "Public Opinion and Political Ideology," in M. Hermann (ed.) *Handbook of Political Psychology* (vol. 2), 1985 (Jossey-Bass).

TOM R. TYLER is Associate Professor of Psychology and Political Science at Northwestern University. He is also a member of the research faculty at the Center for Urban Affairs and Policy Research. During the time this chapter was written he was a Visiting Scholar at the American Bar Foundation. Dr. Tyler is a social psychologist whose research interests include mass media research, political psychology, and psychology of the law. He received a B.A. from Columbia University (1973) and a Ph.D. from UCLA (1978).

DAVID H. WEAVER is Professor of Journalism at Indiana University and Director of the Bureau of Media Research in the School of Journalism. He is the author of *Videotex Journalism* (Erlbaum, 1983), senior author of *Media Agenda-Setting in a Presidential Election* (Praeger, 1981), coauthor of *Newsroom Guide to Polls and Surveys* (American Newspaper Publishers Association, 1980), and author of numerous book chapters and articles on media agenda-setting, newspaper readership, and foreign news coverage. He received his Ph.D. in mass communication research from the University of North Carolina in 1974 after having worked as an editor and reporter on four daily newspapers.